William Neal

An illustrated history of the Missouri Engineer and the 25th Infantry Regiments

William Neal

An illustrated history of the Missouri Engineer and the 25th Infantry Regiments

ISBN/EAN: 9783337221911

Printed in Europe, USA, Canada, Australia, Japan

Cover: Foto ©ninafisch / pixelio.de

More available books at **www.hansebooks.com**

An Illustrated History

OF THE

Missouri Engineer

AND THE

25$\underline{\text{TH}}$ Infantry Regiments

TOGETHER WITH A ROSTER OF BOTH REGIMENTS AND THE LAST KNOWN
ADDRESS OF ALL THAT COULD BE OBTAINED.

Regimental Badge.

EDITED AND COMPILED

BY DR. W. A. NEAL,

ASSISTANT SURGEON 1ST MISSOURI ENGINEERS, SECRETARY AND HISTORIAN OF THE
SOCIETY OF THE 1ST MISSOURI ENGINEERS.

1889:
DONOHUE AND HENNEBERRY
PRINTERS AND BINDERS
Nos. 407-425 Dearborn Street
CHICAGO, ILL.

PREFACE.

THE fact that the greater part of what is called *history* consists of variations of the quarrels and fights of mankind, shows that, after all, the state of war is a natural state, and that the intervals of peace have thus far been merely restraining spells to be used to recuperate for other contests. Is not the most popular maxim to-day, "In time of peace prepare for war"? When the hostilities have actually commenced, the individual is utterly lost in the surging crowd, and even an organization as large as a regiment is of no account except as part of a mass to be controlled by some master mind. Exceptions are rare, especially in such a stupendous machine as was the Union Army in the late Rebellion, so that when a small part, as was the "Engineer Regiment of Missouri," earns for itself a name and place, as did that Regiment, it shows an aggregate of a great amount of talent and physical force, thoroughly organized and well directed.

The Regiment was nearly always separated, on duty in detached portions, so that few of its members knew the whole. It is the province of the compiler and editor of this book to embody the recital of the operations of the different detachments, so that our children can look with pride upon what their fathers have achieved.

Every General under whom the Missouri Engineer Regiment served in its different organizations—as the Engineer Regiment of the West, the Twenty-fifth Missouri Infantry and the First Missouri Engineers—complimented its men and officers, and repeatedly said that there was not another regiment whose officers and men could be compared with us for appearance, health and good conduct! Especially the good conduct.

This history was projected at the first reunion of the First Missouri Engineers, held in St. Louis, Missouri, September, 1887, when about one hundred of that Regiment and the Twenty-fifth Missouri were present. It was there resolved that a joint history of the two organizations should be prepared, and Dr. W. A. Neal was elected secretary and historian of the society of the First Missouri Engineers, and was directed to prepare a creditable book, giving said history, with as complete a roster of both regiments as possible. Lieutenant Parker's Historical Record of the Engineer Regiment of the West to the consolidation, December 31, 1863, with the Twenty-fifth Missouri, has been largely drawn from, and a large amount of manuscript has been furnished by Colonel J. W. Bissell, Lieutenant-Colonel R. T. Van Horn, Captain G. B. Brackett, Captain B. F. Buzard, Lieutenant J. Ricketts, Lieutenant L. R. Lancaster, H. Feuerbach, of Company A, and others. The first thought was to write a book of only one hundred pages or so, but the material accumulated far beyond that, and many of the surviving comrades demanded a handsome and creditable book, that would compare with those gotten out by other regiments, so that the work has grown into a book of four hundred pages, and an endeavor has been made to secure an engraved portrait of every one that could be obtained. The comrades or their friends have borne the expense of these agravings. The maps and other scenes have been engraved expressly for this book.

The large amount of work involved in this undertaking was not comprehended in the start, the roster of three thousand names alone requiring a whole year of research and correspondence to verify and get present addresses. Then the immense amount of correspondence, requiring the inditing of several thousand letters. In the publication of this work there is no prospect of pecuniary gain to any one; the effort has been to please all. The response so far has been fair, and the desire is to see a copy in the hands of every one that served in either the Engineer Regiment of the West, the Twenty-fifth Missouri Infantry, or the First Missouri Engineers. With this end in view, preparations were made for an edition of one thousand copies.

The officers of the Reunion Society of the First Missouri Engineers, Captain B. F. Buzard, President; Lieutenant Joshua Ricketts, Vice-President; Lieutenant Paulus Gast, Treasurer, have acted as a publication committee; and Colonel J. W. Bissell, Captain B. F. Buzard and some others have rendered financial aid, without which the book could not have been gotten out in good form, but it is confidently believed that it will compare favorably with any of the regimental histories that have appeared.

The roster alone is worth all the effort and expense of the publication.

Proud to recall the memory of every comrade, whether living or dead, and of the fact of association with them in the days when they were making a record, and glad of the permission to have been the means of putting in a connected and enduring form some record of their achievements, this book is left to them to approve or condemn.

W. A. NEAL, Historian.

Elkhart, Ind., December 28, 1888.

HISTORY OF THE
FIRST MISSOURI ENGINEERS

PART I.

ORGANIZATION.

THE

"ENGINEER REGIMENT OF THE WEST."

MISSOURI VOLUNTEERS.

IN July, 1861, the following "Proposition to Enroll an Engineer Regiment" was made by J. W. Bissell, Colonel of the then called Tenth Missouri Volunteers, three months.

"I propose, within the next thirty or forty days, to enroll within the States of Missouri, Iowa and Illinois, a full regiment of men who shall be, all of them, either mechanics, artisans, or persons accustomed to work as laborers under mechanics.

"When a full company is formed, they are to be mustered into service at some convenient point, and then sent to the St. Louis Arsenal for military instruction.

"No man shall be mustered until he shall have been examined and approved by the Regimental Surgeon.

"J. W. BISSELL,
"Colonel Tenth Regiment Missouri Volunteers."
I approve of the above.   FRANK P. BLAIR,
    Colonel First Regiment Missouri Artillery.
I concur.   J. C. FREMONT.

Acting upon this authority, he shortly after issued a circular address, calling for volunteer companies for the same, which was to be known as the "Engineer Regiment of the West." The circular held out substantially the following inducements: 1. That, in addition to the regular army pay and allowances the mechanics were to receive forty and the laborers twenty-five cents per day, extra. 2. That the Regiment would not be exposed to the guard duty of other regiments.

Under this call many who had, in consideration of the small pay of soldiers, halted between the convictions of duty to country and family, resolved to avail themselves of the superior advantages of the offer. Companies were raised and organized in the following order: Company A was recruited at St. Louis and East St. Louis, in the early part of July, 1861, and rendezvoused at the St. Louis Arsenal. On the 8th of July it was partly organized by the election of J. H. Vreeland, Captain; E. L. Jones, First Lieutenant, and Frank Daugherty Second Lieutenant, with Richard Ryan, Orderly Sergeant; Louis Young (afterward Lieutenant in Fourth United States Colored Troops) was next Orderly Sergeant, followed by James McClure. On the 20th of the same month the Company was mustered into the United States service by Captain Tracy, United States Army, with a minimum number, which was afterward raised to the maximum.

Like all other companies, A had some exceptionally fine men among its members; iron molders and railroad engineers, with other skilled mechanics. There was James Cunningham, William Cross, William Frazier, Henry Feuerbach and John Lewis, the most intelligent and agreeable of them all. He was killed at Tuscumbia, June 1, 1862, and, next to Sergeant Richard Ryan, was the ablest man in the Company. Probably Lewis or Ryan were more capable to command than the real Captain, but they did not recruit the men, and the system of organizing a regiment was at the time to appoint as officers those who recruited the men.

Company B was recruited in Paris, Edgar county, Illinois, and organized on the 28th day of July, 1861, by the election of Charles T. Rowell, Captain; Jesse D. Anderson, First Lieutenant; John E. Murphy, Second Lieutenant, and Joshua Ricketts (afterward promoted to Lieutenant, Company C), Orderly Sergeant. On the 30th of the same month the Company proceeded to St. Louis, numbering one hundred men, but owing to the large number rejected by the Examining Surgeon, it was reduced to eighty-four, exclusive of officers. With this number it was mustered into service by Captain Tracy, United States Army, at the St. Louis Arsenal, on the night of the 5th of August, 1861. Captain Rowell, refusing to muster, was relieved from duty, Lieutenant Anderson assuming command of the Company. So far as known, neither of them were ever commissioned in the Company.

Company C was recruited at Prairie City, Illinois, and organized August 4, 1861, by the election of Dewitt C. Folsom, Captain; William G. Patten, First Lieutenant, and Asa K. Grow, Second Lieutenant. It arrived in St. Louis on the 17th, and was mustered into the service on the 19th of August, 1861, by Captain Tracy. About seventy men were mustered, but the Company was afterward recruited to the maximum. Prairie City also contributed many men who were recruited for but could not be mustered into this Company.

Company D was recruited partly in St. Louis, though there were recruits from Flora, Olney, Rushville, Carlyle and other places in Illinois. When it came to the organization of the Company there was some clashing of interests. E. M. Hill, representing sixty-six men, and —— Griffith, representing twelve men, each claimed the Captaincy. The twelve men recruited by Griffith refused to be mustered unless their leader was made Captain, and without them an organization could not be effected. The sixty-six men stoutly protested against so unjust a claim, and with a good degree of reason and justice claimed that he who represented so large a majority should be entitled to the honor of the command. It was in this state of affairs that Colonel Bissell interfered, with the statement that the parties could have one hour to compromise the matter, at the expiration of which time, if the different squads were not consolidated, he would take the matter in hand himself. Finding Griffith unyielding, Hill quieted the clamor of his men by quietly admitting the claim of his opponent. The organization which was effected then, stood on the 15th of August, 1861, thus: —— Griffith, Captain; E. M. Hill, First Lieutenant; M. D. Edinger, Second Lieutenant, and Charles W. Morrison, Orderly Sergeant. Colonel Bissell, however, refused to tolerate the injustice of Captain Griffith, and that officer was summarily dismissed without even receiving a commission. On the 31st of October the Company— seventy-eight men—was mustered into the service by Colonel Bissell, and shortly after Lieutenant Hill was promoted to the Captaincy. The vacancy was filled by Charles R. Thompson, who came into the company with a squad, filling it up to the maximum.

Company E was recruited at Adrian, Michigan, and was originally recruited for the First Michigan Engineers, but as there was delay on the part of the Adjutant-General of that State in receiving them into service, it went to St. Louis and on the 19th of August, 1861, offered itself for admittance into Colonel Bissell's Regiment. This company was organized with eighty-four men, on the 13th of July, 1861, by the election of Samuel T. Nicholson, Captain; T. W. Henion, First Lieutenant; Benjamin F. Brown, Second Lieutenant, and Thomas G. Templeton, Orderly Sergeant. On the 23d of August, 1861. it was duly mustered into the service by Captain Tracy, United States Army.

Company F was recruited in Dubuque, Iowa, and vicinity, for which purpose the following statement was issued in a poster, which was substantially the same as the one issued by Colonel Bissell:

"THE ENGINEERING REGIMENT OF THE WEST."

Major-General Fremont has authorized the raising of this Regiment in the Northwestern States, and the undersigned is duly authorized to raise a company for it in Dubuque. Its duties will be more of a mechanical than a military character, although the Company will be armed for its own protection, and drill the same as infantry, when not otherwise employed. Its duty will chiefly consist in building bridges, the mechanical work on fortifications, etc., for which the non-commissioned officers and privates will receive, in addition to the regular pay of $13 per month, 40 cents per day, if mechanics, and 25 cents per day if laborers, thus making the pay of mechanics $24 per month and laborers about $20. All rations, clothing, bounties, and in fact every perquisite that belongs to any other branch of the service, belongs equally to this.

A BOUNTY OF ONE HUNDRED DOLLARS

has been authorized to be paid each recruit at the close of the war. The Government will furnish all tools required. Carpenters, wheelwrights, machinists, blacksmiths, and a few laborers accustomed to work with mechanics, or of marked intelligence, will be received.

It is intended that this Company shall be a first-rate one in every respect, and none will be received less than five feet six inches high, or of a shiftless character. M. RANDOLPH.

DUBUQUE, September 14, 1861.

As no memoranda have been retained, the precise date of the organization of this Company is not known. William Tweeddale was elected Captain, M. Randolph, First Lieutenant; S. W. Mattis, Second Lieutenant, and John McLaren, Orderly Sergeant. About the middle of the same month the Company came to St. Louis, where, after remaining in the receiving camp there a few days it went to the regimental camp near Sedalia, Missouri, and was there mustered into service on the 31st of October, 1861, by Colonel Bissell.

In the meantime the men became dissatisfied with Lieutenant Randolph, and petitioned for his removal, which was granted, and

John D. Rowley presenting himself with a sufficient number of men, enlisted at Bloomington, Illinois, to fill the company to the maximum, was commissioned First Lieutenant in his place.

Company G was raised at Cape Girardeau, Missouri, by M. S. Hasie, who was for a time recognized as Captain. G. L. Werth was elected First Lieutenant; Charles R. Hasie, Second Lieutenant, and Paulus Gast, Orderly Sergeant. The Company was mustered into the service with the full number of men on the 17th of September, 1861, by Colonel Bayles, of the Eleventh Missouri Infantry. About the 18th of November following the Company was sent to Bird's Point, Missouri, opposite Cairo, Illinois, where it was employed on military works until about the 8th of March, 1862, when it joined the Regiment at New Madrid, Missouri, where for the first time the whole Regiment was brought together.

Company H was raised in Paris, Illinois, and was organized about the 15th of September, 1861, with thirty-two men, electing Nathan Sandford, Captain; L. Odenbaugh, First Lieutenant; J. C. Besier, Second Lieutenant, and Nathan Johns, Orderly Sergeant.

This Company arrived at St. Louis, September 23, 1861, but not having a sufficient number of men, Lieutenant Besier was the only officer mustered. Captain Sandford and Lieutenant Odenbaugh returned to Paris, Ill., for recruits, and on the 18th of October returned with about twenty. Captain Sandford did not rejoin the Company and was not mustered or commissioned. About the 25th of October, thirty-three unassigned recruits were attached to the Company by the order of Colonel Bissell, the Company, then numbering eighty-five men, was mustered into the service on the 31st of October, 1861, by Colonel Bissell. The Company was increased from time to time by recruits, until in August, 1862, an enlargement of the number of men to the Company over the infantry maximum having been authorized by the War Department, it reached the number of one hundred and seven enlisted men.

Company I was raised in Iowa, and was recruited in several counties under the supervision of T. J. Dean, a private of the First Iowa Cavalry, who obtained his authority from Colonel Bissell. He was therefore by common consent acknowledged as Captain, and collected his men at Burlington. Twenty-one men were brought from Denmark, Lee county, by G. B. Brackett; twenty-one from Louisa county, enlisted by Frank Bras; eight from McGregor, enlisted by one —— Brant; ten from McGregor enlisted by Solomon Goodrich, and fifteen from McGregor, enlisted by A. R.

Prescott. In the choice of Lieutenants there was a conflict of interests, as might well be supposed from so many representatives of squads. In this condition of affairs, Captain Dean settled the controversy by selecting Brant as First Lieutenant, and G. B. Brackett as Second Lieutenant, on the 3d of October, 1861. Lieutenant Brant took about thirty of the men to St. Louis, followed in a few days by about the same number under Captain Dean, whose squad was immediately mustered into the service by Lieutenant Sandford.

Captain Dean then returned to Burlington with Frank Bras for other recruits, but the Governor of the State of Iowa having issued an order forbidding the enlistment in regiments of other States, it was with difficulty he raised any more there. About the last of October, 1861, Captain Dean rejoined the Company, then at Sedalia, Missouri. In the meantime Lieutenant Brant, who had not yet been commissioned, was summarily dismissed by Colonel Bissell, and Lieutenant Brackett promoted to fill his place. As there was not yet a sufficient number of men to secure the mustering in of Captain Dean, upon his return to the Company he secured the aid of William Hill, who added eighteen men to the roll, whom he had enlisted at Rushville, Illinois, and who was then appointed Second Lieutenant. The first muster of Company I as a full company was on the 31st of October, 1861, by Colonel Bissell, with ninety-six men; afterward increased by recruits to the full maximum. Before mustering a formal organization was made and T. J. Dean was confirmed as Captain; G. B. Brackett as first Lieutenant and William Hill as Second Lieutenant, by a direct vote of the men of the Company.

Company K was recruited at Burlington, Iowa, in September, 1861. Some of the men were also enlisted at other points in the State; twenty men at Wapello, Louisa County, by T. W. Bailey, and about the same number at New London, Henry County by N. W. Wilcox. On the 1st of October the Company was organized by the election of A. J. Merritt as Captain; T. W. Bailey, First Lieutenant; N. W. Wilcox, Second Lieutenant, and A. D. Whitcomb, Orderly Sergeant. Lieutenant Wilcox not being present with his squad, there were only about sixty-five men at the organization of the Company. The 2d of October those present at Burlington started for St. Louis, followed on the 8th by Lieutenant Wilcox with his party. The first muster of Company K was at Sedalia, Missouri, with seventy-six men, afterward recruited to the required number.

The organization of the companies completed and assembled in St. Louis, Missouri, with the exception of Companies A and G, the regimental roll numbered nine hundred and seven enlisted men. The regimental organization was completed October 31, 1861, and officers appointed as follows: J. W. Bissell, Colonel; Charles E. Adams, Lieutenant-Colonel; M. S. Hasie, Major; A. Jacobson, Adjutant; J. D. Ward, Regimental Quartermaster; Charles S. Shelton, Surgeon; Charles Knower, Assistant Surgeon; C. A. Staples, Chaplain; H. E. Hudson, Sergeant-Major; Isaac Y. Fulsom, Quartermaster-Sergeant; William H. Connett, Commissary Sergeant; William A. Neal, Hospital Steward.

THE ENGINEER REGIMENT OF THE WEST IN THE FIELD AT CAPE GIRARDEAU.

The first service required of this Regiment was on the 6th of August, 1861. Companies A and B were ordered to East St. Louis, on the Illinois side of the Mississippi River, to load ordnance and ordnance stores on board the steamer Empress. When loaded, they were started to Cape Girardeau the same evening, arriving there on the 7th. They at once set to work on the fortifications at that place under Captain Henry Flad, of the Topographical Corps of Engineers (Captain Flad was afterward commissioned Captain of Company B). The four works constructed at that place have amply sustained the credit of those who planned and executed them, as, after the garrison had been reduced to a mere handful of men, they resisted successfully every assault of the combined forces of the enemy in Missouri and Arkansas under General Marmaduke.

At Cape Girardeau, as Captain Rowell did not rejoin his Company, B, under orders of Colonel Marsh, of the Twentieth Illinois, Commander of the post, the Company held an election for officers and chose J. D. Anderson, Captain; John E. Murphy First Lieutenant, and Joshua Ricketts, Second Lieutenant, on the 16th of August, 1861. In March, 1862, Captain Anderson resigned and Henry Flad was appointed Captain.

When Companies A and B first arrived at Cape Girardeau there were no tents and Company A was quartered in the town, Company B on board the steamboat Illinois. After several days tents were supplied. A Lieutenant Stone was the efficient Drill Master who taught the men their manual of arms, and was greatly esteemed by them for his kindness and patience, and they will always remember him who taught them to be soldiers. Dr. C. S. Shelton, the Regimental Surgeon, joined the detachment soon after their arrival and remained there until spring, when he moved with the rest to New Madrid.

Nothing very startling occurred during the stay at Cape Girardeau. Attacks were occasionally threatened by demonstrations of small squads of the enemy; one time they approached in force, when the gunboats came up from Cairo and frightened them away. Foraging was strictly forbidden, but this was soon after changed. It was related in camp near New Madrid, in March, 1862, that General Pope stopped in front of the tents of Companies A and B, and pointing to some fat hogs and cattle belonging to a Confederate captain, said: "Soldiers, I don't want you to destroy any property;

Camp of Battalion of Engineer Regiment, under command of Maj. M. S. Hasie, at Cape Girardeau, Mo., going into winter quarters after having built the Fort in the winter of 1861.

but I do not want you to suffer for anything to eat." Three days after that those hogs and cattle had been "put where they would do the most good." Company A refused to take greenbacks from the Paymaster for their first pay, and consequently went without their money until the end of the next two months. The work called Fort George, or Fort A, was first finished; then forts B, C and D were built, commanding the approaches to the town. The forts were well mounted with large twenty-four and sixty-four pound siege guns. The last of October orders were given to prepare to go into winter quarters. (A view of the work and fortifications are given herewith, which was drawn by Captain Tressillion, Assistant Draughtsman.) During the engagement of the troops from Pilot Knob, near Jacksonville, thirty miles northwest of Cape Girardeau, orders were received by Major Hasie to build a bridge across White River to provide for our retreating troops. The orders were received at 7 p. m. and by 11 o'clock that night two companies were on the ground with tools. The only material was the trees standing on each side of the stream; from these the bridge was constructed and completed by 5 o'clock the next morning, just as the troops came up. The bridge was destroyed as soon as the crossing had been effected.

The policy of the Engineer Regiment toward the slave and the fugitive, here, as on all occasions, was to relieve, succor and protect the weak, oppressed and persecuted.

LAMINE BRIDGE.

September 16, 1861.—Those remaining at the St. Louis Arsenal were moved into a camp, about a half mile in a northwest direction, into tents, naming the new camp Genesee. On the 19th all, except a squad to receive recruits as they came in, went by railroad, on the Missouri Pacific, to Lamine Bridge, in Cooper County, Missouri, near Otterville, and named the station Camp Rochester. Headquarters remained here until the 26th of October, 1861. The men worked on the railroad bridge and fortifications to defend it. Such was the urgency for the bridge to be finished that some of the men worked thirty-six hours straight through without rest.

Soon after the arrival at Lamine a detail of Company D was sent to Jefferson City to repair railroad switches, and returned to camp at Lamine October 9th.

October 14th the camp was broken up in St. Louis, and all moved to Lamine. At this camp there were quite a number of cases of typhoid fever, and camp diarrhœa was quite prevalent, many cases becoming chronic, and most of the men being affected to some extent.

It was at this camp near the Lamine Bridge that the "Battle of the Cow Bells" took place. One night a German of Company F was on guard, Sergeant David Armstrong Sergeant of the Guard. He heard a peculiar clicking noise, that seemed to be approaching his beat, and thought that a number of the enemy were approaching stealthily to surprise the camp, taking the clicking noise to be the cocking of muskets. The guard called loudly:

"Halt! Who comes there? Halt, or I shoot!"

The noise still advancing, bang! went the guard's sixty-nine caliber Belgian musket, awakening the echoes of the night.

Sergeant Armstrong, half asleep, jumped up, and in his stentorian voice, that could be heard for miles, yelled, "Turn out the guard!" The whole camp was awakened, and sprang for their guns; the long roll was beaten; the Sergeant and the Officer of the Guard investigated, and found a gentle cow with a cracked bell slowly browsing toward the camp. This engagement was thereafter known as the "Battle of the Cow Bells," and though a trifling affair, furnished a good deal of merriment to while away the tedium of the soldiers in camp.

About the 26th of October, 1861, the Camp at Lamine was broken up and the Regiment removed to near Sedalia, on Flat Creek, naming the camp after the Major, Camp Hasie. The intention at the time was to assist General Fremont's campaign against Springfield, which movement, as is well known, resulted in a failure, and General Fremont was superseded by General Hunter. Our Regiment remained in this camp until the return of the expedition under command of General Hunter. Company F was detailed to run a saw-mill in the neighborhood, and the men worked at getting out timbers for a large bridge and lumber for quartermaster storehouses at Sedalia. The bridge was 700 feet long, but before it was quite completed work was stopped, on the 21st of November, 1861, by order of General Sherman.

While passing through Sedalia the train arrived, about twelve o'clock in the night. Some of the men had to ride outside the freight cars and when they got to Sedalia were cold and benumbed, when they started out, about a dozen of them, to find something to warm them up; went to the New England Hotel, where at first they were refused, though they offered to pay, but, as the proprietor said he kept a bar, the men threatened to break in and help themselves. He said he would open and wait on them. Each took a drink and paid 25 cents. Just then the men were called to fall in and were taken to a loft over a livery stable to sleep. In a few minutes their stomachs began to rebel. Some of the men vomited most of the night, and were very sick the next morning. One, Smith Bradley, was sent to the hospital and died a few days thereafter. The liquor had been poisoned. Lieutenant Randolph thought the men were drunk, and was very angry and had a number of them punished. The victims were very angry at the landlord of the New England House, and threatened to get even with him. About a month after this the house was burned down, and it was never known how it happened; but James Smith and a chum of his passed the night of the fire in Sedalia, and as they were two of the victims and rather reckless fellows, they might throw some light on it. Smith died before the end of the war.

Camp was broken December 11th and the Regiment started to march westward, but was stopped at Georgetown, four miles west of Sedalia, and ordered by General Pope, then in command, to the Cantonment near Otterville, where they went into camp December 19, 1861.

THE WINTER CAMP NEAR OTTERVILLE.

While in camp near Sedalia the measles broke out among the men and was epidemic from November, 1861, to March, 1862, a dozen or more dying from the disease and its effects.

It was at this camp that the first official regimental report was made to the Adjutant-General, on the 11th day of November, 1861, from which the following extract is made:

This is a working regiment composed almost exclusively of mechanics; details are daily made from each company as working parties. The Regiment is provided with every kind of tools and materials, and can do any kind of mechanical work whatever. On the first day of October, 1861, the Regiment had just completed a railroad bridge across the Lamine River, opening the Pacific Railroad to Sedalia; they then furnished the plan and made approaches for teams, and a military road from the country road, occupying about sixty men for two weeks. They constructed at that point a good breastwork for five hundred men, and have got well under way earthworks for three thousand men; have built a permanent hospital and bakery, and got out the most of the material for bullet-proof buildings for one thousand men. A detachment of two companies was at Jefferson City ten days, building extra track for military operations. Twenty men were at Tipton on the same service. Twenty men were at Sedalia making stables and corrals for public horses. Working parties are now engaged every day making a road between Sedalia and Warsaw, for the transportation of military stores. The work includes a bridge and trestle nearly seven hundred feet long, to procure the lumber for which they have prepared and put in operation a deserted saw-mill near the route. From twenty to thirty men are daily employed in repairing broken army supply wagons, to do which they have got out their own timber, burnt their own coal, etc. Thirty men worked at Otterville repairing buildings taken as hospitals for the sick. Regular time books are kept by each Orderly Sergeant, which are daily checked in the Regimental Quartermaster Department.

The above report gives a general outline of the manner in which the Engineer Regiment was employed up to that date; and but little could be added except to specify the particular work assigned to each company. At this time many hours were daily devoted to drill, to discipline the men for the many months of field service that were to probably follow, and the officers as well were wholly without experience.

H. M. Sumner (who was afterward commissioned) was appointed Drill Master.

Work was suspended on the wagon road November 12, 1861, and on the bridge over Flat Creek on the 21st. The movement to Otterville commenced on December 11th, where the Regiment went into camp December 19th naming it Camp Mildred. Company I was left at Sedalia to erect Government buildings and Company F at the saw-mill on Flat Creek, known as Smith's saw-mill and named by them Camp Julia.

As the Regiment was filled and mustered at this camp on Flat Creek for the first time, it might be well to describe the men and relate some of the incidents that occurred there.

WHY THE MARCH TO SPRINGFIELD WAS NOT MADE.

Colonel Bissell had a great dislike and a supreme contempt for a lot of imported officers that General Fremont had about him. This was shared by Colonel Wood, who was really Fremont's right-hand man and did all the work, while the foreigners made all the show. Wood had to conceal his and do the best he could; Bissell's was undisguised.

At the time General Fremont was at Tipton, Missouri, preparing for his celebrated and much ridiculed chase after Price, Mrs. Fremont spoke quite harshly to Colonel Bissell, about the poor clothes he and his men wore while Major Zagonyi and the "body guard" were so well dressed and kept themselves so neat. The reply was that our Regiment was a working regiment and that we could not run a railroad and crowd things as we were then doing and pay much attention to dress. It was a coincidence that after that time Zagonyi never received any more boxes from New York, and after he left, fine overcoats were plenty among our officers, and the Sergeants were not forgotten.

About this time our Colonel was told that the Secretary of War and the Adjutant-General of the army were coming on post haste from Washington, and he was ordered to take a certain house that was pointed out, *ask* the owners to move out for a few days, and then to put it in first-rate order for the distinguished guests. They came in due time, and although their conferences were held under a tree with a faithful guard to care that no one came within ear shot, and though he did not see either of them or go anywhere near them, he is not bound to tell how he knew afterward all that was said. But he did know, as did certain other parties, that Price was way beyond the reach of our forces and that the march would be disastrous, and he made up his mind that this Regiment should not suffer. Fremont started off with his "body guard" and wagons loaded with empty kegs to carry water for the men, and all sorts of fancy arrangements, while we received an order to proceed by rail to Sedalia, there to receive and receipt for a large number of wagons and oxen that were on their way from Kansas for the army, and then to make "a good military road, south toward Springfield." Before the oxen arrived at Sedalia it was well known that the expedition was a failure, and as "a good military road" required a long bridge across the creek and flats south of Sedalia, that was of course built and we hope it stands to this day as a monument marking the spot where our men went through the measles, which were then epidemic among the soldiers.

The name of LeRoy Richardson often appears in these pages. He was a member of Company C. As a forager he was unrivaled, as a shirker of "camp duty" unequaled, but wonderfully faithful in any outside work which he thought would be for the good of the Regiment, especially of his own company, and most particularly for the interest of Mr. Richardson and "Company Q." He could not be induced to keep his gun in order, and one day Captain Patten brought him to the Adjutant's tent with his story that it had been stolen. When told that he would be charged with it at double the Government price for a new one, he asked for a pass for a day, and the privilege of returning a better one. The next day a regiment of Illinois troops passed on the railroad, one company of which was armed with Colt's repeating rifles. Soon afterward LeRoy presented Adjutant Jacobson a new Colt's repeating rifle, and asked to have the account closed.

One day he brought to the Colonel's tent an ill-favored Polish Jew, and said that Mr. Kotowsky had a fine stock of goods which he would sell cheap. Mr. Kotowsky had prepared a price list, which was certainly fair, and LeRoy said that he would see that those prices should not be exceeded, so the permit was obtained to bring the wagon into camp. About a couple of hours afterward a disconsolate peddler complained to the Adjutant that he had no goods! no money!! He could not deny that he had received a fair price in cash for each article and that LeRoy had put all the money into a box standing in the bottom of the wagon, that the box had not been opened as the money had been put through a hole in the top, but the faithful LeRoy had not been able to find out who cut the large hole through the bottom of the box and wagon!! It has never been recorded that LeRoy thrashed any one for cutting the hole either at the top or bottom, but he did afterward admit that he thought at the time it was rather queer that Sergeant Armstrong should have traded out five two-dollar bills that had a corner torn off exactly the same way from each of them.

At one station LeRoy had made the acquaintance of a family a few miles from the camp, where he could always get a good meal and as many pies as he could carry away for one dollar, Confederate and *counterfeit at that;* he could not, however, buy any chickens or turkeys. As it was a standing rule in his mess to have turkey for Sunday dinner, he resorted to an old dodge. One day he told his country friends that the next night there was to be a foraging party out, and that certain roosts had been inspected and marked, so it was agreed that all the fowls in that neighborhood should be gathered in his host's cellar. His quondam friends never saw him again to ask him how it happened that the foragers went straight to this same cellar and nowhere else.

One day while a detachment on the steamboat Crescent City was near Island No. 18, LeRoy came on board and reported that he had discovered and landed a flatboat, in which were a man with his family, and a large number of watermelons. While a soldier ranks watermelons next to chickens, it is always understood that the manner of possession must be surreptitious on the face of it, there was no possible reason why there should be confiscation, and a purchase was not to be considered. LeRoy thought he was equal to the occasion, so an officer was sent to examine and report; when lo and behold! it was found that the boat had a small deep hold, in which were five barrels of whisky, presumably for the use of the rebel scouts down the river. The Doctor added the whisky to his stores and "Company Q," as LeRoy and his adherents were called, feasted upon the melons. Dr. Knower was rather hard, when some of them came and asked for a little whisky, because they had the belly-ache, by answering, that perhaps a little more melon would be effectual.

THE SIXTY-NINE CALIBER.

At Camp Hasie, Flat Creek, every few days the men were put through the battalion drill and practiced firing at a target. The arms were the old-fashioned United States flint-lock smooth-bore musket and Belgian musket, both altered to cap lock and rifled to sixty-nine calibre, and the recoil in firing was fearful. The men had to clean, load and fire them off nearly every day. Jack Sanders, of Company E, declared he did not want his shoulder bruised into a jelly holding his musket, and said to his chum, Soper, of the same company: "Let me fasten it to your back with your belt, and you get on your hands and knees and fire it off that way." "All right," says Soper, and proceeded to put it into action. The muzzle happened to be close to Soper's ear, and when it went off nearly deafened him, and in the recoil the gun jumped back and sideways, just missing Sander's shins and sending Soper sprawling over sideways.

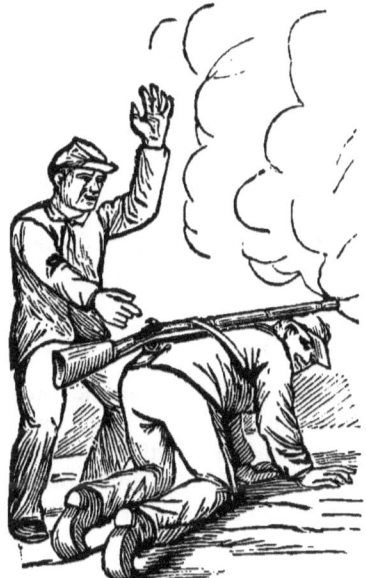

EXPERIMENT OF JACK SANDERS.

The men were raw to the service; army life and food was something new, although plenty and wholesome. One day a new arrival went to Colonel Bissell and told him that he wanted something to eat; that he could not eat those "wide-out" things, meaning the hard army bread or crackers; those served out then were about six inches square and a half inch thick, but with the Engineer Regiment the name, "Wide-out" was adopted in place of hard-tack.

PROMOTIONS DURING DECEMBER, 1861.

December 20, 1861, Henry Flad was appointed Captain of Company B.

January 6, 1862, Lieutenant W. G. Patten was promoted Captain of Company C.

The same date M. Randolph was commissioned First Lieutenant of Company C, and Sergeant W. H. Connett Second Lieutenant.

December 30 1861, Lieutenant Henion was promoted Captain of Company E.

January 1, 1862, H. M. Sumner was appointed Second Lieutenant of Company A.

January 15, 1862, H. E. Hudson was appointed Regimental Quartermaster.

During December and January the following resignations were accepted: December 3d, Captain S. T. Nicholson, and December 23d, Lieutenant B. F. Brown, of Company E; December 30th, Captain D. C. Fulsom and Lieutenant A. K. Grow, of Company C; January 23, 1862, J. D. Ward, Regimental Quartermaster.

Sergeant John McLaren was promoted to Sergeant-Major *vice* Hudson, promoted.

Sergeant A. R. Prescott was promoted Commissary Sergeant, *vice* Connett, promoted.

THE SEVERE WEATHER AT OTTERVILLE.

This winter at Camp Mildred, Otterville Cantonment, was very severe, and the men having no way to have fires in their quarters, which were the Wedge tents, they suffered extremely with the cold. Snow fell in large quantities, and the climate of Missouri, remarkable for its sudden changes at that season of the year, added nothing to their comfort. The measles still continued to be epidemic in the camp.

The continual freezing and thawing, wet or damp feet, and want of comfortable quarters, contributed much to the sickness of the following spring and summer, the foundation for which was contracted at that place.

Up to this time the men had been poorly armed and with guns of different caliber, but these were now replaced with the then new Springfield musket, and which now (1889) would be considered antiquated. On the 29th of January, 1862, Company I was relieved from duty at Sedalia, and rejoined the regiment. On the 7th of February Company F returned from Smith's saw-mill, having made there over two hundred thousand feet of lumber for Government use. February 5th Lieutenant Sumner was detached by order of

CAPTAIN A. J. MERRITT, COMPANY K, ENGINEERS.

LIEUTENANT-COLONEL CHARLES E. ADAMS.

General Pope as Ordnance Officer at Fort Lamine, and remained until February, 1863.

Our men will all probably recollect what a curve there was in the embanked road coming down off the Lamine bridge, and what a lot of stumps there were below. Our excellent Chaplain, whom Adjutant Jacobson used irreverently to style "Captain of Cavalry Staples," (because his rank and pay was that of a Captain of Cavalry) one day saw a train of about a dozen six-mule teams come down the road on a run, and as they reached this turn all go off the bank pell mell together. He was terribly shocked when he saw the "Comanche" begin to whip his team, and worse than that when he heard him swear; but when he found the snarl begin to straighten out and at last the whole train get into perfect order by mere whipping and swearing, he concluded that with mules whipping and swearing were the only remedy, and as such perfectly proper — "strictly medicinal."

It so happened that nearly all of this Regiment were Republicans from the start, and it soon became known that as an organization it could be depended upon to help the colored race. Long before the Regiment went to West Missouri word had been sent in advance to reliable colored men that this Regiment could be depended upon, and they would be helped. In addition to the Colonel, Captain E. M. Hill and Lieutenant Edinger were particularly mentioned, but most of the important messages were to be confided only to "the Kunnel." This reputation preceded them down the Mobile & Ohio Railroad to the center of the State of Mississippi, and there was no time or place when *reliable* messengers could not be had, whose pace was twenty miles per night. The statements brought were always reliable, except as to numbers, then all was at fault; " right smart of them " and " a big heap " covered the whole ground.

The Regiment was often moved out by rail thirty, forty or fifty miles in advance of the main army, but never until the dusky messengers had made their reports, and many a time when our men in Northern Mississippi were called silently at four in the morning to "stand to arms," no one but "the Kunnel" understanding what it meant.

On the first trip South, while working down the railroad south of LaGrange, Tennessee, we were all the time watched by a strong force of cavalry, hoping to find us unprepared and to pounce upon us, but they never dared come within reach. The soldiers did not understand why they were divided into squads of four comrades who were never to separate; that three were to work together while the fourth stood by the stacked guns; nor why the orders were so strict that those on one car were to jump off to the right, the next to the left and instantly form. General Van Dorn is said to have told Lieutenant Connet, after the latter was taken prisoner at Holley Springs, that he never knew any force so thoroughly prepared for everything, and that he could never get his detached commands to attack us. We were never called upon to defend ourselves except once, that was back of Bayou Macon in Northern Louisiana, when six hundred rebs attacked about one hundred of our men and were thoroughly beaten off. We did not lose a man and we brought away the cotton and horses we went for.

When we were ordered to Western Missouri to rebuild the Lamine bridge, the commanding officer at Jefferson City reported to the Department Commander at St. Louis that we were in a very dangerous position; that we had crossed the Lamine River and would have to fight with our backs to the river, that Price, although then besieging Lexington, had a force in our front large enough and ready to cut us up and that Colonel Bissell had refused to obey his orders to recross the River. The officer at Jefferson City, although a Department Commander, did not know that he had no right to give orders to *any* Engineer officer, and he was so informed. At the same time the General at St. Louis sent General J. C. Davis, then a lieutenant fresh from Fort Sumter and General McPherson, then a Captain of Engineers, to examine the situation and report. They were so far from condemning our Colonel that they agreed with him that the proper thing for us to do was to start out in light marching order, with only coffee, salt and ammunition, to attack Price in the rear—six hundred to three thousand! The Captains then at Lamine will now know for the first time why they and their men were so thoroughly and carefully inspected in that Lamine breastworks. Three days would have taken us to the rear of Price, and the friendly negroes in crowds in front would be fleeing from six hundred Yankees. Murphy inside Lexington would have made his sortie and there would have been no surrender of Lexington. So confident was Davis that he remained as a volunteer, and McPherson hurried back to communicate with Murphy as best he could, by way of the north bank of the Missouri. General Sturgis actually appeared on the opposite shore with a small force, and the wonder has always been why he did not make any more demonstration. But he did not hear our gun. Why? Because Sigel, then a newly-fledged Major-General, appeared upon the scene the night before we were to have started and spoiled it all. Nothing could make him believe that we could succeed, and Davis went back to St. Louis in disgust.

When General Pope came up to Otterville all was changed. He took advantage of the information furnished by our friends, and made his expedition, when he captured a large force at a recruiting station and caused his promotion.

THE CONTRABANDS (SLAVES).

Of course our officers had the pick of the country as cooks and waiters, and every company had its good cooks, so that our camp was the envy of the rest of the army there.

When General Halleck took command at St. Louis this was changed; his famous "General Order No. 2" put a stop to all contraband work. Officers were ordered to send all negroes out of their camps. Did we do it? Not a bit. In the first place, Captain Hill had a cave dug under his tent, over the mouth of which was his bed, on the ground; then a strict guard was placed around our camp (which was separate from that of the rest of the army), with Lieutenant Edinger in command. Then, in consequence of the many spies hovering about the camp, Colonel Bissell was ordered, in case any civilians were found near his camp "under suspicious circumstances," to have them arrested and sent, under guard, to headquarters as soon as convenient. As no one came around except to look for stray contrabands, they were there "under suspicious circumstances," and were sent to the guard-house, to be escorted to headquarters; and somehow Lieutenant Edinger always kept them until the next day and often forgot their supper. Of course abundant apologies were offered; but it was not considered a very pleasant job to come near our camp.

One day Colonel Bissell was summoned to a consultation at General Pope's, and it was agreed that he would take the party present straight to the camp, and that if there was a negro there he would be put outside the lines. This was done, but not a sign of one could be found. The secret had been well kept, and Captain Hill recovered from his severe sickness as soon as the searching party had left.

Then followed negotiations, through Mr. Wear, at his store in the village, until finally Captain Patten gave his notes at one, two and three years, for $500 each, and took a clean bill of sale of "one man Jim." He was the only one who could be induced to become a slaveholder.

When the orders came to break camp for the New Madrid campaign, the whole army was marched through the mud to St. Louis, while our Regiment was left to forward the supplies and follow afterward by rail. It took us about ten days to send forward the last of the stores and get away. The Missourians boasted that "now they had us," and the Yankees would know what law was.

At Jefferson City the Superintendent of the railroad came on board and said to our Colonel that as he was an old-time friend and as good an abolitionist, he would talk plain; that these parties had come from Otterville and sued the road for sixteen negroes, which they knew were on board the train, and the damages were $1,500 in each case, which, under the laws of Missouri, the road would have to pay. Of course the cars had to be searched. The soldiers were all in freight cars, and as a searcher was lifted up into the door on one side, somehow or other he did not stop, but landed on his head through the other door. McKissock, the Superintendent, enjoyed it thoroughly; but after the second car, the Missourians did not wish to try any more; it disgusted them. Still they would not dismiss their suits nor release the road. At last Colonel Bissell took McKissock into a private room, and said that they would go up to General T. L. Price (not the rebel), then in command of the city, and get his military order that Colonel Bissell, of the Engineer Regiment, should take sixteen negroes, then on board the train, *as prisoners*, and deliver them *as prisoners* to the Provost-Marshal at St. Louis. This was done. Colonel Bissell gave his receipt for *the prisoners*, the Missourians dismissed their suits, and McKissock was happy. He said he was mighty glad to have his road out of the scrape, but he did not see how the Colonel was to maintain his abolition principles, and it ended in a bet of a hat (which, the Colonel says, has never been paid) that the men would all be taken down the river.

Some things needed attention at Jefferson City, and the Missourians took a passenger train, reaching St. Louis twenty-four hours in advance of the Regiment. When the Regiment reached the station at St. Louis the claimants were there with lots of their friends to see the fun. Lieutenant-Colonel Adams cleared the streets and marched the Regiment to the steamboat in a solid formation with the sixteen *prisoners* in plain view in the center. On the way down, one poor darky became so frightened that he dodged out between the soldiers, when he was grabbed and was seen no more. The others were taken safely on board the steamer Empress, and a strong guard was placed to see that no one passed the gang plank either way.

As soon as the formation was made at the station the Colonel went to the office of the Provost-Marshal, showed him General Price's order, and said that he knew one of these negroes had been bought by Captain Patten, and that the operation in this case was to compel the Captain to pay his note, which was not due for ten months yet; as to the rest he would say nothing, but he wanted an order that Colonel Bissell should summon a court of enquiry, to be held on board the steamer Empress to examine into the status of these fifteen prisoners, and that their report, if approved by the Provost-Marshal and General Halleck, should be binding and conclusive upon all parties.

The court was duly summoned, as the records of the Regiment will show. Captain Hill, the President, read the bill of sale, no one disputed, although all present were called upon. Jim was declared to be the property of Captain Patten.

In the other fourteen cases a bill of sale to some officer was produced, and as it was not disputed the like order was made and entered.

The report was handsomely engrossed, duly tied with red tape, and presented to the Provost-Marshal. He endorsed the same as "approved," and took Colonel Bissell into the other office, where he introduced him to General Halleck. The General wrote "approved," and signed it, and complimented the Colonel upon his obedience to orders, and only wished all the other officers were as obedient.

The boat was pushed out into the stream, before the howling crowd had a suspicion of any action. But before the gang plank was hauled in, Lieutenant Henion, asked permission to step off a moment and just once to knock down the son of a gun who claimed his cook and who stood there "jawing" about his treatment. The Lieutenant hit him once on the jaw and went off in a blaze of glory.

THE EXTRA DUTY MONEY.

Colonel Bissell made frequent application to the Chief Quartermaster for the extra duty money without success, and the men becoming somewhat impatient with reference to it, Captain E. M. Hill was sent under orders to St. Louis, with letters of credit, to represent the importance and urge an early payment of the same.

The Chief Quartermaster at that time being nearly out of funds, Captain Hill met at first with a positive refusal, and many men of less enterprise would have failed in the mission, but having secured the influence of General Cullum, he succeeded in enlisting the interest of the Quartermaster, and on the 23d he telegraphed to Colonel Bissell that he had secured five thousand dollars.

On the 24th of February Captain Hill arrived at Lamine with the money, and on the 25th it was distributed to the companies *pro rata*.

While at Lamine much dissatisfaction existed among the men of the Engineer Regiment, partly owing to the delay of the extra duty money, but mainly at the manner of their enlistments; the demands for their relief became so strong that the matter was referred to General Palmer; but whatever may be said of the merits or the demerits of the complaints made, the subject was dropped after a very brief investigation by that officer. On the 28th of February the regiment mustered for pay, and having received orders, struck camp in the evening for the purpose of going to St. Louis, en route to join General Pope's command at New Madrid. Transportation not being ready, it did not start until the next morning, the men resting on their knapsacks during the night without shelter. As the night of the 28th and the morning of March 1st was cold the men suffered from the exposure.

THE MARCH TO NEW MADRID.

On the morning of March 2d the Regiment arrived at St. Louis and went from the railroad depot immediately on board the steamer Empress. The boat was not ready to start and some of the men, soured by the decision of General Palmer, and provoked by the closeness of the guard, became clamorous, and attempted to force the guard; but the disturbance was soon quieted, and resulted in nothing more than the arrest of the offenders, who were shortly afterward released without charges. On the 4th of March the Regiment started down the river, and landed at Commerce, Missouri, on the 5th, in the morning, where it disembarked, and under charge of Lieutenant-Colonel Adams marched across the country to New Madrid, making the march in three and a half days. This was their first extended march, and the night bivouac was a new experience for the men. The weather in the meantime was extremely severe, especially the first two days of the march. Some of the men found themselves fastened to the ground on awaking in the morning. Having to rest wherever they halted for the night with only a blanket around them, the warmth of the body would thaw the ground under them, which, ere morning, would freeze again fast to the earth and firmly secure the blankets and clothing. The sick and convalescent unable to march were left at Commerce.

NEW MADRID.

On the 8th of March the Regiment arrived in the rear of New Madrid and camped about three miles from the enemy's works, naming it Camp Cullum. New tents of the Sibly pattern, issued

FIRST NIGHT IN CAMP ON THE MARCH.

just before leaving St. Louis, were here used for the first time, and the camp presented a fine appearance; some said the finest in the whole army. Companies A, B and G here joined the rest of their regimental comrades for the first time. They had left Cape Girardeau under Major Hasie as the pioneer corps of General Pope's army in his advance South on the 1st of March, and when the Regiment had arrived at New Madrid, Company A had advanced as far as the rear of Point Pleasant and commenced digging rifle pits and throwing up earthworks for batteries there, while Company B was making fascines and gabions.

After arriving at New Madrid, Captain Flad acted upon the staff of General Pope as Engineer Officer, and an effort was made to retain him permanently in that position, but, Colonel Bissell objecting, he returned to duty as Captain of Company B, on arrival of the Regiment at that place.

March 1st Lieutenant Jones, of Company A, resigned; Lieutenant Jesse D. Anderson, of Company B, resigned, on March 21st, and Captain Henion, Company E, the 26th. March 1st Sergeant John A. Snider was appointed Drum Major.

Captain J. H. Vreeland had some time previous been placed in arrest, charged with embezzling company rations and other offenses, and on the 18th of December, 1861, tried by a general court martial, found guilty and sentenced to be cashiered and dismissed from the service. The finding was approved by the Department Commander March 11, 1862.

Company G arrived on the 8th of March, having marched from Bird's Point, opposite Cairo, Illinois, where they had been employed in constructing defensive works for the Government during the winter. That same evening, just after arriving, Companies D, F and I were ordered to Sikestown to repair the railroad from that place to Bird's Point, for the transportation of army supplies and ordnance, which work was accomplished in a few days, though a storehouse and platform was also built.

General Grant, at a visit to Cape Girardeau, in the fall of 1861, highly complimented Companies A and B for their proficiency and skill in the manual of arms, drill and soldierly appearance, and said that none in Colonel Rose's Seventeenth Illinois or Colonel Plummer's Eleventh Missouri were superior. Just after the two Companies halted in the rear of New Madrid an engagement was expected and every man was ordered into line, Morgan Morgan, cook for Company A, thought he would be exempted but had to go. He asked Comrade Feuerbach to load his gun, which he did amply. There was no engagement, but all were ordered to fire off their guns and clean them, Morgan's gun would not go off, so that he had to draw the load. In place of one he found three charges in his gun! The next day, March 3d, the two companies marched to the rear of Point Pleasant; the enemy opened fire from their gunboats and two men of Company A were killed. A terrible storm of rain drove the men from their tents and the lightning killed several mules in the camp. A twenty-four pound gun was placed opposite Tiptonville eight miles below Point Pleasant, being dragged through by two regiments of infantry.

This gun commanded the landing place of supplies for Island No. 10, which by the river was thirty miles, but by land only seven miles distant.

The Rebels were totally unaware of the gun being placed there, until about sunrise one of their gunboats came along, when there was a puff of smoke from the shore, a boom; a near shot took them by suprise; the gunboat steamed down the river and returned in about an hour with two more; all three opened fire, which they soon saw was not effective at long range. They moved closer, when our "boys," who lay on each side of the gun in sunken rifle pits, gave them a fire all along the line; they stood it for about half an hour, when the boats blew their whistles and off they went, defeated by one smooth bore gun and a support of two companies to three gunboats.

In a few days New Madrid was taken. Colonel Bissell, who had remained behind at St. Louis to transact some business for the Regiment arrived at Sikestown on the 9th of March, the same day the railroad was finished from there to New Madrid; the road was very bad. General Pope, who had ordered some heavy siege guns from Cairo, directed the Colonel to go back for them the next morning, stating that he must have them quickly. Colonel Bissell detailed one hundred of his best men to repair the road to Sikestown and started himself early in the morning of March 10th.

As usual, on arrival at Cairo, he found those at a distance from the front taking things easy and nothing done. At Bird's Point he arrived too late for the ferry that night; could get no bed or supper until the next morning at Cairo.

He got an order from General Cullum, putting all matters under his (Colonel Bissell's) orders, and in two hours he had three twenty-four pounders and one eight-inch howitzer across the river. He then ransacked the magazines for four hundred rounds of ammunition, with his usual energy, so that he had everything at Bird's Point at 4 P. M. of the 11th; on the cars at 6 P. M.; started the train at 9 P. M., arriving at Sikestown at 2 A. M., of the 12th. Colonel Bissell here took possession of all the mules and horses belonging to the troops there, requiring in all one hundred teams for the guns, platforms, implements and ammunition.

The hundred men that had repaired the road, and the railroad and bridge force of the Engineer Regiment already there, made a force of two hundred and eighty men, who assisted the teams and guns through. And a hard job they had of it, one Lieutenant in charge of the barrels, revetments, etc., and Lieutenant J. C. Besier in charge of the ammunition. All arrived just in time to put the guns in position during the night of the 13th and morning of the 14th, and we had to work upon the magazines continuously, until the night of the 14th of March—two days and two nights, without sleep or rest, and thirty-six hours without food; men and officers did appreciate their rest the 15th. During the day of the 13th Colonel Bissell and Major Lathrop, Chief of Artillery, under orders from General Pope, started out to reconnoiter a position to place the guns. Arriving at a brick house in front of an open field, in plain view from the fort, they were discovered in front of a window. A volley was poured into the house, and it is said the two struck it lively through an orchard in the rear of the house for tall timber in a cypress swamp just beyond. The writer knows how it is himself, for the next day he thought during a lull to go to the front, especially as it seemed the said brick house had been out of range some time. No one seemed to be around and he halted there for a few moments for observation, when, whether he was seen or no, the enemy's forts and gunboats seemed to open at once with all their artillery, with grape, cannister, shells, solid shot, round and rifled; directed straight at the brick house. He, too, made good retrograde time through that orchard and "struck for tall timber."

General Pope then sent two regiments of infantry, who drove in the Rebel grand guards about three hundred yards, and established our advance that much nearer and beyond where the position was selected for the redoubts. They were laid out in three sections, one of the heavy guns in each, with curtains connecting them, and a curtain on the flank of the right and one on the flank of the left redoubt, and a bomb-proof magazine for each. All was done by 4 A. M., and the enemy could not have suspected what was going on, as they could easily have driven the men away at any time before 3 o'clock. The works were turned over to the Chief of Artillery at daylight. General Stanley was to assault to the right, and General Hamilton to the left, the rest to make points on the upper works.

The assault was not made, as General Stanley said the Rebels had altogether too many guns, and the river was so high (it was even with the banks) their gunboats could take up any position they chose. He then moved the troops further back.

The men of the Engineer Regiment were kept busy at the batteries keeping them in repair, with a man on watch to cry "down!" whenever one of the enemy's guns were discharged, when the shovels would be again resumed. The guns were worked by a company of the Nineteenth United States Infantry, commanded by Captain George A. Williams. The only casualty at the batteries was from one of the enemy's solid shots striking the twenty-four-pound gun of the right battery, breaking the end off, causing the gun to swing round, killing two men and wounding six others. Three or four other men were killed in the woods and in the road, and about the same number wounded.

Colonel Bissell said : " Of all the army, my Surgeons were the only ones that came out fully prepared. Many regiments made no provision whatever, and the Surgeons of the Engineer Regiment did more than all the others."

The first rifled heavy ordnance used during the war was in this engagement; the Rebels had one long two hundred-pound rifled gun on one of their gunboats, and used it frequently during the day.

After 1 o'clock, Lieutenant-Colonel Adams took charge of the works. The firing was kept up during the whole day, and our works were enlarged during the night, but in the morning the enemy started off double quick, the fort was abandoned, the guns spiked and the gunboats moved off down the river.

General Pope put the Engineer Regiment in possession of the abandoned forts, and our gunsmiths soon unspiked the guns and they were turned to face the other way.

During the engagement Captain Tweeddale with a detail of men was started, by order of General Pope, to Bird's Point for more guns, but was halted at Sikestown by a dispatch announcing the evacuation of New Madrid. The whole force was then set at work strengthening the place against an attack by the enemy's gunboats.

The next problem was the reduction of the enemy's strongly fortified position at Island No. 10, above New Madrid, and for this boats were needed to cross the Mississippi River and attackıthem in the rear.

THE NEW MADRID CANAL, SO CALLED.

We now come to operations that were so original in their conception, so far-reaching in their results, and so successfully carried out, that the credit of originating them has of late been claimed by various persons—John Banvard, General Joseph A. Mower and others. We propose to show that the entire credit of the original idea belongs to Colonel Bissell alone, the details and their execution to Lieutenant-Colonel Tweeddale and the officers and men of the Missouri Engineer Regiment. These operations were the taking of steam transports across the fields and through the woods, around the Rebel fortifications at Island No. 10, to New Madrid, by what has been called the New Madrid Canal. First we will briefly relate the outlines, from orders and documents written on the leading steamboat, the W. B. Terry, on the 31st of March, 1862, and at New Madrid on the 11th of April, 1862, and which are still in existence.

On the evening of March 17, 1862, General Pope directed Colonel Bissell to start for the gunboat fleet, and on the morning of the 18th gave him a letter to Commodore Foote, with full authority for operations, and asking for coöperation. There was no opening on account of the high water and overflow; so he took a dugout canoe, and, with a guide and another man, they pulled through—"running the overflow" it is called—reaching Commodore Foote's at 7 P. M., who called his captains in for consultation. The importance of furnishing General Pope means for crossing the river was laid before them and admitted, but they claimed their boats were not strong enough to withstand the forty-nine guns that they could count, besides those not visible. Colonel Bissell stated a plan for perfectly protecting their sides and stern with bales of hay and cotton, and offered to prepare a boat and certify as Chief Engineer of the Army that it was invulnerable, but, with the exception of Captain Phelps, all voted against it. The Colonel then made a peremptory demand, in the name of General Pope, that they send one boat, which was refused. Colonel Bissell then asked for some tugs to try and get through the bayous, and two were furnished.

On the morning of the 19th an early start was made with the two tugs, and the shore explored for twelve miles, but no opening found with more than two feet of water, while the tugs drew six. In the afternoon the Tennessee shore was explored. No chance of getting in from above was found, but it was learned that the enemy had no communication with the main land, except by steamer from Tiptonville, and that our batteries now commanded that, and that they were now shut in completely.

On Thursday, the 20th, as he landed at the foot of Island No. 8, the thought occurred to Colonel Bissell that a passage might be found for small steamers drawing only two or three feet of water. He hunted all day, when he saw an opening into the woods, used as a farm road. His guide told him this might be enlarged to reach a bayou whose opening was near New Madrid. This seemed to be what he was hunting for, and he reported that evening to General Pope his plan. The General gave full orders, placing everything necessary to carry out the plan in Colonel Bissell's hands, and he started to Sikestown that evening with one hundred men, Captain Tweeddale and Lieutenants Wilcox and Randolph taking Company

G, Lieutenant Werth, along from Bird's Point. The details were eighteen men of Company C, under Sergeant Lape; seven of Company D, under Sergeant Barrow; nine from Company E, under Sergeant Haskins; thirty from Company F; thirty-seven from Company H, under Sergeant Waller; twenty from Company I, under Sergeant West; twenty-five from Company K, under Lieutenant Wilcox; Company G, under Lieutenant Werth—the whole under Captain Tweeddale.

Friday, the 21st, spent in more fully exploring the route for the passage of the boats through the woods and bayous.

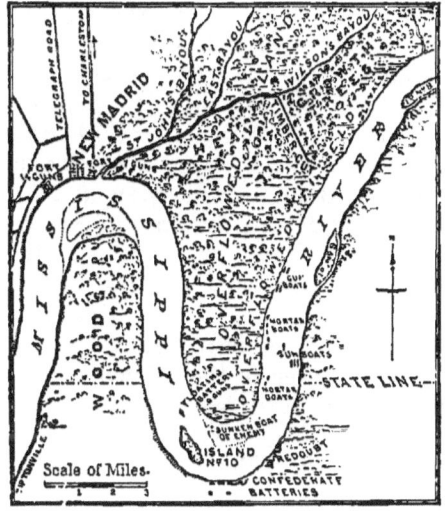

Saturday, the 22d, in getting cutters, lumber and barges and landing all at the levee before dark. The barges were empty coal barges, about sixty feet long and twelve wide, drawing about one foot, the steamers thirty to thirty-six inches of water.

Sunday morning, March 23, 1862, one barge was got through, and the steamboat, R. B. Terry, drawing three feet, started, but the cut in the levee was not deep enough. The levee was cut at an old break a few rods farther up. There were so many stumps and logs that the steamer could not be got through, and was tied up for the night, right in the rush of water above the break. The water of the river was fully two feet higher than below; the rush was fearful, and it took two headlines and six breastlines to hold the steamboat. On Monday, the 24th, the first thing was to cut off about thirty feet more of the levee, to get rid of the stumps and logs, when by means of the lines the boat was let down gently into the cornfield, where the stumps about two feet below the top of the water were so thick that it took all day to get a hundred yards from the levee, but two more barges had been got through the levee.

Tuesday, the 25th, got through to the woods about three hundred yards in about an hour, and worked all day in cutting trees out of the route. The engraving will show how the saws were rigged to cut the trees off four feet under water. After getting fairly into the woods the progress of the machines of the Engineer Regiment was more rapid. General Pope sent five more steamers this day to be taken through, but the men seeing the importance of the movement worked with a will and were proud of it and their share of the honors. Thus the work went on; the first stage was the cut through the woods two miles; the second Wilson's Bayou, about three miles, very narrow and crooked and overgrown with small trees and brush, but no large trees; the third East Bayou, about two miles, very deep, swift and straight; the fourth St. John's Bayou, partly crooked and partly straight, with considerable drift at the upper end.

One morning the Assistant Secretary of War came on board and watched the operations some hours without any one knowing it until dinner time, when he introduced himself to Colonel Bissell, and stated that he had been in the "Canal" the day previous, and had telegraphed to the President that the project was to be a success, and that Island No. 10 would be taken within a week.

On the second Monday, March 31st, the W. B. Terry was half way through Wilson's Bayou, with the expectation that in two days more the boats would be through. Unfortunately the river began to fall, and in the morning many stumps had to be cut off again that were too near the surface, though they had been cut off four feet under water the evening before, so that in place of getting through on the second day of April, it was Sunday afternoon, April 6, 1862, before they got up to near the mouth of the bayou, with the river in front and the way all clear, they were stopped here out of sight, that they might not be seen by the enemy on the opposite shore.

The men took a rest that afternoon and evening. That night the gunboat Carondolet ran past the Island No. 10 batteries and reached New Madrid.

Monday, the 7th, the men were set to work preparing for the crossing of troops. They worked all day and night. About two o'clock on the morning of the 8th the gunboat Pittsburg ran the batteries, having eighty shots fired at her.

Under direction of Lieutenant Randolph, six barges had been arranged as gun barges, with mounted guns. Among them were one eight-inch Columbaid and three thirty-two pounders. After the arrival of the Carondalet and Pittsburg they were not needed.

The enemy on the opposite side of the Mississippi, on the morning of the 8th, were all drawn up in order of battle. They expected the gunboats that had run the batteries to clear out all their small works below the Island, which they did; but that they would cut up in detail the small parties that could be landed by the gunboats. When they saw the four transports loaded with troops round the point, word was given to get out of there as soon as they could, and they started, but being hemmed in nearly their whole force was captured.

THE MISSOURI ENGINEER REGIMENT SAWING OFF TREES UNDER WATER FOR THE PASSAGE OF STEAMBOATS THROUGH THE WOODS.

One of the difficulties encountered in the start was from the levee, which was about forty feet through of solid clay, and though the river was several feet higher than the banks, and the rush of water through was tremendous, it made little impression.

A mishap occurred to Captain Tweeddale, who with seven men, on the night of the 23d, in a small boat were drawn into the rushing water, capsizing the boat, and in the darkness all hands came near drowning.

Colonel Bissell relates the inception and the carrying through of the work as follows:

COLONEL BISSELL'S NARRATIVE.

October 21, 1888.—It gives me great pleasure to comply with the request of Dr. Neal to rewrite the account of the passage of the steamboats through the swamps of New Madrid, thus avoiding the formidable batteries of Island No. 10, without reference to anything I have heretofore published.

In such an operation the public only want to know what was done and how; they take no interest in the fact that Sergeant Prescott never seemed to get tired, or that Devillo Grow was always the first to jump into the water if the saw was "pinched;" the man at the head gets all the credit, while these details, which are often the gist of the whole thing, pass almost or quite unnoticed.

I declined several times to furnish anything for publication, and only consented after I had ascertained that another article had been written which did not give our Regiment due credit.

With my old comrades and in a Regimental Book it is quite different. My great regret is that so many of the names of those good and true men have faded from my memory.

The persons themselves all stand out before me, laboring with an earnestness of purpose and intelligence that was an augury of success, but whether it was Haskins, a Bristow, a Lape or Waller that was doing a particular thing, I can not now recall, but they were all there. It seems to me that McLaren was efficient with the big guns on the barges and that I promised him that he should pull the first lanyard, and that Coy was always particular that his squad should have good coffee and plenty of it.

While the plan was wholly mine, the *entire* credit for its execution should be given to the Regiment. Captain Tweeddale had charge of the work of clearing the timber—I recollect distinctly his explaining to me about working the saws under water—he had done it hundreds of times in piling. At another time, when some one was up to his neck in the water trying to relieve a pinched saw, a man on the raft suggested pulling at the stump with a tackle. This at once relieved the saw and enabled us to double our speed, as the tackle was always rigged ahead of the saws. I think the man's name was Corporal John H. Percy, of Company F. I wish I could remember; he certainly is entitled to great credit.

Captain Randolph transformed the barges into floating batteries with great skill and celerity; Lieutenant Werth was an able assistant. It seems to me that the genial Sergeant Armstrong was always around when hard work was to be done.

LIEUTENANT JOHN McLAREN.

LIEUTENANT JOHN C. BESIER.

We had full command of the Mississippi River at New Madrid and for a few miles below, but could not communicate with Cairo by reason of the heavy batteries and strong force on Island No. 10, and the ridge of clay land on the left bank of the river extending down to Tiptonville, several miles below New Madrid. In the rear of this strong position of the Rebels was Reelfoot Lake and the overflow, extending from above their upper batteries to some distance below Tiptonville. Commodore Foote held the river above with his gunboats and the Rebs could not embark at Tiptonville, because our heavy batteries kept all their fleet below and out of sight. Opposite our position was a fine large field and General Pope said if he were only there he could make the Rebs come and fight him; but how to get there was the problem.

The General stood with me upon the parapets of Fort Thompson and outlined his whole plan, and we agreed that with two gunboats he could cross troops fast enough to carry it into effect. Neither of us doubted but that Commodore Foote would send the boats at once, and we were so confident that a set of signals was then and there arranged to be used as soon as the boats had passed the batteries above. He gave me a very strong letter to the Commodore and a telegram just received from Washington urging a hearty coöperation.

I reached the flag ship that evening about dark. The Commodore did not like to take the responsibility, but consented to call all his captains together that evening, which was done. After the plan was explained, the captains were unanimous in their opinion and vote that two boats should be sent. The Commodore was firm in his refusal to let any of them make the attempt, as he said the boats were fitted solely for fighting "head on," and that if either of them should be captured it could be started hard up stream and whip the whole fleet, lying as they did with their unarmored sterns down stream, and that Cairo would at once be at their mercy. The more I talked to him about protecting the boilers with bales of hay and having hot water nozzles to ward off any boarders the more determined he was, and the fuller he expatiated upon the danger, until finally Captain Phelps said that if he were allowed to start he would stand in the powder magazine and blow the boat out of water rather than that it should fall into the enemy's hands. How well I recollect the horror-struck expression upon the Commodore's face as he turned to the Captain and said, "That would be inhuman; this council is closed."

The telegram from Washington was so strong that I felt authorized to make upon him a peremptory demand for the two boats. This was refused. I then said that all the General wanted was enough boats to get a few of his men across the river at a time and I would at once go to Cairo and run a couple of transports past the batteries. The Commodore said this would not be allowed; that he was in command of the river and would not permit any boats thus to be carried to certain destruction. I at once jumped up and striking my hand upon the table said with considerable emphasis: "General Pope shall have his boats if I have to take them across the country."

I spent the next day upon a tug exploring both banks of the river, the east to see if the enemy were entirely shut in by the over flow, which was found to be the case; then went to ascertain if St. James Bayou, which empties into the river seven miles above Island No. 8, in any way communicated with St. John's Bayou, which had its mouth at New Madrid. Here was found no possible way across.

Here was a dilemma. I had used pretty strong language before the officers of the fleet, and had not as yet found any way of making my words good, when the next morning, standing upon the levee while the guide was bailing out the canoe, I saw an opening in the woods back of the overflowed field, and the thought came over me that this was the way to take the transports through. This was an old wagon road extending half a mile back into the woods; there it terminated. The guide said it was two miles from there to the nearest bayou. I took out my memorandum book and asked him to make a map of the route of this bayou from the nearest point to where we then were to New Madrid. This he did, showing a straight line through the timber of two miles. This we carefully explored and I said to myself, "the Engineer Regiment has talent enough to take a fleet of boats through those woods." The result proves that the old organization could be depended upon for anything.

Upon reaching terra firma I went at once to General Pope's headquarters and reported the refusal of Commander Foote. Those of you who know the General's habit of speech can imagine the blueness of the atmosphere, "blankety-blank" does not begin to express it. The General and his staff had just about finished their supper, and as I was eating mine some one suggested something about a "canal." The General laughed about any "canal" when the whole country was under water ten feet deep. I then took out my memorandum book, and, showing the sketch to the General, told him the whole thing was provided for and that our Regiment would put him across the river in fourteen days. He at once called me into another room, where the whole plan was explained. I knew that he had graduated at the head of his class at West Point, and was distinguished in the engineer service, and when he said the plan was good (" if the regiment could carry it out ") he showed his faith in it by giving me unlimited orders on everybody under his command for every thing that might be asked for.

Captain Tweeddale, Lieutenant Randolph and I sat up most of the night arranging the details, including barges to be fitted with heavy artillery and used as gunboats, and the next morning they started with one hundred men for Cairo to meet me at Island No. 8, with all the material they could get in one day. Lieutenant-Colonel Adams sent a detachment each day thereafter to Cairo to follow the first, until we had about six hundred men at the proposed starting point, with four stern-wheel steamboats, six large coal barges, one columbiad, three siege guns with carriages and ammunition, saws, and all sorts of tools and tackle in abundance and fully two million feet of lumber.

Nearly opposite an old road was a break in the levee about thirty feet wide, this we enlarged about ten feet, and then started across the fields. The way here was clear enough as far as the road extended, then the work commenced. The steamer that had a geared steam capstan went ahead, the others were lashed in single file astern, then the barges and the procession started "to slow music." Captain Tweeddale was the guiding spirit in front, while Lieutenant Randolph was building his gunboat fleet and performing his part equally well. About three hundred men were assigned to each, and all worked from daybreak until dark each day, rain or shine, with a zeal that knew no bounds.

Small rafts were provided upon which were platforms, so that the trees could be cut off about eight feet above the surface of the water. The moment the tree fell another set of men were ready with boats and lines to haul it out of the way. This was done by a line from the steam capstan leading through a snatch block off to one side. This part of the raft was kept several hundred feet ahead of the leading steamer. It took about four sets of lines to prepare the way for the twelve saws which were kept at work on the rafts.

When the space about the stump would admit a raft, this was lashed to the stump and the saw set to work. The sketch will show the manner of working better than any words. With the smaller stumps the saw was quickly worked through, but when the base of the tree spread very much, as in the case with almost all the large trees in that swampy country, it required all the ingenuity of the force to overcome the obstacle, especially as it was about five feet below the surface and the water muddy. The saw would almost always run crooked, and "pinch." If it worked up we notched the top where the saw frame pivoted, and then set the top of the frame farther in; if it run down, we had the tackle ready to spring the stump over away from the saw and relieve it. The great trouble was to ascertain just what was the matter with the saw. A man jumping into the water and feeling down could not always tell. If my recollection serves me, Sergeant Bristow was ordinarily the most correct in his judgment. We would sometimes be two or three hours upon a tough old elm, and in that time all the rest of the saws would have worked ahead several hundred feet. It took eight days to cut through the two miles to the bayou.

We had so far called it hard work, but now it was worse; the river was falling fast and the water running rapidly. The channel was very much obstructed with old fallen timber which had to be removed from the lower side, with all our lines and machinery on the upper side. Small pieces would be removed by men in a yawl, or by a line through a snatch block, but when we reached swamp oak, heavy and tough and deep under water, it would test our tackle. They had to be raised to the surface and held there until they could be chopped up. Once it took eight lines from all four capstans to get one up; three and four lines to a log were almost always in use.

In one place for about two miles every man who was not in a boat had a safety line tied around his waist, and more than one having slipped off a log, was indebted to that for his life.

Not one was hurt or taken sick while in the swamp, but soon afterward, when the excitement was over, many found that they had laid the foundation for chills and rheumatism and were put into Dr. Shelton's small company. When about half way through, Colonel Scott, the Assistant Secretary of War, came on board and said that he had been to the fleet the day before with a yawl from one of the gunboats, and that he had sent a tug up to Cairo and telegraphed to President Lincoln that Island No. 10 would be taken within a week.

While Captain Tweeddale was crowding the work in front Lieutenant Randolph was doing his share well in the rear. The barges were heavy coal barges eighty to ninety feet long, with sides six inches thick, well built of good pine timber. The plan had been to use three steamers in crossing the river. Each one to have a barge on each side and to keep one steamer as a reserve. The Columbiad and the three siege guns were skillfully mounted upon platforms and places prepared to work; several field guns were to be taken on board at New Madrid.

Six hundred of our men using one of the steamers with her two barges were to land at daybreak at the mouth of the slough below Fort Thompson and with their spades make a line of rifle pits as soon as possible. An equal number of picked men from the rest of the army were to be with them to fight or dig, as the exigencies might require; the other two sections of the flotilla were to be filled with good men and were to be landed above or below as deemed best. The reserve steamer to be ready to assist either of the others in case of accident.

As soon as the steamers reached the bayou and were on their way down I returned and reported progress to General Pope. Upon a careful re-examination of the ground from Fort Thompson with our glasses, we could see that the enemy had suspected something and were watching us carefully. The General had a battery of Parrot guns brought to the bank of the river and trained upon a house standing some hundred yards back from the river. The second discharge started the twenty or thirty officers, each provided with a field glass, and they made good time to the timber in the rear. We ascertained that the ground in several places had been moved each night, but the marks were so skillfully covered with weed, etc., that one could not determine just what was done. If they were ready with guns hidden just within the timber and these disturbances of the soil were rifle pits manned every night, they might cause us much trouble; so it was concluded to make the leading boat a fighting boat that could not be disabled and then we could make a landing in spite of them. A large number of empty coal oil barrels were ordered by telegraph from St. Louis and Cairo, which were brought through our channel and reached the fleet in the bayou. They were placed two tiers deep all over the floor of two of the barges, the vacant spaces filled with dry rails and the whole well floored over so that dozens of holes in the barge would not destroy her buoyancy and no shot could go clear through and reach the steamer. The steamer was bulkheaded with timber about the engine and boiler so as to fully protect those vital parts from any damage.

Careful cover was also prepared for a goodly number of sharpshooters.

This improvised gunboat would have covered the debarkation of our Regiment and protected us till we could have dug our rifle pits and been able to take care of ourselves; then it would have been used for the other picked men. The whole were kept concealed in the bayou until all the details could be arranged and the several officers fully instructed just how to act. Late one morning General Pope handed me a roster of the officers he had selected for the expedition, and I had just fallen asleep when a messenger came in great haste, saying that a gunboat had run the gauntlet and we were to show lights for her landing and then have her hauled into the bayou for concealment. The latter could not be done. The Rebs the next morning saw her and began to prepare to dispute our crossing, which they knew was sure to follow. The next night the Pittsburgh successfully run the batteries and a splendid gunboat fight against the shore batteries was witnessed by us all. We know the results.

Several of the captured officers told me that after the gunboats had run the batteries their whole force was withdrawn from about Island No 10, and placed in ambush to pick off the men as they landed from the gunboats, but when they saw our flotilla steam out from the bayou loaded down with men they lost all disposition to fight, and each one looked out for himself. A few succeeded in getting through the overflow, but most of them surrendered without conditions.

As soon as the importance of this work appeared and was spoken of and praised by all in conversation, books and newspapers, both North and South, others began to claim the credit of originating the plan. General Schuyler Hamilton claimed he suggested bringing transports through the overflow. John Banvard, an employee of the Topographical Engineers; General (then Captain) Joseph A. Mower, whose claim is supported by Captain George A. Williams of the Nineteenth United States Infantry, whose Company handled the guns a few days before, in the action against New Madrid, also claim the first credit. But if any one of them thought of bringing transports through in that way, no one heard of it until after the work was accomplished.

To show that no one at the time thought of giving credit to anybody except Colonel Bissell and his Engineer Regiment, the following orders and extracts from publications of the day are introduced.

General Pope in his report to the Government said: "Colonel Bissell having reported that a route could be formed for a channel sufficient for small steamers, I immediately directed him to commence the Canal with his whole Regiment, and to call for any assistance for men or material necessary for the work. It was my purpose to make the Canal deep enough for gunboats, but this it was not found practicable to do within a reasonable period. The work done by Colonel Bissell and his Engineers was beyond measure difficult; the Canal is twelve miles long, six miles through very heavy timber, was made fifty feet wide by sawing off trees four and a half feet under water. Of Colonel Bissell and his Engineer Regiment, I can hardly say too much. Untiring and determined, no labor discouraged them, and no labor was too much for their energy. They have commenced and completed a work which will be memorable in the history of war."

The Chicago *Times* said: "The great feature of this memorable siege, and the immediate cause of the glorious victory which followed, is the transportation of four steamers across the country to the aid of General Pope. Colonel Bissell announced that he was in readiness to attempt the task of taking them across the country. The task of clearing the trees out was one that would have discouraged a sterner heart than Colonel Bissell's but for the engineering experience and natural ingenuity which came to his aid."

From "Leslie's History of the War:" "General Pope, desirous of rendering every aid to Commodore Foote's flotilla, sent Colonel Bissell to ascertain if it were practicable to establish batteries opposite the Island. Three days were spent in the swamps in canoes with negroes as guides, and the project was pronounced impracticable. Colonel Bissell, however, arrived at the conclusion that he could by hard labor get steam and flat boats through the woods and bayous beyond the Island. General Pope at once gave him *carte blanche*, and forthwith he commenced a military canal around Island No. 10."

The New York *Herald* published that "Thousands of trees had to be cut and dragged away in order to allow the upper works of the steamers to pass through; stumps and floating wood without limit have had to be removed, and obstructions almost insurmountable have been met and overcome, such as would have discouraged anyone but a Yankee of the Bissell school, or the untiring and unflinching Western boys whom he commanded. The Colonel is justly proud of his achievement, and his men share with him in self-congratulation."

The Chicago *Tribune* correspondent wrote: "To the Rebels, this last was the unkindest cut of all. They felt sore that General Pope had outgeneraled them out of New Madrid, but the idea of bringing steamboats overland was too much; yes, the cut of that canal was an unkind cut, and they broke and ran in disgust. One rebel officer said: 'We had heard about the canal, but did not believe it could be done.' The idea of cutting a canal large enough for good-sized steamboats, and to saw four feet under water at least one thousand trees from six inches to three feet in diameter, besides removing innumerable snags for a distance of eight miles, is something unequalled in any warfare. Napoleon drawing cannon over icy crags is not equal to it. Colonel Bissell, of the Engineer Regiment, a man of most untiring energy, was the General's right-hand man in executing the enterprise. His men worked thirteen hours per day, while the Colonel himself could scarcely be said to sleep until he had astonished Rebeldom generally."

Just after the surrender of the Rebels, Colonel Bissell said, and the remarks were embodied in a letter written at the time, that no suggestion whatever of anything was made to him by anyone; that as he stood upon the levee opposite Island No. 8, looking at the water all around, the idea came to him like an inspiration; as a flash the whole plan was developed in his mind, and was never changed; that he called to Mr. La Forge, his pilot in the canoe, to get him back to New Madrid as fast as possible. Those of us who know of the twelve miles of water between the levee opposite Island No. 8 and the New Madrid ridge, where the army was encamped, laugh heartily of a canal.

There was no canal, but a way was cleared through the woods to the bayous, which were in turn cleared of stumps, logs and drift. The idea never could have been carried out without just such men as the Missouri Engineer Regiment, and to them should be given the credit.

THE NEW MADRID CANAL.

To Captain (afterwards Lieutenant-Colonel) Tweeddale, who had charge of the details of the work, Colonel Bissell wrote the following letter of acknowledgment:

SIR: While I congratulate each of the officers of the Engineer Regiment that were engaged with me in constructing the canal across the peninsula about Island No. 10, upon the success of the undertaking, I desire especially to express my acknowledgments to you for the valuable assistance rendered by you, for the unfaltering zeal and untiring industry shown by you, as the officer in charge of the work. I was surprised and gratified at the readiness with which you devised an expedient to overcome every obstacle. Trial showed these expedients to be always successful.

Respectfully your obedient servant,
J. W. BISSELL,
Colonel Engineer Regiment.
CAPTAIN TWEEDDALE, Engineer Regiment.

During the clearing of this water route through the woods, Captain Bailey, with detachments from different companies, was engaged in putting the Cairo & Fulton Railroad in repair as far as Sikestown. Captain (afterwards Lieutenant-Colonel) E. M. Hill, was charged with the improvement of Fort Thompson and made it impregnable from attack by water. Company B was making fascines and gabions, while Company A, with detachments from other companies, remained at Point Pleasant and below, constructing batteries under Lieutenant-Colonel Adams.

While here one man of Company A was accidently killed by the discharge of a gun. His comrades, while preparing to bury him, were fired upon, and an exploding shell set the hotel where he was killed on fire; when the fire was put out his body was found to be badly burned, but faithful to their comrade in arms, they took the remains to another building, where they found a beautifully lined coffin supposed to be the property of the Masonic fraternity. In this they deposited the body, which was then taken to a covenient spot and buried with all the honors of war.

FORT PILLOW.

On the 12th of April the whole of the regiment, excepting Companies A and I, went on board the steamer McDowell, and the men received their pay for the months of January and February before proceeding down the river, which they did with the army of General Pope on the 13th and disembarked in Arkansas opposite Fort Pillow, where they enjoyed the music and stings of the myriads of musquitoes for one night.

TO CORINTH.

The next day the whole army re-embarked, going up the Mississippi River and the Tennessee River to Hamburg, Tennessee, where they arrived April 22, 1862.

As the successful operations of the Engineer Regiment had been published in all the papers, the passage up the Ohio River was a continual ovation, especially at the towns of Mound City and

Metropolis. The streets were crowded with an enthusiastic people, who with cheers and the waving of thousands of handkerchiefs bade the Regiment "Godspeed."

On this trip Colonel Bissell, who had already become well known for his summary method of treating matters, turned the Captain, clerks, pilots, servants, and in fact every one except those of his own Regiment, out of the cabin, closed the bars, put his own servants in charge of the cooks galley and conducted his own mess, the officers of the boat taking rooms and eating in the Texas. This treatment was owing to some impositions of the boat officers, but was Colonel Bissell's usual way of disposing of such cases. There was but one pilot, and Sergeant David Armstrong, who had experience in that line, took his turn at the wheel half of the time on this trip

The work in the water taking the steamboats through the woods had been very fatiguing, and the men had been greatly exposed, Company G especially suffered, one or another of the men either had to get into the water up to their necks to adjust a saw, tackle, line or something, or fell in dozens of times a day. Probably one-half of the men engaged contracted rheumatism or chronic colds, laying the foundation of permanent disabilities. So also on the trip to Hamburg, taking eleven days, it rained almost continually, with nearly a thousand men crowded upon one boat, filling every nook and corner of it. Few could secure shelter, and by far the larger number had to brave the tempest and endure their wet clothing, many sleeping in pools of water. April rains are cold in that latitude. The facilities for cooking were so poor that some could get but one meal a day. The suffering and sickness caused thereby will be remembered by all. The result of the exposure from these two sources was that by the time the men arrived at Hamburg about one-half were on the sick-list, and some days it took until night for the Surgeons to get through the morning sick call.

Companies A and I were detached at New Madrid, by order of General Pope, to build a magazine and to make inventory of ordnance stores; to remove the heavy guns from the detached batteries below to Fort Thompson, and from the main land above to Island No. 10, all of which they accomplished by the 4th, and rejoined the Regiment before Corinth on the 8th of May.

The following changes and promotions were made during the months of April and May, 1862. April 12th, Lieutenant and Adjutant Jacobson returned from recruiting service, and was on the 25th appointed Ordnance Officer on General Pope's Staff, assuming the duties at once.

Captain Dean, of Company I, resigned, and his resignation was accepted by General Halleck, to take effect on the 25th, and about the same time Lieutenant Dougherty, of Company A, who had been under arrest since the 27th of January, was dismissed the service.

On the 29th of May, Lieutenant Thompson, of Company D, was detached and appointed Post Quartermaster, by order of General Pope. About the same time, the resignations of Chaplain C. A. Staples and Lieutenant Charles R. Hasie were tendered and accepted June 6th.

Soon after arriving at Hamburg, Tennessee, it was discovered that the corps of Pope and Buell, were separated by a deep creek or bayou, and would in case of an attack be unable to communicate with each other. Companies D and F were detailed under Captain Hill to build a bridge, which was commenced about dark on the evening of the 23d of April, and finished about daylight the next morning, after an all-night's work.

The next day, after arrival at Hamburg, Colonel Bissell asked a few of his officers if they did not wish to go out to the front and reconnoitre. Putting on old clothes and riding good horses, they, five of them, started for the picket lines on the Farmington road, which were on a ridge crossing the road, one branch of the road leading to Shiloh Church, about a half mile off to the right in plain sight. The Sergeant with the party said the vidette was on the left about a quarter of a mile in advance, just over the ridge. So sure was he that there was no enemy near that they concluded to take their chance for a good look at the famous church. The Colonel explained the lay of the country before starting, so that in case they became separated, they could make their way back to camp. Just as they reached the church a party of fully a hundred cavalry attacked the picket, firing a volley. Before the party could get behind the church they were discovered. The enemy started for them with a yell, fifty to five. The Colonel and his party started for the Owl Creek ford; the Colonel with his roan thought he could keep ahead, but had to be second, as one of the others had a better horse. After a breakneck ride of two miles, not hearing pursuit, they halted, and now, being in old clothes, they had to be on their guard not to be fired on by Buell's pickets.

They soon discovered the welcome blue uniforms. The Colonel dismounted, threw both hands up and advanced; the picket guard of about twenty all brought their guns to a ready; the Sergeant stepped in front with his pistol cocked and levelled; the Colonel marched up as though he was going to bite off the end of the Sergeant's pistol and did not stop until within about a foot of it.

He afterwards said that pistol looked larger to him than a hundred pound Parrott gun. The Lieutenant coming up, the whole party was placed under guard and marched to General Buell. It was night when they reached camp, where the report was current that they had all been captured.

On the 25th of April the Regiment moved six miles inland, and from this time until the 30th of May was actively engaged with the left wing of the army in the siege of Corinth.

But a slight conception of the amount of work performed can be entertained, except by a person who has passed over the road and witnessed the untiring industry of the men of this Regiment, who alone were relied upon to open the way for the army and make many of the entrenchments for the siege. The distance is twenty-two miles, much of it over a swampy country. The recollection of that spring is that it was very rainy, rendering the roads, as they were, impassable for an army.

To transport the siege trains and supplies the whole road had to be corduroyed and enlarged to a double track for the passage of long wagon trains in opposite directions; making nearly forty-four miles of corduroy road. This was done by cutting down young trees, splitting them in two; using these puncheons as a road bed. Much of the way it was impracticable to work teams in the road building, and these heavy logs and poles were carried by the men to the place required. All the men were engaged upon this and work of the kind, and as each company was taxed to its utmost capacity, sustained equal credit in this campaign. Not only were the men worked during the day, but in the still hours of the night, while other soldiers were enjoying such rest as could be obtained on the field, considering the unsettled condition of affairs; this regiment was actually employed building bridges, or building roads, preparatory to the next day's advance by the army. As they neared the enemy's strongly intrenched position near Corinth, other duties arose.

From Farmington the ground was strongly contested by the enemy, and the further advances were made at the cost of a series of skirmishes which might be magnified into so many battles.

In addition, therefore, to keeping the roads in repair, batteries had to be constructed, and heavy guns placed in position. It was in the construction of one of these batteries on the 28th of May that the enemy opened a cross-fire and made a dash with a brigade of men upon the workmen under Lieutenant Randolph. This battery was being constructed on a high knoll and was armed with two thirty-pound Parrott guns, and from which point the church steeples in Corinth could be seen. The brigade that charged the battery was from Hardee's division; the guns were not yet in place and were consequently useless, and the dash was so sudden and unexpected that our men did not have time to retire or get out of the way of our own guns, two or three batteries of which were unlimbered in the rear. The men, therefore, lay down flat and let our men fire at the advancing enemy who came on with the Rebel yell (Ki! yi! yi! yi!)

Richard Ryan, Orderly Sergeant, Company A, was killed. Private Carver, Company A, recieved a canister shot in his right foot and died from the effects about a week later. Private Thomas E. Bivins, Company C, was wounded in his right leg near the knee joint and the leg was amputated above the knee by Surgeon Shelton. Sergeant Ryan was shot, seemingly by a shell, through the shoulder and left breast, tearing the whole left side of his chest open, one leg and arm broken, killing him outright. He was one of the brightest, bravest and noblest of the men of Company A. He was buried where he fell. Sergeant Young and many of his comrades wept like women as they buried him. One of his comrades says, though twenty-six years have elapsed, many times his form comes up before the memory with an effect to even now start the tears afresh, as the thoughts of his loving, kind and helpful nature is recalled. Sergeant James McClure was taken prisoner. One killed, two wounded and one prisoner were the casualties of the Engineer Regiment in this affair.

The last battery finished by the Regiment during this siege of Corinth was a large one of thirty-pound Parrot guns by Companies C and H, under charge of Captain Patten, Lieutenants Odenbaugh and Besier. The order for its construction was received and the work commenced late in the afternoon of the 27th of May, and before daylight the next morning the whole work was completed and the guns in position; so rapidly and creditably was the work done that Generals Rosecrans and Smith on the following day extended a flattering compliment to the builders.

An incident of the campaign illustrating the fertility of the resources of the Engineer Regiment was a remarkable observatory erected in a tall oak tree near Farmington, from the top of which a full view of the enemy at Corinth could be obtained; the height of the tree was increased by a framework of tall poles on which was built a platform.

Captain Hequambourg, of Company G, had on the 24th of April been assigned to the command of Company E.

In a skirmish on the 3d of May, near Farmington, Lieutenant-Colonel Adams was captured by the enemy and did not rejoin the Regiment until November.

On the morning of the 30th of May it was found that the enemy had evacuated Corinth, and the army was ordered in pursuit. The Engineer Regiment was the first to march in pursuit, except one regiment of cavalry, leaving tents, hospital and train behind, taking nothing that would impede rapid movement. About dark the Tuscumbia River was reached, at a point where the enemy had destroyed the bridge and had placed a batttery with infantry support to dispute the passage. The Engineers, being in advance, were the first to receive their fire. Company A, under Captain Randolph (who was always hasty, inconsiderate and pushing), was marched right up to the burning bridge without reconnoitering or deploying skirmishers, and when within fifty feet of the bridge the Rebels opened with artillery and infantry. All who could, ran back; but four of the Company, among whom were Sergeant John Lewis and Corporal Whitson, were killed; two, Henry Feuerbach and Platt Griffith, were taken prisoners. Feuerbach afterward escaped, and his adventures are given elsewhere. The result of this reception was that the whole Regiment was thrown on the defensive without support and were compelled to retire about two hundred yards, where they reformed and were deployed as skirmishers and advanced, forcing the enemy back to the river, where a battery was brought into position and Company B, under Captain Flad; Company C, under Captain Patten; part of Company H, under Lieutenant Besier; and Company I, under Captain Brackett, coming up, they were ordered to support the battery, which they did. Darkness coming on, the whole command rested on their arms until morning. The next morning the enemy was still obstinate and the troops were unable to effect a crossing. An order was made to construct a bridge under their fire, and a portion of the day and the succeeding night was passed in getting out material to have everything ready to lay the bridge with as little delay as possible.

In the morning, everything being in readiness, the men moved with the material to the river, prepared to meet a shower of bullets; but, contrary to expectation, the enemy had withdrawn, and the bridge was built without further hindrance.

While the whole Regiment was obedient to orders and did its duty faithfully, the conduct of Company A, together with Company F, being more immediately engaged, was particularly creditable.

It was near this bridge that Captain Merritt, while in charge of Company K as escort to the wagon train, was fired at by the Rebels in ambush, one of the bullets penetrating his canteen, and as the day was very hot and he felt the warm fluid trickling down his legs, he got off his horse to examine, though he felt no wound, when he found in place of his own blood it was from a wound in his canteen. Some of his teasing comrades started the story that he had fainted from the fancied loss of blood.

Upon leaving Corinth the orders were very strict about straggling, foraging, or any appropriating of property by the men, and Colonel Bissell had told the men that on no account would they be permitted to leave the ranks or to help themselves to anything belonging to the inhabitants. It so happened that the day was very hot, the roads dusty and the men thirsty. The head of the column had been halted at a pump, each man getting water as he passed; Sergeant Aaron Clark stepped to the side of the road and reached through a fence to pluck some blackberries. The Colonel observing him and thinking he was attempting to straggle, shouted to him to take his place in the ranks. Clark either did not hear the Colonel, or did not know that it was himself called to, and paid no heed. The Colonel without consideration raised his revolver and fired towards Clark, the bullet entering near the middle of his abdomen on one side, passed just beneath the skin and out on the other side, without wounding the bowels at all. A clear case of misunderstanding on both sides, and the Colonel was certainly hasty. The Sergeant made a quick recovery.

COLONEL BISSELL'S VERSION OF THE TUSCUMBIA BRIDGE FIGHT.

Colonel Bissell, in his version of the Tuscumbia affair, says: "After the evacuation of Cornith our Regiment was sent to overtake the wagon train of the column that had taken that route ; one company of Cavalry was added. Just at dark we reached the narrow valley through which the Tuscumbia runs, here a small stream. The cavalry were ordered not to go faster than the men on foot who swept the woods on each side, to keep the men out of any ambuscade. But they would push ahead, and when they reached within point blank range of the bridge, they were treated to a round of grape and canister that sent them back in a hurry. By this time a formation could be made, the bridge was burned and the Rebels took to their heels. Several wounded men were taken to Dr. Knower and cared for. There was one whose head appeared so much mashed, and who seemed so very dead that the Doctor thought he would eat his supper before attending to him; but when the Doctor came back, the man was groaning feebly, showing that there was at least a little life left in him. Some water was heated and the Doctor carefully washed off brains and blood, washing from the neck upwards very carefully, and no wound, until at last the top of the man's head was reached and found to be perfectly sound; it was the brains and blood of the man's horse that had been dashed into his face by a cannon shot, and the only hurt was a bruise on the shoulder caused by the fall with the horse."

When the Regiment went from New Madrid to Hamburg, Companies A and I were left behind. Concerning their duties, Captain Brackett says:

"The operations of General Pope's army soon resulted in the capture of Island No. 10; after which our Regiment, with General Pope's whole command, was ordered up the Tennessee River to reinforce General Grant after the battle of Shiloah. Two compaines (A and B) were left under my command, with a steamboat, to gather up all the ordnance and ordnance stores for the purpose of fortifying the lower end of Island No 10. After this was accomplished, we proceeded up the river to joint the Regiment. When we reached Cairo, I landed and reported to the Post Commander for further orders. It was while here that Lieutenant Randolph, of Company A, came near being killed by his men. Although a strong guard was placed on the gangway of the boat, many of his men got ashore, some by jumping into the river on the outside of the boat and swimming, and after becoming intoxicated, they returned to the boat as furious as wild beasts. I was at the Post Quartermaster's Office drawing clothing for the men when a messenger, in great haste from the boat, informed me that there was a meeting going on, and on hastening to the boat, I was just in time to save Lieutenant Randolph from massacre. He had undertaken to tie some of them up, when they

APT. G. L. WERTH, CO. G, MO. ENGINEERS.   CAPT. ALEX. G. HEQUAMBOURG.

MAJ. M. S. HASIE, MISSOURI ENGINEERS.   DR. CHARLES KNOWER,
ASSISTANT SURGEON MISSOURI ENGINEERS.

became infuriated; they had got him down amidship and were on the point of bayoneting him. I quelled the riot as soon as possible, and after getting all on board we proceeded up the Ohio River; but it took all of Company I to guard Company A that night; but by the time we joined the Regiment, Company A had sobered up, and Lieutenant Randolph again resumed his command, feeling thankful that he had escaped from what at one time appeared to be certain death from a bayonet charge by his own men.

CORINTH TO JACKSON, AND THE OPERATIONS AT AND AROUND JACKSON, TENNESSEE.

When the bridge across the Tuscumbia was finished, the Regiment returned to Corinth, where the headquarters, hospital and corral had been located according to orders. The Regiment was then ordered to open the Mobile & Ohio Railroad to Columbus, with headquarters at Jackson, Tennessee. Company E remained behind at the ordinance magazine; a part of the regiment halted at Purdy for about a week, quartered in vacant buildings. It did not take long to repair the railroad from Jackson to Corinth, whence the camp equipage was sent by rail from Corinth. The headquarters arrived at Jackson about the 6th of June, 1862.

When the Regiment moved from Corinth to Jackson, Company E was left near Farmington in charge of the magazine and ordnance stores. On the 6th of June Lieutenant Edinger left for St. Louis, Missouri, on a furlough, and Captain Hequambourg, of Company G, was assigned to the command of Company E. The Company remained at Farmington until June 23d, when the ordnance stores were moved to Corinth.

At this time it was easy for citizens to enter Corinth to sell supplies, until one day a man with a wagon, selling buttermilk, was found to have in the wagon a lot of United States muskets, bayonets, cartridge boxes and belts; and a few days later another citizen peddler was arrested with a lot of letters on his person.

Owing to the carelessness of the Provost Guard the morals of Corinth became very low, until about the 13th of August Lieutenant Edinger arrested all the lewd women in the town and sent them to Cairo, when tranquillity was restored.

Captain Hequambourg did not long remain in command of Company E, but resigned July 2d to accept promotion as Lieutenant-Colonel of Fortieth Missouri Infantry, and on June 18th Lieutenant

William Hill was placed in command of the Company, with orders to take charge of the military work shops at Corinth, where he remained until October, creditably representing the mechanical skill of the Missouri Engineer Regiment, constructing several large warehouses, an addition to the railroad depot, a turn table, a car shop, a number of platform cars and all the mechanical work which the interests of the place demanded.

The detachment proved so useful that General McPherson, who was then Military Superintendent of Railroads, complimented them and Lieutenant Hill with his favor and approbation.

About September 16th two men of Company E were captured near Burnsville, a few miles east of Corinth. On the 30th of September the Company was ordered to join the rest of the Regiment at Jackson, leaving a small detachment under Lieutenant Thompson at Corinth.

On the 3d and 4th of October, 1862, occurred the second battle of Corinth. The small detail of Company E was all of the Engineer Regiment in that action. Lieutenant Charles R. Thompson, at a critical moment when the enemy had penetrated to the town and were forming on the streets, greatly distinguished himself by taking possession of a section of a battery that had been abandoned, and, with a few of our men, turning the guns upon the line of the enemy that was forming, thereby causing them to scatter and soon after retreat and abandon the contest.

For this gallant action Lieutenant Thompson was highly complimented by General Rosecrans, and soon after appointed Captain and Aide-de-Camp on his Staff, and a few months later Colonel of the Seventeenth United States Colored Troops.

In the early part of July the "extra money" due the men was paid over to the company commanders pro rata, and by them transferred to the men entitled thereto.

On the 1st of July Quartermaster-Sergeant Hudson was appointed Lieutenant and Regimental Adjutant, Sergeant E. Winegar was promoted to Lieutenant and Quartermaster; Sergeant-Major McLaren was promoted to Second Lieutenant, Company A; Lieutenant Jacobson to Captain, assigned to Company E; Second Lieutenant Wilcox to First Lieutenant, Company I; Sergeant J. P. Brooks to Commissary Sergeant; Sergeant Frank Bras to Sergeant-Major; Sergeant John A. Points to Quartermaster-Sergeant; Lieutenant Randolph to Captain, Company A; Second Lieutenant William Hill to First Lieutenant, Company A; Private L. W. Coy to

Second Lieutenant, Company F; Lieutenant L. Odenbaugh to Captain, Company H; Second Lieutenant J. C. Besier to First Lieutenant, Company H; Sergeant D. G. Parker to Second Lieutenant, Company G; Sergeant D. B. Sherwood to Second Lieutenant, Company I; Second Lieutenant S. W. Mattis to First Lieutenant, Company C; First Lieutenant G. L. Werth to Captain, Company G; Second Lieutenant John E. Murphy to First Lieutenant, Company B; Sergeant Joshua Ricketts to Second Lieutenant, Company B; First Lieutenant G. B. Brackett to Captain, Company I; Sergeant A. D. Whitcomb to Second Lieutenant, Company C; Second Lieutenant W. H. Connett to First Lieutenant, Company G. July 7th Sergeant J. P. Brooks was again promoted, from Commissary to Second Lieutenant of Company K, and Sergeant John F. Anderson appointed as Commissary. The above promotions were all in the first week of July, 1862.

The resignation of Lieutenant John D. Rowley was tendered on the 10th of July and accepted August 8th, to take effect from July 14, 1862.

While the Missouri Engineer Regiment was located at Jackson, Tennessee, nearly every branch of manual and mechanical labor demanded by the military service was carried on. One detachment of the men under Lieutenant Besier was engaged in clearing obstructions from the railroad track, which they did along the whole road from Corinth to Columbus, a distance of one hundred and forty-four miles.

Captains Flad, Tweeddale, Patten and Bailey, assisted by a half score of lieutenants with large detachments of men, were actively employed constructing bridges and trestles over the many rivers and swamps with which that country abounds. The bridges over the Obion and Deer rivers constructed this season were extremely creditable to the builders.

Lieutenant Sherwood had charge of a saw-mill at Jackson, which he operated with a detail from Company I, assisted by Lieutenant Mattis with a squad of negroes; they manufactured a large amount of lumber for the Government.

About thirty men were daily under Lieutenant McLaren constructing an improved lattice bridge, which was framed at the machine shop in Jackson and taken on cars to the crossing of the Obion River and there put in place for the railroad bridge. This bridge was pronounced an ornament to the road and a lasting credit to the Regiment. Another detail under Lieutenant Coy was engaged erecting Government buildings, while still another under Lieutenant Whitcomb was engaged in constructing cars, and built one of the finest passanger coaches in this country. This car was afterward transferred to the Memphis & Charleston road, and was only used on special occasions. The painting of this car would recommend Artificer Graves to a creditable place among the members of his craft.

THE ISLAND NO. 10 WRECKING DETAIL.

On the 21st of July Captain E. M. Hill, assisted by Lieutenant Parker, with a detail of sixty-five men from the various companies, was ordered on a wrecking expedition on the Mississippi River, among the boats, barges and floating batteries, sunk or destroyed by the Rebels in their surrender of Island No. 10 and New Madrid. This detachment reached Columbus, Kentucky, the same evening and embarked on board the steamer Crescent City about 11 o'clock P. M. Next day they went down the river to a small sand island opposite Point Pleasant, where the Rebel floating battery had drifted in April previous. It was cut loose by them on the day of the surrender of Island No. 10, hoping it would float past the Federal forces and thus be saved to them for future use.

The water was high at the time and it passed nearly over the island and was caught upon the highest point; the falling river had left it high and dry and half buried in the sand. This battery was a formidable affair and mounted sixteen guns, some of them sixty-four pounders, and carried two large engines for propelling, which were protected by a bomb proof. It was not a difficult job to remove the guns, but in order to get at the machinery the bomb proof had to be torn away; this was a work of patience and labor. It consisted of twenty-four inches of timber, covered by a thick iron plating, firmly secured by bolts. The men were engaged nearly three weeks at this work, which was anything but a pleasant experience, as the burning heat of a July sun on a barren sandbar, rendered doubly tedious and oppressive by the heated sand, was soon felt, and its effects told in the increasing sickness of the men. At the same time myriads of mosquitoes held high carnival during the night and added to their discomfort. Only one small boat was left with which to communicate with the main land, and that was soon useless because of the low water. There was a short relief afforded in a trip down the river to Memphis on the Crescent City, with a partial load of guns and ammunition from New Madrid, which were taken down for the defense of Memphis. This trip, although a relief from the sun and mosquitoes, was very fatiguing to the men in the working detail. The loading and unloading of heavy guns under a burning sun was by no means an enviable job; nevertheless any employment or position almost was preferable to a barren sandbar.

On the way up the river on this occasion the boat was landed at Island No. 18, by order of Colonel Bissell, who was on board, for the purpose of breaking up a camp of the enemy said to be in that vicinity. No such camp was found, the squad sent out reporting the destruction of a quantity of salt, a ferry boat used by the enemy, and the capture of a number of horses and mules, only one of which was retained.

On the 16th of August the detachment removed to Island No. 10, where it was employed nearly two weeks removing guns and amunition from the Rebel batteries to the landing for shipment. Upon this island they had the advantage of shelter and shade, but being covered with luxuriant vegetation it was unhealthy, and sickness increased. Dr. Knower who was on duty with the detachment had his hands full, but was equal to the emergency, and by his untiring labor won the confidence and esteem of all.

After this work was finished the detail crossed the river to the Tennessee side, where it remained until about the 20th of October at work on the wreck of the steamer John Simons, when it was taken on board the Belle Memphis and returned to ¡Columbus, and the next day to Jackson, rejoining the Regiment after an absence of two months and a half.

COLONEL BISSELL'S RIVER PATROL.

While this detachment was at Island No. 10, Colonel Bissell fitted out another for the purpose of patroling the river, keeping down Guerrilla bands and making a chart of the Mississippi River and its tributaries. The charting of the river was assigned to Captain Flad, while the Colonel himself, with a detail of a few selected men, undertook the patroling duty.

For this purpose the steamer Emily was placed at his command and made several trips to Memphis, once extending the trip to near Helena. Captain Flad met the boat at Memphis on the second trip down and at once commenced the work of mapping. From Memphis the boat proceeded down the river, and when opposite Harkerodes Landing, was fired into by a large party of Guerrillas, who were lying in ambush on the bank. Two men were killed and a third wounded. Instead of attempting to avoid them Colonel Bissell accepted the issue and immediately rounded to and landed the boat. No sooner had the boat touched the shore than every man sprang to the beach, musket in hand, and charged up the embankment. The enemy, finding they had caught a Tartar, beat a hasty retreat and made good their escape, with the exception of one man, who was caught and immediately tried by "drum-head" court-martial. He was found guilty and sentenced to be hanged immediately. While the gallows was being prepared, however, Captain Flad made a proposition to hear some additional testimony in the case, which was assented to, and some facts being revealed more favorable to the prisioner, his sentence was commuted to three years in the penitentiary.

Search was then instituted among the numerous houses of wealthy planters in that locality, in one of which was found the muster roll of the whole party, disclosing the fact that nearly every man living in that section of the country was connected with this band engaged in outlawry. A letter was found, written that day, notifying certain members of the gang that a boat (doubtless meaning the Emily) was coming down, and to "hasten down and have some fun," but the laugh proved to be on the other side, as upon this disclosure a general bonfire ensued in which was consumed houses, stables, lumber, cotton gins, in short everything of value, and ere the boat was ready to depart no shelter was left within a radius of five miles for assassins or bushwhackers.

This, in connection with kindred transactions, soon rendered the boat a prominent object and the name of Bissell a terror to the Rebel sympathizers along the river. The story was at once put in circulation that the Emily crew had hung thirty men and sacked the whole country, and a general edict was published by the enraged Rebels declaring that no quarters would be granted to any one on board that boat in case of capture. Such threats had no terror to Colonel Bissell, who continued his operation until the chart was completed and he was warned that his time for operating on the river was up.

Many other events worthy of note occurred. Sometimes the boat would land, under pretense of wooding up, or some other cause, and while there manage to have a number of men slip into the canebrakes and secrete themselves, or to take ambush on some public road leading to the landing. The boat would then shove off and be gone a number of hours. As soon as the boat would disappear, guerrillas, and often regular Confederate soldiers, supposing no one left behind, would resume their active operations, but only, in a number of cases, to find themselves picked up and made prisoners when they least expected it. On one occasion six were caught by this piece of strategy, by an equal number of our own men under Sergeant David Armstrong, who posted his squad in a high canebrake on each side of the road. Among the squad was one Frazier, of Company A, generally known as Comanche, standing about six feet six inches, and proportionate in other respects. Sergeant Armstrong was not much behind him in size, and it must be acknowledged that they were pretty *heavy* representatives of "Northern mud-sills," in every way qualified to command the respect of their opponents. A Rebel officer who was captured on that occasion stated that when Sergeant Armstrong arose from the brakes and demanded a surrender, the first impulse was to make his escape. In a moment Comanche was on his feet, towering above the canebrakes on the other side of the road. This was too much, and concluding that the whole Yankee army was composed of giants, he at once surrendered, with his five companions in arms. Much property was also captured in this expedition, and turned over at Memphis. Colonel Bissell having completed his business, returned to Jackson. The map made by Captain Flad on that occasion was furnished to General Grant, and a copy was afterward solicited by General Sherman.

Before Captain Hill's detatchment returned to the Regiment, and while yet at work on the John Simons, Lieutenant Besier, with another detachment of twenty-seven men from Company H, was ordered, September 29th, to Point Pleasant, to complete the work on the Rebel floating battery, which had been abandoned some time previously on an account of the low water; having completed this business about the latter part of October they returned to the Regiment.

TO JACKSON, TENNESSEE, AGAIN.

To return to the main body of the Regiment at Jackson, where matters of interest were transpiring. July 25th, four hundred of the Engineer Regiment were at work on a railroad bridge near Bolivar on the Mississippi Central, which had been burned by roving partisans of the enemy. Colonel Bissell arrested two citizens suspected of being engaged in burning the bridge. The report got out that the Colonel hung them to a bent of the bridge, but this was not true, he only threatened them and they were let loose after a scare.

On the 28th of July a small bridge, two miles north of Carroll Station, on the Mobile & Ohio Railroad, about ten miles north of Jackson, was burned by a force of Rebel cavalry, and a large detachment of the Engineer Regiment, under Colonel Bissell, hastened out to repair the damage. Upon inquiry, it was found that J. D. Beadle, a citizen living near by, was strongly implicated in the affair, and was guilty of other offenses, as were explained in Colonel Bissell's own report to General Grant.

The Colonel ordered a drum-head court-martial, consisting of Captains Tweeddale, Odenbough and Werth, to hear and determine the case. In the meantime, considering the case a foregone conclusion, he ordered Lieutenant Wilcox to prepare a gallows, while the balance of the party were seeking information in regard to, and practicing on a hangman's knot, in the presence of the culprit. The court being somewhat tardy in its proceedings, Colonel Bissell relieved the members from further responsibility and sentenced the prisoner to be hung that evening at four o'clock; whereupon, it was said, he detailed Captain Odenbough to administer spiritual consolation to the prisoner. Having finished this part of the proceedings, he sent out parties and burned Beadle's house, together with those of two of his relatives. From some cause, however, the execution did not take place, and his case was referred to a Military Commission at Jackson, who, after hearing the case there, jointly entered an informal complaint against the act of burning, but failed to name the officers implicated. This complaint was forwarded to Major-General McClernand, through General Logan, and was soon returned by that officer, indorsed: "No action can be taken on account of the names of the parties not being furnished. The Commission will therefore furnish the names. By order of Major-General McClernand."

To which the reply was returned that: "The houses and property were burned by and under orders of Colonel Bissell, Engineer Regiment, and his officers. Their names are not known. J. W. Haynes, President of Court."

With this additional information, the case was referred to General Grant, indorsed:

"HEADQUARTERS DISTRICT OF JACKSON.
"JACKSON, TENN., August 4, 1862.
" Respectfully referred to Major-General U. S. Grant for his consideration: If Colonel Bissell ever invades my District again, and usurps authority which belongs to me, and not to him, he will be made to answer for it in a very exemplary way.
"JOHN A. McCLERNAND,
"Major-General Cavalry."

From General Grant it was returned to Colonel Bissell, directing him to report through General McPherson and return the papers.

Under date of August 8, 1862, Colonel Bissell reported in substance that: About noon of July 28th a train bound north returned reporting that a train had been burned, and a large force of Rebels was in the vicinity, that fighting had occurred, etc. Colonel Bissell called in his details, put them under arms, and telegraphed to General McPherson, who directed him to report to General Logan, receiving verbal orders, to load his men, tools, etc., on the train, go with them personally to the spot and to take such action as deemed best, Captain Tressillian, A. D. C. to General McClernand, going along to give advice and authority in case harsh measures were taken. At the bridge four men were found under arrest. An investigation was made proving that J. D. Beadles ran some two hundred yards to meet a party of Rebel cavalry, letting down his fence for them to pass to the bridge, and furnishing them with two axes. After the bridge was burned, they formed an ambush in the fields where the three houses and gin houses were burned. A troop of United States Cavalry was saved from this ambush by five negroes owned at these houses, but not soon enough to avoid receiving the fire of the Rebels, whereby three men were wounded and four horses killed.

Beadle, himself, and one Thomas Harris saw the United States Cavalry pass, and did not warn them of the ambush. In the gin house were found secreted three United States Cavalry sabres and one bayonet, and in the house a holster belonging to one of the United States Cavalry who was unhorsed, and a carbine belonging to another United States Cavalryman. After this investigation, the buildings were burned, with the full concurrence of Captain Tressillion, A. D. C. Colonel Bissell disclaimed any wish—though he named Captain Tressillion—of throwing responsibility on him; he wished to take the responsibility as the officer commanding the expedition.

The Colonel's report appears to have been satisfactory, as no further action was taken in the matter.

August 10th, Captain Odenbaugh went home on recruiting service, and Captain Werth, on the same duty, on the 16th. Lieutenant Whitcomb was transferred from Company C to D. Lieutenant Bailey was detailed as roadmaster, and Lieutenant Brooks to Cornith to assist Leuitenant Wm. Hill. August 31st, the resignation of Major M. S. Hasie was accepted.

About the first week in August, 1862, at Jackson, Tennessee, a notice was published that: " The regiment was to be changed under a new law from an extra duty Engineer Regiment to a regular Engineer Regiment, and increased to twelve companies of one hundred and fifty men each, with ten Sergeants at thirty-four dollars per month; ten Corporals at twenty dollars per month; sixty-four Artificers at seventeen dollars per month ; sixty-four Privates at thirteen dollars per month ; two Musicians at twelve dollars per month.

" The Regiment has been in service since July 26, 1861, and in consequence of the men having no guard or picket duty the deaths have to this time (August 1, 1862) been only about twenty, while the number on the sick list has generally been about one-fourth that of others in the same department. No men will be received as recruits under twenty-one years of age, nor less than five feet eight inches in height."

This change caused a good deal of dissatisfaction among certain restless spirits among the men, and caused the Colonel and other officers a good deal of trouble for a time ; one of the agitators, Sergeant J. Y. Folsom, was arrested, tried by court-martial and sentenced to be dishonorably discharged.

Under this law Privates would get about $8, Artificers and Corporals $12 less and Sergeants $2 more per month, than under the extra duty allowance ; hence the discontent.

During September, 1862, sixty-six recruits were received. A detail under Captain Randolph and Lieutenant Wilcox was sent out on the Mississippi Railroad, who built two large bridges near Bolivar, Tenn.

THE SECOND BATTLE OF CORINTH.

On the evening of October 3d, 1862, the whole available force of the Regiment was ordered to march to and reinforce the garrison at Corinth, as that place was threatened by the combined forces of

Price and Van Dorn. The Regiment moved by rail that night as far as Bethel, where it halted for the night to await the arrival of other troops from Jackson. At daylight the next morning, the other forces having come up, the whole command, under General McPherson, moved on by rail about ten miles further and then marched by turnpike to Corinth, where it arrived a little before dark.

The weather at that time was exceedingly hot, and the men had marched but a few miles when they commenced relieving themselves of blankets, overcoats and everything burdensome, excepting their guns and accoutrements. The distance marched that day was about twenty miles, and many of the men, having new shoes, badly blistered their feet.

They did not arrive, however, in time to participate in the engagement at Corinth, the Rebels having been repulsed and then in full retreat.

The whole army was immediately ordered in pursuit. About one hundred of the Engineer Regiment, under Captain Tweeddale, accompanied it as a Pioneer Corps as far as Ripley, Mississippi, building several temporary bridges on the route. While at Ripley, Lieutenant William Hill obtained a human skull, which was inscribed :

"This poor Yankee was killed at the battle of Bull Run, July 21, 1861."

Lieutenant Hill kept this as a relic to show to his friends and sent it home.

The rest of the Regiment, under Captain Flad, started the next day, October 5th, to return to Jackson, arriving there the 6th ; six miles north of Corinth they rebuilt a bridge destroyed by the enemy the day previous, and at the same point where they had constructed one a few months before. The night of the 5th they quartered at Bethel.

The army having abandoned the pursuit, the detachment under Captain Tweeddale returned to Jackson, having marched on foot one hundred miles.

About this time Colonel Bissell obtained orders and went to Washington on business connected with the Regiment.

October 3d, Captain Tweeddale was promoted Major; 13th, Lieutenant Bailey to Captain, Company F; 15th, Lieutenant McLaren to First Lieutenant, Company A, and Sergeant-Major Bras to Second Lieutenant, Company B; 17th, Lieutenant Whitcomb promoted to First Lieutenant, Company D, and Sergeant J. S. Cunningham to

Second Lieutenant, Company H; 18th, Sergeant Solomon Goodrich to Second Lieutenant, Company K; 20th, Second Lieutenant William Hill promoted to Captain, Company E; 26th, Sergeant R. G. Smith to Second Lieutenant, Company F. October 30th, Sergeant A. R. Prescott was appointed Sergeant-Major, the last to fill this office in the Regiment.

October 17th, Captain Brackett and Lieutenant Bras were detailed on recruiting service, by order of General Grant; the same date Captain Flad, Captain Bailey (who had been relieved as Roadmaster), and Captain Odenbaugh were detached with Companies B and H, to improve the fortifications at Corinth, which, under their labor, were soon declared impregnable. October 18th, Captain E. M. Hill, who had been sick since his return from the wrecking expedition on the Mississippi River, was removed to Trenton with the view of recruiting his health. October 20th, Lieutenant Ricketts was detailed to the assistance of Captain William Hill at Corinth. The same date Lieutenant Sumner, who was absent in Missouri as Assistant Adjutant-General on the Staff of General Ben Loan, was transferred to Company A. Lieutenant Brooks from K to D, Lieutenant Mattis to Company F, and Lieutenant Wilcox from Company I to G.

While the Engineer Regiment was encamped at and near Jackson with the Regimental Headquarters and Hospital there, there was a good deal of sickness, caused by the variety of exposure and the unusually hot weather of the summer of 1862. Dysenteries were frequent and a number of cases fatal; there were a great many cases of remittent fever and some pernicious fever, typhoid fever, chronic diarrhea and rheumatism; inflammation of the eyes was epidemic, a special dark-room hospital was built that at one time contained thirty patients. One of the first victims to this epidemic inflammation of the eyes was Colonel Bissell himself, who was taken about the 10th of June and could see but little for about two weeks.

THE NEGROES AND THEIR EMPLOYMENT.

The management of the contrabands gave some trouble at Jackson, the difficulty was solved by Colonel Bissell and Captain Brackett. Related by Captain Brackett as follows:

"A matter which, I think, is worthy of record in reference to employing slaves in army operations. I believe I was among the first, if not the first, to press them into service, and it was in this wise: After the taking of Corinth our Regiment had camped at Jackson, Tennessee, and was engaged in repairing the Mobile & Ohio Railroad, I was ordered to select a dozen men with tools and proceed with two hand cars to a stream one mile north of Trenton and build a bridge over it. When we reached there we found the bridge, a Howe truss had been burned and dropped into the river. I concluded at once that my force was not sufficient to do the work in time, and, instead of putting my men into the water to remove the wreck, I determined to press in help from the surrounding country, and so sent out a corporal's guard with instruction to notify the citizens to send in their slaves with three days' rations. I thus obtained about forty good hands, who went at their work most cheerfully, and, when their day's work was done, they would have a grand social time, dancing and singing till midnight. It was a taste of liberty, such as they had never before enjoyed, and it was with sad faces that they returned to their old masters when the work was done. In the meantime, while they were removing the wreck, I found a lot of timber hewn out for the railroad company near by, which I caused to be hauled to the river by the citizens with ox teams, and which my men soon had in readiness and our bridge finished in just one week from the time we left camp, and a little sooner than a bridge back of us of same length had been built by a whole company of men, who commenced a week sooner than we did. This was all due to the help of our colored friends."

"Soon after this Colonel Bissell obtained orders to press into the service the slaves whenever the emergency required, and, I think, it was due to what I had done in this case that another bar was added to my shoulder straps."

After we had rebuilt the railroad from Corinth north and established our camp at Jackson, Tennessee, General Quinby, then in command at Columbus, the northern terminus, told our Colonel that he had great trouble with his laborers brought at great expense from St. Louis—that they would not half work, and demanded exorbitant wages. A remedy was soon devised. Our Colonel went to General Grant at Corinth and obtained an order to impress such persons as he thought best, to work upon the railroad or at either terminus and to keep a roll of all such and send a copy to the Quartermaster at Columbus. The next day a train load of willing darkies was started, followed soon by others, till General Quinby had supplanted his whole force of white laborers with colored, who were glad to work for their rations.

General Logan was at that time in command of the Military District at Jackson, and, as he was fresh from Southern Illinois, he had not yet got his eyes open, and was still a believer in the "divine institution;" at any rate he was in favor of letting it alone; while he could not override General Grant's order, he insisted upon controlling the manner of its execution, his wish being, practically, to nullify it. He only succeeded in one instance: Lieutenant Brackett stopped one day at the station in town with his train, when the General, who happened to be on the platform, had it unloaded and the darkies put outside the camp. Of course they at once found their way back to us at the round house, and the next day, as they moved slowly through town, a goodly number of soldiers were on the tops of the cars singing "John Brown."

The General immediately sent an order for the Colonel to "report" to him. This the Colonel declined to do; then a staff officer came with a like "order," and said that the General would send down an armed force to enforce the order if this was not obeyed. A couple of hours later when a company came they found twice as many ready to receive them, so they marched back. General McClernand, who ranked General Logan, was appealed to by the latter and went to Corinth where he was told that he had better let the Engineer Regiment and its officer alone, and he did.

The personal relations between our officers and those of General Logan's staff were very friendly and this little episode did not cause any interruption. One day Captain Tressillion came in and said that we had a man Edward and a yoke of cattle from Mrs. Brown's place and that if we would send them back Mrs. Brown would give him a fine horse, then hid out in the woods. This was agreed to and Edward consented to take his cattle back, while the Captain was charged to get a receipt for so much cash paid for the horse. The next day the Captain paid us a visit on his new horse, a beauty, and he exhibited his receipt. Edward proved unfaithful and was at work the next week at our saw-mill with his cattle.

Continued intercourse with those people soon made General Logan a convert, and he afterwards told Colonel Bissell that by his zeal as an abolitionist he proposed to atone for his past errors.

On the 1st of November the Secretary of War, by a formal order, carried into effect the authority previously given, as contained in Colonel Bissell's card, and practically received the Regiment as a part of the Engineer arm. Each company was therefore authorized to have an additional First Lieutenant, and the Regiment being divided by the same authority into three battalions, created an increase of two Majors. The Staff officers, however, had to be taken from the line, and therefore Adjutant Hudson was assigned to Company H, and Quartermaster Winegar to Company K, November 1st, but still retained in their former positions as Staff officers. By the same order a portion of the Non-commissioned Staff was abolished, and therefore Sergeants Prescott and Snider were returned to their companies, while Wm. H. Ward was appointed Quartermaster-Sergeant, and M. K. Webster Assistant Commissary-Sergeant, on the same date.

THE HOLLY SPRINGS CAMPAIGN.

On the evening of the 8th of November, the Engineer Regiment received marching orders to accompany General Grant's expedition to Grenada, and the next morning the camp equipage was loaded upon the cars and everything put in motion; the greater part of Companies C and G having already preceded the Regiment to build some important bridges at Bolivar. Part of Company I, under Captain Brackett, was left to run the saw-mill and prepare material for bridge work, while the balance of that Company under Lieutenant Sherwood went with the Regiment. All the detachments at Corinth had been relieved from duty there and rejoined their Companies at Grand Junction. The corral was ordered across the country by pike, and all the sick and convalescent turned over to the Post Hospital.

When we arrived at Bolivar it was found that one of the bridges was not finished. The train was halted and Companies H, K, and a part of two others, took up the march and camped in a grove that night ten miles further on, the balance remaining to complete the bridge.

During the night the bridge was completed and in the morning the train started, stopping on the way to take up the advance companies, arriving at Grand Junction a little before daylight, going into camp about two miles south of town.

The next day, November 10th, the Regiment, pursuant to orders, went to Moscow, Tennessee, to build a large bridge across Wolfe River near there and remained there until about the 14th, when orders were received to open the Mississippi Central Railroad south from Grand Junction, Companies C, G and a part of D were left. A short halt was made near Grand Junction to build a small bridge, and on the 16th, Headquarters was moved to Davis Mill, where three large bridges had been destroyed. On the 17th Colonel Bissell returned, accompanied by First Lieutenants Horace B. Hooker and James W. Hooker, and Second Lieutenant Josiah H. Bissell, who had been lately appointed to commissions in the Missouri Engineer Regiment. Lieutenant H. B. Hooker was assigned to Company B, Lieutenant J. W. Hooker to Company I, and Lieutenant Bissell to Company C, and was detailed as Assistant Adjutant. Lieutenant-Colonel Adams rejoined the regiment at this place, after an absence of seven months as a prisoner of war. Colonel Adams only remained a day or two, being in poor health he tendered his resignation and pending its acceptance went to St. Louis and did not rejoin us. The three bridges at Davis Mill having been completed, Lieutenant Goodrich, with a detachment of men, was detailed to run the sawmill, build tanks and other work, the balance of the regiment moved under orders to near Moscow again on the Memphis & Charleston Railroad, and commenced the re-construction of the road, about one and a half miles of which had been destroyed by General Sherman's forces, the summer previous.

About this time the attempt was made to divide the Regiment into two battalions; the first under Major Tweeddale with Regimental Headquarters, for which no additional Staff officers were appointed; the second consisting of Companies B, E, H and G, under Captain Flad, who appointed Lieutenant H. B. Hooker Adjutant, and Lieutenant D. G. Parker Quartermaster.

This organization, however, owing to the confusion caused by the details required in carrying on the duties of the Regiment was shortly abandoned.

On the 19th of December, Company E (except a detachment under Lieutenant Edinger), having been relieved from the Ordinance department, rejoined the Regiment. Lieutenant Edinger had a short time before been appointed Ordnance Officer on General Schuyler Hamilton's Staff. About the same time Lieutenant Murphy returned with his detachment from the Obion River, having completed the bridge over that stream. After completing the railroad east of Moscow, which required the cutting and hewing of ties, transportation of iron and the rebuilding of the road entire, the men again went to the bridge over Wolfe River; it was partly completed, when, on the 27th of November, we were ordered to resume

LIEUTENANT D. G. PARKER.

CAPTAIN JOHN E. MURPHY.

operations on the Mississippi Central, and went on a construction train to a partially destroyed bridge at Hudsonville, about ten miles in advance of all other troops, the greatest caution was exercised to avoid ambush or surprise. For this purpose, after halting at Lamar for dinner, two companies were deployed as skirmishers, Company B under Captain Flad in advance to near Hudsonville.

The advance of the Army did not bring relief for three days. On the 25th Companies H and G under Captain Odenbaugh and Werth were ordered on a scouting expedition and returned with some captured contraband property.

While at Moscow Company A under Captain Randolph was detailed for fitting up ponton trains, and Adjutant Hudson was sent to Bloomington, Illinois, on recruiting service. Henry Feuerbach, of Company A, who had been taken prisoner at Tuscumbia May 30th, and escaped, making his way six hundred miles through the enemy's country, to the gunboat fleet, rejoined the Regiment at Moscow. His adventures written by himself are given elsewhere.

November 12th, Second Lieutenant Ricketts was promoted First Lieutenant, Company C. On the 30th Companies H and G, Captain Werth and Lieutenant Besier, were ordered on a scout, and captured five prisoners of war, nineteen horses and mules, together with a large quantity of Quartermaster's supplies; the other companies doing the bridge work while they were absent.

December 1st the whole camp was moved to the Coldwater, where a long and high trestle had to be constructed; there were many others, however, of less note at short intervals along the whole road, and the work of building them was assigned by companies. Four companies, the same day, advanced beyond the Coldwater, to work assigned them, and Company B even entered the town of Holly Springs, taking up quarters in vacant buildings.

December 3d, the bridge over the Coldwater having been completed, the Regimental camp was removed to Holly Springs, from which place it again advanced on the 6th, the first battalion moving about five miles beyond, while the second proceeded to the Tallehatchie River, a distance of about twenty miles, over extremely rough roads, and arriving at that place at a late hour in the evening.

At this point there was a bridge and trestle about half a mile in length, and which had been completely destroyed by the retreating Rebels. Besides this, there were a great many others of less dimensions between it and where the first battalion was camped.

The Regiment becoming short of rations, a foraging party was detailed nearly every day by each battalion, which proceeded ten or twelve miles into the country, and sometimes brought in prisoners, besides their forage and provisions. These excursions were frequently enlivened by amusing events, and the party often made the officers in command the butt of their jokes. On one occasion they reported him as having made a speech, dictating a code of orders, in which he told them there should be no "private pilfering except for the officers."

The Regiment continued employed in this business until the 20th of December, when Holly Springs was captured by Van Dorn's Rebel cavalry, the first battalion moving, in the meantime, twice— the last time locating about one mile south of Tallehatchie River, in an open field. The second battalion being encamped on the north side, and the Rebels having taken some Federal soldiers prisoners within a few miles of the river, it was deemed prudent to move camp to within supporting distance of other troops, which were nearly all on the south side. The camp was therefore moved to the same field occupied by the first battalion. The Regiment, however, being badly exposed in case of an attack, moved next day to the bank of the river, where the Rebels, previous to their retreat, had made strong fortifications, and which were then in a good state of preservation. Lieutenant Edinger having previously removed his Ordnance stores to Holly Springs, they were, of course, captured by the enemy, together with his whole detachment of about twenty men, which had been detailed from the Regiment; Captain Wm. Hill being then on temporary duty, and Lieutenant Connett, who was acting conductor of a construction train, were each captured. Doctor Shelton was also taken prisoner, but on learning his position in the army, he was released and returned to the Regiment the same evening. All the other prisoners were paroled on the spot, and were soon after forwarded to St. Louis by way of Memphis, to rendezvous there until exchanged. A full car load of tools designed for the Regiment were also captured and destroyed.

On the 28th of November the Regiment was strung along the Mississippi Central Railroad for ten miles, building bridges and repairing the road; December 1st, headquarters moved to Walls Station; December 5th, moved into Holly Springs. While unloading the cars there Jack Dodds, of Company F, in pulling his gun toward him, was shot through the head and instantly killed. On the 6th the headquarters moved again, to Lumpkin's Mill, where there were eight railroad bridges to build within a mile or two.

While at the work along here quite a number of the men were badly injured by falling from bridges, timbers falling on them, and in a train accident; among others, Lieutenant-Colonel Tweeddale. December 15th, moved to the large Tallahatchee bridge, three-fourths of a mile long, where the most of the men were when Holly Springs was taken. On the 24th, moved into Holly Springs, except Company G, left to keep the bridges in repair until the whole army had re-crossed; 26th, Company G returned to Holly Springs in a severe rain storm. December 25th, Company H was sent to Davis' Mill, and on the 28th the whole regiment started under orders for Lagrange, Tennesssee, stopping a short time at Davis' Mill. December 29th the Regiment, agreeable to orders, moved from Lagrange to Moscow again, and on the 31st completed the bridge over Wolfe River near there.

The Regiment then moved about five miles further west to rebuild two or three small bridges. While here rumors were current that the enemy were to attack, and everything was put in readiness to give him a proper reception by preparing a fort with cordwood and destroying all the pike road bridges. The enemy failed to make his appearance, and the command finished the bridges without disturbance. This was carried out and managed by Captain Flad, who was in command in the absence of Colonel Bissell at St. Louis, and Major Tweeddale, who was at Jackson, Tennessee, with Captain Merritt and Lieutenant Sherwood. January 2, 1863, the Regiment moved by rail to Lafayette, where Colonel Bissell, who had arrived with a wagon train from Memphis, was met.

MEMPHIS.

January 3d, Companies D, H and K were ordered to Memphis, with instructions to repair the railroad as they went, which they did. Company G was ordered to Jackson, Tennessee, going the same evening and reporting to General Webster, Superintendent Military Railroads. On the 4th, Captain William Hill went home on recruiting service. Company E remained at Moscow until the 24th, when it was ordered to Memphis. On the 5th the Regimental Headquarters were moved to Lagrange, escorted by Company F, and from there to Jackson, Tennessee, to the camping ground of the previous summer, the Regimental Hospital remaining at Lagrange until the 17th, when it also was moved to Memphis. On the 5th Companies I and F were ordered to the Obion River, and were soon joined by Company F. Company A had been on duty at Jackson with a part of Company I, who were running the sawmill there when the road was broken by the enemy, and were both ordered to the Obion River, to assist in the repairs, but the former was relieved soon after the arrival of the other companies, and proceeded to Jackson on the 12th, and from there to Memphis on the 17th, while the latter was rejoined by the rest of the Company at the Obion River. Company G, having reported to Colonel Webster, was ordered to Carroll Station, about nine miles from Jackson, for the purpose of constructing block-houses, and proceeded there on the 4th, where it remained employed in that duty until the 25th, when it was ordered to Memphis and rejoined the regiment on the evening of that day, having been preceded by Regimental Headquarters. The four companies employed in the Obion Bottom, having been driven out by the sudden rise of water on the 15th, located their camp at Kenton, and remained there until the 27th, when the severe rain and snow storms having overflowed the bottom land, rendered further work impracticable, and the companies were ordered to rejoin their regiment at Memphis. During this storm, the most of which occurred on the 14th and 15th, the men suffered extremely with cold and exposure. Snow fell rapidly to the depth of eight or ten inches, followed by rain; which, together with the melting snow, suddenly overflowed the only available camping ground in the Obion Bottom, and rendered it necessary for the four companies to beat a hasty retreat to Kenton, as before mentioned, which they did on the night of the 15th. Arriving at midnight, they were compelled to occupy their snowy bed which everywhere covered the ground, and with no covering or shelter except the army blanket, in which they rolled themselves as best they might. Add to this the fact that the command was eighteen hours without food, and there is nothing in the situation to make it desirable or attractive. A great quantity of mechanical tools were said to have been lost in the bottom land by this overflow.

On the 18th Colonel Bissell proceeded to St. Louis, on business, accompanied, or followed shortly after, by Major Tweeddale, Lieutenants Whitcomb, Mattis and Cunningham, under orders from General Grant. While at Kenton, on his way thither, the former telegraphed to Captain Werth to remove Company G to that place; but the dispatch having been referred to General Webster, the order was countermanded, and the Company continued on stockades until the 25th of January. Between the 20th and 25th the Regiment was paid up to the 31st of August, 1862. Companies D, H and K, during all this time, were employed in building side-tracks, etc., at Memphis.

On the 15th, seven and a half inches of snow fell in Memphis, and, on the 21st, a larger part of the Regiment and the Headquarters and Regimental Hospital having arrived, camp was made in the northeast part of the city; going into tents in the snow without straw and boards, it was very disagreeable and caused much sickness.

The 21st of January, at Moscow, a scouting party of Company E, who were out, had two of their men captured, Privates Joseph Soper, Jack Sanders, James Wilson, D. F. Smith and Finch escaping.

While at Memphis the Regiment was employed taking up iron and ties on the Memphis & Ohio Railroad, excepting such details as were necessary for camp guard. Companies A and I were employed in repairing the pontoon train designed for use in the Mississippi expedition against Vicksburg.

Lieutenant Wilcox had previously been detailed with a detachment of men, and was employed at Point Pleasant removing siege guns to Memphis, which he accomplished, and rejoined the Regiment early in February. Lieutenant Besier was also absent at Cairo on special duty, by order of General Grant.

THE VICKSBURG CAMPAIGN.

On the 11th of February the Regiment embarked on board the steamer Crescent City, with the exception of Company C, which took passage on the Sam Young, and after receiving two additional months' pay, proceeded on the 12th, at 4 A. M., down the river, and arrived at Young's Point on the 14th day of the same month. On the way down the river, it having been ascertained that boats were frequently fired into at Bulah, and that a party of guerrillas frequented and rendezvoused at that town, Colonel Bissell determined to chastise them; and having a ten-pound Parrott gun on board, prepared to shell the place in case of any demonstration. On approaching the town, a suspicious gathering presented itself on the bank of the river, and satisfied that it would be a difficult matter to injure an innocent party in that loccality, the gun was wheeled into position and opened fire on them. Of course there was a scattering, and ere the boat reached the landing, no living inhabitant was to be seen. Two companies were immediately landed and deployed as skirmishers, while the rest stood to arms and were held in readiness to support them. Those two companies had hardly passed out of sight ere a scattering musketry fire ensued, and Colonel Bissell ordered a third company to reinforce them. Soon after, however, the firing ceased, and the companies returned, reporting that they met with a band of about thirty guerrillas, but the latter escaping beyond a marshy strip of land difficult to cross, they had abandoned the pursuit. In the skirmish with them, however, one man, John Senthouse, of Company H, was wounded. There being no other means of affecting the offending parties, it was decided to reduce the town, and soon the rising smoke and flames added another to the many cautionary lessons the rebels had received from Colonel Bissell. Having captured and taken on board about twenty-five bales of cotton, the boat proceeded down the river. In the meantime Company C had landed from the Sam Young near the lower end of Turkey Bend, with a view of flanking the force which it was expected would retreat from Bulah upon the landing of the other companies, but having skirmished some distance inland without meeting with the enemy, the company returned on board the boat and proceeded down the river. Arriving at Young's Point, opposite Vicksburg, the regiment was at once employed cutting a road through timber from army headquarters to the canal in course of construction across the point.

This work occupied two days; during one of which it rained in torrents. The men, however, worked during the whole time, and while constructing one bridge leading to the river embankments, were compelled to stand to their waists in water. There not being sufficient ground outside the levee to admit of a camp, the regiment remained on board the boats. In the meantime, Colonel Bissell submitted a plan for opening the contemplated canal across Young's Point, which, as it proposed abandoning the work already done there, was not adopted. Having completed this work all the Companies except F and I moved, under orders, to Lake Providence, La., by the steamer Crescent City, under command of Colonel Bissell; Company C having been transferred from the steamer Sam Young to the former boats, while the latter received on board in exchange the two companies already mentioned, and which were left at Young's Point.

The Regiment arrived at Lake Providence early on the morning of the 30th, and Companies D and G, under Captain E. M. Hill, were immediately ordered to Baxter Bayou, distance eight miles, and proceeded there on foot the same day, making camp near the mouth of the bayou on a flat piece of ground. There two companies were subjected to the most trying ordeal the two succeeding days, by rain, which fell in torrents and covered the entire ground upon which the camp stood to the depth of several inches, leaving no place upon which one could stand dry-footed. The whole locality was also under a state of cultivation, leaving no turf, and the ground being saturated with water, there was no possible means of stepping without sinking knee-deep in the loam.

In the meantime Company C, under Lieutenant Coy, made an expedition to Old River, but met with no incident worthy of note, and soon returned to the steamer.

On the 25th the Regiment moved to Baxter's Bayou, and continued the work already begun by Companies D and G, of clearing out that sluggish stream, the object being to open a communication through that channel to the Macon Bayou, and from there to the Mississippi River below Vicksburg through the Black and Red Rivers. On the 27th, Companies D and G moved camp a few miles further down the bayou, and on the 28th was mustered for pay by Colonel Bissell.

On the 12th of February Lieutenants Brooks and McLaren were detailed and left at Memphis to apprehend deserters, and for other purposes; Lieutenants Mattis and Wilcox were also left there on business connected with the Regiment. Charles C. Wood was commissioned Second Lieutenant, to rank from the 20th December, 1862, and assigned to Company I. He was captured at Holly Springs, on his way to join his regiment, in consequence of which he was not entered upon the return of the Regiment until February, 1863.

While at Baxter's Bayou, a large quantity of cotton was discovered hid among the canebrakes, amounting to about 500 bales, and marked C. S. A. Of course it was taken charge of as captured property, and Lieutenant Ricketts, with Company E, detailed to open a wagon road to it, and to guard the same until the infantry teams could haul it out. Colonel Bissell becoming satisfied that it would result in a useless attempt to effect a passage through Baxter's Bayou, expressed his convictions to General McPherson; but that from a previous examination, he was confident that an attempt at Ashton to effect a passage would be more hopeful. At that point Bayou Macon took its rise, within a short distance of the Mississippi

River, and by cutting the levee, would produce a fall of about seven feet, and a consequent inundation of the country to a sufficient depth to pass boats into the bayou. Having obtained an order for this work, he proceeded therewith the Regiment on the 3d day of March, and commenced operations; leaving, however, Company G at Baxter's Bayou to collect the regimental tools and to keep in repair the road leading to the cotton above mentioned.

On the 5th the Regiment cut the levee at Ashton, and on the 6th the water had overflowed the banks of the bayous to such an extent that the troops were obliged to abandon the work on Baxter's Bayou and seek a place of encampment on the higher banks of Lake Providence. At Ashton there was little or no camping ground excepting the levee, and the Regiment was obliged to extend itself upon that narrow belt of *terra firma* in detached companies; the Crescent City, in the meantime, plying back and forth between them, and was placed fully at the disposal of the Regiment.

Several breakages were made through the levee at this place, and ere the Regiment left, the openings through the same made more than a quarter of a mile in the aggregate, and had inundated over fifty thousand square miles of the finest agricultural country in the Rebel dominion. The manner of cutting the levee, which was by a process of blasting, is also worthy of note. A small hole was dug perpendicularly into the levee to the depth of six or eight feet, or until the filtering water prevented a further progress; this done, a keg containing one hundred pounds of powder was thoroughly plastered over with mud to prevent the powder gathering dampness from the water. It was then lowered to the bottom of the hole, having first connected with it a fuse-pipe made of cane, long enough to reach the top of the embankment, filled with fine powder, and it connected with the keg so carefully made and protected with mud as to prevent the water reaching the powder through the vent. The hole was then filled up to the top, and the earth closely packed. A train of powder was then extended from the cane pipe, a distance of several rods, and the sudden rush of workmen to get beyond the reach of the convulsion was a signal that the train was about to be lighted. The eruption which followed the explosion of one hundred pounds of powder deeply buried in the earth can be easily imagined. A quick, distant, rumbling sound, and the next moment a sheet of fire and smoke leaped from the spot toward which all eyes were turned, shaking the ground like an earthquake, and sending missiles almost beyond the range of sight in the air. By this means a per-feet breech would be made in the embankment and pulverizing the earth for many yards around, causing it to yield easily before the action of the rushing water.

On the 13th Company G returned to the town of Lake Providence and embarked on board the Crescent City. The same day it proceeded to Ashton, and rejoined the Regiment in the evening.

On the 15th of March the resignation of Lieutenant Smith, which had been previously tendered, was accepted. Also on this date the trial trip was made through the opening in the levee, and the steamer Sam Young successfully passed over the falls into Bayou Macon, as a proof that what a dozen or more regiments had failed to accomplish at Lake Providence by way of opening navigation through Baxter's Bayou, this Regiment had successfully performed alone, and within a space of a few days, near Grand Lake, in securing a direct entrance from the Mississippi into Bayou Macon, and an uninterrupted communication to the Red River, which led again directly into the Mississippi.

But owing probably to the great distance through the enemy's country before again reaching the Mississippi River, and hazardous undertaking of navigating those bayous and small rivers, the trial was never made.

On the 17th the Regiment embarked on board the Crescent City, and toward evening proceeded down the river to Young's Point, leaving Companies A and C on board the Sam Young to get that boat back again into the Mississippi River.

On the 21st the regiment again made a trip up the river to Grand Lake on the Crescent City. On the way one man from Company G was accidentally lost overboard and drowned. Landing at Grand Lake, two companies were ordered to scout on that side of the river, while the boat crossed with the balance of the regiment to the Mississippi side and spent the remainder of the day, several companies going some distance in the country. Meeting with no enemy, however, nor making any discovery worthy of note, they returned to the boat and re-crossed the river, where the other two companies re-embarked, and the boat again proceeded to Young's Point.

In the meantime companies H and I had been detailed, under Major Tweeddale, to work the dredging machine in the Young's Point canal, to which they steadily applied themselves from the time the Regiment first went to Lake Providence until on or about the 16th of March, when the enemy having constructed a battery at the point nearly opposite, and which enfiladed the work, it was deemed advisable to withdraw out of range.

March 16th Major Tweeddale was sent with Company F and one hundred and fifty negroes to open Black Bayou, and proceeded up Steel's Bayou to Muddy Bayou, where they were to take up a portion of General Stuart's command, who were crossing from Eagle's Bend. While there Colonel Bissell sent across companies D and H as a reinforcement. The expedition, however, having failed, the whole command returned; the three companies under Major Tweeddale by the steamer Pocahontas, and arrived at Young's Point on the 27th, where they found the rest of the Regiment engaged constructing batteries in the levee opposite Vicksburg.

While engaged in these various works, the additional amount of extra duty money was obtained and paid over to the companies *pro rata* on the 24th, amounting to $24,167, making the sum of $64,167 received by the Regiment over and above its ordinary pay and allowances, and which completed the pay for extra services up to the 1st of November, 1862, at which date the extra pay was suspended by reason of the reorganization of the Regiment.

The difficulties attending the payment of the last sum of money is worthy of note.

A few weeks before leaving Jackson, the extra pay-rolls to that time were duly made up and certified to by General McPherson, as "late Superintendent of Military Railroads." Upon this, General Grant ordered the payment by Captain Dutton, Q. M., at Columbus, Ky. This officer, however, declined payment until the signature of General McPherson could be changed by leaving out the "late." In the meantime the army was on the advance down the Mississippi Central Railroad, McPherson's corps taking the lead; consequently, in order to make the change in the rolls, Lieutenant Winegar was obliged to make a trip on horseback (the railroad not being then open) to Oxford, to which General McPherson had advanced his headquarters. Upon returning, another obstacle presented itself. An order had just been received by Captain Dutton from the War Department, suspending the payment of the money, for some cause unknown; and thus matters rested until sometime in the early part of February, when a second order was received authorizing the payment of the money.

Upon the arrival of the Regiment at Young's Point from Memphis, Colonel Bissell immediately obtained an order from General Grant, pursuant to an order from Washington, on Captain Dutton (who had in the meantime removed to Memphis) for the payment of the full amount due. The rolls were accordingly completed, and Lieutenant Winegar proceeded to Memphis the next day for the purpose of obtaining the same. In due time he returned with the funds which were paid to the companies as before mentioned.

To the benefits of "extra pay" may be added the fact that no regular sutler was ever tolerated in the Regiment, and therefore the men were spared the impositions usually practiced by this *leech* of the soldier's pocket.

On the 24th Colonel Bissell having conceived the idea of constructing case-mated batteries by cutting into the levee opposite Vicksburg, obtained an order to proceed with the work. On the night of the 25th it was commenced, by taking all the material there under the cover of darkness and depositing it behind the embankment out of sight.

The companies were then set at work by reliefs, and no man was permitted to speak above a whisper. Ere morning the whole command returned to camp to avoid attracting the attention of the enemy, where they remained until the succeeding night, and in that manner the work progressed without even attracting the suspicion of the enemy until the morning of the 28th, when they were completed and ready to mount two 30-pounder Parrott guns. Before mounting them, however, important changes were made in the army; and among others, Colonel Bissell, with six companies of the regiment, was ordered back to Memphis to open the Memphis & Charleston Railroad to Corinth. Before leaving for Memphis, however, another trip was made by the Regiment to Ashton on the Crescent City, where it arrived on the 31st, and a detachment sent down the chute leading to the bayou some distance, where a large quantity of corn in sacks was found stored, and the same taken for Government use. In the meantime the balance of the Regiment occupied the day preparing boats and barges for an expedition to Macon Hills.

On the 1st of April, all things being in readiness, the whole command started on the contemplated expedition, supported by two pieces of artillery, one a 12-pounder brass mountain howitzer, mounted on a gunboat barge, and the other a 10-pounder Parrott, mounted on a raft or scow prepared for that purpose. Sergeant, afterward Lieutenant, Gast, with a portion of Company G, worked the former, while the latter was manned by volunteers from the other companies. The Regiment was transported there by means of a large coal barge temporarily decked over, and which was propelled to the place of destination by means of warping with a long rope, one end of which was taken out some distance ahead from time to time, with the aid of a boat's crew detailed for that purpose, as the occasion required, and hauled in again by them on board the barge. On approaching Macon Hills, the pickets of the enemy were discovered, and their busy movement gave rise to apprehensiveness that the Rebels were there in some force. The two mounted guns were therefore brought into requisition, and the scattering that was made on shore by a few well directed shots induced the belief that no severe opposition would be made to the landing of the troops.

Lieutenant Coy, with Company C, instantly obeyed the call upon him to take the advance, and left the barge in an open boat for the shore, while yet some distance from it, and although they met with no opposition from the enemy, yet it must be confessed the attempt was a hazardous one; and the handsome manner in which every man sprang to the shore and instantly deployed in line of skirmishers, showed their apprehension of danger, and that they had prepared to meet it. The other companies landed in quick succession, and immediately made such dispositions as were necessary for defense in case of an attack. It was soon ascertained, that all the strength of the enemy in that locality consisted in a company of one hundred and twenty-five men, who were camped near the landing, but who fled at the first discharge of artillery They could, however, considering their position and the inconvenient approaches to the shore, have greatly embarrassed the landing of the regiment had they made the effort to do so. Having obtained a large amount of commissary supplies and taken on board thirty bales of cotton, the expedition returned in the evening to the Crescent City.

On the 3d the Regiment proceeded down the river again, arriving at Young's Point on the morning of the 4th. On the 30th of March, official information was received of the promotion of Lieutenant Thompson to Captain, and Aid-de camp on the Staff of General Rosecrans, which had been made by the President and confirmed by the United States Senate on the 7th previous. Lieutenant Thompson, after having served as Post Quartermaster at Hamburg, Tennessee, which fact has already been mentioned, was appointed Ordnance Officer on General Rosecran's Staff at Corinth, and was serving in that capacity when the great battles of the 3d and 4th of

October, 1862, took place, in which he so far distinguished himself as to receive the favorable mention of his General in the report of that officer. On this date, also, Lieutenant Besier returned from Island No. 10, where he had spent much of the winter in removing Government property from that island.

Captain Merritt, while the Regiment was at Memphis, became detached and was employed on railroad work under direction of General Webster. He was afterward appointed on General McPherson's Staff, and was finally mustered out of the service as a supernumerary officer upon the consolidation of the Regiment with the Twenty-fifth Missouri Volunteer Infantry.

In consequence of the absence of Captain Merritt, Lieutenant Goodrich was placed in command of Company K, and continued in charge until July following.

On the 14th of March Second Lieutenant Parker was promoted to First Lieutenant of Company C, to rank from the 17th of February, but was detached on duty in Company G, where he remained until October following. Sergeant A. R. Prescott was promoted to Second Lieutenant of Company F, to rank from the same date.

On the 25th of March, J. G. Kappner was commissioned First Lieutenant in Company B, but was never with the Regiment, and on the 29th of May resigned to accept a Colonel's commission in a colored regiment.

On the 4th of April, after having detailed Companies A, D, F and I under Major Tweeddale to remain with the army in front of Vicksburg and denominated the Second Battalion, the balance of the Regiment, under Colonel Bissell, moved from the Crescent City on board the steamer City of Alton, and proceeded up the river the same night.

March 21st Lieutenant Ricketts resigned. On the way down the river to Young's Point February 13, 1863, while rounding to at Eagle Bend to report to General McClernand, one of the men fell overboard and was lost. On the 6th of March, while at work enlarging the break in the levee at Ashton, Louisiana, Adolphus Hall, of Company C, fell into the water and was swept away. On the 8th of March thirty-nine men of Company C came near being washed away; they were on a short strip of the levee, which had been cut each side of them, and the water unexpectedly commenced to rapidly wash both ends of the strip; they were finally rescued, when there was only just about enough of the levee left for them to stand on.

At Grand Lake, after the cut in the levee had overflowed the corn fields, large numbers of buffalo fish, weighing from six to twenty-five pounds each, literally filled the water in the fields; the men in skiffs easily scooped up boat loads of them, until all were bountifully supplied.

From about the 25th of March to the 1st of April, a detail of Company E, under Lieutenant-Colonel Flad was building a battery at the extreme apex of Young's Point, opposite Vicksburg. Owing to the continual fire from the guns in Vicksburg, the men had to work mostly at night, towing timbers and using iron from the old railroad terminating there; the battery was made by cutting through the levee, which was about thirty feet thick at the base and fifteen feet high; the earth removed was used in making the bomb proofs. It made a very good redoubt with little work as the clay silt of which the levee was made was very tenacious and about ten or twelve feet wide at the top. The 25th of March, about four o'clock in the morning, the gunboats Lancaster and Switzerland attempted to run past the Vicksburg batteries. The Switzerland got through with a hole in her boiler, but the Lancaster was sunk near the shore and near where Company E was making the casemated battery in the levee; two of their men were drowned and two badly scalded, one had a leg taken off with a shell after reaching the levee. Some company E men went out in boats and picked up the crew.

During the operations in the neighborhood of Vicksburg, the headquarters and hospital of the Reginent remained on board the boat Crescent City, but April 3d, before going up the river, was moved to the City of Alton.

YOUNG'S POINT TO POCAHONTAS.

On the 6th those companies now denominated the First Battalion arrived in Memphis about 2 o'clock P. M., and proceeded with camp and garrison equipage the same evening to the Memphis & Charleston Railroad. April 7th, took the train at 1 o'clock P. M., and proceeded to Grand Junction, where it arrived about 7 o'clock.

Lieutenant Prescott was temporarily detailed in charge of Company E, he having been detached from Company F, near Vicksburg, for that purpose.

April 8th the battalion made camp about one mile from Grand Junction, and a party sent east on the railroad to reconnoitre, who returned in the evening and reported that road in good condition fifteen miles; also a few men accidentally left in Memphis on the 17th rejoined the Regiment.

April 9th, battalion took a train and proceeded to the Mobile & Ohio Railroad after timber; arrived at Jackson and halted for dinner; after which the battalion proceeded to Humboldt and stopped for the night. April 10th, moved on to Dyer's Station and loaded two trains with timber, which proceeded back, leaving Companies C and G to make a scout to Dyersville. At the first tank station north of Trenton Companies E and K were left with instructions to do what scouting they could until the train returned.

April 11th one train was again loaded near Dyer's Station, and taking on the companies which had been left the day previous, proceeded to Trenton, where a part of the command quartered in vacant houses for the night, having become thoroughly wet with rain which fell that afternoon; the rest of the command returning to Jackson with the train.

April 12th, at 10 A. M., the train again arrived at Trenton and loaded with bridge timbers, and took on board those left there the evening previous; then proceeded to Jackson, stopping several times on the way for bridge timber and ties, and arrived at Jackson about 7 o'clock P. M.

April 13th the battalion again started north on the cars, and was immediately followed by another train to load with timber, stopping at tank north of Trenton for dinner; the battalion proceeded on that evening as far as the Obion Bottom, where the road was found to be somewhat damaged, and stopped for the night, during which it rained hard, and nearly the whole command got wet. Next morning, having repaired the track, the train proceeded on to Union City, where the battalion quartered in vacant buildings; the Colonel, with a small escort of men, proceeding through to Columbus, but returned that evening. It was upon this trip that some complaint being made to the Colonel relative to the men obtaining hams from the neighboring smoke-houses, he declared there must be some mistake about it, as his men "never eat hams."

April 15th battalion started early in the morning back to Jackson, where it arrived about 5 o'clock P. M., and met Lieutenant-Colonel Adams, who, however, did not rejoin the command for duty.

April 16th the Colonel and Lieutenant-Colonel started for Memphis, after having ordered the command to proceed north again for timber; shortly after, however, Company C was ordered to Grand

Junction, the rest of the command fulfilling the previous order, going to Dyer Station.

April 17th Lieutenant Wilcox, with a detachment of men, accompanied General Smith to the Coldwater as a pioneer party, who returned the next day, as also that portion who were collecting timber on the Mobile and Ohio road.

April 20th the battalion was paid for four months, and Major Flad returned from St. Louis; Company H ordered out on a scout; while Companies B and C went to Porter's Creek on a reconnoissance.

April 23d Colonel Bissell went to Memphis, and returned again on the 26th.

April 25th a detachment of Company H went out on a scout mounted. During the day a dispatch was received from Colonel Bissell directing a guard to be furnished the train when it arrived at Jackson, and Lieutenant Parker, with a detail from Company H, was sent, who returned the next day. There being rumors of a force of the enemy near, in the evening Major Flad deemed it prudent to move camp nearer to the fort, which he did.

April 26th Lieutenant Coy, who had obtained leave of absence on the 10th, returned. Company H was ordered to Saulsbury, with instructions to strongly picket the place, and to hold in *duress* all the inhabitants untill the battalion arrived.

April 27th the command moved by railroad to Saulsbury, repaired the road near that place, and remained all night, quartering on the train and in vacant houses. While here several hogsheads of sugar were taken possession of for Government use.

At this point Colonel Bissell called a meeting of the citizens, at which he informed them that they would be held responsible for any mischief done to the road by guerrillas, and that although they were at liberty to fight the battalion, or any portion of it, at any time they thought it safe to do so, yet any disturbance of the railroad or telegraph would be met by retaliation upon the property of citizens down to the tenth degree of relationship.

The roving partisans between Corinth and Grand Junction at this time gave a great deal of trouble in opening up and keeping open the railroad. Eighty of the men were mounted and kept scouring around the country, managing to keep these guerrillas at a distance and in fear of the Engineer Regiment. The telegraph was kept open from Jackson to Columbus, Ky., without the aid of infantry, as the Generals at Memphis did not think it safe to reduce their force.

Colonel Bissell called the men at each town together, and told them the road and telegraph *should be kept intact* without a guard, and, if either were touched, he would burn every building within five miles of the road on either side, that, the second time, he would add five miles more. The result of this threat was that eighty-seven miles of road was secure without a soldier; the one hundred miles between Jackson and Memphis, guarded by 10,000 soldiers, was cut nearly every day.

General Hurlbut did not believe the road could be kept clear on Colonel Bissell's plan, but gave him absolute control outside of his own line. The Colonel fined and imprisoned the citizens as he thought best for the object in view, and the people found that his word was good and his hand heavy; he fined one man $500 for taking up Dr. Shelton's horse and not returning it to camp, but keeping it until the guerrillas took it. The man threatened to appeal to the Colonel's superiors, as he had taken the oath of allegiance to the Union. Colonel Bissell replied, that if he had known of his taking the oath he would have gone up the first tree. A week on hard bread and cold water brought the man to terms.

We never could get these roving guerrillas to stand for a fight, though they met them dozens of times in the neighborhood of Saulsbury, and almost always two or three to one of us, but they never failed to run as fast as their horses could carry them, and one day two men of Company K drove thirty of them more than a mile.

THE NIGHT HAWKS.

In this part of the country, west of Corinth, in North Mississippi and Southern Tennessee, the Union men were about as numerous as the Rebels: they were organized into bands and called themselves Night Hawks, and retaliated every time they were molested by the Rebel element. The spirit and feeling between them was as terrible as any to be read in the histories of the middle ages. The Union Night Hawks were mostly poor men; not one in twenty ever owned a slave; the soil is poor and hilly, the men ignorant, the women use (dip) snuff immoderately. An unusual experience was that these men were not afraid to fight. The Rebel partizans (guerrillas), on the other hand, would not stand up to a fight. Colonel Bissell said, " with four hundred of his men he would not hesitate to meet four thousand of them; that strategy was good in its place and sometimes necessary, but is not to override energy and vigor." The condition of things and movements here are better stated by Colonel Bissell himself as follows :

COLONEL BISSELL'S STATEMENT IN REGARD TO THE TENNESSEEANS AND THE OPERATIONS AROUND POCAHONTAS.

" The worst class of people with whom we came in contact were the 'stay-at-homes' in Northern Mississippi and that part of Tennessee bordering upon the Mississippi line. They had been small slave-holders before the war and took the loss of their slaves more to heart than did the large planters further south. Their 'chattels' were so near the border line, and escape was comparatively so easy, that it required an extra number of blood-hounds to be kept on hand, and a greater degree of vigilance in watching the movements of strangers and wandering colored people. All the young men who could be coaxed or driven into the Rebel army were there ; the others were to them as *outlaws*, and if found in the neighborhood were hunted and treated as such. While professing strict neutrality and peacefulness, they were constantly on the watch to do us harm and to convey to the enemy all the information they could. They were notified that open hostility would be permitted and received in a soldier-like manner, but that firing upon trains and guerrilla warfare would be met with the severest punishment, and that if any of our trains were fired upon or any of the men ambushed, every building within five miles of the spot would be at once burned. The effect was salutary, and not a circumstance of that kind occurred to call for punishment.

" Once a train was stopped by a flag and the men all carried off as prisoners, but none of them were injured nor was the train harmed. Lieutenant Goodrich, who was in command, said that his captor was civil, and that as he was taken South his guard was changed at nearly every house ; the men being enlisted for this particular raid, which was supposed to be upon a paymaster's train. The Lieutenant had time to slip his money under his shoe lining, so his captor did not get even that. Our faithful allies here were the 'night hawks,' a band of about twenty Union men who were not allowed by the 'stay-at-homes' to remain upon their places and who thought they could do more good as scouts than as regular soldiers in our army. They had succeeded in killing nearly all the bloodhounds, and our doctors furnished them with strychnine, so that the remainder were soon disposed of. We remounted them with good horses from our surplus stock, and furnished part of them with repeating rifles. When General Sherman was marching from Corinth to Memphis and tearing up the railroad, one of his brigades lost its way. The officer in command stopped at a house upon the road and wanted a boy about twelve years of age to show him the road to the main route. His mother begged with tears that he might not be taken, his father was a Union man in the Union army, and if the boy went the family would be made to suffer. The officer said that his letter stating that the boy was *forced* to go would protect them, and he gave it in the strongest language.

"But within a week this boy was hanged to a tree in the front yard in the presence of the family by the very neighbors who to us professed to be so neutral. When the 'night hawks' had obtained their new horses and guns, they hung the boy's murderers to the same tree, and gave such notice that neither this nor any other Union family was molested, at least while our army was in Western Tennessee.

"Soon after this two officers came from Corinth with a letter from the officer in command there, asking for the services of an efficient 'night hawk.' Their story was that in a skirmish a few months before they were wounded, and crawled into a fence corner and were not found when the rest of the wounded were carried away; that the next day some of the people in the neighborhood came around, and finding that they were alive, stripped them of their clothes, and amused themselves by using them as targets. Fortunately the powder was poor, and they received no fresh wounds, though they made a fearful yell at each shot. After dark some negroes took them to a Union camp, and they were now well, but not strong. They had carefully noted the face of each one of their tormentors, and knew they would be able to identify them. They did find every one of them, and started for Corinth with the 'night hawks' as escort.

"One day a man came to the camp with this story: that he was a Union man, that he was forced into the Rebel army, that he deserted and returned home, that he worked upon his little farm on bright nights, keeping hid in the woods during the day, that one of his rich and influential neighbors, with a military title (we will call him Major Jones), suspected that he was around and hunted him up with dogs, caught him, tied him to a tree and whipped him and then sent him back to the Rebel army; that he had again deserted and had now enlisted in a Tennessee loyal Regiment. Without letting his family know, a Lieutenant was sent to his house, when his story was fully confirmed. Our Colonel sent for Major Jones, constituting himself a court martial, and appointing this Lieutenant judge advocate. The Major denied the whole story and every part thereof, said his dogs (which where now all dead) were only for hunting deer. When one of the 'night hawks' was called in the Major admitted that once, and only once, his dogs had been used to hunt a 'worthless nigger' who was prowling about the woods. The Lieutenant was relentless, and he finally recollected that his pack had been used a second time for negroes; but never, no, never, to hunt up any white man. When his receipt for so much money paid by a Quartermaster C. S. A., for the use of his dogs was produced, he wilted, and as the phrase is, 'threw himself upon the mercy of the court.' He would not admit that he had ever known 'Mr. Smith,' although he had heard there was or had been such a man in the neighborhood. When Mr. Smith stepped out from behind a screen the gallant Major nearly fainted away, and it took a stiff drink of Dr. Shelton's best brandy to revive him. When asked to go to Corinth with Mr. Smith and deny his story there, he earnestly asked to be excused; and when told that he *must* go, he went so far as to get down upon his knees and beg not to be put in the power of 'that man.' Several of the 'night hawks' volunteered as escort, and the procession started. An hour or two afterward Mr. Smith came back and applied for a couple of wagons to bring his family and effects to the camp, these were furnished and they were all safely started for Memphis.

"The Sergeant of the picket put on the Corinth road reported that outside the lines he saw a man start out from a party and try to run away, that when called to stop he only ran the harder, when the party fired upon him and he fell.

"While rebuilding the railroad about forty miles east of Memphis, General McArthur, who was in command of a brigade near by, tried hard to find out what became of some of his men. Every few nights a small squad would be missing and never again heard from. One of our men by the name of Logan, from Paris, Illinois, was detailed to work the matter up; he soon reported that about two miles north of us was a small private still, the whiskey from which was the temptation. The soldiers who obtained the liquor were mum and the fact that once or twice a week the whole party were run off to Rebeldom did not deter others from going.

"One night one of our Captains, with a couple of hundred men started to investigate. The premises were surrounded and proceedings begun. The dwelling was a very large one, well finished and furnished. Repeated knocks brought a woman to an upper window; she declared that she was alone, that there was no one but herself in the house. Threats of breaking the door brought her down. There was no trouble in finding plenty of candles, by the light of which it was found that it was a regular manufactory of clothing for the Rebel army, the cloth being smuggled through the lines from Memphis. The negroes upon the place were first supplied with whatever they wanted and the rest was distributed among the men of the Expedition. In the still house no liquor was found, but the mash tubs were full of the 'beer' from which the whiskey was distilled. This was made from persimmons and the men who had been eating freely of honey found in some 'bee gums' in the yard, found it very palitable. Shall I tell the effect of honey and persimmon beer? Every one who partook was on the sick list for about three days. The celebrated 'Tennessee quick-step' was nothing in comparison.

"Several fine mules and a number of bales of cotton were found. These were all given to the negroes of the place and they were all sent to a trusted man in Cincinnati. He sold the cotton for about a dollar a pound, bought a farm in Southern Ohio for the men where they were made contented and happy.

A few years after the war closed, the owner of the place presented his account to the Court of Claims in Washington fortified with sundry affidavits of his loyalty and devotion to the Union cause—the sum was quite large, over $20,000. All the papers were referred to Colonel Bissell who reported to the Court that the items as reported were correct but the account was not full enough; to it should be added —— yards grey cloth smuggled from Memphis, —— Rebel uniforms partly finished, —— uniforms complete, —— $—, being $— each for over fifty Union soldiers decoyed by whiskey and sent prisoners to Rebel prisons."

TEMPERANCE IN THE MISSOURI ENGINEER REGIMENT.

Colonel Bissell had determined from the start that he would have a temperate, if not a temperance set of men, by keeping liquor away with a firm, vigorous policy.

The entire officers of the Regiment also, looking at it as an organization formed to accomplish certain results, and thinking it might be called upon to do important duties, concluded that, if conducted upon temperance principles, it would be the best course, they therefore took the stand, the wisdom of which was often demonstrated. The Surgeon and his assistant contributed greatly to the success of what was certainly, in army life, an experiment. The men were told just what was expected of them, and that if any of them thought they really needed a drink, they could always have the very best liquor at the Doctor's tent without charge. They were put upon their honor whenever they had passes to visit any village, and they always kept their word. There might have been some cases of overstepping the bounds, but they were so rare and so well concealed that none of them reached headquarters.

A person can not realize how great is the thirst for liquor in some men and the methods to which they will resort and the prices they will pay to get it, unless he has been with a body of men like an army, when so many of the men have been hard drinkers in cities and villages. During the early part of the war whiskey was worth about twenty cents a gallon. As it sold readily in the camps for a dollar or more a bottle, the temptation was great to take advantage of this market. The officers might issue all manner of orders, but the smugglers found many ways to pass the lines, especially when the bribe would be so tempting to the guard.

The Regiment took the field when it was about half full, and its first duties were to assist the Quartermaster's department and the Missouri Pacific Railroad in the repair of that road and the movement of trains. They started out upon very short notice and entirely without blankets or overcoats, trusting to the promises of the Quartermaster at St. Louis for a supply to be sent. None came, and the nights were getting cold, but as the men used the buildings of the railroad company and as September had not yet passed there was no great inconvenience.

One day a new Missouri Regiment came up the road finely equipped, as their colonel was a politician and in favor with the authorities. They stopped one day at Jefferson City, but the next day when they were to start there were about half of them missing. About two hundred of our men were there, who were given the task of "shipping" the laggards while their Colonel started up the road with the remainder. The stragglers were all found "lying around loose," a rather *tight*, and they were duly *shipped*, a car load at a time, but it was noticed that the whole detachment of the Engineer's Regiment had new overcoats and good blankets.

While General Pope's command was stationed at Lamine Bridge, great complaint was made by the Colonels of some of the regiments that liquor was smuggled into their camps in spite of the most stringent regulations and the utmost care. The Sixth Missouri was in the worst plight, as sometimes they would have dozens of men drunk at a time. General Pope called in Colonel Bissell and gave him full authority in the matter. The Colonel first went to all the Sutlers and told them that if they sold a drop of liquor, or any was found upon their premises, their whole stock would be confiscated. This helped the matter; but as nothing more was said, and no notice taken of the new drunks, they concluded it was all talk, and soon the plague was about as bad as ever. But our Colonel had not been idle; he had called in Le Roy Richardson, of Company C, and told him that if he and "Company Q" would find out where the liquor came from, and would prove it, they should have the spoiling of the Sutlers' tents. Le Roy soon reported that the liquor all came from the Sutler of the Sixth Missouri, that it was smuggled in milk cans made double. At the proper time Captain Patten, with his full company, "interviewed" Mr. Jew Sutler and found the liquor as reported. Our Colonel kept his word, and several hundred dollars' worth of nice goods made glad the hearts of Company C, and no more liquor was to be had about that camp.

After the battle of Shiloh large reinforcements were sent to General Grant by steamboats, all of which took their final clearance from Cairo. At this port the boat captains were uniformly told that they must in no circumstances take a particle of wine or liquor with them, and they all agreed faithfully that it should not be done, but the sequel shows that the temptation of great profits was too strong. General Grant was often complaining of the bad effects of whiskey continually present, until one day he said something about it to General Pope, who answered that he had an officer who could locate the liquor. Our Colonel was called in and given full authority, as in the case at Lamine. He first went to each boat, and, calling the captain, clerk and bar-tender, told them that he suspected they had liquor on board, that he would give them two days to "disinfect" the boat, and that, if after that time a single drop of liquor or wine was to be found, everything in the ship, of stores brought for sale would be confiscated; the inevitable Le Roy Richardson and "Company Q" were then given the hint.

Every bartender had laid in a large stock of tobacco, candy, canned goods, etc., some of them several thousand dollars' worth, and it was hoped that the warning would be heeded, as their loss would be heavy if the threat were carried out. Some of them sent off a few cases, most of them nothing.

In due time Le Roy reported that every boat had liquor on board and most of them were selling, though the price had risen to $2 a bottle.

The next morning a strong guard was placed on each boat, and the fun began. The *poison* all went overboard into the water on one side of the boat, the *spoils* were thrown among the soldiers on the other. Before work was finished on the first boat there were thousands of them waiting and ready to catch the boxes of cigars and all sorts of good things that were thrown out as fast as they could be handled. The captains raved and stormed and threatened, but it was of no use, and by the time the twentieth boat had been *disinfected*, there were that number of captains, clerks and bartenders who had found out how strong was the military arm. That raid is a tradition of "the River" as is "black Friday" one of Wall street. When the command of the Regiment devolved on Colonel Flad, he also carried out the policy of excluding liquors; not allowing even beer to be sold in the vicinity of his camp.

April 28th, the Regiment was sent to Porter's Creek, where a large trestle was found nearly destroyed, which the battalion completed on the 3d of May.

On the 30th the battalion was mustered for pay. Company E sent to Saulsbury.

May 1st Lieutenant Goodrich was captured by a band of guerrillas together with the train under his command, a short distance west of Saulsbury. This was accomplished by one of the band dressing in Federal uniform and signalizing the train to stop. Not suspecting the strategy, the train was stopped immediately and came to a "stand still" within a deep cut, when to their astonishment thirty or forty desperadoes came pouring down over the banks. and left no alternative but an unconditional surrender. On his person was about $1,000, which he managed carefully to secrete and secure against their vigilant search. He was taken some miles into the interior (after they had first started the locomotive back to Grand Junction under a full head of steam), when the band was overtaken by a party of the Sixth Iowa Cavalry, and, in the melee which followed Lieutenant Goodrich, together with the other prisoners, made his escape, and returned to the battalion on the 3d. In the mean time Captain Werth had gone to Saulsbury, under orders to investigate the matter, and to discover if possible whether the citizens of that place were implicated in the capture.

May 4th, Colonel Bissell again went to Memphis, and did not return until the 6th. The battalion moved to Muddy Creek, near Pocahontas, where a large iron bridge had been destroyed, and made camp on the east side on a high piece of ground; Company E, under Lieutenant Prescott, remaining on the west side.

The train used by the Regiment for bringing timbers and other materials required, was fitted out with a guard of boiler iron for the Engineer on the locomotive, and a flat car was fitted up with a timber guard faced on the outside with boiler iron, and carrying a ten-pounder Parrott gun with a train guard of fifteen men, they called this bullet-proof car their gunboat.

May 8, 1862, details from Companies B, H and G, accompanied by the Home Guards of Pocahontas, were ordered out on a foraging expedition, and proceeded about twelve miles into the country, to what is known as Ray's planation (a noted Rebel), where a large amount of corn and commissary stores were obtained. While there it was ascertained from the negroes that two guerrillas had remained there the night previous, having in charge a Federal soldier, and had left but a short time before. Upon hearing this, Lieutenant Bras started in pursuit with a few picked men, and in one hour returned with the guerrillas and the rescued men, having overtaken them about five miles distant.

May 11th Company G moved into Pocahontas, and the citizens of that place exhibited a strong Union and friendly feeling. The next day the news was received that Richmond was taken, and so reliable did it appear, that in the evening the battalion celebrated it with cannon, musketry and bonfires.

Colonel Bissell and Adjutant Hudson started for Vicksburg the same day, May 13th, the other companies of the battalion moved to Pocahontas and made camp. Lieutenant Parker was appointed Provost-Marshal of the post, and filled that position until relieved by the arrival of Colonel Meisner's Brigade, June 6th.

There remained but one important bridge to complete, viz.: that of the Hatchie, before meeting the workmen from Corinth, and the battalion, now under Major Flad, applied itself to the work, and although the bridge was a very large one (formerly built of iron), it was completed and the train passed safely over the whole road on the 12th of June. In the meantime, a great deal of other work presented itself. It was found that the whole road was badly out of repair. The ties had become rotten, and all the smaller bridges and culverts useless; so much so that on the 17th a locomotive broke through a small trestle at Middleton, and was injured so fbadly as to render it useless. Lieutenant Wilcox was therefore detailed, with a large detachment of men, to carefully examine and put in repair all small bridges and trestles of doubtful security.

May 19th, it having been ascertained that a large force of guerrillas was near, and there being no other troops within supporting distance, all other work was, for a time, suspended, and the work of fortifying the place commenced. A fine earthwork was soon constructed, in which was mounted, shortly after, four guns.

May 22d, Sol. Street, with his band of guerrillas, made a demonstration against the place, but after a reconnoisance of our position, withdrew. His band, however, was attacked that night and completely broken up for a time; more than half of his men were killed and wounded.

On the 27th, while at Vicksburg, Colonel Bissell resigned, and while waiting action on his papers, obtained leave of absence from the Regiment. His resignation, however, having been accepted, he did not rejoin.

On the 2d of June the resignation of Lieutenant Connett, which had been previously tendered, was accepted.

On the 6th of June, a brigade having arrived to garrison the place, the whole command was turned over, and the battalion was thereafter devoted exclusively to engineering.

June 14th an engine, one car and the gun car, with a detail of the Regiment on board, ran into a chasm where a bridge had been burned; the shells and two hundred pounds of powder on the gun car exploded. A Lieutenant Morgan and one man were killed and fourteen wounded belonging to a Tennessee regiment; the fireman was so badly injured that he died. June 24th the men captured and paroled at Holly Springs, December, 1862, returned to duty having been exchanged. July 15th, Companies E, H and K moved to a camp five miles east of Pocahontas, at Tuscumbia River bridge, and operated a steam sawmill there; left August 24th with a regiment for Memphis, but returned to the sawmill, September 18th, and remained until October 4th.

September 23d, Rev. E. L. Hunt, a Baptist minister, was elected Chaplain of the Regiment, and served until December 31st, when he was mustered out at the consolidation of the Engineer Regiment of the West Missouri Volunteers, with the Twenty-fifth Missouri Infantry.

June 10th notice was received that the resignation of Lieutenant-Colonel Adams, which had been previously tendered, had been accepted on the 25th of May; the following day Lieutenant Wilcox was transferred from Company G to the charge of Company K.

The battalion remained at Pocahontas, engaged in getting out ties, timber, constructing fortifications along the line of the road, scouting, etc., until the 21st of August, when it moved under orders to Memphis, with a view of rejoining the First Battalion at Vicksburg. While at the former place, however, a countermand order was received, and after going into camp long enough to supply a deficiency in the camp equipage and receiving four months' payment, it returned to Pocahontas again on the 30th.

While at the latter place the battalion did considerable scouting, and for this purpose Lieutenant Bras was detailed, who, with a detachment of about thirty men, principally from Company K, prepared themselves with a mounted outfit. Becoming somewhat familiar with the cavalry drill, they acquitted themselves creditably in every encounter with the enemy. On one occasion, while returning with a forage train, the rear guard was fired into from an ambuscade, and one mule wounded. But they were promptly attacked in return, and compelled to beat a hasty retreat. At another time, having passed up a narrow lane in search of forage, upon their return, the end of the lane was found to be fenced up, and ere they had time to remove the same or to conjecture the cause of the obstruction, they received a full volley from a neighboring thicket. No one was hurt however, and the next moment a party of rebels were bounding away before the reckless dash of our men.

At another time (August 11) the party was attacked by Street's guerrilla band, while the former were in the act of crossing Muddy Creek; the Rebels rushing up from their ambuscades upon the rear guard with one of those demoniacal yells for which they have always been celebrated, and with the evident intention of throwing the whole in confusion, but our men had too long subjected themselves to the discipline of soldiers to be surprised by bushwhackers. Lieutenant Bras was on hand, and the men prompt to obey his calls. A part of the command, under Sergeant Carlin, was immediately sent to cross at a lower ford and to attack the Rebels in flank while the remainder attracted their attention in front. No sooner did they find a force on their flank, than they broke in confusion, in the midst of which there were two killed and seven wounded. The rest scattered in every direction. Street was himself so closely pursued that he was obliged to leap from his horse and escape to the thicket, his horse, blankets, muster-rolls and everything falling into the hands of our men.

July 10th, the resignation of Lieutenant Bissell, which had been previously tendered, was accepted, followed by that of Lieutenant J. W. Hooker, on the 11th.

July 30th, Major Flad received commission of Lieutenant-Colonel, vice Adams resigned, having been mustered out by Lieutenant Hoffman for that purpose on the 10th of the same month.

August 24th, notice of the acceptance of Dr. Shelton's resignation was received, which occurred on the 30th July previous.

TO IUKA AND CORINTH.

Upon the return of the Regiment from Memphis, as already mentioned, it engaged in the same line of duty as before, and remained until the 3d of October, when the battalion broke up camp at daylight and proceeded on the train to Corinth; leaving, however, Companies G and K to finish some business already commenced. Company H, although detailed to proceed with the battalion, did not go up on the same train, but arrived in Corinth the same evening. On the way the battalion narrowly escaped a catastrophe, the enemy having burned a small unguarded bridge, notice of which was given by a friendly citizen in time to stop the train. It was, however, the work of only a few hours to replace it, and the command proceeded on.

At Corinth the battalion was joined by Dr. J. C. Book, who had been commissioned Surgeon in the Army and assigned to this Regiment, and who was mustered on the same day, October 3d.

October 4th, the battalion moved from Corinth to Glendale, repairing the road as it went, where it remained until the 6th, when it moved to Burnsville. The object of the expedition was to open the Memphis & Charleston Railroad east from Corinth, in advance of General Sherman's march over that line to reinforce General Grant at Chattanooga.

October 12th, the bridges were all completed to Iuka, and the train passed through and returned in the evening.

October 14th, the Battalion moved to Iuka and made camp a little north of the town.

October 16th, moved camp to Clear Creek, where it remained until the 23d of October, when it removed in the midst of a severe rain storm to Buzzard Roost.

October 28th, moved camp to Dixon, from which place on the following day the Battalion returned again to Bear Creek, having accomplished all that was desired, and going as far as General Sherman designed to proceed on that line. It was said, and with a good degree of truth, that the Battalion constructed bridges on this march as fast as the Rebels could burn them, and until frightened at the rapidity with which their mischief was repaired, began the complete destruction of the whole road by adding the burning of ties and bending of iron. During the march the Battalion was divided into detachments and assigned to the different branches of work along the road. In that manner half a dozen bridges would be in course of construction at the same time, many of which were very large. While at Burnsville the battalion was rejoined by Company G, which Company, under Captain Werth, was charged with the construction of a large bridge at Iuka.

October 20th, Company K arrived while the Battalion was at Clear Creek, and was charged with the construction of the bridge over Bear Creek, a work of three hundred feet in length, which had to be piled the whole distance, and which was finished in seven days, principally by that Company. Several amusing incidents occurred while on that expedition. At one time, while encamped at Glendale, one of the Lieutenants, with a small party went out on a turkey hunt, of which game that country abounded. It happened that an old lame mule, of little service in the teams, had been turned out that morning to graze and recruit, and had strayed some distance into the timber. As the Lieutenant made the ascent of a sharp hill, he discovered the top of the mule's head, as that animal stood in fancied security on the other side of the crest. Having much the appearance of the fowl so prominent in his imagination, the Lieutenant secured a good place to aim, and the next moment the whole party were convulsed with the laughter that the scene foced upon them, as they discovered that the shot designed for what they supposed a turkey had penetrated the head of the mule in question.

Upon another occasion, while the Battalion was at Burnsville, some of the men were in want of flooring to spread their blankets upon. For this purpose they had taken charge of two doors, and were about to proceed with them to camp, when the Provost Guard, who had been instructed to have nothing disturbed in town, interfered and stopped the arrangement. But they were not to be thus baffled. In a few moments one of them was taken *violently sick*, and had to be taken to camp. Of course something was required to carry him on, and accordingly he was stretched upon one of the doors (that being the most convenient), a blanket spread over him, and in this way conveyed to camp by his comrades, upon reaching which it was found that they had *accidentally* taken both doors, one having been laid immediately above the other. It is also a remarkable fact that the sickness of the man was of short duration, and *urgent* business prevented the doors from being taken back.

First Lieutenant Sherwood died at Jefferson Barracks, Missouri, August 8, 1863.

October 28th notice of the previous appointment of Rev. E. L. Hunt as Chaplain of the Regiment was received.

October 9th Captain E. M. Hill was commissioned Major, *vice* Flad, promoted, and First Lieutenant Wilcox commissioned Captain of Company D, *vice* Hill, promoted; also Sergeant David Armstrong promoted to Second Lieutenant of Company C, *vice* Bissell, resigned.

Lieutenant-Colonel Flad had made a bet that he could get all the bridges repaired and a train through to Iuka by the 12th, and won the bet.

October 16th Lieutenant-Colonel Flad was promoted to the rank of Colonel.

October 30th the Battalion returned to Iuka, after having furnished guard for the Bear Creek Bridge, the night previous all other troops having accompanied General Sherman. Two men from Company K having proceeded a short distance from camp, were left and fell into the enemy's hands, who advanced to the bridge shortly after the battalion left. The same evening Company C was ordered to guard a bridge near Burnsville, while Lieutenant Parker, with a detail from the same, proceeded to Glendale to ship some ammunition belonging to the Regiment to Corinth, and which had been stored at the former place for safe keeping.

October 31st the whole battalion removed to Corinth and quartered in what was known as the barracks of the Fifty-seventh Illinois Infantry, which had just been vacated by them.

November 2d, Lieutenants Winegar, Coy and Parker went to Memphis, and the latter returned to the battalion on the 7th. The two former proceeded to Vicksburg on business, returning on the 6th of December. The battalion remained at Corinth actively engaged in drill, guarding trains and repairing fortifications at that place, until the 26th of December, when it was moved by orders to Nashville, under command of Major Hill, for the purpose of consolidation with the Twenty-fifth Missouri Volunteer Infantry, Colonel Flad having previously gone to St. Louis for that purpose.

The works constructed while at Corinth, particularly Batteries Williams and Robinett, were fine specimens of engineering skill, and declared to be impregnable.

November 13th notice of the promotion of F. Tunica to First Lieutenant Company B was received; the promotion, however, having been made on the 17th of August, 1863.

The battalion arrived at Memphis on the evening of the 26th of December, and was furnished transportation on the steamer America. The trip will long be remembered by all on board, for its hardships and exposure. The record will furnish but few instances wherein the weather was of greater severity, while six companies were obliged to be crowded upon a boat of the smallest class, without fire, and little or no facilities for cooking.

At Cairo the battalion reported for orders, and it excites but little surprise that the men, after having been thus exposed united for a while in what is termed a "good time."

On the 31st of December the Battalion arrived at Smithland, Kentucky, where the cold became so intense that the boat was unable to proceed, and the men nearly perished with its severity. In this state of affairs Major Hill refused to proceed any further until an improved condition of the weather would warrant it. The boat was therefore made fast, and all who were unable to procure shelter in the cabin were quartered in vacant buildings.

On the 4th of January, 1864, the battalion arrived at Nashville, and immediately went into camp for the purpose of effecting the consolidation.

While at Iuka, Mississippi, the men were exposed a good deal to cold rains without proper shelter, and a severe type of dysentry broke out among them. James V. Hampton, of Company K, died of that disease there on the 18th of October, and his body was sent home to New London, Iowa, by his comrades.

October 24th, at the camp near Bear Creek, General Sherman, on his way to Chattanooga, passed part of the day and the following night, and while in conversation with Colonel Flad, the writer heard the General make the remark that he was preparing his men so that he could pick the whole command up (making a scoop-like motion with his two hands) and go anywhere with them, cutting loose from all the railroads and living off the country. This was verified just a year afterward in "Sherman's March to the Sea."

THE CAMP IN CORINTH, MISSISSIPPI.

While in camp at Corinth, the work done besides repairing the fort was repairing bridges between Corinth and Memphis. Company E worked at building a Cotton Gin, and enlarging the Regimental Hospital.

December 6th. While Companies H and E were repairing the bridge at Moscow, the enemy tried to surprise and capture them, and there was quite a lively fight for a time; Lieutenant Goodrich took charge of the Artillery during the fight.

December 18th, a detail of one hundred and fifty, from four companies, were sent to Glendale, east of Corinth, to repair a saw-mill; they found it burned, and loaded the machinery and some timbers on the train and brought them to Corinth, where they erected the saw-mill.

THE TRIP TO NASHVILLE.

On the trip up the river to Nashville the boat arrived at Smithland, the mouth of the Cumberland River, about 9 A. M., December 30th, weather very fine until afternoon it commenced to rain, and about 5 P. M. the wind changed to the northwest with snow and rapidly growing colder, until about 9 P. M. Colonel Flad, fearing his men would freeze to death, took Companies B, H and K, to a brick church in the village, making fires with the fencing.

January 1, 1864, the thermometer on the boat registered eighteen degrees below zero. The boat started up the Cumberland River at 3 P. M. The cold was so severe the first night on the Cumberland River that the men nearly perished, the boat was so crowded that the men could not all get into the cabin, every state-room, bunk and floor was full, and the cabin floor, tables and under the tables, was crowded as close as candles in a box. The hurricane deck was protected as much as possible by hanging up tents for curtains, still the men of Companies C, D and G, who were quartered out there, suffered terribly with the high wind and the thermometer ten to fourteen degrees below zero.

HENRY FEUERBACH, CO. A, 1st MISSOURI ENGINEERS.

FOUNTAIN FOX, CO. B, K and A ENGINEERS.

When we arrived at Nashville on the 4th it was not much better; four degrees below zero, seven inches of snow on the ground, no wood, straw or boards to be had. Withal a great deal of trouble and red tape to get the sick into the General Hospitals. The private citizens were not much better off for fuel, as wood was fifty dollars a cord and coal not to be had. Among the men, as a result of this exposure, nearly one-third of them came down with coughs, colds and lung fever, with quite a number of rheumatisms and bowel complaints, that made them invalids for the rest of their lives. The weather did not moderate until the 10th of January; no regular supply of wood until the 9th, when ten cords were obtained, and on the 10th a detail of fifteen men of Company G went down the river with a flat boat and returned with thirty-five cords.

About the 1st of January the men commenced re-enlisting as veterans, and by the 20th they were re-enlisting quite rapidly.

THE SECOND BATTALION AT VICKSBURG.

Having followed the record of the First Battalion, we will now return to the Second, which was left with the army in front of Vicksburg, working at the Duckport Canal, to which it had removed on the 31st of March. Companies A, D, F and I were left under Major Tweeddale, Dr. Knower as Surgeon.

Leaving Company I and a detail from Company F, under Captain Brackett, at Duckport to fit up dredges, barges, etc., the battalion moving out on Walnut Bayou, and were engaged in clearing out stumps, trees, etc., until the 13th April, when the water was let into the canal, and three dredges were sent in.

On the 20th the steamer Victor and two barges were also sent in and passed Richmond on the 27th, having been delayed by the great amount of work in Brashy Bayou.

On the 29th April the expedition arrived at Parker's plantation and were ordered to proceed through Bayou Vidal to New Carthage, with dispatches for General Grant.

On the 30th the Battalion moved back to Parker's plantation. The water in the bayou began to fall very rapidly, and as it ran off through Roundaway Bayou at Richmond, Captain Prime, Chief Engineer on General Grant's Staff, directed that a drain be built at Richmond.

Companies A, D and F were engaged at this until May ,9th when the battalion moved to Milliken's Bend, by order of General Sullivan.

On the 11th of May, Major Tweeddale received, on behalf of the Engineer Corps, a complimentary letter, of which the following is an extract:

"General Sullivan directs me to say that the energy and perseverence manifested by the Engineer Regiment in the construction of the road from Sherman's Landing to Bower's Landing deserves the highest commendation, and should not be allowed to pass unnoticed. The work was one of vast importance to our brave soldiers in the front, and the General commanding the army in the field shall not go unadvised of the amount of praise to be awarded to the Engineer Regiment."

On the 9th of May General Grant having communicated with the Gunboat Fleet by way of Chickasaw Bayou and Yazoo River, the battalion received orders the same night to proceed to Chickasaw Bayou and open a road to the bluffs.

On the 20th of April four gunboats and two transports ran past the Vicksburg batteries and received but little damage. On the 25th, six transports ran past, one, the Henry Clay, was burned. The 28th, one tug and two barges were lost trying to run the batteries.

May 18th a detachment of Company D left Young's Point for Grand Gulf to repair the steamer Anglaze; the balance of the battalion at Miliken's Bend, Young's Point and Chickasaw Bayou.

It remained thus employed until the 25th, when the following order was received, which is inserted for the reason that it more clearly defines the duties upon which the battalion was called to act:

CAMP IN FRONT OF VICKSBURG,
25th May, 1863.

MAJOR TWEEDDALE,

Commanding Battalion Eng. Reg't of the West.

MAJOR: On receipt of this you will move your Battalion at once to this side of the river, leaving a Sergeant and necessary details to guard your property at Young's Point.

You will leave a Lieutenant and twenty men at the landing on the Yazoo, who will take charge of the Pontoon Train and road leading to the landing. The Lieutenant will report to General Sherman's Headquarters, and obtain all necessary instructions and details for the work under his charge. With the balance of your Battalion you will take position on the side of the bridge beyond the graveyard on the road leading from General McClernand's command to Warrington. You will attract as little notice as possible from the enemy, locate the position of his work between McClernand's left and Lauman's right, and also explore the country with respect to opening a road for Infantry between those two points in front of the road now in use. As soon as you are in position you will send an officer to report the fact to me at General Grant's Headquarters.

BY ORDER OF MAJOR-GENERAL GRANT, &C.

In pursuance of the above order, the Battalion moved on the day of its issue, and was engaged upon the work therein indicated until the 28th, when it moved under orders to Haines' Bluff, for the purpose of constructing fortifications at that point, and was thus engaged until the 1st of July, when it was ordered to take position with the army in the rear of Vicksburg, while Captain E. M. Hill was detailed with twenty men to mount the guns in the works completed.

May 27th the detachment repairing steamer at Grand Gulf moved to Warrenton, where they were mostly kept until Vicksburg surrendered, when they moved in July 5th.

On the 2d the Battalion moved in pursuance of the order of July 1st, and reported to Captain Comstock, Chief Engineer of the Department.

On the surrender of Vicksburg, the Battalion moved inside the line of works, and was employed in destroying the works constructed during the siege by the Federals until August, when a new line was commenced, and to obtain lumber for the profile and revetments a sawmill near Snyder's Bluff was called into requisition.

The logs were obtained from the Yazoo River, being a part of the raft that was constructed across the same at Snyder's Bluff by the Rebels to obstruct its navigation. On the withdrawal of the Federal troops for the Big Black River, the mill was abandoned, the logs floated down to Vicksburg, and a new sawmill erected by the battalion.

August 14th a detachment of Company D was moved out of Vicksburg four miles to repair a railroad bridge, and remained there until August 24th.

The Battalion, under Major Tweeddale, was kept at work on the fortifications of Vicksburg, and other engineering work there, until January 15, 1864, when orders were received to go to Nashville and join headquarters, to be present at the consolidation with the Twenty-fifth Missouri Infantry; they arrived at Memphis January 23d, left there the 25th, arrived at Cairo the 27th and left the 30th.

The Battalion arrived at Nashville February 2, 1864, and went into camp with the main body of the Regiment.

On the 4th, the two regiments perfected their consolidation with each other; but as it is the purpose only to give here a record of the Engineer Regiment of the West up to that time, the history of the New Organization will not be entered upon further than to append a list of its officers.

The greatest strength shown by the returns at any one time was in the month of December, 1861, when it numbered - - - - - - - - 939 men.
Enlisted since, - - - - - - - - 192 "
Company L, added in December, by order of the Secretary of War, - - - - - - - 56 "

Total, - - - - - - - - 1,187 "

The last company was transferred from another regiment, and as it was never with the Regiment until the consolidation, its history would add but little interest to the record here.

From the above can be taken the following:
Died from disease, - - - - - - - 80
Discharged for disability, - - - - - - 130
Deserted, - - - - - - - - 78
Reported at the date of consolidation. - - - - 795

Total, - - - - - - - - 1,083

Leaving a discrepancy of 104 men to be accounted for by "missing in action" and from other causes.

With reference to this Regiment the Adjutant-General of Missouri, in his printed report, makes the following complimentary remark in 1863:

"The honor of the citizens of Missouri is due to this working regiment, an emblem, as it is, of the noble spirit of labor, while it glorifies the spirit of war by engaging in it only when the nation is attacked by a portion of its citizens with the design of prostrating it at their feet. It may also be added that, by general orders, the Regiment was authorized to inscribe upon its banner the name of New Madrid, Island No. 10 and Corinth, as an acknowledgment of the important part taken by it in the reduction of these strongholds of the enemy."

THE CAPTURE AND ESCAPE OF HENRY FEUERBACH.

May 29, 1862, occurred the evacuation of Corinth by the Rebels, who were running trains and blowing up their magazines, for we could hear them. May 30th, next day, we followed them on a hot and quick march, the whole Regiment in line with Colonel Bissell in command. Just at sunset we came up to the Rebel rear guards down in the swamps, in which ran Tuscumbia River. Our

Company in advance, with Captain Randolph in command, who marched us up to a burning bridge, which had all the appearance of danger, in place of halting the Company and deploying one platoon as skirmishers, so as to gradually feel our way, which would have developed what was in front of us; but, no—on we marched, four ranks in double file, up the road, until within fifty feet of the bridge, when the Rebels opened out on us with a fire of cannon and infantry, which drove back all who could get back—three or four killed outright. John Lewis, brave, noble soul; Corporal Whitson, and two others, whose names I have forgotten. Two of us were taken prisoners—Platt Griffith and myself. I was on the edge of the river bank and fell down; some roots sticking out, my right leg caught and held me firm. From there early next morning we were taken south to Mobile, Alabama; thence to Macon, Georgia. At Mobile we were kindly treated under the command of General Forsythe. A Rebel officer, who was a native of Florida, came in one day while I was lying on the floor and reading "Shakespeare" with two friends. He asked me all about what my opinion was in reference to our army or the policy of our Government. I told him frankly that we would gradually take possession of the country, one city after another, and capture the entire South; that it would take years, but that we would succeed in the end. Then he asked me what I thought would become of their negroes. I told him that it was my opinion that all would be freed by us; that our banner meant freedom to all who came under it. He was partly drunk, and, after I said that the negroes would be free, he raved, swore, threw his arms out, right and left, as if he would like to lick a whole army. He left, but in a few day's after he tried to have me put in a dark cell or guard house, as he swore he would. General Forsythe sent one of his staff officers, who was a native of New York; he asked me all about it, and, after he heard my version and made inquiries among the men, whether my statement was correct, he released me with a friendly good-bye. General Forsythe came to see us one day, to look after our treatment. In the papers was an account written by one of their men, a prisoner at Camp Douglas, that we "Yank's" were treating them so kindly "as a matter of policy," so as to demoralize them so none would return South again. I asked the General if he had read it. He said, yes. I told him he could try that experiment on us, if he thought it would have a like effect. He looked at me, smiled and went away.

After we left Montgomery, Alabama, on our way to Macon, Georgia, the second station on the train ahead of us were a lot of Rebels to reinforce Lee, for the second battle of Bull Run had just been fought. A lot of Alabama ladies were on horseback, with flowers to give their men as an encouragement of "Southern Chivalry." I thought the flowers would also be an encouragement to us Yankees, so I called to them that they should fairly distribute them among us all. One fair lady rode near our car, threw me a bouquet, for which I thanked her. The officer in charge of the guard told her the mistake she made; that we were "Yanks." That officer spoilt all of the pleasure of those ladies for *that* day. On the same train a fruit dealer came to sell us peaches. I bought them all with a label from a bottle of Mexican Liniment; any bill that was decently engraved with a horse or a railroad train you could pass. Every town or business house, no matter how small, had its own paper money; such was free trade in Confederate paper money.

At Macon there were all of the Shiloh prisoners, with our Lieutenant-Colonel Adams, who was taken prisoner at Farmington. Adams had all the refined character of a soldier and gentleman, but upon his return he resigned and returned to St. Louis, where he died before the war ended, with consumption, honored and respected by all who knew him.

While in prison our whole time was occupied in thinking and planning how to make our escape, because if we remained prisoners among them all hope and courage was lost, or if one was taken sick, the last hope was gone. I have helped to bury many of our comrades, who, when they took sick, if they could have been sent home among their friends, would have been restored to health. If any men deserve a pension, there are none more deserving than those who were prisoners. It was starvation from the time you were taken until you left. I hardly need to state the account of rations per day—corn meal, about a pint cupful, a piece of bacon as large as your hand and full of maggots; with the corn meal we made coffee by browning it. I was Captain and cook of our mess. One day a Rebel guard, who had a great amount of confidence in me, asked me in confidence about those gunboat cars which we had that run on our railroads; he wanted me to describe them to him, which I did in an enlarged shape. I told him they could run on the rails or could, if found necessary, walk on land; the machinery on the inside was so arranged as to throw hot water, or throw out long arms and draw in a whole company. As green looking as he was, that lost me his confidence; he raised his musket to make a pass with his bayonet at me, but I quickly got out of his road. Our men, who knew of the devilment, during our talk had gathered around and laughed at him so loudly that he thought I had sold him, and he never came in among the prisoners again to gather information.

Finally the time came for action; our plans were made—to stay longer in prison would only reduce our physical strength, for every man had vermin more or less on him; the very ground was covered with them. I have seen the lice crawl up the trees. I have seen our comrades who died in the Rebel hospital covered all over with lice.

On September 10, 1862, a splendid warm afternoon, toward sunset, three of us, Robert Timmons, of the Thirty-fourth Indiana, and Alvin Q. Bacon, of the Fourteenth Illinois Infantry, watched our chance at the rivulet which ran in and out of the prison pen where the water closets were. The guard's route was inside near the fence; the warm sun made him sleepy, so down the ravine we went. While our men sat on the seats watching us, we crawled outside of the fence, kept alongside and crawled in the high weeds, and lay there until long after dark; up we ran along the road toward the Ocmulgee River. It commenced to rain and thunder. We met some Confederate soldiers, who were out stealing apples; each had a load on his shoulders. We passed them with a reply that we were on the same errand. No more was said by them or us, for when one is on an illegal mission, such as stealing apples, the less said the more apples you bring to camp. Toward morning we got tired from tramping all night, as we saw in front of us a cotton gin. I proposed we take a rest until near daylight; Timmons opposed it as dangerous, but my orders ruled; we lay down for a few minutes; it nearly cost us our liberty; we were awakened by hearing the negroes singing on their way to work; it was broad daylight; we ran as fast as possible toward the timber, not forgetting to take along some green ears of corn. When we got in the timber, which was in a swamp, we lighted a fire and roasted the ears for our morning meal. Then we started toward the river. We in some places had to crawl through underbrush; in one place, over our heads, crawled a long water moccasin, but we kept on, as we were not after snakes. Finally we came to a large bayou. On some logs on the other side sat some Confederate soldiers fishing. Timmons said we were lost. I told him to get behind the tree, pull off his blouse and put it on inside out, so they could not tell we were Union soldiers by our uniform. Bacon and myself had on nothing to indicate our nationality. I boldly stepped out and hallo ed over: "Here is your old mule," which was a common expression among the Rebel soldiers; they answered "all right." I asked them how fishing was, they said good. I asked them where we could cross, as we wished to go to the river bridge to fish; they told us to go about half a mile up, then we could cross on some logs. I bid them "good-bye," and invited them, in case fishing got bad, to come to us at the bridge. I asked them what command they belonged to; they told us Colonel Ross' Regiment. I told them we belonged to Major Rylander's Battalion, which was part of the command that were guarding us at the prison; they said "all right." If they came to the bridge they never found us, as we surely did not want to see them again. The ruse worked well, and I hope they never up to this day found out how bad they were fooled by the "Yanks." After crossing we made for the brush near the river. During the afternoon, toward evening, we heard a negro come along singing the old Southern songs; we needed something to eat. I crawled out to the edge of the undergrowth until I was sure that he was a negro, then I called him. He looked as if we were men fallen from another world. I spoke to him, took him to my comrades, told him we were making our escape, that we wanted something to eat, as we had nothing but a few ears of corn all day, that he should bring us something after dark. True as steel came our old gray-headed darky friend after dark. At first he whistled softly, then louder; we replied. When he found all safe he opened his basket full of eatables, well cooked; if I mistake not, a stewed chicken. A negro in the South during the war never betrayed a Union soldier; at least I have never heard of one. They in all cases were our friends and helped us in every possible way, even to stealing their master's eatables for our benefit. That night we took from a small lake a flat-bottom boat about sixteen feet long and square at each end, hauled it about 600 feet to the edge of the river bank and launched it. When we tried to get in the boat it leaked so badly that one of us had to continually bail out the water to keep from sinking. We floated along down stream with a strong current, as the Ocmulgee River near Macon, Georgia, is narrow. We passed one house after another by drifting with the current and laying flat in the boat. About 12 o'clock on the river bank we saw a fine canoe about eighteen feet long and three feet wide. We "honorably" exchanged with the owner by leaving ours in place of it, while he slept and dreamed of victories which their armies were gaining daily. Next morning we landed below a rope ferry on an island where the trees were full of a very large grape, which we ate to satisfy our hunger. In about three hours Timmon's bowels began to loosen, so much so that he got frightened. He thought that the large plum-grapes had poisoned him, as none of us had ever seen any before. The effect was only temporary, though.

That night we went to the main shore to see if we could not get something to eat for a few days ahead, we slept in a corn crib, and toward morning we heard the hogs grounding, so up we jumped, got a few ears of corn and threw it to the nearest hog which snatched it. I caught it by the hind legs, threw the hog over my shoulder and ran to the river bank with the hog squealing as loud as hog could. At the bank we bled it and took it to our island home; that gave us the finest fresh hog meat we had since we left our lines. There was nothing of unusual interest occurred until we came near the first railroad bridge, which was guarded by Rebels; how to get under it was a problem; some five or more miles above the bridge we camped in the cane brake; on the opposite shore was the Southern steamer, "Southern Belle," which had been run out of the reach of our army. We usually camped back from the bank, so that we could not be seen; we pulled our canoe in the weeds or hid it under them; we traveled altogether at night; one of us would sleep while two paddled; we became so used to the starry sky, that we could tell the time of night, especially was it the case with the sister stars or dipper. We cut cane enough to cover our canoe over, then we drifted along until we came squarely opposite the center span, then the last one, "myself" crawled under the cane and floated with the stream gently along under the bridge; our canoe struck one of the piers and I heard one guard ask what time it was, and another answered, about twelve o'clock; they never knew how near the "Yankees" came to that bridge; below it were one or two forts, which had outside of them pickets with fires; we saw them and crawled under our cane again out of danger. One day in trying to get information, we stopped near a rope ferry; the road leading to it was a very fine one; in the distance we could hear a song as if a negro were singing; on being sure of the color of the man depended our safety, and the information we wanted; we laid alongside the road near the landing in a deep gully; the man was singing as joyfully as a lark, but he never knew that because he was white he came near being killed, for Simmons had a short ax, with which he wanted to kill him or take him prisoner. I would not allow it for it would have resulted in an injury to us, as it would have impaired our safety in making our escape. Some ten miles below we stopped at an old warehouse; I went, or sneaked along the fence until I came upon some negroes working happily along in rows of cotton, singing their usual negro songs.

After seeing that no white person was near, out I came boldly and called them to come to me. I told them we were Union soldiers making our way to our gunboats; that we wanted something to eat. That night in that old one-room warehouse gathered the most joyful lot of male and female blacks in all Georgia. They brought us cooked meats, corn bread, bacon and chicken. We were the first Union soldiers they had ever seen. They put to us question after question of how our army was getting along; would we ever come their way, and what kind of a man was Lincoln. They had been told that he was a mean tyrant who would murder them if they ever were caught. That was the kind of yarns the Southerners were telling their blacks to keep them well under control. That kind of stories had but little effect, as Sherman's army soon came along and settled all such hobgoblin stories. Some ten miles below were falls in the river; at the bottom of those rapids was Hawkinsville; the negroes told us the falls were dangerous, and that we should keep near shore; when we came to them the current was so strong that I told our comrades that we might as well take our chances and let her go, which we did, and got over safely. We did not know how many houses there were in town, as we kept on the opposite shore. Finally we came nearer and nearer to the mouth of the river. As we were drifting near our journey's end, the river widened. The first alligators we heard was as I was sleeping, and Timmons woke me up, as he said he heard the roaring lions in the woods, but it was a large alligator who was growling loudly, and it frightened him so that he would not stay in the rear of the canoe and steer; I had to take his place, and under no circumstances could I prevail upon him to take this place again, telling him that there was no danger. Finally the wind made the surface of the river so dangerous that we were compelled to seek the shore and land.

As the morning's grey dawn appeared, we found we had landed on a plantation. Above us was an orange tree; we picked oranges from it but they were sour, not sweet. My comrades were afraid that we would be captured, but I proposed that we explore. To our surprise, we found a fine plantation; none on it but a few old grizzled unserviceable negroes, none of whom could speak good English. They had been brought from Africa late in life, and never learned much English. They did their talking to us mostly by signs; as they told me by signs and pointing to the sky, that when the sun was so bright the superintendent would come. They had honey plenty, and fixed up a good meal for us. Long after the war, in reading a book of her Southern life by "Fanny Kemble Butler," I found that this was the plantation where she had spent a part of her married life with her husband, Colonel Butler. I agree with her in all she says of this plantation. Rice fields are numerous from here to the coast. Opposite is the old town of Darien, which is one of the oldest settled towns on the Southern coast, so Bancroft says. It was settled with Scotch in 1640, or about that time. The river here divides, one arm running to St. Fernando, the other passed Darien, out at Doboy Inlet or Altamaha Sound. Information from the darkies we could not get, as they could not speak English, so about eleven o'clock we were determined to find out which way we had to go to get to our nearest blockading steamer. Here is where I committed the only error of our whole trip, for under my advice we rowed up to an old sawmill below Darien, in place of keeping on the river where we were unobserved. But I was the captain, on we paddled, struck the shore by the mill. Out stepped two partisan rangers, so they called themselves, fully armed with Sharps' carbines. Timmons and Bacon looked at me as much as to say we are again prisoners.

All our long journey was in vain; we would be brought back to Macon, or likely shot, as had been the case with hundreds before us, but I did not think that. The Rebels asked where we were from. I told them Butler's plantation, which they could see some three miles across. The pickets went to one side to talk together; that gave Timmons and me a chance to consult. We agreed, that under no circumstances would we be taken prisoners without a desperate struggle. I told Timmons to watch me closely, and if I did not succeed, that he should help me; they returned, and wanted us to go as prisoners to their camp with them, some three miles away. I talked them out of that, by telling them we were barefooted and could not walk over the ground as it was full of thistles. They wanted to know what we were doing on Butler's plantation. I told them we were old overseers, and were spending a few days on the old place a fishing, on furloughs which we had left there, and that if they would give us a chance, or go with us, we would show them, so that they could see we were old Confederate soldiers; that we belonged to the Twelfth Georgia Infantry; had been fighting the "Yanks" and had killed numbers of them; told them what battles we had been in, how brave and great we were. I could see their eyes sparkle. I did not forget to tell them, we thought in about six months the war would be over, as England would help us, then we would gain our independence. I think I used all the eloquent conversational powers I possessed to charm them (and those who know me will credit me with some powers in that direction). While I was entertaining them, Timmons picked up a piece of iron about one foot long and three inches wide, which he hid up his shirt sleeve, ready for service if need be. I told the Rebels that one of them should stay and guard us, as we had on nothing but pants, shirt and hat, not even shoes, and under no circumstances could we harm them, as they had the best of arms; and for the other one, to go quickly to camp, bring their Lieutenant along, and him we would satisfy that we were Johnnies by taking him over to the plantation and showing them our furloughs. They thought that an excellent idea, and locked our canoe. Off he went as fast as his horse could carry him, while I had his partner take me up on the run of the mill, where all the sawing was done; on top we could look all over the country, for it is all level and the tide overflows it. I asked him all about how each arm of the river ran, and how far it was to our gunboats, which he told me with childish glee, and much more information that we did not want, but which was very valuable.

Timmons was behind us a few feet standing with his iron ready to do his part if required. I looked at the Confederate time and again; he held his carbine in both hands partly resting on his knees; my heart was beating with anxiety; the desperate deed had to be done; it was man to man. With one quick jump I snatched his gun from him, he hallooed and ran. I cocked the carbine and told him to stand or I would shoot him. He did so, and slowly got down the slide, on which we went up. When on the ground, he told me or begged me not to kill him; that he told his partner his suspicion was that we were "Yanks," and now he was sure of it; I told him that he was right, but that my talk had thrown them off their guard. We took all his tobacco, for we had none for over a month, and tobacco to us was worth more than gold just then. I made him get on his knees and swear that under no circumstances would he tell who we were or where we were going or anything about us, when his partner and the officer came back.

We promised we would not hurt a hair of his head. He swore like an old professional. Bacon broke the lock and chain with the ax, which let the canoe free. I took all the ammunition he had, threw it in the river, took the load out of his carbine and told him I would give it back; that he should tell them we had hunted for our passes and found them, and that he let us go. Off we started and paddled as hard as our physical strength would allow; the sun seemed fearful hot.

When looking with my memory back to that September month, in 1862, my mind brings the occasion before me as vivid as the day it took place, twenty-six years ago. Still we kept on, rounded a sharp bend in the river from where we could not be seen. After that I took Timmons' advice. We pulled our canoe in the high canebrake, as the tide was low, away from the river so none could see us; for Timmons said they would surely come after us, which proved to be the case. About nine o'clock that evening we could hear the sound of rowing coming nearer and nearer. We felt safe, for we knew that from the river they could not see us, unless they came on the edge of the canebrake with torches, for there was no moon to light up the scene, and if there had been a moon, we had crawled out of sight, too far for any one to see us even in daylight in a yawl. After they passed on down, I thought we had better get out and start for the gunboat, as the tide was at its highest. Timmons said : "No, they have gone down to look for us and will not find us, so they will come back, and we must not leave until they return." Such proved to be the case, for in about two hours we again heard the rowing, at first gentle, but as they came nearer, louder and louder until they passed out of hearing. We could hear them talk as they passed by. Knowing that our time had come, we pulled our canoe through the canebrake into the river, it being then about one o'clock. As we floated along, we struck upon a riff or shoal of fish. They were so thick that by the bottom of our canoe striking them many jumped inside. Finally we thought it was near morning, and we felt a sense of knowledge that we were nearing the mouth of the Altamaha River; so in the darkness, on the left bank, we landed at an old warehouse with a lot of one-story houses in the rear. Not a dog barked at our coming; we thought not a soul was near. The first door I came to, with Timmons and Bacon by me, with such weapons as we had for use in case of danger, I knocked at the door. A voice inside answered, "Who are you?" I said "friends." A light was made, the door was opened, the man looked at us with surprise. We watched every movement of his body as we went in the room; he had been fast asleep. He asked us were we not the "Yanks" who had made our escape from the Rebels that day; we told him yes. Then he told us he was from New York, and that we could trust him; that away from the Rebels he was a strong Union man, but that he was in their country or power, and had to keep a very close mouth; that he was one of the men who were in the large skiff or yawl after us; that there were six of them, heavily armed and determined to capture us, and that it would have fared badly with us if they had caught us, as the pickets at Darien were partisan rangers, or in other words guerrillas. He related how bad they felt in not being able to capture us, as they knew we had not or could not pass out of the river without him seeing us, as he acted as a spy for them. Then he told us to get away from his place as quick as possible, for if the Rebels saw us at his place his life would not be safe thereafter. He gave us some corn bread and a large china meat-dish full of cooked bacon. In getting into our canoe the bank was so slippery that I fell down and broke the dish. I picked up the meat and bid our loyal New Yorker, their Rebel spy, now strongly reconstructed back in the Union, good bye. Daylight was fast making its appearance, the mouth of the river was before us, the gunboat "Western World" lay in Doboy Inlet near the light-house.

When we again saw the "star-spangled banner" waving from her mast-head, our hearts were so full of joy that we would take our turns in standing up in our narrow canoe and wave our old hats and halloo with might and strength. The "Western World" let down a cutter filled with armed marines and came to us, which was a blessing, for the waves were so high that our frail craft would not stand it. They took us on board and asked us if we were not escaped Confederates; as they saw us in the distance they expected we were making our escape from them. I told the Captain who we were, and all about our trip. We were kindly treated, and those who were aboard will remember the tall young soldier with sandy hair and blue eyes, who wanted to take them up to Darien and whip those partisan rangers, whom the Captain always took for an escaped Confederate officer, and who was no other than the writer of this sketch.

A few words about those who made their escape with me on that trip:

Robert Timmons was a member of an Indiana regiment, the Thirty-fourth, I think, a splendid, brave man, whom you could only frighten with alligators, wild beasts or ghosts ; he had been a raftsman on the Upper Mississippi, and who was just the man for such a trip. I have never heard from him since we parted at New York, each to go to his regiment. Alvin Q. Bacon was killed at the charge, on May 22, 1863, at Vicksburg ; a good, kind soul, but during the trip had been of little service, as he was mostly sick from the imprisonment at Macon. He was a member of the Fourteenth Illinois Infantry. A few days before he helped charge the works at Vicksburg, where he was killed, he came to see me in our camp by Butler's Canal, opposite the city. He had his pockets full of candy and oranges, and was as glad to see me as if I were to be his lover and companion friend forever.

Your Comrade,
HENRY FEUERBACH.

PART II.

THE

TWENTY-FIFTH MISSOURI INFANTRY.

IT has been difficult to find anyone that knows accurately concerning the earliest organization of those who served in the Twenty-fifth Missouri Infantry, but according to the official records:
"This Regiment was first organized in June, 1861, from the Home Guard Battalions of Major Peabody, Major Van Horn and Major Berry, and was then known as the Thirteenth Regiment Infantry Missouri Volunteers. It was re-organized in the fall of 1861, and designated the Twenty-fifth Regiment of Infantry Missouri Volunteers."

The records do not show what portion of the Regiment belonged to Major Berry, his full name or what became of him. It is certain that Major Berry did not serve as an officer after the union of the three Battalions, either in this Regiment or any other Missouri regiment.

VAN HORN'S BATTALION.

R. T. Van Horn, Major; Joshua Thone, Surgeon. Company A—Captain William Von Daun; Lieutenants, Fredrick Loos and Fredrick Klinger. Company B—Captain William Millar; Lieutenants Daniel Cahill and David O'Neil. Company C—Geo. C. Bingham, Captain; Henry Spears, First Lieutenant; Theodore S. Case, Second Lieutenant. This Battalion consisted of three companies of Infantry, and was organized by authority of Brigadier-General Nathaniel Lyon, in the month of May, 1861. On the 10th of June, 1861, Captain W. E. Prince, in command of two companies of Regular Infantry, a squadron of Cavalry, with one twelve-pounder howitzer, landed and took possession of Kansas City. Immediately after this,

ROBERT T. VAN HORN, LIEUTENANT-COLONEL 25th MO.

JOHN T. BERGHOFF, SURG. 25th MO.

COL. CHESTER HARDING, 25th MO.

this Battalion was organized, armed, equipped and mustered into the United States service for three years, by Captain A. F. Bond, U.S.A., June 24, 1861. On the 18th of July, 1861, Major Van Horn received orders to take two of the companies of this Battalion and march to the relief of Colonel Nugent, who was threatened with a superior force at Austin, Cass county, Missouri. On the 19th inst., while camped on Smith's farm, five miles north of Harrisonville, in Cass county, he was attacked by a large force of Rebels, under a Colonel Duncan, and after a very spirited fight of about two hours, mostly skirmishing, the Rebels withdrew, with a reported loss of fourteen killed and wounded; the Union loss was one killed. Breaking up camp in the night, the Rebels being in strong force at Harrisonville, and hourly increasing, he by a night march succeeded (after losing most of their subsistence in crossing Grand River, which was over its banks) in reaching camp, on the State line, near Jonesville. Here they were joined by reinforcements from Kansas, under Colonel Weer, and by the command of Colonel Nugent, the united forces then marched on Harrisonville, which, after a short engagement, was captured, and the entire Rebel force broken up and scattered, when the expedition returned to Kansas City. In the early part of September, 1861, the Rebels, under Colonel Roult and others, to the number of two thousand, were encamped at Blue Springs and near Lone Jack, with the intention of attacking Kansas City. Colonel Peabody, with the Thirteenth Missouri Volunteers, was ordered from St. Joseph to reinforce Major Van Horn, and arrived at Kansas City about September 1st. As soon as his arrival was known, the Rebel forces broke up camp and marched to Lexington to attack that post. Learning this, Colonel Peabody, with his command, joined by Major Van Horn, with two companies, B and C, took steamer for Lexington, arriving there in time to relieve the garrison. This was the beginning of the operations which ended finally in the surrender of the entire force under Colonel Mulligan to Sterling Price, September 21, 1861. Through the entire fifteen days the Battalion was constantly on active duty; was part of the force which had the severe fight in the lane, on the 12th, four companies, under Major Van Horn, meeting and engaging the whole of Price's force, in the severest fight of the siege. Companies B and C were respectively commanded by Captain Miller and Lieutenant Spears, and both officers and men behaved with distinguished bravery. On the 19th Colonel Peabody was wounded, and the command of the whole devolved upon Major Van Horn, who continued in command until he was wounded and taken to the hospital, about two hours before the surrender. After the exchange of prisoners, in December, Colonel Peabody's Regiment and Van Horn's Battalion were consolidated, and then formed the Twenty-fifth Regiment Missouri Infantry Volunteers, until in 1864, when it was again consolidated with the First Missouri Engineers, closing their service with the close of the war. Thus they commenced their organization under the brave Lyon, and were mustered out at the close of the Rebellion.

The Thirteenth Missouri Infantry, so far as this title applies to Colonel Peabody's command, never existed as a completed organization. There was at that time no Governor in Missouri—Governor Jackson having joined the Rebellion—and all troops had to be raised under special orders of either the War Department or some army officer. Peabody's and Van Horn's commands were authorized by General Lyon, in the same order and at the same time. Peabody soon after made the effort to increase his battalion to a regiment, to be called the Thirteenth, but before it had attained completion the surrender at Lexington stopped everything, and the number "13" was taken by another organization. That is the true status of the Thirteenth as connected with Colonel Peabody's name. Its history, up to the siege of Lexington, is thus briefly given in the report of the Adjutant-General of Missouri for 1866 on page 206: "The Regiment was employed in guarding a portion of the line of the Hannibal & St. Joseph Railroad and upon garrison duty, until it was ordered to Lexington, in the latter part of August. Colonel Mulligan, who commanded at Lexington, surrendered the post to General Sterling Price on the 20th of September, 1861, who paroled the officers of the Thirteenth, and released the men upon their oaths. Exchanges were subsequently effected, and the Regiment was re-organized as the Twenty-fifth, with Everett Peabody as Colonel, Robert T. Van Horn as Lieutenant-Colonel, and James E. Powell as Major. In March, 1862, the Regiment was sent to General Grant, at Pittsburg Landing, and was brigaded in McKean's Brigade, Prentiss' Division. It participated in the battle of Shiloh, losing very heavily in killed and wounded; among the former were the Colonel and Major. Captain Frederick C. Nichols was subsequently promoted to the Majority, and Chester Harding, Jr., was appointed Colonel.

"In the advance upon Corinth, the Regiment was constantly upon picket duty, or engaged in the construction of earthworks.

During the summer of 1862 the Regiment constructed a chain of forts south and west of Corinth. It was ordered to Missouri for the purpose of recruiting, in September, 1862, but, on its arrival at St. Louis, was sent to Pilot Knob; thence to Patterson, where it was assigned to Brigadier-General J. W. Davidson, and became part of the Army of Southeast Missouri.

"It remained with this army during the winter campaign. Upon returning to Iron Mountain, in March, 1863, it was ordered to St. Joseph, Missouri, and was actively employed by detachments in clearing the district of Northwest Missouri from bushwhackers until June, when it was sent to New Madrid, where it reconstructed the fortifications, which had been dismantled, and constituted the garrison of the post."

LEXINGTON, BY MAJOR VAN HORN.

On our arrival at Lexington, we marched at once to Warrensburg to relieve Colonel Grover at that place, and here we met the advance of General Price's whole army. Falling back to Lexington we found there the command of Colonel Mulligan. On comparing dates of commission, Colonel Mulligan was found to rank Colonel Peabody a very few days, and was in consequence recognized as in chief command. The fighting opened on the 12th, and the surrender occurred on the 21st. The troops engaged, besides the commands of Colonel Peabody and my own, were fragments of regiments commanded by Colonel Grover and Colonel White, of Missouri. Mulligan's Regiment from Chicago, and Marshall's First Illinois Cavalry, the latter not yet armed with carbines, having only sabres and old-style holster pistols and numbered in all only a little over 2,700 men. Price's army was over 25,000 of all arms. All Western Missouri flocked to him with such arms as they could get, and one of his staff officers with whom I was acquainted told me that the morning after the surrender they fed 40,000 people, or issued rations to that number. Of course these were not all armed as soldiers, but they had, most of them, something to shoot with.

During the siege many noted acts of bravery occurred. One of the most daring things of the war was the re-taking of the hospital, a large brick dwelling about a hundred yards from our works. The Rebels got possession of it, and as it commanded the inside of our breastworks they were picking off our men rapidly. The task of retaking it was confided to Captain Schmitz, Company B, of Colonel

Peabody's command, from St. Joseph, Missouri, which was composed entirely of Germans; and Captain Gleason's Company, of Mulligan's command, from Chicago, and composed of Irishmen. They charged the whole distance over open ground, exposed to a heavy fire from the hospital roof and windows, and from supports outside, but in less time than it takes to write it, the brave fellows had driven the Rebels from the building with the bayonet. It was one of the most gallant and desperate things I saw during the war, and ought to be preserved in story.

After Lexington, General Fremont ordered the muster out of all Missouri troops engaged and captured. After the exchange I went to Washington, and laid the matter before the Adjutant-General of the Army, and General McClelland rescinded the order and the Twenty-fifth was then organized.

THE TWENTY-FIFTH MISSOURI IN THE BATTLE OF SHILOH.

Lieutenant James M. Newhard says that "the part taken by the Twenty-fifth Missouri in the battle of Shiloh has never been correctly written; that Company B, Captain Schmidt; Company H, Captain Dill, and Company E, Captain Evans, went out before daylight on Sunday morning, April 6th, under command of our noble little Major Powell. We quietly passed through our single line of pickets a short distance in front of our camp guard, drove in Johnston's pickets, and fell onto his whole army about a mile and a half from our camp. They had laid on their arms during the night, ready to attack us first in the morning.

"We sounded their reveille by opening up fire on them, and it was not many minutes before that whole army of 65,000 men were in motion and the 'woods were full of them.' We stood long enough for most of the men to use up their forty rounds of ammunition, which, with the hot volleys they turned loose on us, gave good and convincing warning to our slumbering army to 'fall in' on short notice. Even our skeptical General Prentiss shook himself out of his blankets when he heard the racket, and was shortly convinced that Colonel Peabody was right when he said the evening before that he believed Johnston was moving on us and would likely attack in the morning, which at that time Prentiss would not listen to.

"Colonel Peabody, being so firm in this belief, did not go to sleep at all that night, and after mature deliberation decided to do as above stated—attack, and thus give the alarm to those in our rear, so that they could turn out and make some resistance to the overwhelming force, and not be captured or attacked in their quarters. This move seemed to be the only way to convince General Prentiss that there was an army between us and Corinth.

"General Prentiss commanded our Division and Colonel Peabody our Brigade—Sixth Division, First Brigade. Our Division was on the outer line to the left, and rear of Shiloh Church; Uncle Billy Sherman's on our right; hence we were the first to take the medicine, and we got it in heavy doses. Our Regiment and Division were badly handled from the start. Colonel Peabody was killed when our first line was broken, and we were driven back through our camp. When we regained our camp on Monday, after having driven the enemy back over our ground, we found Colonel Peabody lying on the line of the officers' tents, and near the tent where he had passed the night before. It was too bad that he was not allowed to live and get the credit he was entitled to, as it is beyond the question of a doubt that the action he took that morning in opening fight and giving the alarm to the troops in the rear in time to prepare for the attack, was what enabled our army to make the resistance it did, and hold out until Buell and Nelson came to the relief.

"All this he did on his own responsibility. General Grant was still at Headquarters at Savannah, and General Prentiss could not be convinced or made to believe as Peabody did, nor could he be persuaded to make any preparations for an attack.

"The rest of that stubborn-fought battle from this, the commencement, to the finish, has been written up hundreds of times, by as many different writers, each from his own standpoint. I only want to get this part of the service of the Twenty-fifth Missouri and its gallant and wide-awake commander properly on record with the credit due. After we woke up Johnston's army and were falling back to camp, we met Colonel Moore, of the Twenty-first Missouri, with half of his Regiment. He would not believe that it was Johnston's whole army; said: 'It was only a skirmishing party;' and insisted on our Major 'facing about with his command, and we would finish them up in no time.' It was not long until he found out what we already knew. He filed us off to the left, into a cotton-field near at hand, and brought us to a front. By this time the *Johnnies* were up to the fence in *our* front; a very formidable looking 'skirmishing party.' We made a fine target for them, which they seemed to fully realize. About the first volley Colonel Moore himself was a recipient of their favor by way of a shot in one of his legs (which was afterward amputated). Our Major then took command, and ordered us to cease firing and marched us at a double quick back to the Division line, which by this time had formed ready for the attack, which shortly followed.

"This was the way the battle of Shiloh began; by Colonel Peabody and three companies of his Regiment, the Twenty-fifth Missouri.

"Major Powell, Captain Evans and myself were with Colonel Peabody from about twelve o'clock that Saturday night until we went out in front; Colonel Peabody informed me that as the two Lieutenants of my Company (E) were at St. Louis, I should take the position (though only Orderly Sergeant at the time) of Acting Lieutenant, as the Company needed another officer. When we went into camp the Captain and I tented together. The Colonel would often come to our quarters and stop for an hour or so and make himself at home with us. On this Saturday night, before the battle, he came to our tent, about twelve o'clock, and woke us up, saying, he 'had not slept yet, and did not intend to, as he had business to attend to, hoping it would be no intrusion to sit up with us for a while.' We made him easy on that score, made a light, dressed, took out some cigars, smoked and talked.

"He told then that he 'thought we were lying in the face of a powerful enemy, in a very careless and unguarded position, liable to be surprised and overwhelmed at any time. He had spoken to General Prentiss about it the evening before, and urged that instead of lying idle, as we were at that time, we ought to put ourselves in some condition to resist an attack, in case one should be made by Johnston, and which was liable to happen at any time. He had asked for one of the batteries that were in park to be put in position in front of our Regiment, and had urged the necessity of being better prepared for defense. General Prentiss, instead of giving it the consideration due, hooted at the idea of Johnston attacking us. The Colonel told us he believed they were moving on us, and that if we did not look out, we might be taken by surprise almost any time. He said that he did not intend to be taken by surprise himself; that he would act upon his own responsibility and judgment. He asked me to call Major Powell up and ask him to come to our quarters.'

"Lieutenant-Colonel Van Horn was not with us at this time, he was still disabled by a wound received at Lexington. The Colonel told the Major his views and plans, and directed him to go about three o'clock to Brigade guard Headquarters, take a squad and go in front beyond the pickets and reconnoitre. We had only one line of pickets out about one-fourth mile in front.

"The Major returned in about an hour and reported that he had passed our pickets, and about a mile further on came to a strong line of Rebel pickets; that, in his opinion, a strong force was camped in their rear. The Colonel said he was satisfied it was Johnston's army, and that they would move forward and attack us early in in the morning; 'but,' he said, 'they shall not surprise us; there is but one thing for me to do; that is, to send a small force out and attack *them*, and so give the alarm to our army. I can not say anything more to General Prentiss, but he will soon see how near I was right. I must do this upon my own responsibility, but I will not live to receive censure or credit for doing so.' He then asked me to wake up Captain Schmidt, of Company B, and Captain Dill, of Company H, to come to our tent. When they reported he told them to get up their companies as quietly and as quickly as possible, and see that each man had at least forty rounds in his box, directing me to turn out our Company (E), also. In a very short time the three companies were ready, and, under Major Powell, struck the pickets at break of day.

"The Union army had not yet shaken the leaves off. The Colonel's instructions to the Major were to 'drive in the guard and open up on the reserve, develop the force, hold the ground as long as possible and then fall back to the command, which was done. The Colonel shook hands with us as we started out to the front, bade us good-bye, stating he would be killed that day. A firm presentiment which proved too true; he was killed about two hours from that time, by a gunshot wound in the head. We buried him, the best we could, in a coffin made from boxes at the Quartermaster's, at sundown on Tuesday after the battle. His remains were placed in a metallic casket by his friends about three weeks later and removed to Boston, Massachusetts.

"This is as true an account of the opening of the battle of Shiloh as can be given by any living man, and shows what the Twenty-fifth Missouri did at that time, and the great good it accomplished, through the clear-headed vigilance of its noble and self-sacrificing Colonel."   JAMES M. NEWHARD.

Lieutenant-Colonel Robert T. Van Horn says of Colonel Peabody: "He was a gallant officer, and one of the most accomplished gentlemen that the service knew. I saw his tablet in Memorial Hall, Harvard College; he was a graduate of that institution."

Captain Joseph Thompson says of him: "He was possessed of the finest scholarly attainments, reading readily and speaking fluently the German, French and Spanish languages. He was a noted mathematician, a ripe scholar and a true and polished gentleman; of fine personal appearance, pleasing address and commanding presence. He promised the attainment of high work in the service of his country."

From Volume X, Part 1, Rebellion Records:

No. 82.

Report of Lieutenant-Colonel Robert T. Van Horn, Twenty-fifth Missouri Infantry.

HEADQUARTERS TWENTY-FIFTH MISSOURI VOLUNTEERS,
FIRST BRIGADE, SIXTH DIVISION,
ARMY OF WEST TENNESSEE.

NEAR PITTSBURG LANDING, April 9, 1862.

CAPTAIN: I have the honor herewith to submit a report of the part taken by the Regiment under my command in the battles of the 6th and 7th instant. The Regiment occupied the right of the First Brigade, commanded by Colonel Peabody, Acting Brigadier-General, and had the honor of opening the fight on the 6th, the attack being made on its front at 3 o'clock in the morning. By order of the Acting Brigadier-General, three companies—Captains Schmitz, Company B; Evcans, Company E; Dill, Company H—under Major Powell, were dispatched to engage the enemy's advance, which was successfully done until re-enforced by the Twenty-first Missouri, under Colonel Moore. The fighting now became general and heavy, and I was ordered to support with the whole Regiment. The enemy had now reached within the distance of half a mile of the encampment, where they were checked and held until near 7 o'clock, when our force fell back to the line of encampment, where another stand was made. The fighting was very severe until 8 o'clock, when we were compelled to fall back still farther behind our encampments on the Division, which had by this time formed in line of battle on an elevation in our rear. My Regiment had by this time become badly cut up, but they rallied and took position on the right of the Twelfth Michigan, with the loss of several of my most valuable officers. The fighting now became most determined, and continued with little intermission for three hours. The enemy, being thrice repulsed, finally moved to our left.

It was in this part of the engagement that Major James E. Powell, a most valuable officer and brave soldier, fell mortally wounded, and Sergeant Matthew Euler, color-bearer, was killed clinging to the staff until it had to be disengaged from his grasp by Sergeant Simmons, who took his place. My command was after this detached to Colonel Hildebrand, Acting Brigadier-General, where it remained without taking any decisive part in the engagement for the remainder of the day.

On the 7th I was placed with the First Missouri Battery near the river, except one company, under Captain William Millar, who was attached to the Seventh Iowa (Colonel Crocker), where, I am gratified to state, this brave officer rendered efficient service.

Captains Wade, Millar and Donnelly, and Lieutenants Bradshaw, Newberry, John H. Miller and Singleton, deserved special mention for bravery displayed in the most trying periods of the fight; but where so many did well it is difficult to discriminate. I mention these as coming particularly under my own observation. All will bear testimony to the distinguished bravery of Major James E. Powell, who fell in the hottest of the battle, cheering on his men. He was an officer in the Regular Army.

I have to report Surgeon John T. Berghoff as missing, but whether a prisoner or not it is impossible to say, as he has been in camp once since the battle. He was at the hospital in front on yesterday, but supposed to be cut off by Rebel pickets.

I have the honor to be, very respectfully, your obedient servant,

R. T. VAN HORN,
Lieutenant-Colonel, Commanding Twenty-fifth Missouri Volunteers.

CAPTAIN HENRY BINMORE,
Assistant Adjutant-General, Sixth Division, Army of West Tennessee.

THE CAPTURE OF SURGEON BERGHOFF.

It afterward transpired that Dr. Berghoff, Surgeon of the Twenty-fifth, whose whereabouts were unknown for a time after the battle of Shiloh, was a prisoner in Corinth, caring for our own wounded, under the following agreement:

GENERAL HOSPITAL OF THE FIRST ARMY CORPS,
IN THE FIELD, April the 10th, 1862.

This convention made and entered into this day between the undersigned, representing the two Governments, witnesseth, that as there are many wounded men belonging to each party unable to be removed, they shall remain in hospital here, and be attended by their respective Surgeons and Hospital Attendants. It is further agreed that such Surgeons and Hospital Attendants and patients are to be respected by both armies, and are not to be held as prisoners of war or otherwise, but are to be removed without hindrance or molestation, at their own will and convenience. It is further agreed that the wounded, Surgeons and Attendants are to be subsisted mutually, with such supplies as can be furnished. It is further agreed that the private property of these is to be respected by both parties

Signed in duplicate—

S. M. D. LYLE,
Surgeon C. S. A., Medical Director of the First Corps, Army of the Mississippi.

JOHN T. BERGHOFF,
Surgeon First Brigade, Sixth Division, U. S. A.

Approved—

JOSEPH WHEELER,
Colonel Nineteenth Alabama Regiment, Commanding Rear Guard.

April 10, 1862.

As the wounded referred to within and now within my lines can not be removed without endangering their lives, I have allowed them to remain in hospital here, and do hereby approve this agreement made by the Surgeons of the respective parties.

JOHN C. BRECKINRIDGE,
Brigadier General Commanding Confederate Troops.
MAJOR-GENERAL LEWIS WALLACE, U. S. A.

I certify that the foregoing agreement is a true copy of the original.

F. M. ROSEGATE,
Commander of Custer Post, G. A. R., St. Joseph, Missouri.
December 17, 1888.

There were in said hospital three Surgeons, four Hospital Attendants and fifty-six wounded belonging to the United States Army, in charge of Surgeon J. T. Berghoff, which, through his management, were liberated, and not held as prisoners.

Colonel Van Horn's recollection of the operations of the Twenty-fifth Missouri is that, in March, 1862, the Regiment was sent to General Grant, at Pittsburg Landing, and was assigned to Prentiss' command, forming the extreme right of his Division. In the battle of Shiloh, Colonel Peabody was in command of the Brigade and Lieutenant-Colonel Van Horn commanded the Regiment. The loss was heavy in killed and wounded. Among the killed were Colonel Peabody, Major Powell, Captain C. A. Wade, Company C, and Lieutenants John J. Bramble, Company D, and S. M. Penfield, Company H. It is a fact, now settled by the record, that Prentiss' Division was the first attacked, and the Brigade commanded by Colonel Peabody the first engaged in the battle of Shiloh, and the Twenty-fifth first of all was engaged with the enemy's advance as early as daylight on the 6th of April. The facts are these:

" On Saturday evening General Prentiss reviewed his Division in an old field in front of the line of encampment. Major Powell, who was a Regular Army officer, was field officer of the day, and did not take part in the review. After the review was over he reported to Colonel Peabody, that during the review, while out in the woods in front, he had noticed a party of mounted men, too numerous and similarly mounted to be citizens, and they were not Union troops, and requested authority to make a reconnoissance to see what could be learned. He was directed to take two companies and do so. On his return he reported that he had gone a mile or more to the front to 'an old cotton field,' where he met some negroes who told him there had been a body of 200 Rebel Cavalry there in the afternoon. He was then directed, when the grand rounds were made at one o'clock in the morning to take four companies and station them out on the advanced picket line to await eventualities at daylight.

This was done, and when daylight came they found themselves confronted by the Rebel force and firing began. The Twenty-first Missouri was ordered out to support this advance, then the Twenty-fifth, Twelfth Michigan, etc., till the whole line was engaged. This was the opening of the battle of Shiloh. Frederick Klingler, Second Lieutenant of Company B, Twenty-fifth Missouri, was wounded at day dawn, the first man wounded in the battle. After the capture of the left wing of Prentiss' Division and of General Prentiss himself, the remaining regiments were assigned to other bodies of troops— the Twenty-fifth, holding the extreme right, was for the balance of the first day attached to Colonel Hildebrand's Ohio Regiment, till sundown, and then placed as support to the line of Artillery formed near the Tennessee River to check the Rebel advance—and remained on that duty during the night and succeeding day, which was without special incident.

"In the advance on Corinth the Regiment made such an efficient record that it was, after possession of that place, entrusted with the construction of a series of earthworks or forts, south and west of Corinth, which constituted its defensive works in the battle at that place in the following October. In September the Regiment was ordered to report to General Logan, at Jackson, and was after sent to Missouri to recruit. But on arriving at St. Louis, was ordered to report to General Davidson, at Pilot Knob. From there it was ordered to Patterson, and became part of the Army of Southeast Missouri, for the winter. In March, 1863, it was ordered to St. Joseph, Missouri, to recruit, and for about three months, while engaged in that work, did active duty, operating in detachments in clearing Northwest Missouri from bushwhackers. In June it was ordered to New Madrid, Missouri, where it reconstructed the fortifications which had been dismantled, and formed the garrison of the Post till in November, when it was ordered to Columbus, Kentucky immediately preceding its consolidation with the Engineer Regiment of the West.

"During this time I had been but part of the time with the Regiment. In 1862, while at Corinth, I was elected to the Missouri Senate, and attended the session of that body in the winter of 1862-3. After the Regiment went to New Madrid, I was ordered by General Schofield to report to General Thomas Ewing, commanding the District of the Border, with Headquarters at Kansas City, during the execution of Order No. 11 — removing the disloyal population from the counties of Jackson, Cass and Bates — and remained on that duty till the meeting of the Legislature in the winter of 1863-64, during which time the consolidation took place. I was in the fall of 1863 elected to Congress, previous to the consolidation.

"This constitutes, as near as I can now recall, the history of the Twenty-fifth, from April 7, 1862, to December, 1863.

"R. T. VAN HORN."

COMPANY L.

This Company was raised principally in Central Missouri, by Captain J. D. Voerster and Lieutenant John E. Hensler, in September, 1861, as an Independent Company of Sappers and Miners.

By Special Orders No. 43, Headquarters State of Missouri, March 18, 1862, this Company was consolidated with the Fifth Regiment Missouri Volunteers Infantry as Company I.

By Special Orders No. 217, December 3, 1862, Headquarters State of Missouri, this Company was transferred to the Thirty-fifth Missouri Infantry Volunteers as Company I, Captain John E. Hensler.

The Company was again transferred in December, 1863, this time to the Missouri Engineer Regiment as Company L, Captain C. Lochbiler, Lieutenants Henry Hennings and Max Fraude; on consolidation with the Twenty-fifth Missouri it was transferred with Company G to Company I, Captain Lochbiler.

PART III.

THE
FIRST MISSOURI ENGINEERS.

THE CONSOLIDATION OF THE TWENTY-FIFTH MISSOURI AND THE ENGINEER REGIMENT OF THE WEST MISSOURI VOLUNTEERS AS THE FIRST REGIMENT OF ENGINEERS MISSOURI VOLUNTEERS.

ON the 4th of February, 1864, the consolidation of the two Regiments was effected, in pursuance of the following order, they having rendezvoused at Nashville, Tennessee, for that purpose:

> HEADQUARTERS DEPARTMENT OF THE MISSOURI,
> ST. LOUIS, Mo., December 28, 1863.
>
> SPECIAL ORDERS)
> . No. 355.   )
>
> 15. In accordance with Special Order No. 520, Current Series War Department, A. G. O., of November 23, the Twenty-fifth Missouri Volunteers and the Regiment of Volunteer Engineers heretofore known as "Bissell's Engineer Regiment of the West," are hereby consolidated into a Regiment of Engineers, the numerical designation of which will be fixed by his Excellency, the Governor of Missouri. All Officers of the two Regiments rendered supernumerary by the organization as herein announced will be honorably mustered out of the service, to date from the first day of January, 1864. All officers promoted in the new organization, above the positions held by them in their old Regiments, will, upon being duly commissioned by the Governor, be mustered out of the old grade and into the new. The pay, as Engineers, of that portion of the Regiment which has heretofore been Infantry, will commence on the first day of the ensuing year.
>
> BY COMMAND OF MAJOR-GENERAL SCHOFIELD:
>
> O. D. GREENE,
> *Assistant Adjutant-General.*

On the 4th of February, as above stated, the two Regiment moved into camp together, and were afterward known only as the First Missouri Engineers. The following assignments of officers and men were announced:

FIELD AND STAFF.

Henry Flad, Colonel; William Tweeddale, Lieutenant-Colonel; Hamilton Dill, Fredrick C. Nichols, Eben M. Hill, Majors; John C. Book, Surgeon; Charles Knower and William A. Neal, Assistant Surgeons; Lieutenant-Colonel Van Horn, Quartermaster; J. D. Henderson, Surgeon; John T. Berghoff and Assistant Surgeon John Q. Eggleston, of the Twenty-fifth, Chaplains; Alpha Wright, of the Twenty-fifth, and L. E. Hunt, of the Engineers, going out, and Adjutant Giseke, of the Twenty-fifth, promoted to Captain of Company L, First Missouri Engineers.

Company A was composed of Companies C and D of the Twenty-fifth; Captain, James Dunn; Lieutenants, L. R. Lancaster, George G. Bayne and William Claxten; Lieutenants Henry Carlisle and Timothy Darby retiring.

Company B of Company C and part of K, Engineers; Captain, W. G. Patten; Lieutenants, Lucien W. Coy, Daniel G. Parker and David Armstrong.

Company C of Companies I and part of D, and K of Engineer Regiment; Captain, G. B. Brackett; Lieutenants, Eli Winegar, H. B. Hooker and Max Fraude.

Company D of Companies H and part of K, Engineer Regiment; Captain, Lisbon Odenbaugh; Lieutenants, John C. Besier, J. S. Cunningham and Soloman Goodrich.

Company E of Company A and E, Engineer Regiment; Captain, William Hill; Lieutenants, Haynes E. Hudson, John McLaren and Porter J. Brooks; Captain Randolph retiring.

Company F of Companies F and part of D, Engineer Regiment: Captain, Thomas W. Bailey; Lieutenants, S. W. Mattis, M. D. Edinger and Alvah R. Prescott; Captain N. W. Wilcox retiring.

Company G of Companies E and K of the Twenty-fifth; Captain, Benjamin F. Coleman; Lieutenants, John P. Morton, Benjamin R. Tanner and Gustavus Salsman.

Company H of Companies F and I, Twenty-fifth; Captain, Benjamin F. Buzard; Lieutenants, William W. Brown, William A. Morton and James M. Newhard; Captains Hawley and Thompson and Lieutenant Marcus Morton retiring.

Company I of Companies G and L, Engineer Regiment; Captain, Christian Lochbiler; Lieutenants, A. D. Whitcomb, Anthony Kilp and Paulus Gast; Captain Louis G. Werth and Lieutenant Henry Hennings retiring.

Company K of parts of Companies A, B and K, Engineer Regiment; Captain, John E. Murphy; Lieutenants, Francis Tunica, H. M. Sumner and Frank Bras; Captain A. J. Merritt retiring.

Company L of Companies B and G, Twenty-fifth; Captain, Herman Giseke; Lieutenants, William K. Lyle, John Murphy and Stephen S. Brown; Captain William Millar and Lieutenant George W. Shinn retiring.

Company M of Companies A and H, Twenty-fifth; Captain, Oscar F. Storey; Lieutenants, Addison N. Glenn, William E. Hight and Stephen T. Lucas; Captain Robert C. Bradshaw and Lieutenant W. J. Hahn retiring.

The Regimental non-commissioned staff is not entirely known, but John A. Points and William H. Ward were Quartermaster-Sergeants. Charles Dunsford, Ralph B. McClary and John S. Starr were Hospital Stewards.

THE JOHNSONVILLE CAMPAIGN — NASHVILLE TO JOHNSONVILLE.

There was considerable disappointment among the Sergeants. Some of them thought that the supernumeraries would be mustered out as the commissioned officers were, but it was held otherwise, and some of them had to return to the ranks. Sergeant William Vogel, of Company G (I), was made so despondent over it that he took his life the morning of the 4th of February, by shooting himself through the head with his musket.

Sunday, February 12, 1864, the whole Regiment, about twelve hundred men, were drawn up in line for inspection.

The 10th, details from the Companies were made for work on the Nashville fortifications.

Thursday, 18th, the Regiment broke camp and marched ten miles out of Nashville in a southwest direction.

19th, marched eighteen miles west.

20th, marched eighteen miles—to about three miles west of Charlotte.

21st, marched twelve miles. Third Battalion went into camp at Station 57, nine miles east of Waverly, and the Second Battalion seven miles east of the same place.

22d, First Battalion, with Headquarters, marched into Waverly, Tennessee, on the Nashville & Northwestern Railroad, one company going on seven miles further west to Johnsonville, on the Tennessee River.

The 26th of February the small-pox broke out among the men and was quite serious for several months, some half dozen dying from the disease.

March 3d there was a snow storm. Snow three inches deep on the night of the 6th, with a rain and sleet so heavy that the trees broke down with the weight of ice, and as the tents at Station 57 were in the woods, the falling limbs crushed many of the tents and injured several of the sleeping men. Altogether it was very disagreeable weather.

March 2d and 3d details were sent to the river at Johnsonville, and to the farm of a Dr. Gross near there to operate a steam sawmill. At this time rations ran short and the men were put on one-fourth allowance. Measles broke out, and cases of lung fever and severe colds were very frequent. The 15th there was another snow storm; the weather remained cold for a week or more.

The men, in the meantime, were kept busy building the railroad, warehouses and side-tracks, and were assisted by a large force of mechanics and laborers in the employ of the U. S. Quartermaster Department.

April 16th the railroad was completed from Johnsonville to Waverly, and an engine that had been brought up the river to Johnsonville ran over the track. On the 7th of May the railroad was finished through from Nashville to Johnsonville, and on the 19th of May an excursion train brought Governor Andrew Johnson, with a number of distinguished guests, among whom was General Daniel E. Sickles. Both Governor Johnson and General Sickles made congratulatory speeches to the men.

May 4th a detachment of ninety men from the First Battalion, under command of Captain Brackett, was sent out to hunt for forces of the enemy's cavalry, said to be hovering about. A team taken along got swamped in Tracy Creek, and the teamster was drowned. Captain Brackett, in describing this expedition, says of this and other incidents at and around Johnsonville:

"We left Nashville, after the consolidation of the two Regiments, on the 18th of February, 1864, and marched to Box Mills, Tennessee; camped 23d, where we remained the rest of the month and the month of March, when we moved to Waverly, Tennessee. We were

COLONEL EVERETT PEABODY, 25TH MO.

ASSISTANT SURGEON 25TH MO.

engaged in building the Nashville & Northwestern Railroad, warehouses and blockhouses. On the 20th of May the First Battalion moved to Section 51, and the Third Battalion was ordered to Johnsonville, Tennessee, and I was placed in command of it, and also commander of the Post. We finished the Nashville & Northwestern Railroad on the 10th of May, and the first train came over the line from Nashville on that day. While at Johnsonville the Thirteenth Regular Infantry (colored) reported to me for duty, and with the First Kansas Battery and two companies of Tennessee Cavalry and our Third Battalion, constituted the force at the Post. The men were engaged in building forts, warehouses, etc.

BOTH PARTIES MISTAKEN.

"While we were camped at Box's Mills, on the Nashville & Northwestern Railroad, which we were constructing from Nashville to the Tennessee River for the purpose of opening a shorter line of transportation than via Louisville, I received orders to go to the terminus of the road, which we named Johnsonville, and where Captain Coleman's Company was stationed, and superintend the landing of a locomotive and some cars from a steamer and barges. I made the trip on horseback, a distance of six or eight miles, going in the morning and returning at night daily. On one occasion, when I was returning, as I turned at right angles into a long lane, running across Flat Creek, fenced with rails on both sides, I saw two men about a quarter of a mile ahead dodge back into a fence corner out of sight. It was so near dark I could not distinguish their uniforms, and, as this was a place frequented by bushwhackers, I concluded that they belonged to that class of the Southern chivalry, and as there was no other way for me to reach camp but by passing them, I determined to take my chance in the unequal contest, and give them the best I had, so after drawing my trusty six-shooter from the holster, and seeing that it was in good order, I proceeded cautiously on my way keeping a close watch on the place where they disappeared. As I neared the spot I heard the click of their guns as they cocked them. My revolver was firmly grasped, and in readiness for the emergency.

"The next moment they sprang from their ambush, but before any harm was done we recognized each other; they were members of my Company who had slipped away from camp in search of game, and when they saw me enter the lane they mistook me for a guerrilla, and, though not the kind of game they were looking for, concluded to take me in. After a hearty laugh over the mistake of both parties, and congratulating ourselves that this little affair had terminated no worse, we soon found our way to camp.

NO MISTAKE THIS TIME.

"While in command of the Post of Johnsonville, which was garrisoned by the Third Battalion of our Regiment, one regiment of Colored Troops, the First Kansas Battery, and two companies of Tennessee Cavalry, we were greatly annoyed by bands of guerrillas which were made up of citizens living around us.

"On one occasion, as some of our teamsters were riding along the road about a mile from camp, they were fired on by a band of three bushwhackers, from ambush, wounding one man and a mule. As soon as they reached camp and informed me of the affair, I started in pursuit with one company of Cavalry, but after a half-day's ride we returned to camp without having seen one of these outlaws; but having learned that it was useless to continue this mode of warfare, we decided to change our tactics and use a little strategy, so I issued an order holding the citizens of the neighborhood responsible for all depredations by whomsoever committed in the vicinity of the camp.

"This had the desired effect, for soon after this I was awakened from my sleep one night by the voice of a citizen, who came to inform me that a band of guerrillas was in the neighborhood, led by one Rodgers, who lived near by our camp. I immediately called out one company of our Battalion, and by previous arrangement with Captain Cronin, of the gunboat Key West, which lay in the river near by, it was taken up the Tennessee River and landed above the mouth of Duck River, a small stream running into the Tennessee about eight miles above us, and across which there was a ford about two miles from its mouth, where the bushwhackers were in the habit of crossing, when pursued. It was at this place that the company was ordered to go and lie in waiting until morning, and until we should drive the game into the trap. With these arrangements all completed, I returned to my tent and rested quietly till morning, when with one company of Cavalry we commenced the drive. When we reached the ford we found that the company that had been sent around had already bagged the game. As usual, this band, when they found we were in pursuit, had attempted to cross the river, and were all captured.

"We placed them under charge of the Rear Guard, with orders to take good care and not let them escape, and with a few hints in regard to the mode of warfare these outlaws carried on, and the unnecessary expense of sending them to Nashville, we left them and moved on to camp. That was the last we ever saw of those guerrillas.

"A similar attempt soon after this did not turn out so successful. I received orders from Headquarters of our Regiment, at Section 57, to take two companies on board the gunboat and go down the river about twenty miles, and land and remain until they should make the drive from Section 57.

"We landed soon after daybreak, and at once sent out pickets to various points with orders to arrest all citizens that should be found, so that they would not spread the news that we were there, but one of our Lieutenants (I will not mention his name) came to a school-house and took the school-master prisoner and turned the scholars all loose, to spread the news far and wide.

"Of course, the game was up; we could do nothing more than wait for the Cavalry, which was to make the drive from Section 57, to come in, which did not reach us till long after dark, and when they found they had failed to drive in any game, the mystery was explained to them, and though greatly disappointed over the result of our day's work, all joined in a round of laughter at the expense of the Lieutenant. The question now turned upon how we were to get back to camp. A fleet of transports under convoy of a gunboat was expected up about midnight. As there was time for the men to rest a while, they rolled themselves in their blankets and laid down some distance from the river while a few of us took our position on the bank to watch for the boats. It was not long after midnight when they hove in sight, and when within the sound of our voice, we hailed them and asked them to take us on board, but as this was a place where boats had been fired on by guerrillas they were suspicious of us, and so the Captain of the gunboat which was in the advance dropped his boat back and ordered me to get my men all up in line on the bank of the river where he could see them. We could hear the officer on the boat giving orders to the gunners to load their guns and prepare for action and then they approached us very cautiously until they became satisfied we were not enemies. We were soon on board and steaming up the river toward our camp, where we landed about daylight, tired and disgusted with our grand expedition, but the farce of capturing the school-master furnished laughing stock for the Battalion for a long time.

"While I was in command of the Third Battalion and commander of the Post of Johnsonville, Tennessee, the guerrillas or bushwhackers became very troublesome, many of them living in the neighborhood.

"One Sunday some of our teamsters, without consent, took mules from the corral, and rode into the country, and when some two miles from camp near the forks of the road they were fired on from ambush, and one mule and rider wounded; the others returned to camp much faster than they went out, and reported the case to me. I immediately ordered one of the companies of Tennessee Cavalry under my command to be in readiness at once, and we commenced the pursuit, but after a hard day's ride we returned without any game. It was a heavily-timbered country, and one after another of these miserable wretches would strike off on some bridle path until the whole squad had escaped.

"Another little incident occurred while at Johnsonville, which helped to break the monotony of camp life. One day a squad of colored soldiers belonging to the Regiment under my command came to me for a pass to go out in the country to get some vegetables. While they were out they captured an old man taking mail across the lines and brought him to camp with the mail. He was examined and placed in the guard-house. When we were constructing the railroad from Nashville to Jacksonville the slaves along the line were liberated and many of them employed on the road. And a few miles from the terminus of the road there lived an old man, a widower, and his two daughters. They had quite a number of slaves, who, of course, followed in our wake with the other colored citizens of African descent, leaving poor Mr. Barfield to do his own work out of doors, and the young ladies to learn how to cook and do housework. In the mail that was captured by the colored soldiers I found a letter written by one of these young ladies, Miss Sallie Barfield, directed to her brother in the Rebel army in which she said that the "Yanks" had taken his shot-gun, but did not get his rifle. So I commissioned Lieutenant Tanner, a gallant young officer of Captain Coleman's Company, who was well acquainted with the Miss Barfields, to go and get the rifle spoken of in her letter. Taking the letter with him he boarded the first train going east, which soon landed him at the Barfield house, where he made known his orders to take the rifle, greatly to the surprise of Miss Sallie who seemed to know nothing about it, but the Lieutenant said that he knew the gun was there, and his orders were such that he could not return without it. She then wanted to know his authority for saying the gun was there, when he produced the letter with her signature to it. She owned up, and said the gun was secreted about eight miles from there, but she would get it and bring it to camp. True to her promise, a few days after that she rode up to my tent on horseback with the rifle on her shoulder and delivered it.

"And now for the old man that was captured with the mail.

"The next day after the old man was put in the guard-tent, his wife, a good motherly-looking old lady, came into camp and made an earnest plea for her husband's release. My sympathy was touched, and I told her I would release him on condition that they would both take the oath of allegiance. She wanted to know what it was, so I read her the iron-clad document, and after listening very attentively she shook her head and said she could not do it, but begged hard to have me grant the release; when she found it was of no use she went home — the next day she returned with her daughter, a fine, rosy-cheeked, red-haired maiden of eighteen summers. Thus reinforced they opened on me with smiles and tears, with pleading and begging, and importuning me with all the language they could command, but when they found it of no effect the old lady yielded to the demands; when I told her that there was a new factor in the conditions, that the young lady must also take the oath, it caused another hitch, but they finally consented, and the old man was brought out, and after they all went through that dreadful ordeal of taking the oath, they left camp for home, for all this they were very kind to me, often bringing me vegetables and stopping to have many a pleasant chat, and when we received marching orders the old man came to bid us good-bye and expressed a great deal of sorrow to have us leave. I think the acquaintance of these people with the "Yanks" (as they called them) gave them new ideas, they did not find them, as they expected, with horns and cloven feet.

"I have narrated the above incidents to show the different phases of army life, and add a little spice to some of the stern realities of war."

"G. B. BRACKETT, *Captain Company C.*"

May 30th the Government employees in the Quartermaster's Department struck for an increase of wages. June 3d they became mutinous, Company M was ordered to form a cordon around them with loaded guns; the mutineers were then disarmed and Company M escorted them to the State's Prison at Nashville.

June 8th Colonel Flad, with eight companies of the Regiment and Surgeons Book and Neal, went on an expedition about nine miles up the Tennessee River from Johnsonville; rumors of a force of the enemy in that direction had been brought to the Post, but none were found.

About June 20th Assistant Surgeon W. A. Neal was put on duty as Post Surgeon and organized a Post Hospital.

June 24th five hundred and fifty of the Engineer Regiment, with two companies of the Second Tennessee Cavalry and a section of Kansas Battery, crossed the Tennessee River in flat-boats, reaching Camden at eleven o'clock P. M. the next day, going into camp five miles south of that place about daylight. Afternoon of the 26th started back by another route, marching eight miles; 27th reached the Tennessee River at noon, and crossed to Johnsonville before night.

July 2d the Second Battalion was moved to Section 53. During the months of July and August the men were broken up in squads engaged in building blockhouses along the line of the Nashville & Northwestern Railroad. July 15th the guerrillas raided a station, killed two track hands, burned up their tents and threatened the rest with death.

About the 20th of July, the Post at Johnsonville was threatened with a force of the enemy's Cavalry. Colonel Flad, becoming alarmed, sent Alfred Craig, of Company F, with dispatches to the Colonel of the Twenty-fifth Wisconsin, near Waverly, for assistance. About three miles from camp, Craig rode into a squad of Rebel Cavalry, was shot, and fell from his horse, and one of the squad rode up to where he lay and deliberately emptied his revolver into Craig, leaving him for dead.

Word was brought to camp and Craig was found to be alive with one bullet in his head, one in his shoulder and one in his left leg; after a long siege he recovered. The Post was not attacked.

July 27th the Second Battalion was moved from Section 53 to section 28.

About the 1st of August, the three years' term of the men began to expire; on the 1st, thirty of Company E were mustered out.

THE ATLANTA CAMPAIGN.

August 15th the Regiment was ordered to go to the front near Atlanta; loaded on the cars 17th, the Second Battalion marching by the road. After turning over all surplus baggage, Quartermaster stores and tents, and placing the sick in the General Hospitals, the Regiment reached Nashville on the 18th, leaving on the 20th, of August, at 2 p. m., reaching Chattanooga, Tennessee, at 9 a. m., 21st. There were no quarters to be had here; the men turned out of the cars and laid down on the floor of the new machine shop, so sleepy and tired that it was with difficulty they could be aroused. They staid there all that day and the next night, but on the morning of the 22d went into camp one mile from base of Lookout Mountain; 23d, were ordered to pack up for marching; stood around all day in a heavy fog, and laid down at night in the same spot near the depot. On the morning of the 24th the Regiment started in three trains, reaching Marietta, Georgia, at sundown. The trains remained there all night, starting early in the morning, reaching the Chattahoochee River bridge at 10 a. m., then marched three miles to the front, taking some siege guns on the train, returned to the north side of the Chattahoochee bridge.

The Twentieth Corps was camped near here and manning the fortifications in the front, keeping up an occasional fire from the siege guns into Atlanta, the pickets keeping up a continual skirmish.

It was noticeable that many of the headlogs on top of the earthworks, eight inches or more in diamater, were filled with lead. At points some of them nearly cut in two with the bullets fired at the picket behind them, so long and close had been the siege.

The Regiment remained at the bridge, getting tools and supplies, until Monday, August 29, 1864; the teams were loaded up, and all but the convalescent sick (who were left at the bridge) started, reaching Sandtown, eighteen miles, at 2 p. m., the men halting, the teams keeping on as fast as the long train in front would permit. The men started early on the morning of the 30th, coming up with the wagon train at 2 p. m.; heavy firing heard in advance all day in the southeast direction. We kept up with the wagon train of the Fifteenth and Seventeenth Corps all day, all night, and all the next day (August 31st) until 5 p. m., when we halted in a field a half-mile in the rear of the infantry—forty-eight hours without a halt.

There had been a severe fight the day before, and this day the Fifteenth and Seventeenth Corps engaged the Fifteenth suffered most. The men slept well, not noticing the heavy firing with artillery and small arms that was kept up all night, some of the shells coming very near our camp. The men had been marching continuously thirty-six hours without removing their knapsacks; the teamsters and some of the officers, sixty hours without sleep.

The firing in front was increased; as daylight, September 1st, appeared, the shells were dropping very near our camp. At one time in the afternoon the enemy brought out a battery of six-pounder guns in an open field, about a mile directly west of our camp, and in plain sight—about a mile away, we could watch their maneuvers without being in danger. Later in the afternoon the Fourteenth, supported by the Fourth Corps, charged the enemy and drove them from their works into Jonesboro.

A DETAIL OF THE FIRST MISSOURI ENGINEERS DESTROYING A RAILROAD IN GEORGIA.

September 2d. It was found this morning that the enemy had retreated, leaving only a small Rear Guard. About noon we marched through Jonesboro, and the men were set at work tearing up the railroad track, which they did by placing a company along one side of the track with levers and hooks. They would lift about 150 feet of the track at one side and turn it over, then taking crowbars and sledge hammers would knock the ties free from the rails, lay them in piles of fifty or so, set fire to them, and place the rails with their center across the burning ties until they were red hot, then two men at each end of a heated rail would seize it with a pair of tongs, give it a twist, take it to the nearest small tree and wrap it around, making an iron collar for the tree. This day we went into camp three miles south of Jonesboro. This night there was a very heavy rain, and having no shelter all were well soaked. About two o'clock in the night or morning of the 3d, heavy explosions were heard in the direction of Atlanta, about twenty miles away; the impression prevailed that Atlanta had been abandoned. This proved to be correct, and the explosions were from the blowing up of the Confederate ordnance stores.

September 4th, the men all engaged in destroying track, repairing wagon roads and building earthworks. In the afternoon work was ordered stopped, and in the evening we marched back to Jonesboro and beyond, where we lay in camp until the evening of the 5th; camp was moved about one mile. On the 5th we marched five miles, repairing wagon roads as we went.

September 7th, in camp at Gaines' Mill; the roads are badly out of repair, the men busy repairing them. Just at dark we were in motion again and marched ahead two miles; rained all right.

Tuesday, September 8th, the main part of the Regiment marched to East Point, took a short rest, and marched two miles farther toward Atlanta and encamped.

September 9th Companies E and G were just before dark ordered back to East Point, the balance of the Regiment with the headquarters having marched into Atlanta.

The detachment at East Point was worked in details at fortifications there, burning coal and other work there. The time of a great many of the men expired, and they were discharged and went home from that place, twenty-seven of Company E in one day, September 27th, and as many from Company G.

About October 1st the whole Regiment was gathered in one camp in Atlanta. The men while there, during the month of October, were engaged in building and strengthening the fortifications.

This Regiment was left at Atlanta during the whole of the time General Sherman was north with the main part of his troops after Hood. While there we were cooped up some six weeks with no rations except hard bread and fresh beef; all the bacon was reserved for the long march to follow. There was no feed for the horses or cattle, the beeves becoming very thin and poor, and as fast as they became too weak to stand they were killed and dressed, and they made about as tasteless meat as men ever tried to eat; we all got very hungry for a little fat. It was unsafe to venture outside the lines to forage, as roving companies of the enemy were moving around in the vicinity all the time, though once a strong escort was sent out with teams to forage; they brought in a few wagon loads of sweet potatoes, which were a great treat and were devoured all too soon. One day, about the middle of the month of October, a Cavalry company of the enemy, with a section of Artillery, made a bold dash through the outer fortifications south of Atlanta, just as we were sitting down to breakfast. Their onset was with the then familiar " Rebel yell;" the shells from their guns came sailing beautifully over and beyond our camp. We watched them and went on with our breakfast as though it was an every-day occurrence, with no danger for any one; their small arms, which made a great rattling, all appeared to fall short of where we were; it was a grand sight! A display of noisy fireworks in the day time. They did not remain long, as our infantry and forts soon woke up and were at them. If any one was hurt on either side it was not made known.

THE BATTALION CONSOLIDATION.

About the 31st of October the terms of some five hundred of the men expired and they started home, and the Regiment was by this time reduced from thirteen hundred to six hundred. When by Special Orders No. 246, Department and Army of the Tennessee, dated October 31, 1864, the veterans and recruits were consolidated into a battalion of five companies.

The order consolidating into five companies was as follows:

HEADQUARTERS DEPARTMENT AND ARMY OF THE TENNESSEE, }
ATLANTA, GEORGIA, October 31, 1864. }

Special Orders No. 246.

I. 1st. In compliance with General Orders No. 86, War Department, Adjutant-General's office, 1863, the First Regiment Engineers, Missouri Volunteers, is hereby consolidated into five companies, and the following will be the organization:

William Tweeddale, Lieutenant-Colonel; Eben M. Hill, Major; John C. Brook, Surgeon; William N. Neal, Assistant Surgeon.

COMPANY A—William Hill, Captain; Francis Tunica and Heywood M. Sumner, First Lieutenants; Stephen S. Browne, Second Lieutenant.

Eight sergeants, ten corporals, sixty artificers, fifty-three privates—total, 131.

COMPANY B—Thomas W. Bailey, Captain; George G. Bayne, First Lieutenant; Lucien W. Coy, First Lieutenant.

Eleven sergeants, ten corporals, three musicians, sixty artificers, fifty-two privates—total, 136.

COMPANY C—Benjamin F. Coleman, Captain; John McLaren, First Lieutenant; John P. Morton, First Lieutenant; James M. Newhard, Second Lieutenant.

Twelve sergeants, nine corporals, one musician, sixty-four artificers, fifty-two privates—total, 138.

COMPANY D—Benjamin F. Buzard, Captain; Benjamin R. Tanner, First Lieutenant; William A. Morton, First Lieutenant; Solomon Goodrich, Second Lieutenant.

Ten sergeants, eleven corporals, one musician, fifty-nine artificers, fifty-three privates—total, 134.

COMPANY E—Oscar F. Storey, Captain; Ashael D. Whitcomb, First Lieutenant; William K. Lyle, First Lieutenant; Stephen T. Lucas, Second Lieutenant.

Eleven sergeants, ten corporals, two musicians, fifty-three artificers, fifty-nine privates—total, 135.

One sergeant of Company B will be transferred to the non-commissioned staff.

One musician of Company B will be transferred to Company A.

One sergeant of Company C will be transferred to the non-commissioned staff.

One sergeant of Company C will be transferred to Company A.

One corporal of Company D will be transferred to Company C.

One sergeant of Company E will be transferred to Company A.

2d. The following named officers, rendered supernumerary, will, on the 12th day of November, 1864, be mustered out of the service of the United States:

Colonel Henry Flad.
Major N. C. Nichols.
Captain James Dunn, Company A.
Captain William G. Patton, Company B.
Captain Haynes E. Hudson, Company D.
Captain Christian Lochbiler, Company I.
Captain John E. Murphy, Company K.
Captain Herman Giseke, Company L.
First Lieutenant Littleton R. Lancaster, Company A.
First Lieutenant Daniel G. Parker, Company B.
First Lieutenant Eli Winegar, Company C.
First Lieutenant Horace B. Hooker, Company C.
First Lieutenant Silas W. Mattis, Company F.
First Lieutenant John Murphy, Company L.
First Lieutenant William E. Hight, Company M.
Second Lieutenant William C. Claxton, Company A.
Second Lieutenant Gustavus Salzman, Company G.

BY ORDER OF MAJOR-GENERAL O. O. HOWARD.

JOHN H. MUNROE, *Assistant Adjutant-General.*

THE CENTRALIA, MISSOURI, MASSACRE.

About the 22d of September, 1864, Sergeant Goodman, who had, previous to the consolidation, served in Company K of the Twenty-fifth Missouri, and Valentine Peters, Josiah Connor, Charles

T. Hildebiddle, James Mobley, Cass Rose and James Thomas, who had all served in the Twenty-fifth Missouri, and whose homes were in Northwestern Missouri and Southwestern Iowa, received a furlough. Although the word furlough expressed a good deal to a soldier, much more than can be conceived by a mere civilian, they little imagined what they would undergo on the trip.

The following is compiled from a little book of sixty-six pages, published by Sergeant Thomas Goodman, the only survivor of the Centralia massacre, where twenty-seven discharged and furloughed soldiers and Major Johnson's command of 120 men were massacred by deceit, in cold blood, after surrender:

At Big Shanty, thirty-five miles from Atlanta, the track was found torn up. Many of those on the train belonged to the First Missouri Engineers, and they went to work with a will, and in the course of four or five hours the eighty rods or more of destroyed track was repaired. No more incidents occurred on the trip to Louisville except the delay of the trains, and the time was passed away by the comrades in telling experiences and yarns, and in discussing the Tennessee ladies, which all agreed were "up to snuff." It is said that many of the men at the stopping places, Chattanooga, Nashville, etc., visited various institutions where liquids are dispensed for a consideration, trying to elevate their own spirits by pouring liquid spirits down; this, and it is said with sorrow, was a weakness common at that time with a good many soldiers. As they approached Louisville, Kentucky, some one of them cries: "Hurrah! near God's country at last." "Bully for God's country," says another. "Won't I have a square meal before long?" says a third. "Now for refreshments and substantials," say all; and they went for them as only soldiers who have lived on bacon, beans and hard tack for months know how.

They left St. Louis, Missouri, on the morning of September 27th. Before leaving the depot they heard warnings that it was not safe for the United States mails and unarmed soldiers to pass over the North Missouri Railroad, as the route was infested with guerrillas, and that large bodies of them had been seen within a few days at Centralia and other points; further warning that the guerrillas were upon the road was received at St. Charles, but as other soldiers got on board there, the increase in numbers gave them more courage. Still all were uneasy and in evident excitement with an expectant anxiety of expression, such as marks the soldiers' features upon the eve of bat   though happily unconscious of the fate that awaited them. As all said guerrillas were on the road, the conductor was asked if he had a train guard on board, answered that he had twenty-seven old soldiers—their uniforms alone would scare off guerrillas.

Upon the approach of the train to Centralia, it became evident that the fears of an attack were not groundless. Quite a large body of mounted and dismounted men were to be seen around the station. Some of the boys noted peculiarities in the crowd that stamped them as guerrillas and our natural enemies. The train was moving rapidly and it was hoped the conductor would pass without stopping, but he failed to make the attempt. When the whistle sounded for the stop, a soldier of the First Iowa Cavalry, looking out of the window, said: "There are guerrillas there, sure!" A moment more the train was inside a line of blazing, murderous weapons, and volley after volley was poured into the train until it came to a stop. The men on board were totally unarmed. With shouts and yells the guerrillas in a body rushed toward the cars, the doors were burst open, the captors shouting, "Surrender!" The boys had collected about the center of the car, looking as though they intended resistance. One of the guerrillas said: "Surrender quietly and you shall be treated as prisoners of war." Some one of the boys answered: "We can only surrender, as we are totally unarmed."

In a moment the spirit of our captors was changed. On learning our defenseless condition, the promise of humane treatment was withdrawn, and those half-cowed wretches of a moment before became lawless and inhuman monsters. For each guerrilla to present his revolver to the man singled out and demand the money or life of his victim was the work of a moment; evidently a pre-arranged matter, so quickly and quietly was it done. Not a man escaped.

They were ordered to fall into line, with hearts filled with vague apprehensions, which, when ordered to strip off their clothes, became certainties, and they began to contemplate death as the speediest deliverance from a worse fate. The fatal line was formed, twenty-seven soldiers, unarmed, defenseless men, before these *demons*, to expiate their crime of loyalty to their country! History has no parallel to the monstrosity of this act. Honor and loyalty are brave, cheering words in the hour of death; great and good men have died for them. It would be difficult to find in history or fable an instance where men prepared for death so calmly as those brave men. No faltering, no emotion, no entreaty, only a fixed determination to meet cruelty with sublimity, and in the presence of *devils* to die like *men*. Stripped to their underclothing, in line they calmly waited the fatal signal. Anderson, the chief of the guerrillas, approached. As his eyes wandered over the doomed men, he suddenly said: " Boys, have you a Sergeant in your ranks?" No one answered; they wondered what the inquiry would lead to. The chief repeated the inquiry. Silence pervaded the rank. In a louder tone he asked the question, adding : " If there be one, let him stand aside."

Sergeant Goodman, knowing that the stripes on the coat taken from him would designate his rank, and fearing to keep longer silent, stepped out, wondering the purpose of the demand. Anderson directed two of his men to take charge of and remove the Sergeant from the spot. He was at once conducted to the rear. He had hardly reached the place when a volley from the revolvers, with yells of the guerrillas, mingled with cries and moans of pain and distress, were heard. The line had disappeared; most of his comrades lay dead on the ground, others groaning in the agony of their wounds, some making a last struggle for existence, or trying to avoid further injury.

One brave man, Sergeant Peters, made a desperate struggle for life, and succeeded in felling a number of his assailants and obtained a temporary respite by hiding beneath the station-house, which was fired at once, and they succeeded in killing him; after the last one was killed, the train was fired and started up the track.

The civilians stood trembling by, fearing to speak for dread of a like fate.

Sergeant Goodman could not conceive why he was saved, and kept waiting in anxiety and suspense for the ordeal he supposed he was to pass through, and which he fancied would be only more horrible torture than his comrades had passed through. The guerrillas, each time, they passed heaped abuse and curses upon him; some would place a revolver carbine close to his head, with the threat. I would like to kill the———Yankee ; " hell fire is too good " and other expressions, vile, obscene and abusive; the guard could only save their prisoner by the threat to call Anderson. Goodman made no reply as the guard told him they were trying to get some provocation for killing him. The guerrillas finally mounted and began to march in a northwesterly direction ; Goodman was placed on a mule with a guard on each side; the Union soldiers were left lying where they had fallen. Just after leaving Centralia a freight train arrived which was burned by twenty or thirty who turned back for that purpose. Their camp was about two and a half miles from Centralia. There Goodman heard one of the band remark: "I say Bill, I wonder how in h——l Anderson has let that d——d Yankee live so long?" "Dunno; can't say, lest like t'was a Providence; for t'aint like Old Bill, is it?"

Anderson was a man without pity, without emotion. Goodman was the first man who wore the Federal blue that he *ever* spared; his band was mostly deserters, renegades and outlaws.

They had been in the outlaws' camp but a short time, when word was brought of a Federal force under Major Johnson of one hundred and sixty men, who were approaching to give them battle. Goodman was ordered to mount a horse and the guard instructed that if he tried to escape in the battle to kill him instantly. Anderson divided his force, sent one-half of this one hundred and twenty men around to the left, the other half to the right and led the others to the direct attack on the center, which he did with a yell. The two flanks at the same time appearing, yelling like demons, dashed forward on the little line of dismounted Federals; defeat was inevitable, though the little handful in blue showed true courage; there was no flinching; their conduct was worthy of emulation ; they did all they had time to do — gave the rabble one volley ; they were surrounded before they had time to do more; the guerrillas were riding through their ranks shouting: "Surrender, surrender."

Yes, they surrendered. As did the unarmed men on the train a few hours before, as prisoners of war, were disarmed and rendered defenseless. No sooner was this done than "hell" was let loose; even the horrors at Centralia were outdone in the infamous conduct of these bloody demons; men's heads were severed from their bodies, exchanged to other lifeless bodies and labelled with rough and obscene inscriptions; lifeless heads were stuck upon carbine points, on fence stakes, on stumps, and tied to saddle bows. The detachment, twenty-five men holding the horses of Johnson's command, sought safety in flight as soon as the flanking party appeared. They were hotly pursued, from five to ten men chasing one Federal soldier; not more than two or three it is said of these men escaped, and about one hundred and twenty men of Johnson's command were slain on this occasion.

The band then started to Centralia to massacre the escort left with the wagon train. Some of the soldiers saw them coming and mounting escaped ; a few were captured and killed. One man who shut himself up in an outhouse, proposing to defend himself, was told that Major Johnson and all his men were prisoners, and was assured by everything sacred that he would not be harmed, but would be treated as they had been, which was true in one thing—as soon as he opened the door he was shot dead—*treated as his comrades had been.*

On the return to the camp, three hours were allotted for rest to the band, and the march was taken up toward the Missouri River, as Anderson said "the land will be swarming with blue coats by tomorrow evening." The march was continued all night, halting at daylight, after a rest it was taken up by by-roads and through brush until noon; a halt was made until nightfall, when the march was again continued, halting at midnight with orders to rest until daylight.

In the morning Sergeant Goodman was ordered to curry and saddle Anderson's horse, which, though against the grain, he did with a blacksmith's energy. Anderson in passing about an hour later, said to him: "Well old fellow, how are you getting along?"

"Very well, sir," was the reply.

"You are the first being whose life I ever spared, who was caught in Federal blue."

"That's so, Colonel," shouted twenty or more of the guerrillas, as Anderson rode forward.

A fine looking man rode up, addressing the guard: "Who is this man?"

"A prisoner, taken at Centralia, sir," was the reply.

"I thought you took no prisoners?"

"This *one*, Colonel, reserved by Anderson's orders!"

"Aha, I understand, Anderson was right."

This man was an officer of Price's army.

Some ten or fifteen miles further on a halt was made. Scarcely ten minutes later a cry was raised: "The Yankees are coming! Ride as if hell was after you!"

Without orders each sprang to his saddle, led by Anderson, they dashed into the road.

Goodman's hope arose as the boom, boom, of a field piece was heard and a six-pound shell burst one hundred yards to the right and another in nearly the same line set them in rapid motion by the left to the rear. They had been badly frightened, but emerging on the prairie they galloped to an eminence from which the entire country seemed dotted over with Federal Cavalry! Now the chase began. The bold leader saw at a glance their peril.

LIEUTENANT ADDISON N. GLENN.

LIEUTENANT L. W. COY.

With a shout, understood by his men, Anderson wheeled and dashed by the column to the rear halting by Goodman's side. In a second, excepting Anderson and eight men, the entire column was dashing over the prairie in squads of from five to eight men, each taking a different course to mislead the Federals.

Goodman thought his time had come, as he did not hope to be carried a prisoner through their peril. After a time Anderson turning said : "Prisoner, you must ride for your life! Boys, we all must!"

Away for hours they rode in retreat. Stopping about half-past four in a heavy piece of timber the squads began to come in, some with badly wounded men. This was their rendezvous. They began to drink and soon were wild, except two men who never drank, who were guarding Goodman.

The force was here divided into squads. The country was so excited over the Centralia acts they could not hope to keep together in safety any longer. The squad with Anderson took charge of Goodman, and gave him an old coat, putting on a Federal officer's uniform. After several days' march through the brush the Missouri River was reached near Maxwell's Mill. The band was here recruited and prepared again for action, and the order for march was given October 6th, with the reported intention of crossing near Rocheport. The first point reached not suiting Anderson, they passed through Rocheport to three miles below ; the night was dark and Goodman determined to escape in the confusion of crossing the river. But eight men could cross at once and he and his guards were the last.

The men were in the boats leading the horses to swim them, some of whom proved restive, all was excitement ; one of the guards said to the other, "you watch the prisoner, I want to see the start." A moment later some sudden and increased excitement at the river and the other guard moved about a rod in that direction ; Sergeant Goodman seized the opportunity and walked rapidly away directly into the crowd of men and horses near, passing carelessly through, struck into a dense mass of bushes and brushwood on the river bank, pausing to listen after going some two hundred yards, hearing nothing, he struck in the direction of the North Star, to reach the Post at Fayette. At daylight a signboard showed he had only made eight miles, though he had walked at least twenty. He hid in an old tobacco shed, and at night resumed the journey. When nearly exhausted from fatigue and want of food he met an old negro, who told him that he was only one mile from Fayette, and only three or four hundred yards from the line of the Federal pickets. Thoughts of liberty, friends, home, caused him for a time to forget himself and his guerrilla dress, as he was rushing forward, the command "halt there!" greeted him, and he stood within twenty paces of a cavalry man in blue; the sentinel convinced, and listening to his story the Corporal was dispatched to Post Headquarters, Captain Eaton, Ninth Missouri Cavalry. The next day word was brought that Anderson and Shelby was marching against Fayette. Another trusty scout was sent out to obtain further information. He returned in a very brief time, stating there was barely time to save themselves from a fate like that at Centralia. The march

THE FIRST MISSOURI ENGINEERS DESTROYING A RAILROAD SHOWING THE USE OF HOOKS MADE BY THEM FOR THE PURPOSE.

to Macon was at once taken up, and home was reached in safety. Sergeant Goodman died in Santa Barbara, California, in the summer of 1887.

INCIDENTS AT ATLANTA.

While yet at Atlanta, news of Price's raid through the central part of Southern Missouri, and of how some of our Regiment who had parents, wives, brothers and sisters there were despoiled, their homes fired, the last crust or covering taken, and other atrocities. These men became greatly embittered, and, it is said, to in a measure get some revenge on Confederates, they afterward assisted in spreading the conflagration at Columbia, South Carolina.

Soon after coming to Atlanta, Lieutenant W. K. Lyle was detailed to go to Nashville and procure new material for a pontoon train and other engineer supplies; he returned to Atlanta on the last train over the road. During the first two weeks in November at Atlanta, the Battalion was engaged in drilling on the ponton, and getting it in complete order, making and repairing necessary engineer and pioneer tools for an extended march, and in tearing up the railroads east and south of Atlanta.

November 13th and 14th one Lieutenant and ten men were making ox-yokes, details making hooks for destroying railroads; the balance of the men tearing up the Atlanta & Macon Railroad under direction of Captain Poe, Chief Engineer. It was found that forty men with hooks and levers could tear up and destroy four-fifths of a mile per hour. (See engraving on opposite page.)

THE MARCH TO THE SEA.

NOVEMBER 15, 1864, the Battalion, under command of Lieutenant-Colonel Tweeddale, left Atlanta with the army; transportation and the roads very bad. One company was detailed to repair roads and one to assist teams over bad places. We arrived at South River about 6 P. M. The train in advance was stalled on Moore's Hill. Two companies were sent to help the train up the hill; went into camp two and a half miles beyond at 11 P. M; distance marched, thirteen miles.

16th. Ordered to start at daylight; sent one company to build a bridge across a creek near camp, and did not get started until near eleven A. M., having to wait for train in front to move. One company was detailed to assist Captain Buzard with ponton train; camped within one mile of McDonough, at 11 P. M. The last of ponton train did not reach camp until 1 A. M.; distance marched, sixteen miles.

17th. Department Headquarters' orders were to march at 6 A. M. Captain Buzard's orders from General Blair were to march at 5 A. M. The ponton train marched in advance of the Regiment; two companies were detailed to assist the ponton train over the hills and bad places. Arrived in camp across the Tassahaw river, near Hendrick's Mill, about 7 P. M., having marched that day twenty miles. Orders came that evening to push forward one section of the bridge to Nolling's Factory and have it thrown across the Ocmulgee river as soon as possible. The mules of the train having failed very much, Captain Reese directed that mules be obtained from General Smith's Division, Seventeenth Corps.

18th. Started at 5 A. M. in advance with a section of thirty wagons of the ponton train, drawn by thirty of the best mule teams, with three companies of the Regiment as a guard; arrived at the Ocmulgee river, near Nolling's Factory, at 11 A. M.; bridge 275 feet long; ready at 1 P. M. The second section not coming up, Colonel Tweeddale went back and found it was delayed by the mules giving out and the road being blocked by the trains of the Fifteenth Corps. The road was cleared and the section arrived at the village at 2 P. M; waited one hour to have the road cleared to the river. The second bridge was ready for crossing at 5 P. M.; length of this bridge, 264 feet; depth of water, thirteen feet; distance marched, twelve miles.

19th. One company was sent across the river to repair the roads, and details sent to obtain mules for the ponton train. In the afternoon the balance of the Regiment moved across and camped on the top of the hill. Fires were built on that side from the river to the top of the hill to enable the teams to get over the road in the dark.

20th. The Army having crossed, except the cattle of the Fourteenth and Twentieth Corps and the rear guard, one bridge was taken up at noon and the train started at 1 P. M.

The ponton train used by the First Missouri Engineer Regiment on this march was of skeleton frame boats, covered with canvas, using sixty wagons, with six mules to each wagon, which was afterward increased to eight mules to a wagon. Besides our train there were twenty-five hundred wagons and six hundred ambulances in the Army train.

The pontons were composed of two skeleton sides and two end pieces of 3x3-inch wood, about twenty feet long and three feet wide. The sides, end pieces and braces were separate, and were put together and held with hooks and staples, the canvas, which for each boat was just a large square sheet of very heavy duck, tarpaulin or sailcloth, was drawn up at each end and tied, making a boat very strong that did not leak a drop. The boats were then taken out into the stream and anchored about six feet apart, the first two from stakes on shore, as well as the last two on the far side, the balance with iron anchors weighing near two hundred pounds in the stream; the boats were also tied diagonally across from end to end. As soon as a boat was placed the beams or balks, four in number, were laid, first from a plank on shore to the far edge of the first boat, then from the shore edge of the first boat to the far edge of the second boat, and so on. The planks or chesses were then laid as fast as a boat was anchored and the balks laid on it. As each twelve feet of the chesses were laid, the guard-plank was put down and tied at the end to the chesses, and so on until the bridge was completed. The chesses and guard-plank were about one and one-half inches thick, six inches wide and twelve feet long; the balks, six inches square and twelve feet long. See the engraving below:

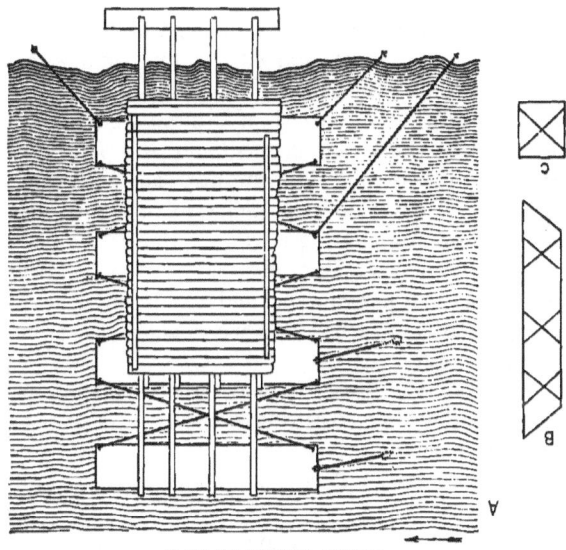

PLAN OF PONTON BRIDGE.
A—Bridge.   B—One skeleton side.   C—End piece.

One boat with the frames, canvas, anchors, ropes, braces, balks (beams or sills), chesses (planks for flooring), and guard-planks made a load for one wagon, and is the lightest, strongest and quickest laid ponton in use.

The roads on the 20th of November were found generally good until within one mile of Monticello, where they were very bad through a clay ravine, and it became difficult to get along in the darkness and rain; went into camp a half mile south of the village. Captain Buzard, having a number of surplus citizen teamsters, organized them into a pioneer corps and sent them in advance of the ponton train to repair roads; marched ten and a half miles.

21st. Started at 5:30 A. M. It had rained all night, making the roads very bad; moved very slow; within one mile of Hillsboro the roads became impassable; at 5 P. M. went into camp, having marched nine and a half miles; worked until 8:30 repairing roads; weather cold, with frost.

22d. Started men in advance at 6 A. M., the train at 6:45; the weather cold, with snow, and roads miserable; got four wagons through to Clinton, the balance of the train scattered along for two miles. We worked until 11 o'clock P. M., when, finding it impossible to get farther, went into bivouac alongside the wagons; distance marched, fourteen miles.

23d. On account of the wagons being frozen fast in the mud, it was late before the train was started. A by-road was found which had not been cut up by the trains. The train was got up the hill at 1 P. M. About three miles south of Clinton we received fifty-five six-mule teams from the Headquarters train, and put eight mules to each wagon and pushed on. The infantry advance turned off on the wrong road. About 5:30 P. M. General Corse sent an aid to tell us that "there were no troops in advance; that if we desired to go further and would not wait, he would send a guard." He also stated that "the General was in camp one and a half miles in rear of us." We then went into camp where we were, six miles from Gordon; marched thirteen miles.

24th. Started at 6 A. M. Colonel Tweeddale went in advance to Gordon, and at Headquarters was ordered to divide the train and the Regiment into two sections, the first section to report to the Fifteenth Corps; the second section, under command of Captain Buzard, to report to the Seventeenth Corps, to fill up the second section with the best eight-mule teams and harness and send them immediately on the Jackson ferry road, the Seventeenth Corps having already gone; to obtain transportation for the first section from the Fifteenth Corps. Companies A and E were detached to report to Captain Buzard, whose section was filled up and started at 1 P. M. There were now but forty-one mules left, and they were unserviceable. Transportation for the whole of the first section was obtained from Colonel Fort, Chief Quartermaster Fifteenth Corps. Started again at 3 P. M. on orders from General Osterhaus, commanding Fifteenth Corps; arrived at Irwinton at 8 P. M.

25th. At 6:30 A. M. ten teams reported from the First Division, and ten from the Second Division, at 7. The train was still two teams short, so the ponton supply wagons were each filled with six ponton train mules, and one boat-wagon with team from the regimental train, replacing them with eight mules from ponton train. Started at 7:15 A. M., and arrived within one mile of the Oconee river at Ball's Ferry at 1 P. M.; at 5 P. M. four boat-wagons, one chess-wagon and eighty men were sent to the river a half mile above the ferry. The stream was very rapid, the boats unwieldy and there was considerable difficulty in getting a rope across. A rope was finally attached to a tree above, the boat got across, and a Lieutenant and thirty men ferried troops across. This day marched fifteen miles.

26th. At 6 A. M., a detail of a Lieutenant and some men were sent to bring up the boat and chess-wagons to where the train was. At 7:15 A. M. orders were received to lay the bridge across the Oconee River at Ball's Ferry. Owing to the delay in getting the wagons up that were used the evening before, when the troops were ferried across, the bridge was not ready to cross until 11 A. M.; length of bridge 236 feet, depth of water ten feet. Orders were received to divide the train, pontons and appurtenances. Lieutenant Lyle was assigned to receive ten eight-mule teams from Lieutenant Morton with harness and everything complete. Company A was ordered to report to the first section and relieve Lieutenant Tanner and detail from first section. The second section was then loaded up and sent forward with the Fourth Division Fifteenth Corps, in charge of Lieutenant John P. Morton; Company C and twelve men, four boat-wagons, two chess wagons, two Lieutenants and twenty men were detailed to take charge of the bridge during the night.

27th. At 7 A. M. the bridge being still down, and no crossing since 3 A. M., Captain Buzard had taken up the bridge of the Seventeenth Corps early in the morning; permission was obtained for the loan of mules and harness to take this train to the camp of the Seventeenth Corps, a distance of two miles. The regimental train was then sent across, and parked one mile in advance; the bridge was taken up at noon, and the train started at 1:25; the roads were generally good, but delay was caused by cattle of the Fourteenth and Twentieth Corps; arrived at Irwin Cross Roads at 6:30 P. M., having marched eight and a half miles.

28th. Were assigned a position in rear of the Third Division of the Fifteenth Corps. Owing to some misunderstanding the Second Division train got in before us, delaying us nearly three hours in starting, during which time we sat around, in weary waiting, and making our progress slow, owing to the long train in advance of us on the same road, besides we had several bad swamps to cross. We were delayed so long at a swamp that finally we went into camp at 9 P. M., one mile in rear of the Second Division, and nearly four miles in rear of Third Division, near the Little Ohoope River; distance marched this day, thirteen miles.

FORAGING IN GEORGIA.

29th. Started the train 5:05 A. M.; pushed forward and arrived at Headquarters, Third Division, at 7:15; we were delayed by the Third Division until 8:20; roads generally good during the forenoon; about 10 o'clock the trail of the Seventeenth Corps opened parallel with the main road. About 1 P. M. we struck off to the right into a circuitous road that led through the woods and swamps, arriving in camp at 8:30 at Luther Sand's Mill, on Sartain's Creek, having marched twenty miles.

30th. We started at daylight. The men were sent forward to build a bridge at the mill. The teams fell into the rear of the Third Division, whose pioneers we found repairing the road occupied yesterday by the Fourth Division in our rear. The Second Division passed us on a road across a swamp, and our men assisted

E. M. HILL, LIEUTENANT COLONEL 1st MISSOURI
ENGINEERS, FROM MAY, 1865.

W. A. NEAL, Asst. Surg. 1st Mo. Engrs., 1861.   Dr. W. A. NEAL, Elkhart, Ind., 1889.

approaches. The troops having all crossed at 5 p. m., the bridge was taken up, and they started for Raleigh, arriving in camp at 2 a. m., 15th, having marched eleven miles.

15th. Advanced and marched four miles; went into camp on the Hillsboro road.

16th. Under orders returned to same camp at Raleigh.

18th. Rumors were circulating that Johnson's Army had surrendered.

20th and 21st. There was a grand review of the Tenth and Twenty-third Corps.

24th. The word is circulating in camp that General Sherman's terms to General Johnson receiving his surrender are rejected at Washington, and that General Grant had arrived in person to direct the campaign.

27th. It was duly published to the army that General Johnson had surrendered, and that General Grant had returned to Washington, and the feeling in the army is that the war is over.

THE MARCH TO WASHINGTON.

April 29th. The whole army left Raleigh for Washington, our Regiment arriving in Manchester, opposite Richmond, Virginia, May 9th, crossing the James River, and marching through Richmond May 11th. We arrived in Alexandria in sight of Washington May 19th; staid in camp there until May 24th. We took part that day in the grand review of Sherman's Army, and at the close of the review encamped out on Fourteenth Street, near Columbia College. We remained in Washington until June 3d. In the march from Raleigh to Washington we had made some very rapid marching, at one time we marched with the ponton trains of sixty wagons, forty-four miles within twenty-four hours.

RUSHVILLE, ILLINOIS, December 18, 1865.

Colonel Samuel P. Simpson, Adjutant-General of Missouri:

SIR—In compliance with your request, I would state that the First Missouri Engineers were at Savannah, Georgia, on the 1st of January, 1865, building fortifications and repairing the pontons of the Army of the Tennessee, preparatory to the great campaign with Major-General Sherman through the Carolinas to Raleigh, North Carolina, where General Johnston surrendered.

We were in charge of the pontons of the Army of the Tennessee. The first great work was bridging Broad River, near Beaufort, South Carolina. We marched with the Fifteenth and Seventeenth Army Corps, sharing all the dangers, hardships and exposures incident to the campaign, often putting bridges across streams under fire of the enemy's guns; were at the destruction o

Columbia, South Carolina, then at Fayetteville, North Carolina, and at the battle near Goldsboro, North Carolina. Marched thence to Raleigh, North Carolina, on the 29th of April, 1865. Left Raleigh, North Carolina, for Washington, D. C., by way of Petersburg, Richmond, Fredericksburg and Alexandria, Virginia, and took part in the grand review at Washington, D. C.

We were next ordered to Louisville, Kentucky, where we arrived June 7, 1865; went into camp and passed satisfactory inspection by General Reese, Inspector-General, Army of the Tennessee.

On the 22d of July were mustered out of the service of the United States, and ordered to St. Louis, Missouri, for final discharge, where we arrived on the 24th of July, 1865, and were discharged on that day, after a four years' campaign, from our original organization as the Engineer Regiment of the West, under Colonel J. W. Bissell, to date of muster out.

I have the honor to be, very respectfully, your obedient servant,

WM. HILL,

Late Lieutenant-Colonel First Missouri Engineers.

TO LOUISVILLE AND THE MUSTER OUT.

June 3, 1865, we all started for Louisville, Kentucky, on the Baltimore & Ohio Railroad. Arriving at Parkersburg, West Virginia, on the 6th, we were transferred to a steamboat on the Ohio River, and arrived at Louisville on the evening of the 7th, going into camp two miles above the city. We remained in Louisville until July 22d, when, just before evening, we marched to New Albany, and took the cars there about 9 P. M. for St. Louis, Missouri, arriving there on the afternoon of the 24th and were quartered in Jefferson Barracks; mustered out, and the last of the Regiment paid off July 28, 1865, although the muster rolls are all dated Louisville, Kentucky, July 22, 1865.

The following, from the report of the Adjutant-General of Missouri for the year 1865, is appended:

HISTORICAL MEMORANDA.

The First Regiment of Engineers, Missouri Volunteers, remained at Nashville during the month of January and the fore part of February to perfect the reorganization of the Regiment. It was then ordered to complete the western portion (twenty miles) of the Nashville & Northwestern Railroad. During the following two months the Regiment constructed several large bridges and trestlework—among others, one seventy-five feet high and nearly 1,000 feet long; laid the track, and constructed platforms, switches, turnouts, etc. At the same time small forts were built at Johnsonville and Waverly. After the completion of the road the Regiment commenced the construction of blockhouses for the protection of the numerous bridges and trestlework, and had nearly completed them from Johnsonville to Kingston Springs, when, about the middle of September, it was transferred to the Department of the Tennessee, and ordered to report to Major-General Howard, before Atlanta. It participated in the flank march to Jonesboro and Lovejoy, resulting in the evacuation of Atlanta, when it was ordered to Atlanta to construct an inner line of fortifications. It had completed several forts on the south side of Atlanta, when General Sherman commenced his march to Savannah. The Regiment had, in the meanwhile, by expiration of the term of service of a great many enlisted men, been reduced from 1,360 enlisted men to 600, and it was, therefore, necessary to consolidate the twelve companies into five. In consequence of this consolidation the Colonel two Majors and the line officers of seven companies were honorably mustered out (November 17, 1864), while the remaining five companies, under Lieutenant-Colonel Tweeddale, accompanied the Army of the Tennessee on its march to Savannah.

PART IV.

ROSTER

OF THE

FIRST ENGINEERS AND TWENTY-FIFTH MISSOURI INFANTRY.

HE names are in alphabetical order and numbered consecutively, with rank following the name; then the various companies served in by letter and regiment, whether the Engineer Regiment, the Twenty-fifth Infantry, or both, followed by date and place of enlistment, date and place of discharge, and the History, as far as known, lastly the present address. Of many survivors the addresses could not be found, nor anything learned about them.

To condense as much as possible, the following abbreviations are used:

Col., for Colonel; Lt.-Col., Lieutenant-Colonel; Maj., Major; Capt., Captain; Lt. or Lieut., Lieutenant; Sur., Surgeon; A. Sur., Assistant Surgeon; Sergt., Sergeant; Cor., Corporal; Q. M., Quartermaster; Com., Commissary; Co., Company; P., Private; Eng., Engineer Regiment, 25th, Twenty-fifth Infantry; e., enlisted; disch., discharged; dis., disability; ad., present address; res., resigned.

To find a comrade's history, recollect the name. To find where the name is forgotten, trace by the company letter, the oldest companies are first in order. It is in contemplation to issue an annual or bi-annual correction sheet of this Roster. The survivors of the Engineer Regiment or the Twenty-fifth Infantry finding any errors, omissions, or knowing of any changes of residence or deaths will please notify the Historian. The address of every survivor is wanted. Dr. W. A. Neal, 431 Main Street, Elkhart, Indiana Historian.

THE ROSTER

1. Abbott, Stewart, P. Co. G, 25th; e. March 1, 1862, Lexington, Mo.
2. Abernathy, Moses F., P. Co. F, Eng.; e. Sept. 21, 1861, Dubuque, Iowa; disch. Feb., 1862, Otterville, Mo.; dis. lung disease.
3. Abraham, Michael, P. Co. A, Eng.; e. July 20, 1861, St. Louis, Mo.
4. Ackerman, Christian, P. Co. B, 25th; e. June 13, 1861, St. Joseph, Mo.
5. Ackerman, Joseph, P. Co. B, 25th; e. Nov. 1, 1861, St. Joseph, Mo.
6. Ackerson, Garrett, P. Cos. C, K, Eng.; e. Aug. 4, 1861, Prairie City, Ill.; disch. Sept. 8, 1864, Madison (Ind.) Hospital; ad. Smithfield, Ill. Was 41 years old when enlisted; is a pensioner.
7. ADAMS, CHARLES E., Lt.-Col. Eng.; e. October 31, 1861, St. Louis, Mo.; res. May 5, 1863, for dis.— lung disease. *History* — Was born in Lyons, N. Y., October 31, 1838. He was the youngest son of General W. H. Adams, of the War of 1812; a brother, Colonel Alex. D. Adams, was a Colonel of the Twenty-seventh New York. After graduating from college, in the fall of 1858, he removed to St. Louis, and when the war broke out entered the Fourth Regiment United States Reserve Corps, as Captain of Company A, May 8, 1861; assisted in the capture of Camp Jackson, May 10, 1861; marched his Company to Rolla, May 16, 1861; thence to Waynesville until June 30th, garrisoning that place with Company B, Captain A. G. Hequembourg; marched to Springfield, July 9th; thence to St. Louis, 17th; thence to Pilot Knob, August 18, 1861; was mustered out at the end of the three months' term; October 31, 1861, was appointed Lieutenant-Colonel First Missouri Engineers, and served with them until he was captured, about May 3, 1862, in front of Corinth, he was held by the enemy in various prisons until November he was exchanged; he was there with General B. M. Prentiss, who, with all his comrades in captivity, testified that as in his Regiment he won the love and esteem of all with whom he came in contact for his gentlemanly deportment and devotion to their welfare; to some he seemed strict, and needlessly neat and rigorous in his police system, but they were soon brought to see that he was working for the benefit of all, and loved him the more for his strictness. He was nearly starved, and his health broken in the Southern prisons, and being unable for duty, resigned May 5, 1863; returned to St. Louis, and was employed in the County Clerk's office; died in St. Louis, Mo., January 11, 1866, of lung disease, contracted in prison; was buried at Lyons, N. Y. His sister, Mrs. Henry J. Ruggles, 524 West 153d street New York City, is the last of the family.
8. Adams, John, Corp. Cos. D, F, B, Eng.; e. Aug. 17, 1861, Greenville, Ill.; Veteran Feb. 4, 1864.; disch. July 22, 1865, Louisville, Ky.; was 25 years old when enlisted; ad. Greenville, Ill.
9. Adams, Eli D., P. Co. H, 25th; e. Aug. 14, 1861, Nodaway Co., Mo.; ad. King City, Mo.
10. Adams, Geo. W., P. Co. D; e. May 1, 1864.
11. Adams, Henry C., Corp. Cos. I. 25th, H, D, Eng.; e. Aug. 10, 1861, Pleasant View, Mo.; disch. July 22, 1865; ad. Flag Springs, Mo.
12. Ad in, Stephen B., P. Co. D, 25th; e. July 13, 1861, St. Joseph, Mo.
13. Agnew, Mathew, P. Co. G, 25th; e. July 13, 1861, Leavenworth, Kan.
14. Ahlers, Henry, P. Cos. H, 25th, C and D, Eng.; e. Nov. 7, 1861, St. Louis, Mo.; disch. July 22, 1865.
15. Ainsworth, Lionel, P. Cos. I and C, Eng.; e. Sept. 9, 1861, Ft. Madison, Iowa.

16 Alden, Andrew A., Sergt. Cos. A and E. Eng.; e. July 24, 1861, St. Louis, Mo.
17 Alexander, C. S., P. Co. H, 25th; e. Nodaway Co., Mo.
18 Alexander, Geo. L., P. Co. F, Eng.; e. Sept. 9, 1861, Dubuque, Iowa.
19 Allen, James, P. Cos. A and E, Eng.; e. July 7, 1861, St. Louis, Mo.; ad. Newton Co., Mo.
20 Allen, John, P. Co. C, Eng.; e. Aug. 4, 1861, Prairie City, Ill.; died St. Louis, Mo., Aug. 24, 1861.
21 Allen, Orlando, P. Cos. H, 25th, M and E, Eng.; e. May 4, 1863, Andrew Co., Mo.; disch. July 22, 1865.
22 Allen, Thomas, P. Co. C, 25th; e. Aug. 20, 1861, St. Joseph, Mo.
23 Allers, Henry, Sergt. Cos. G and I, Eng.; e. Sept. 9, 1861, Cape Girardeau, Mo.; disch. Sept. 28, 1864, Atlanta, Ga.
24 Alternus, John, P. Cos. I and C, Eng.; e. Nov. 5, 1862, Denmark, Iowa.
25 Ambaugh, Peter, P. Co. E, 25th; e. Dec. 24, 1861, Holt Co., Mo.
26 Amlin, James, P. Cos. K, D and C, Eng.; e. Sept. 9, 1861, Burlington, Iowa.
27 Ambros, Frederick, P. Co. E, 25th; e. Nodaway Co., Mo.
28 Amlung, Henry, P. Cos. G, I and D, Eng.; e. Sept. 9, 1861, Cape Girardeau, Mo.; disch. July 22, 1865; is a pensioner.
29 Amos, James E., P. Co. K, Eng.; e. Sept. 4, 1861, Burlington, Iowa.
30 Anderson, Benj. F., Sergt. Co. B and Com.-Sergt. Eng.; e. July 28, 1861, Paris, Ill.
31 Anderson, Charles B., Sergt. Co. K, Eng.; e. Oct. 5, 1861, New London, Iowa; dead.
32 Anderson, David, P. Cos. K and B, Eng.; e. Oct. 5, 1861, New London, Iowa; is a pensioner; ad. Ashland, Neb.
33 Anderson, E. W., P. Cos. B and K, Eng.; e. July 28, 1861, Paris, Ill.
34 ANDERSON, JESSE D., Lieut. Co. B, Eng.; e. July 28, 1861, Paris, Ill.; res. March 21, 1862.
35 Anderson, John P., P. Cos. I and C, Eng.; e. Sept. 19, 1861, Burlington, Iowa.
36 Anderson, John, P. Co. D, 25th; e. Aug. 8, 1861, Andrew Co., Mo.; died at Mill Brook, Kan.
37 Anderson, Robert, P. Cos. A, 25th, M and D, Eng.; e. June 14, 1861, St. Joseph, Mo.
38 Anderson, Samuel F., P. Co. B, Eng.; e. July 28, 1861, Paris, Ill.
39 Anderson, Thomas, P. Co. D, 25th; e. July 18, 1861, Andrew Co., Mo.
40 Andrew, Aminidab, P. Co. H, 25th; e. Aug. 14, 1862, Nodaway Co., Mo.
41 Andrew, Abivardi, P. Cos. H, 25th, M and E, Eng.; e. Aug. 14, 1862, Nodaway Co., Mo.; disch. July 22, 1865.
42 Appleby, Franklin, P. Cos. H and D, Eng.; e. Oct. 1, 1861, Vermillion, Ill.; dead.
43 Appleby, Robert C., Cor. Cos. H and D, Eng.; e. Sept. 15, 1861, Kentucky, Ill.; ad. Brocton, Ill.; is a pensioner.
44 Appleby, James, P. Cos. A and E, Eng.; e. July 20, 1861, St. Louis, Mo.
45 Arheart, Charles, P. Cos. H, 25th, M and E, Eng.; e. Feb. 1, 1862, Gentry Co., Mo.
46 ARMSTRONG, DAVID, Lt. Cos. C and B, Eng.; e. Sept. 16, 1861, Avon, Ill.; res. Sept. 20, 1864, Atlanta, Ga.; is a pensioner; ad. Avon, Ill.
47 Armstrong, Wm., P. Cos. A, 25th, M and E, Eng.; e. July 18, 1863, Clay County, Mo.; disch. July 22, 1865.
48 Arnett, Wm., P. Co. C, 25th; e. July 2, 1861, Gentry Co., Mo.
49 Arnold, Alex., P. Cos. A and E, Eng.; e. July 20, 1861, St. Louis, Mo.
50 Arnoldin, Peter, P. Co. G, 25th; e. June 27, 1861, Kansas City, Mo.
51 Arterburn, Wm. J., P. Co. D, Eng.; e. Sept. 14, 1861, Flora, Ill.; disch. Nov. 2, 1862, Jackson, Tenn.; dis.
52 Ash, David C., P. Cos. H and D, Eng.; e. Sept. 20, 1861, Paris, Ill.
53 Ash, Newton, P. Cos. A and E, Eng.; e. July 28, 1861, St. Louis, Mo.
54 Ashley, Bladen, Sergt. Co. I, 25th; e. July 27, 1861, Victoria, Mo.

THE ROSTER.

55 Ashworth, Edward, P. Co. G, 25th; e. June 27, 1861, Kansas City, Mo.
56 Ashworth, Wm., P. Co. H, 25th; e. June 27, 1861, Kansas City, Mo.
57 Asp, John, P. Cos. I and C, Eng.; e. Sept. 21, 1861, Toolsboro, Iowa.
58 Atkins, Bartlett, P. Cos. C, 25th, A and B, Eng.; e. Jan. 13, 1862, St. Joseph, Mo.; dead.
59 Aughinbaugh, John, P. Co. C, 25th, A, Eng.; e. Aug. 1, 1861, Easton, Mo.; ad., St. Joseph, Mo.
60 Austin, Hiram, P. Co. B, 25th; e. Aug. 1, 1861, Linneus, Mo.
61 Austin, Moses, P. Co. I, 25th; e. Aug. 12, 1861, Cameron, Mo.
62 Avery, Alanson, P. Co. K, Eng.; e. Sept. 18, 1861, Roseville, Ill.
63 Avra, Jonathan, P. Cos. B and K, Eng.; e. July 28, 1861, Paris, Ill.
64 Avra, Wm., P. Cos. B and K, Eng.; e. July 28, 1861, Paris, Ill.
65 Averman, Jos., P. Co. K, 25th; e. Feb. 1, 1862, Montgomery County, Mo.
66 Aylesbutt, Jas. J., P. Co. E, Eng.; e. Feb. 18, 1864.
67 Baer, Franz, P. Cos. L, I and D, Eng.
69 **BAILEY, THOS. W. CAPT.**, Cos. K, F and B, Eng.; e. Sept. 1, 1861, Wapello, Iowa; disch. July 22, 1865; was brevetted major, June 12, 1865; died near Burlington, Iowa, April, 1887.
70 Bailey, Geo. W., P. Cos. H, 25th, M and E, Eng.; e. July 28, 1863, Nodaway County, Mo.; disch. July 22, 1865.
71 Bailey, Jas. M., P. Cos. B and K, Eng.; e. July 28, 1861, Paris, Ill.; disch. Aug. 4, 1864.
72 Bailey, John, P. Cos. H, 25th, M and E, Eng.; e. July 1, 1863, Nodaway Co., Mo.; disch. July 22, 1865.
73 Bacon, Ira, P. Co. E, Eng.; e. Aug. 13, 1861, Adrian, Mich.; disch. Aug. 14, 1864; ad., Blissfield, Mich.
74 Bacon, John W. Sergt. Cos. A and E, Eng.; e. July 21, 1861, St. Louis, Mo.
75 Bacco, Felix, P. Co. G, 25th; e. Aug. 12, 1861, Santa Fe, N. M.
76 Bair, John, P. Co. G, 25th; e. June 27, 1861, Kansas City, Mo.
77 Baker, Andrew, P. Co. H, 25th; e. Aug. 14, 1861, Nodaway County, Md.; ad. Barnard, Mo.
78 Baker, Bolin, P. Cos. F, 25th, H and D, Eng.; e. Dec. 21, 1861, St. Catharines, Mo.; disch. Dec. 31, 1864; ad. Given, Iowa.
79 Baker, Brice V., P. A and E, Eng.; e. July 20, 1861, St. Louis, Mo., disch. Aug. 1, 1864.
80 Baker, Daniel B., P. Cos. F, 25th, H and D, Eng.; e. Jan. 4, 1862, St. Catharines, Mo.; ad. Vancouver, Wash. Ter.
81 Baker, Francis M., P. Cos. F, 25th, H and D, Eng.; e. Jan. 22, 1863, St. Catharines, Mo., ad. North Salem, Mo.
82 Baker, Geo. W., P. Cos. F and D, Eng.; e. Sept. 23, 1861, Bloomington, Ill.
83 Baker, Geo. W., Cos. F, 25th, H and D, Eng.; e. Dec. 21, 1861, St. Catharines, Mo.; is a pensioner; ad. Sedgwick, Mo.
84 Baker, Geo. H., P. Cos. F, 25th, H, Eng.; e. Dec. 21, 1861, St. Catharines, Mo.; ad. St. Catharines, Mo.
85 Baker, James, P. Cos. F, 25th, H and D, Eng.; e. Dec. 21, 1861, St. Catharines, Mo.; ad. Winigan, Mo.
86 Baker, James, Jr., P. Cos. F, 25th, H and D, Eng.; e. July 21, 1861, St. Catharines, Mo.; ad. Adams, Ore.
87 Baker, James A., Cor. Cos. F, 25th, H and D, Eng.; e. Sept. 22, 1862, St. Catharines, Mo.; is a pensioner; ad. North Salem, Mo.
88 Baker, James B., P. Co. F, 25th, e. Mar. 20, 1862, St. Catharines, Mo.
89 Baker, James R., Sergt. Cos. F, 25th, H. and D, Eng.; e. July 22, 1861, St. Catharines, Mo.; ad. Greencastle, Mo.
90 Baker, John, P. Cos. A and E, Eng.; e. July 20, 1861, St. Louis, Mo.
91 Baker, Lafayette, Sergt. Cos. F, 25th, H and D, Eng.; e. July 22, 1861, St. Catharines, Mo.; ad. Vancouver, Wash. Ter.
92 Baker, Lucius P., P. Co. E, Eng.; e. Aug. 13, 1861, Adrian, Mich.; is a pensioner; ad. Adrian, Mich.
94 Baker, Morris, P. Cos. F, 25th, H and D, Eng.; e. Dec. 21, 1861, St. Catharines, Mo.
95 Baker, Robert J., P. Co. F, 25th; e. Dec. 21, 1861, St. Catharines, Mo.

96 Baker, Samuel T., Corp. Cos. A and E, Eng.; e. July 21, 1861, St. Louis. Mo.
97 Baker, Sylvester, P. Cos. I and C, Eng.; e. Oct. 26, 1861, McGregor, Iowa; disch. Oct. 31, 1864.
98 Baker, Wm., P. Co. C, 25th; e. March 2, 1862, St. Joseph, Mo.
99 Baker, Wm., P. Co. F, 25th; e. Dec. 21, 1861, St. Catharines, Mo.; ad. Vancouver, Wash. Ter.
100 Baker, Wm., Jr., P. Co. F, 25th; e. July 22, 1861, St. Catharines, Mo.
101 Baker, Wm., Jr., Corp. Co. F, 25th, H and D, Eng.; e. Jan. 19, 1862; disch. July 22, 1865; is a pensioner; ad. Knobel, Clay County, Ark.
102 Ball, Oscar C., P. Co. F, Eng.; e. Sept. 23, 1861, Dubuque, Iowa; ad. Holden, Mass.
103 Ballard, Thos., P. Co. E, 25th; e. July 22, 1861, Oregon, Mo.
104 Ballard, Wm., P. Co. E, 25th; e. July 22, 1861, Oregon, Mo.
105 Balsey, Geo. H., P. Cos. B, K and A, Eng.; e. July 28, 1861, Paris, Ill.; is a pensioner; ad. Vermillion, Ill.
106 Balzecker, Fred, P. Co. B, 25th; e. June 13, 1861, St. Joseph, Mo.
107 Barman, W. W., P. Cos. B and K, Eng.; e. July 28, 1861, Paris, Ill.
108 Bamblitts, John W., P. Co. H, 25th; e. Aug. 14, 1861.
109 Bancot, Nicholas, P. Co. B, 25th; e. June 13, 1861, St. Joseph, Mo.
110 Bank, James E., P. Cos. I and C, Eng.; e. Oct. 16, 1861, McGregor, Iowa.
111 Bannister, Wm., P. Co. G, 25th; e. Feb. 12, 1862. Gentry Co., Mo.
112 Barker, Chas. F., P. Co. E, Eng.; e. Aug. 13, 1861, Adrian, Mich.; ad. Adrian, Mich.
113 Barker, Chas. N., P. Co. H, 25th; e. Sept. 2, 1862.
114 Barnes, Cyrus, P. Co. C, 25th; e. July 28th, 1861, St. Joseph, Mo.
115 Barnes, David, P. Co. D, 25th; e. June 18, 1861, St. Joseph, Mo.
116 Barnes, Elisha, P. Co. D, 25th; e. July 12, 1861, St. Joseph, Mo.
117 Barnes, Harrison, P. Co. D, 25th; e. July 12, 1861, St. Joseph, Mo.
118 Barnes, James, P. Co. D, 25th; e. July 12, 1861, St. Joseph, Mo.
119 Barnes, Thos. J., P. Co. D, 25th; e. July 12, 1861, St. Joseph, Mo.
120 Barney, Joseph, P. Cos. I and C, Eng.; e. Sept. 9, 1861, Rushville, Ill.; ad. Canton, Ill.
121 Barrett, Henry, Sergt. Co. F, 25th; e. July 12, 1861, St. Joseph, Mo.
122 Barrett, Wilson, P. Co. I, 25th; e. Aug. 30, 1861, Kansas City, Mo.
123 Barrington, Richard, Sergt. Co. G, Eng.; e. Sept. 13, 1861, Cape Girardeau, Mo.
124 Barrow, Wm. H, Sergt. Cos. D, F and B, Eng.; e. Aug. 17, 1861; vet.; e. Feb. 4, 1864; disch. July 22, 1865; ad. Carlyle, Ill.
125 Barrow, Samuel, P. Cos. A and E, Eng.; e. July 20, 1861, St. Louis, Mo.
126 Barshaw, John, P. Cos. K and B, Eng.; e. Sept. 28, 1861 Wapello, Iowa.
127 Barkoff, William, P. Cos. K and B, Eng.; e. Sept. 24, 1861, Wapello, Iowa; ad. Wapello, Iowa.
128 Bartholomew, Peter, P. Co. B, 25th; e. June 13, 1861, St. Joseph, Mo.
129 Bartlett, Phin., P. Co. D, 25th; e. July 12, 1861, St. Joseph Mo.
130 Barto, James S., P. Cos. H and D, Eng; e. Sept. 20, 1861, Kentucky, Ill.
131 Bassard, Joseph, P. Cos. L, I and D, Eng.; e. June 5, 1862.
132 Batcheller, James W, Musician, Co. E, 25th; e. Dec. 2, 1861, Oregon, Mo.; ad. 206 S. 17th st., St. Joseph, Mo.
133 Bates, Wm. H., P. Co. C, Eng.; e. Aug. 4, 1861, Prairie City, Ill.; died St. Louis, Mo., Sept. 20, 1861.
134 Banker, Geo. W., P. Co. E, 25th; e. Jan. 5, 1862, Holt Co., Mo.
135 Baucum, James, P. Cos. F, 25th, H and D, Eng.; e. Jan. 11, 1862, Independence, Mo.
136 **BAYNE, GEO. G.**, Lt. Cos. C, 25th and A, Eng.; e. June 16, 1861, St. Joseph, Mo.; ad. Denver, Colo.
137 Bay, Adam, P. Co. B, 25th; e. June 13, 1861, St. Joseph, Mo.
138 Bays, Stewart B., P. Cos. C and B, Eng.; e. Sept. 16, 1861, Avon, Ill.; disch. Nov. 4, 1864; ad. Lewistown, Ill.
139 Beal, Dexter, P. Co. F, Eng.; e. Oct. 18, 1861, Cedar Rapids, Iowa; disch. Aug. 13, 1863, Vicksburg, Miss., dis.
140 Beale, James, Sergt. Co. C, 25th; e. July 12, 1861.
141 Beakey, David C., P. Co. E. Eng.; e. March 2, 1862.
142 Beauchamp, Sanford, P. Cos. G, 25th, L and C, Eng.; e. October 3, 1863, Clinton, Mo.; disch. July 22, 1865.

143 Beauchamp, Thos. J., P. Co. G, 25th; e. Feb. 14, 1862, Clinton, Mo.; disch. July 22, 1865, Louisville, Ky.
144 Bradbury, Geo. W., P. Co. A, 25th; e. June 20, 1861, St. Joseph, Mo.
145 Beck, William, P. Cos. G, 25th, L and E, Eng.; e. June 20, 1861, Wyandotte, Kas.; ad. Argentine, Kas.
146 Beckner, John, P. Co. D, 25th; e. July 19, 1861, St. Joseph, Mo.
147 Bebee, Jeremiah S., P. Cos. C and B, Eng.; e. Aug. 4, 1861, Prairie City, Ill.; disch. Aug. 14, 1864.
148 Beeler, Geo. H., P. Cos. E, 25th, and G, Eng.; e. July 22, 1861, White Cloud, Kas; a pensioner; ad. Logan, Kas.
149 Bebee, Geo. W., P. Cos. H and D, Eng.; e. March 3, 1863, Vermillion, Ill.
150 Beeman, Wm., P. Cos. A and E, Eng.; e. July 20, 1861, St. Louis, Mo.; draws a pension.
151 Behle, Jacob, P. Co. B, 25th, e. June 13, 1861, St. Joseph, Mo.
152 Bell, James M., Cor. Cos. D and F, Eng.; e., Oct. 10, 1861, Olney, Ill.; disch. Oct. 31, 1864; a pensioner; has a small farm: a broom-maker; ad., Olney Ill.
153 Bell, John H., Sergt. Cos. D and F, Eng.; e. Aug. 15, 1861; Olney, Ill.; disch. Aug. 18, 1864; ad. West Plains, Mo.
154 Bays, Frank, P. Cos. C and B, Eng.; e. Aug. 4, 1861; Avon, Ill.
155 **BELL, JOHN A.**, Lieut. Co. H, 25th; e. Aug. 14, 1861; Maryville, Mo.
156 Bell, Wm., P. Co. E, 25th; e. Sept. 22, 1861; Oregon, Ill.
157 Belzer, Richard, P. Co. F, 25th; e. Feb. 21; 1862; St. Catharines, Mo.
158 Beuel, James, Musician (fifer), Cos. C and B, Eng.; e. Aug. 18, 1861; Prairie City, Ill.
159 Benel, Adam, P. Cos. C and B, Eng.; e. Sept. 6, 1861; Prairie City, Ill.; disch. Aug 14, 1864; ad. Prairie City, Ill.
160 Benel, Robert M., P. Cos. C and B, Eng.; e. Sept. 6, 1861; Prairie City, Ill; ad, Moline, Ill.
161 Becket, T. S. S., P. Cos. H, 25th and M, Eng.; ad. Galva, Kas.
162 Benedict, Benj. W., P. Cos. C and B, Eng.; e. Sept. 24, 1863; Pocahontas, Tenn.; ad. Pontiac, Ill.
163 Bender, Peter, P. Cos. L and I, Eng.
164 Bender, David, W., P. Co. H, 25th; e. Aug. 14, 1861, Andrew Co., Mo.
165 Bender, Philip, P. Co. H, 25th and M. Eng.; e. Aug. 14, 1861, Holt Co., Mo.; ad. Maitland, Mo.
166 Benne, Joseph, P. Co. K, Eng.; e. Oct. 5, 1861, New London, Iowa; dead; widow ad. Birmingham, Iowa.
167 Bennie, Andrew, Cor. Co. F. Eng.; e. Sept. 23, 1861.
168 Bennett, Alfred, P. Co. D, 25th; e. July 2, 1861, St. Joseph, Mo.
169 Bennett, Geo D., P. Cos. I and C, Eng.; e. Oct. 1, 1861, Dubuque, Iowa; ad. Dubuque, Iowa.
170 Benson, Christ, P. Cos. L and I, Eng.
171 Benton, Geo. D , P. Co. H, 25th; e. Sept. 1, 1862, Stewartsville, Mo.
172 Berdel, Wendlin, Cor. Cos. C. and B, Eng.; e. Aug. 4, 1861, Prairie City, Ill.; vet. Jan. 18, 1864.
173 **BERGHOFF, JOHN T.**, Sur., 25th; e. June 13, 1861, St. Joseph, Mo. Was born in Germany, immigrated to the United States, reaching Galveston. Tex., April 15, 1846, and October 16, 1846, reached St. Louis, Mo. Having studied pharmacy in Germany, he opened a drug store in 1850, at the same time attending lectures in the Medical Department of the University of St. Louis, graduating March, 1855; serving as assistant in the St. Louis City Hospital for three years. In 1860 he moved to St. Joseph, Mo., and was one of the 400 original Republicans who voted for President Lincoln, and whose names were published in the newspapers that sympathized with the Rebellion. The Secession element greatly preponderated in St. Joseph at that time, and it was not safe to express Republican sentiments. When the war broke out he entered the service of the then called Thirteenth Missouri Infantry, Colonel Everett Peabody. In the battle of Lexington, Mo., he was taken prisoner, September 21, 1861; paroled and sent with the wounded to St. Louis. He was again taken prisoner on his way home by the Quantrell gang, at Centralia, Mo., but showing his parole from General Price, was released. During the fall and winter the Regiment was reorganized as the Twenty-fifth Missouri Infantry, and he again rejoined as Surgeon. On the 6th day of April,

the first day of the battle of Shiloh, he was again taken prisoner, taken to Corinth and placed in charge of the wounded prisoners. While there he was successful in negotiating an agreement (given elsewhere) allowing freedom to the surgeons and wounded. After release he served with the Twenty-fifth until its consolidation with the First Missouri Engineers, his discharge dating January 30, 1864, at Nashville, Tenn. He was afterward commissioned Surgeon of the Eighty-seventh Missouri Enrolled Militia, and in 1865 a Surgeon of the Missouri Militia. He was for two years, 1868 and 1870, coroner of Buchanan county, Mo. In 1868 appointed United States Pension Examining Surgeon, serving until 1884, when the Democratic administration came into power. He has held, since 1879, the chair of professor of surgery in the Northwestern Medical College at St. Joseph, Mo. He lives at No. 215 South Sixth street, St. Joseph, Mo.

174 Bergen, Abe A., P. Cos. A and E, Eng.; e. July 20, 1861, St. Louis; ad. Stone Fort, Ill.
175 Berry, Isaac N., P. Cos. K, D and C, Eng.; e. Sept. 30, 1861, Burlington, Iowa; is a pensioner; ad. South Pueblo, Colo.
176 Berry, John, P. Co. G, 25th; e. Feb. 22, 1862, St. Joseph, Mo.
177 Bertsch, Joseph, P. Co. B, 25th; e. June 13, 1861, St. Joseph, Mo.
178 **BESIER, JOHN** C., Lieut., Cos. H and D, Eng.; e. July 28, 1861, Paris, Ill. *History*—Was in business at Vermillion, Ill., when the war broke out; assisted in raising Companies B and H of the original Missouri Engineer Regiment; was appointed a Sergeant in Company B, and September 15, 1861, First Lieutenant of Company H. On consolidation of the Regiment, was transferred with his Company to Company D, and was mustered out October 31, 1864. He rendered efficient service at the battle of New Madrid, March 14, 1862. The evening before the battle, under special orders from General Pope, he rode from the battle-field to Sikeston, twenty-two miles, in one hundred and thirty minutes, for a supply of shot and shell, returning with it before daylight; went right into the trenches, where he had charge of the ammunition at the left flank magazine; he had started without supper, got no breakfast or dinner the next day, and was complimented in orders by General Pope. He is now in good circumstances; draws a pension; ad. Vermillion, Ill.
179 Bessler, Philip, Sergt. Co. D, 25th; e. Sept. 25, 1862, St. Louis.
180 Best, David, P. Co. E, 25th; e. Jan. 25, 1862, Holt Co., Mo.
181 Bethards, James, P. Co. D, 25th; e. Nov. 11, 1861, St. Joseph, Mo.
182 Beyer, Edward, P. Cos. L and I, Eng.
183 Beyer, Joseph, P. Cos. L and I, Eng.
184 Biggar, Thomas, P. Co. F, Eng.; e. Oct. 10, 1861, Dubuque, Iowa; a pensioner; ad. Nashua, Iowa.
185 Billeter, John, P. Co. B, 25th; e. June 13, 1861, St. Joseph, Mo.
186 Billings, James P., P. Co. H, 25th; e. Aug. 14, 1861, Nodaway Co., Mo.
187 Bills, Jonathan, P. Co. E, Eng.; e. July 13, 1861, Adrian, Mich.
188 **BISSELL, JOSIAH** W., Col. Eng.; e. July 26, 1861, St. Louis; res. June 2, 1863; ad. 12 Globe bldg., St. Paul, Minn. *History*—Colonel Bissell was born at Rochester, N. Y., May 12, 1818; enlisted as a private in one of the companies of the "Home Guard" at St. Louis the day after the firing upon Fort Sumter; elected Second Lieutenant same day, the next day First Lieutenant; a day or two afterward was appointed Quartermaster upon the staff of General Sweeny; soon afterward was appointed Assistant Adjutant-General to same General with rank of Lieutenant-Colonel; about the same time was commissioned Colonel of Tenth Missouri Volunteers, but retained this latter commission merely for the purpose of holding the place for Chester Harding, who was at that time the confidential secretary of the Governor of Missouri, and wished to take the field as soon as the Regiment could be filled up and organized by the Lieutenant-Colonel.
189 **BISSELL, JOSIAH** H., Lt. Co. C, Eng.; e. Nov. 12, 1862; res. June 29, 1863; was a son of Col. J. W. Bissell and acted as Assistant Adjutant; is a prosperous lawyer; No. 52 Major Block, La Salle st., Chicago, Ill.
190 Bissinger, Mathias, P. Cos. K and B, Eng.; e. Sept. 24, 1861, Wapello, Iowa.
191 Bittman, Peter, P. Co. A, 25th; e. Dec. 15th, 1861, St. Joseph, Mo.

192 Bivins, Thomas E., P. Co. C, Eng.; e. Aug. 4, 1861, Prairie City, Ill.; wounded with loss of leg at Farmington, Miss., May 28, 1862; disch. Jefferson Barracks July 28, 1862; is a wagon-maker by trade; carries on a shop at Prairie City, Ill.
193 Bixler, Israel, P. Cos. I and C, Eng.; e. Oct. 5, 1861, Trenton, Iowa; ad. Rogers, Benton Co., Ark.
194 Bixler, Levi, P. Cos. I and C, Eng.; e. Nov. 6, 1861, Trenton, Iowa; ad. Trenton, Iowa.
195 Black, Alex., P. Co. I, 25th; e. Aug. 12, 1861, Gallatin, Mo.
196 Black, John G., P. Co. I, 25th; e. Aug. 3, 1861, Gallatin, Mo.
197 Black, Leroy, P. Cos. I and C, Eng.; e. Sept. 11, 1861, Rushville, Ill.; pensioner; ad. Monroe City, Mo.
198 Black, Samuel, P. Cos. I, 25th, H and D, Eng.; e. Jan. 3, 1861.
199 Black, William, P. Cos. B and K, Eng.; e. Aug. 5, 1861, Paris, Ill.
200 Blackwendt, Chas., P. Cos. G and I, Eng.; e. Sept. 9, 1861, Cape Girardeau, Mo.; pensioner; ad. Cape Girardeau, Mo.
201 Bladen, Ashley, Sergt. Cos. I, 25th, H and D, Eng.; e. July 27, 1861, Victoria, Mo.; vet. Feb. 5, 1864.
202 Blagg, Francis M., P. Co. H, 25th; e. Sept. 13, 1862, Nodaway Co., Mo.; ad. Barnard, Mo.
203 Blagg, Geo. W., Corp. Cos. H, 25th, M and E, Eng.; e. Nov. 10, 1861, Guilford, Mo.; ad. Barnard, Mo.
204 Blanchard, John, P. Co F., Eng.; e. Sept. 14, 1861, Cedar Falls, Iowa; pensioner; ad. Blencoe, Iowa.
205 Blanchard, Geo. A., P. Cos. C and B, Eng.; e. Aug. 12, 1862, Grand Rapids Mich.
206 Blake, Asa W., P. Co. K, 25th; e. Feb. 1, 1862, Hawleyville, Iowa.
207 Blandy, John M., P. Co E, Eng.; e. Nov. 20, 1861.
208 Blanton, Anton, P. Co. G, 25th; e. June 13, 1861, St. Joseph, Mo.
209 Blayney, John M., P. Co. G, 25th; e. Feb. 18, 1862, St. Joseph, Mo.
210 Bledsoe, John, P. Co. E, 25th; e. Jan. 11, 1862, Holt Co., Mo.
211 Bledsoe, Wm., P. Co. E, 25th; e. Jan. 11, 1862, Holt Co., Mo.
212 Bliss, William, P. Co. C, Eng.; e. Sept. 6, 1861, Avon, Ill.; died Jefferson City, Mo., of typhoid fever, Nov. 17, 1861.
213 Blossom, Wm. A., P. Co. F, Eng.; e. Sept. 21, 1861, Chillicothe, Ill.; disch. January, 1863, for loss of thumb coupling cars at Holly Springs, Miss., December, 1862
214 Babington, Jeremiah, P. Co. E, 25th; e. July 21, 1861, Holt Co., Mo.
215 Bock, Christian, P. Cos. G and I, eng.; e. Sept. 13, 1861, Cape Girardeau, Mo.; a pensioner; ad. Cape Girardeau, Mo.
216 Boden, Wilkerson, P. Co. H, 25th; e. Aug. 11, 1861, Nodaway Co., Mo.
217 Bodington, John, P. Co. C, 25th; e. Nov. 28, 1861, St. Joseph, Mo.
218 Boehm, Chas., P. Co. B, 25th; e. June 13, 1861, St. Joseph, Mo.
219 Bolen, Patrick, P. Co. K, 25th, and G, Eng.; e. June 17, 1861, St. Joseph, Mo.
220 Bolin Wm. H., P. Co. B, 25th; e. Feb. 1, 1862, Andrew Co., Mo.
221 Bolton, James, P. Co. G, 25th; e. March 1, 1862, Gentry Co., Mo.
222 Bond Richard A., P. Cos. H and D, Eng., e. Aug. 22, 1861, St. Louis, Mo.; deserted.
223 Bones, Royal M., Cor. Cos C and B, Eng.; e. Sept. 6, 1861, Prairie City, Ill.
224 **BOOK, JOHN C.**, Sur., Eng.; e. Oct 3, 1863, Corinth, Miss., died Stewartsville, Mo., April 16, 1882.
225 Boon, Joseph, P. Cos. H and D, Eng.; e. Sept. 20, 1861, Paris, Ill.; ad. Parsons, Kas.
226 Bosteder, C. C., P. Cos. F, C and B, Eng; e. Sept. 25, 1861, Epworth, Iowa ; pensioner; ad. Laporte, Neb.
227 Boulger, Wm., P. Co. D, 25th; e. July 13, 1861, Nodaway Co., Mo.
228 Bowers, John, P. Co. A, 25th; e. June 30, 1861, St. Joseph, Mo.
229 Bowman, A. J., P. Co. D, 25th; e. Nov. 28, 1861, St. Joseph, Mo.
230 Boyd, Alex. W., P. Co. A, 25th; e. July 28, 1861, St. Joseph, Mo.
231 Boyle, James, P. Co. A, 25th; e. Feb. 15, 1862, St. Joseph, Mo.
232 Boyle, Peter, P. Co. A, 25th; e. June 19, 1861, St. Joseph, Mo.
233 Boyle, Wm., P. Co. C, 25th; e. Dec. 11, 1861, St. Joseph, Mo.
234 Boyles, Jeff., P. Co. I, 25th; e. Aug. 28, 1861, Cameron, Mo

235 Boylan, Martin, P. Cos. C and B, Eng.; e. Sept. 6, 1861, Prairie City, Ill.; pensioner; ad. Swan Creek, Ill
236 Bostwick, —, P Co. —, 25th; ad. Oregon, Mo.
237 **BRACKETT, G. B.**, Capt. Cos. I and C, Eng.; e. Sept. 15, 1861; Denmark, Iowa; pensioner; ad. Denmark, Iowa; is president of Iowa State Horticultural Society.
238 Brakey, David C., P. Co. G, 25th; e. March 20, 1862; St. Joseph, Mo.; ad. St. Catharines, Mo.
239 Bradley, Frank M., P. Cos. I and C, Eng.; e. Sept. 30, 1861; Burlington, Iowa.
240 Bradley, Smith A., P. Co. F, Eng.; e. Aug 28, 1861; Dubuque, Iowa; died February, 1862, at Otterville, Mo., from effects of poison in liquor, at Sedalia, Mo.
241 **BRADSHAW, JAMES T.**, Lieut. Cos. A, 25th, M and E, Eng.; ad. Lebanon, Mo.; a newspaper publisher.
242 Bradshaw, Nelson, P. Co. A, 25th; e. Jan. 1, 1862; St. Joseph, Mo.
243 **BRADSHAW, ROBERT C.**, Capt. Co. A, 25th; e. May. 16, 1861; promoted Col. 44th Mo. Inf. Sept. 26, 1864; ad. St. Joseph, Mo.
244 Bradshaw, Thomas, P. Co. A, 25th; e. Jan. 18, 1862, St. Joseph, Mo.; ad. Holton, Kas.
245 Brainard, Menzo, P. Cos. C and B, Eng.; e. Sept. 6, 1861, Avon, Ill.
246 Brainard, Wm., P. Cos. C and B. Eng.; e. Sept. 6, 1861, Avon, Ill.
247 **BRAMBLE, J. J.**, Lieut. Co. D, 25th; e. June 4, 1861, St. Joseph, Mo.; killed in Battle Shiloh, Apr. 6, 1862.
248 Brandeberry, P. Co. K, Eng.; e. Sept. 4, 1861, Burlington, Iowa.
249 **BRAS, FRANK**, Lt. Cos. B and K, Eng.; e. Sept. 13, 1861, Burlington, Iowa; dead.
250 Bras, Horace T., Corp. Cos. A and E, Eng.; e. July 20, 1861, St. Louis, Mo.; ad. Dexter, Mich.
251 Brasington, Wm. H., Sergt. Cos. D and C, Eng.; e. Aug. 19, 1861, St. Louis, Mo; dead
252 Bray, John R. C., Corp. Cos. D and C, Eng.; e. Sept. 25, 1861. Otterville, Mo.; a pensioner; ad. Mt. Vernon, Ill.
253 **BREY, JULIUS**, Asst. Sur. 25th; e. Mar. 5, 1862; disch. dis. July 23, 1862.
254 Breiner, Louis, P. Cos. C and B. Eng.; e. Aug. 12, 1862, Prairie City, Ill.
255 Breeden, William, P. Co. E, Eng.; e. July 13, 1861, Adrian, Mich.; pensioner; ad. Adrian, Mich.
256 Brennan, Alvin J., P. Co. I, 25th; e. Oct. 5. 1862, Gallatin, Mo.
257 Brennan, Geo. W., P. Co. I. 25th; e. Oct. 16, 1862, Gallatin, Mo.
258 Brennan, Jerry, P. Co G, 25th; e. June 13, 1861, St. Joseph, Mo.
259 Brennan, John, P. Co. G, 25th; e. Aug. 13, 1861, Kansas City, Mo.
260 Brennen, Owen, P. Co. G, 25th; e. Feb. 10, 1862, Kansas City, Mo.
261 Bridges, Jesse D., P. Cos. K, 25th, G and C, Eng.; e. Apr. 15, 1862, St. Joseph, Mo.
262 Bricker, Nelson F., Sergt Co. F, 25th; e. Jan 1, 1862, St. Joseph, Mo.; ad. St. Joseph, Mo
263 Brinkley, Wm. T., P. Co. G, 25th; e. March 1, 1862, Plattsburg, Mo.
264 Brinkhoff, Fred, Sergt. Cos. G and I, Eng.; e. Sept. 13, 1861, Cape Girardeau, Mo.; ad. Cape Girardeau, Mo.
265 Brisbin, Edwin, P. Co. E, 25th.
266 Bristorf, John, P. Co. F, Eng ; e. Aug. 28, 1861, Gilbertville, Iowa; died in Regimental Hospital, Atlanta, Ga., Oct. 1864.
267 Bristow, Geo. W., Sergt. Cos. I and C. Eng.; e. Sept. 15, 1861, Denmark, Iowa. He has been in County Clerk's office, Des Moines county, several years; ad. Des Moines, Iowa.
268 Broderick, Wm., P. Co. B, 25th; e. June 13, 1861, St. Joseph, Mo.
269 Broecker, Bernard, P. Co. G, Eng.; e. Sept. 13, 1861, Cape Girardeau, Mo.
270 Breuning, Fredk., Cor. Cos. G and I, Eng.; e. Sept. 13, 1861, Cape Girardeau, Mo.; pensioner; ad. Cape Girardeau, Mo.
271 Breuning, Louis, P. Cos. G and I, Eng.; e. Sept. 13, 1861, Cape Girardeau, Mo., dead.
272 **BROOKS, JOSHUA P.**, Lt. Cos. D, I, K and E, Eng.; e. Sept. 15, 1861, Denmark, Iowa; dead.
273 Bronght, Chas. G., P. Co. A, 25th; e. June 17, 1861, Holt county, Mo.

274 BROWN, B. F., Lt. Co. E, Eng.; e. August, 1861, Adrian, Mich.; res. Otterville, Mo., Dec. 24, 1861.
275 Brown, Calvin, P. Co. D, 25th; e. Aug. 19, 1861.
276 Brown, Chas. W., P. Co. E. Eng.; e. Aug. 13, 1861, Adrian, Mich.; a pensioner; ad. Carthage, Mo.
277 Brown, David C., P. Cos. D, 25th A and B, Eng.; e. Nov. 30, 1861, St. Joseph, Mo.; veteran, Feb. 1, 1864.
278 Brown, E. F., P. Co. D, 25th; e. Dec. 24, 1861, St. Joseph, Mo.
279 Brown, Frank M., P. Co. F, 25th; e. Jan. 15, 1862, Stewartsville, Mo.
280 BROWN, HILTER W., Lieut. Cos. B and A, Eng.; e. July 28, 1861, Paris, Ill.; ad. Pratt Center, Kas.
281 Brown, James, P. Co. D, 25th; e. July 19, 1861, St. Joseph, Mo.
282 Brown, John D., P. Co. G, 25th; e. Dec. 16, 1861, Wyandotte, Kas.
283 Brown, Marcus L., Cor. Cos. K, 25th, G and C, Eng.; e. Feb. 2, 1862, Hawleyville, Iowa.
284 Brown, Marcus M., P. Cos. F, 25th, H and D, Eng.; e. Nov. 26, 1861, Douglas, Mo.; ad. King City, Mo.
285 Brown, Oliver P., P. Co. E, 25th; e. Feb. 17, 1862, Polk Co., Iowa.
286 Brown, Robert, P. Cos. I and C, Eng.; e. Sept. 15, 1861, Denmark, Iowa.
287 BROWN, STEPHEN S., Lieut. Cos. G, 25th, L and A, Eng.; e. Jan. 23, 1862, Omaha, Neb. *History*—Was born at Schenevus, Otsego County, New York, November 14, 1828; was a delegate to the first Free Soil Convention that nominated Martin Van Buren, which nomination lost New York to the Democrats; defeating General Cass. He afterwards resided in Missouri, Iowa and Nebraska, and was living in St. James, Cedar County, Nebraska, when the war broke out. Considering it his duty to enlist and do his part in saving the Union, he traded his wheat crop for a horse, saddle and bridle; he went first to Sioux City, Iowa, then to Omaha, where he enlisted in Captain Wm. Millar's Company G, Twenty-fifth Missouri Infantry and followed the fortunes of that Regiment to Shiloh; was out with Major Powell and a squad at the front on the evening of the 5th of April, found the enemy at the first house; Major Powell not being satisfied, they returned the same night and about two miles at the front were fired on from the timber while crossing a field; several were killed and wounded, who were brought back to camp, just at sunrise and as the long roll was sounded calling all to arms. Thus the Twenty-fifth Missouri furnished the first victims in the battle of Shiloh. He was promoted to Sergeant for his bravery on the first line of battle, being the last one of the Brigade to fall back, not then until ordered to do so by his superior officer. During the siege of Corinth he was sick with malarial fever, down until the middle of July, and not able for duty until October, 1862. From that time until muster out he was constantly on duty. January 1, 1864, on consolidation with the First Missouri Engineer Regiment, he was promoted from Orderly Sergeant to Second Lieutenant, and to First Lieutenant January 27, 1865. He was absent on furlough at the muster out July 22, 1865, at St. Louis, but returned and was mustered out at St. Louis in August, 1865; is in business at Bath, Ill.; address, Bath, Ill.
288 Brown, Thomas B., P. Cos. I and C, Eng.; e. Sept. 11, 1861, Rushville, Ill.; ad. Industry, Ill.
289 Brown, Thos. H., P. Cos. B and K, Eng.; e. July 28, 1861, Paris, Ill.
290 Brown, Wm. W., Sergt. Co. F, 25th; e. Aug. 14, 1861, Douglas, Mo; ad. Kansas City, Mo.
291 Broyles, Jefferson, P. Cos. I, 25th, H and D. Eng.; e. Aug. 26, 1861, Cameron, Mo.; vet. Feb. 1, 1864.
292 Broyles, Wm., P. Co. H, 25th; e. June 1, 1863, Nodaway Co., Mo.
293 Bruce, James, P. Co. G, 25th; e. June 26, 1861, Leavenworth, Kas.
294 Brummet, Syrene, P. Cos. H, D and C, Eng.; e Aug. 8, 1862, Vermillion, Ill.
295 Brunk, Elijah E., Cor. Cos. I, 25th, H and D, Eng.; e. Dec. 7, 1861, Gallatin, Mo.; vet. Feb. 9, 1864; ad. Linwood, Kas.
296 Brunk, Samuel. Sr., P. Co. I, 25th; e. Aug. 20, 1861, Gallatin, Mo.
297 Brunk, Sam'l, Jr., P. Co. I, 25th; e. Jan. 1, 1862, Gallatin, Mo.
298 Brunk, Wm. C., P. Co. I, 25th, H and D, Eng.; e. Aug. 12, 1861, Gallatin, Mo.
299 Brummett, Andrew, P. Cos. B and K, Eng.; e. Aug. 28, 1861, Paris, Ill.
300 Buch, John, P. Co. G, Eng.; e. Sept. 13, 1861.

301 Buckingham, Geo., Sergt. Co. K, 25th; e. Nov. 11, 1861, Hawleyville, Iowa.
302 Buckingham, John F., P. Cos. K, 25th, G and C, Eng.; e. Feb. 1, 1862, Hawleyville, Iowa.
303 Buckingham, Joseph, P. Co. K, 25th; e. Nov. 29, 1861, Hawleyville, Iowa.
304 Buckley, Jas., P. Cos. D, H and B, Eng.; e. Aug. 15, 1861, St. Louis; dead.
305 Buckley, Michael, P. Cos. L and I, Eng.
306 Buckley, Michael, P. Cos. F, 25th, H and D, Eng.; e. Jan. 28, 1862, St. Catharines, Mo.
307 Budin, Geo., P. Cos. D. 25th, A and B, Eng.; e. July 28, 1862, St. Joseph, Mo.
308 Bull, Geo. T., P. Cos. F, 25th, H and D, Eng.; e. April 14, 1863, St. Catharines, Mo.; ad. Vancouver, Wash. Ter.
309 Burns, Daniel, P. Co. G, 25th; e June 12, 1861, Kansas City, Mo.
310 Burns, Daniel, 2d, P. Co. G, 25th; e. July 10, 1861, Westport, Mo.
311 Burns, Edward, P. Co. G, 25th; e. July 22, 1861, Westport, Mo.
312 Burns, Wm. Mc. K., P. Cos. E, 25th, G and C, Eng.; e. Jan. 2, 1862, Sonora, Mo.
313 Burge, Wm. H., P. Cos. K and F, Eng.; e. Oct. 5, 1861, New London, Iowa.
314 Burget, Aaron J., Sergt. Cos. D and C, Eng.; e. Aug. 15, 1861, Flora, Ill.; ad. Bloomfield, Ind.
315 Burke, John, P. Co. E, Eng; e. Aug. 13, 1861, Adrian, Mich.; ad. Ottawa Lake, Mich.
316 Burnett, John, P. Co. G, 25th; e. Dec. 25, 1861, Wyandotte, Kas.
317 Burr, Stephen O., P. Co. H, 25th; e. Oct 27, 1861.
318 Busey, James, P. Co. E, 25th; e. Jan. 12, 1862, Brown Co. Kas.
319 Busenbark, John, Sergt. Cos. E and D, Eng.; e. Aug. 15, 1861, Adrian, Mich.
320 Bush, Wm. C., P. Cos. C and B, Eng.; e. Aug. 14, 1861, Galesburg, Ill
321 Burtner, Geo. T., P. Cos. H and D, Eng.; e. Oct. 1, 1861, New Goshen, Ind.
322 Burton, Otis H., P. Co. A, 25th; e. July 10, 1861, Rushville, Mo.
323 Burton, St. Clair T., Cor. Cos. D and F, Eng.; e. Aug. 15, 1861, Flora, Ill.; ad. Nineveh, Ind.
324 Butler, Benj., P. Co. H, 25th; e. Nodaway Co., Mo.
325 Butler, Cyrus W., P. Co. C, Eng.; e. Sept. 6, 1861, Prairie City, Ill.; died typhoid fever, Otterville, Mo., Oct. 17, 1861.
326 Butler, Elias, P. Co. D, 25th; e. Feb. 17, 1862, St. Joseph, Mo.
327 Butler, Jas., P. Cos. A and E, Eng.; e. July 20, 1861, St. Louis, Mo.
328 Butler, Oliver P., P. Co. G, 25th; e. July 7, 1861, Savannah, Mo.
329 Butterfield, Jas. L., P. Co. D, 25th; e. July 19, 1861, Andrew Co., Mo.
330 **BUZARD, BENJ.** F, Capt., Cos. F and K, 25th, and H and D, Eng.; e. Aug. 12, 1861, St. Joseph, Mo. *History*—The Captain with others assisted in raising Company F for Colonel Peabody's Battalion at St. Joseph, Missouri and vicinity followed the fortunes of that Company until December 8, 1862, when he was promoted First Lieutenant Company F, Twenty-fifth Missouri, and May 3, 1863, was promoted to Captain of Company K, Twenty-fifth; was transferred to Company H, First Missouri Engineers at the consolidation, January 1, 1864, and when the Regiment was consolidated into a battalion of five companies he was assigned to the captaincy of Company D; was mustered out on expiration of his term of enlistment, at Savannah, Ga., January 4, 1865. During the march to the sea he had charge of one section of the ponton train. Since the war he has been in the West and Texas in the cattle-raising business, and is vice-president and manager of the Neuces Land and Cattle Company. The ranch is near Uvalde, Uvalde County, Texas; is considered wealthy; address St. Joseph, Mo.
331 Buzard, Michael, G., Sergt. Cos. F, 25th, H and D, Eng.; e. Aug. 12, 1861, Oregon, Mo.; disch, July 22, 1865.
332 Buzzell, Joseph, P. Cos. C, 25th, A. Eng.; e. Aug. 1, 1861, St. Joseph, Mo.
333 Byington, John, P. Co. K, 25th, e. April 15, 1862.
334 Bradshaw, Thomas, P. Co. A, 25th; e. Jan. 2, 1862, St Joseph, Mo.
335 Byrd, Harmon, P. Cos. I and C, Eng.; e. Oct. 5, 1861, Trenton, Iowa; ad. Audubon, Iowa.
336 Bronkhorst, John, P. Cos. G and I, Eng.; e. Sept. 13, 1861, Cape Girardeau, Mo; ad. Cape Girardeau, Mo.
337 **BINGHAM, JOHN,** C., Capt. Co. C, Van Horn's Battalion; e. June 27, 1861, not accounted for after Lexington.
338 Cain, Eben H., P. Cos. A and E, Eng.; e, July 20, 1861, St. Louis, Mo.

339 Cahill, John, P. Cos. A and E, Eng.; e. July 20, 1861, St. Louis, Mo.
340 Caldwell, David, P. Cos. E, 25th, G and C, Eng.; e. July 22, 1861, Holt Co., Mo.
341 Caldwell, Francis M., P. Cos. F, 25th, H and D, Eng.; e, May 1, 1863, Chillicothe, Mo.
342 Caldwell, Thomas, P. Cos. C and B, Eng.; e. Sept. 6, 1861, Prairie City, Ill.
343 CAHILL, DANIEL, Lieut. Cos. B, C, Van Horn's Battalion; e. June 27, 1861; not accounted for after Lexington.
344 Call, Thos. C., P. Cos. F, 25th, H and D, Eng.; e, April 4, 1863, Chillicothe, Mo.
345 Callahan, Charles, P. Cos. H and D, Eng ; e, Oct. 15, 1861, Paris, Ill.; dead.
346 Callahan, Dennis, Musician, Cos. A and B, Eng.; e, Oct. 1, 1861, St. Louis, Mo.; ad. 2825 Madison ave., St. Louis, Mo.
347 Callahan, Edward, P. Co. A, 25th; e. June 25, 1861, St. Joseph, Mo.
348 Callicott, John T., P. Cos. K, 25th, G and C, Eng.; e. Sept. 23, 1862, Hawleyville, Iowa.
349 Callicott, Wm. R., P. Cos. K. 25th, G and C, Eng.; e. Oct. 14, 1862, Hawleyville, Iowa.
350 Cambe, Lewis D., P. Co. D, Eng.; e. June 25, 1864.
351 Camp, Fredrick, P. Cos. G and I,Eng.; e. Sept. 13, 1861, Cape Girardeau, Mo. ad. Lebanon, Ill.
352 Campbell, Francis, Cor. Cos. H and D, Eng.; e. Sept. 15, 1861, Terre Haute, Ind.
353 Campbell, Frank, P. Cos. A and E, Eng.; e. July 20, 1861, St. Louis, Mo.
354 Campbell, Hamilton, P. Co. F, Eng.; e. Oct. 9, 1861, Bloomington, Ill.; deserted.
355 Campbell, Henry, P. Co. B, Eng.; e. July 28, 1861, Paris, Ill., ad. Vermillion, Ill.
356 Campbell, Mathew D., P. Co. K, Eng.; e. Nov. 23, 1861, Sedalia, Mo.
357 Canton, Patrick, P. Co. B, Eng ; e. July 28, 1861, Paris, Ill.; pensioner; ad. Soldiers' Home, Dayton, Ohio.
358 Cansy, Peter C., P. Cos. G, 25th, L and E, Eng.; e. July 10, 1861, Kansas City, Mo.; ad. Cansy, Dak.
359 Carback, Henry, P. Co. E. 25th; e. Sept. 21, 1862, Atchison, Mo.
360 Carey, Abel O., P. Co. G, 25th; e. Jan. 6, 1862, Omaha, Neb.
361 Carey, Albert P., P. Co. G, 25th; e. Jan. 6, 1862, Omaha, Neb.
362 CARLIN, JAMES, Lieut. Cos. K and B, Eng.; e. Sept. 10, 1861, Burlington, Iowa; dead.
363 CARLILE, HENRY C., Lieut. Co. C, 25th; e. Feb. 1, 1862, Shelburne, Mo.; disch. Jan. 1, 1864.
364 Carleton, Chester M., Sergt. Cos. D and C, Eng.; e. Aug. 15, 1861, St. Louis, Mo.; a pensioner; ad. Haverhill, N. H.
365 Carolus, Geo., Cor. Co. B, 25th; e. June 13, 1861, St Joseph, Mo.
366 Carr, Charles, P. Co. E, Eng.; e. Aug. 15, 1861, Adrian, Mich.; a pensioner; ad. Soldiers' Home, Dayton, Ohio.
367 Carr, Jas., P. Co. G, 25th; e. June 24,1861, Wyandotte, Kas.
368 Carr, Robert, P. Cos. K, 25th, G, Eng.; e, May 26, 1863.
369 Carriker, Jacob, P. Cos. F, 25th, H and D, Eng.; e. Jan. 27, Bucklin, Mo.; ad. St. Catharines, Mo.
370 Carroll, Dennis, P. Cos. H, D and C, Eng.; e. Feb. 10, 1863, Vermillion, Ill.; a pensioner; ad. St Mary's, Ind.
371 Carroll, Ferdinand, P. Co. G, 25th; e. June 20, 1861, Lexington, Mo.
372 Carroll, John, P. Co. D, 25th; e. July 22, 1861, St. Joseph, Mo.
373 Carroll, John, P. Co. G,25th; e. Jan. 9, 1862, Kansas City, Mo.
374 Carroll, J. J., P. Cos. B and K, Eng.; e. July 28, 1861, Paris, Ill.
375 Carroll, Price L., P. Cos. H, 25th, G, and E, Eng.; e. Aug. 14, 1861, Nodaway Co., Mo.
376 Carroll, Wm. P., P. Co. B, Eng.; e. Sept. 1, 1861.
377 Carroll, Wm. R., P. Co. K. Eng.; e. Sept. 4, 1861, Prairie City, Ill; died in 1887.
378 Carson, Lafayette, P. Cos. A and E, Eng.; e. July 20, 1861, St. Louis, Mo.
379 Carver, Addison, P. Cos. H and D, Eng.; e. Sept. 8, 1861, Paris, Ill; died June, 1862, from wound of foot in action at Farington, Miss., May 28, 1862.

380 Carter, Erastus, P. Co. E, Eng.; e. Aug. 15, 1861, Adrian, Mich.; a pensioner; ad. State Soldiers' Home, Grand Rapids, Mich.
381 Carter, John A., P. Co. H, 25th; e. Mar. 28, 1862.
382 Carter, Philip, P. Cos. D and C, Eng.; e. Oct. 22, 1861, Camden, Ill.; a pensioner; ad. Hannibal, Mo.
383 Carter, G. W., P. Co. C, Eng.; ad. Lester, Kas.
384 Carteron, Edward, P. Co. A, 25th; e. June 19, 1861, St.Joseph, Mo.
385 Case, Aaron, P. Cos. A and E, Eng.; e. July 28, 1861, Paris, Ill.
386 Case, C. C., Sergt. Cos. B and K, Eng.; e. July 28, 1861, Paris, Ill.
387 Case, Pleasant, P. Cos. C, 25th A and B, Eng.; e. Dec. 14, 1861,Harrison Co. Mo.; ad. Ridgeway, Mo.
389 Case, George, P. Co. C, 25th; e. June 28, 1861, St. Joseph, Mo.
390 **CASE, THEODORE**, Lieut. Co. C, Van Horn's Battalion; e. June 28, 1861; promoted Capt. and A. Q. M. Vols. June 9, 1862; appointed Q. M. Gen. of Missouri, Jan. 13, 1865.
391 Casey, George W., P. Co H, 25th; e. July 30, 1862, St. Joseph, Mo.
392 Casey, Hugh, P. Co. H, 25th; e. July 30, 1862, St. Joseph, Mo.
393 Casey, Wm., P. Co. H, 25th; e. Sept. 30, 1862, St. Joseph, Mo.
394 Casey Ivy, P. Co. H, 25th; e. Feb. 11, 1862, St. Joseph, Mo.
395 Cassidy Hugh, P. Co. C, 25th; e. July 5, 1861, St. Joseph, Mo.
396 Cassidy, Wm., P. Co. D, 25th; e. July 12, 1862, St. Joseph, Mo.
397 Cates, Wm., P. Co F, 25th; e. March 7. 1862, Bucklin. Mo.
398 Catois, Clement, P. Cos. F and B , Eng; e. Sept. 28, 1862, Gilbertsville, Iowa; pensioner; ad. Laporte City, Neb.
399 Cavanaugh, John, P. Cos. C and B, Eng; e. Aug. 4, 1861, Prairie City, Ill; pensioner; ad. Macomb, Ill.
400 Cecnhead, John W., Cor. Co. E, Eng.
401 Chamberlain, Ira, P. Cos. H, 25th, M and E. Eng.; e. July 29, 1862, St. Joseph, Mo.
402 Chamberlain, J. J. C., P. Cos. H, 25th, M Eng.; e. Oct. 27, 1861, Stewartsville, Mo.
403 Chamberlain, Philip, P. Cos. C and B, Eng.; e. Aug. 4, 1861, Prairie City, Ill.
404 Chamberlain. Thomas, P. Co. E, Eng.; e. August 15, 1861; Adrian, Mich.
405 Chaplin, Henry, P. Co. F, 25th; e. Dec. 26, 1861; North Salem, Mo.
406 Chapman, Arthur, P. Cos. I and C, Eng.; e. Oct. 15, 1861; Camden, Ill.; dead.
407 Chapman, Geo. C., Sergt. Cos. H and D, Eng.; e. Sept. 15, 1861; Paris, Ill.; a pensioner; ad. Stratford, Mo.
408 Chapman, John H., P., Cos. H and D, Eng.; e. Sept. 15, 1861; Paris, Ill.; a pensioner; ad. Paris, Ill.
409 Chapman, Leonard, P. Cos. I and C; Eng.; e. Sept. 13, 1861; Rushville, Ill.; draws a pension; ad. Pittsburg, Ill.
410 Chapman, Robert P., P. Cos. H and D, Eng.; e. Sept. 13, 1861; Paris, Ill.; ad. Orange, Ill.
411 Chapman, William, P. Co. G, 25th; e. June 27, 1861; Kansas City, Mo.
412 Chapman, Wm., P. Co. I, 25th; e. Jan. 27, 1862.
413 Chapman, Wm. B., P. Co. I, 25th; e. Aug. 25, 1861; Pleasanton, Kas.
414 Chase, Alfred, P. Co. D, 25th; e. Aug. 6, 1862; St Joseph, Mo.
415 Chastian, Joseph F., P. Cos. H, 25th, M and E, Eng.; e. Nov. 24, 1861; Nodaway Co., Mo.; has pension; ad. Decatur, Neb.
416 Chenowith, John M., P Cos. F, 25th, H and D, Eng.; e. Jan. 5, 1863; DeKalb Co., Mo.; ad. St. Joseph, Mo.
417 Chenowith, Wm. M., P. Co. A, 25th; e. July 28, 1861; St. Joseph, Mo.
418 Cherublm, Rudolph, P. Cos. A and E, Eng.; e. July 20, 1861, St. Louis, Mo.
419 Chipman, Geo., P. Co. E. 25th; e. Jan. 10, 1862, Donaphan. Kas.
420 Christ, John, P. Co. B, 25th; e. June 13, 1861, St. Joseph, Mo.
421 Christian, John, P. Co. A, 25th; e. July 9, 1861, Platt Co., Mo.
422 Chronic, Wm. W., musician, Co. B. Eng.; e. July 28, 1861, Paris, Ill.; ad. Scottsville, Kas.
423 Churchill, Henry, P. Co. B, 25th; e. Nov. 1, 1861, St. Joseph, Mo.
424 Clabaugh, David, P. Co. D, Eng.; e. Oct. 17, 1861, Mt. Sterling, Ill.; died Jan. 2, 1862, Otterville, Mo.
425 Claproth, Henry, P. Cos. G and I, Eng.; e. Sept. 13, 1861; Cape Girardeau, pensioned; ad. Cape Girardeau, Mo.

426 Clark, Aaron M., Sergt. Co. D, Eng.; e. Aug. 17, 1861, Carlyle, Ill.; wounded in abdomen and disch. Aug. 2, 1862; dead.
427 Clark, David, P. Co. K, Eng.; e. Sept. 28, 1861, Wapello, Iowa.
428 Clark, John, P. Co. B, Eng.; e. July 28, 1861, Paris, Ill.; ad. Paris, Ill.
429 Clark, John C., P. Co. K, Eng.; e. Sept. 24, 1861, Burlington, Iowa.
430 Clark John W., P. Cos. A and E, Eng.; e. July 26, 1861, St. Louis, Mo.
431 Clark, Levi, P. Cos. G, 25th, L and E, Eng.; e. Dec. 23, 1861, Omaha, Neb.
432 Clark, Morrell, Mus. Cos. I and C. Eng.; e. Oct. 10, 1861, Burlington, Iowa.
433 Clark, M. J. L., P. Cos. B and E, Eng.; e. July 28, 1861, Paris, Ill.; ad. Paris, Ill.
434 Clark, Theodore, P. Co. D, Eng.; e. Aug. 17, 1861, Carlyle, Ill.; disch. Oct. 25, 1862, for defective vision.
435 Clark, Ward A., P. Co D, Eng.; e. Sept. 10, 1861, St. Louis, Mo.; disch. dis. Otterville, Mo., Feb. 6, 1862.
436 Clark, William, P. Co. K, Eng.; e. Sept. 28, 1861, Wapello, Iowa; is pensioned; ad. Wapello, Iowa.
437 Clarke, W. L., P. Co. E, Eng.; e. Aug. 15, 1861, Adrian, Mich.
438 Clary, John, P. Co. C, Eng.; e. Aug. 4, 1861, Prairie City, Ill.
439 **CLAXTON, WM.**, Lieut. Cos. I, 25th, and A, Eng.; e. Nov. 1, 1861, Hannibal, Mo.
440 Claybourne, James, P. Cos. E, 25th, G and C, Eng.; e. Nov. 23, 1861, Holt Co., Mo.; ad. Sidney, Iowa.
441 Claywell, James, Cor. Cos. F, 25th, H and D, Eng.; e. Jan. 13, 1862.
442 Cleary, John, P. Cos. G, 25th, L and E. Eng.; e. Feb. 13, 1862, St. Joseph, Mo.
443 Cleetouet, N. B., P. Cos. F, 25th, H and D, Eng.; e. Oct. 1, 1862, Pleasant View, Mo.
444 Cleinion, Thos. C., Mus. Cos. G, 25th, L and E, Eng.; e. Dec. 26, 1861.
445 Clemens, Anthony, P. Co. E, 25th; e. Feb. 27, 1862, Sidney, Iowa.
446 Clemens, Nicholas, P. Co. E, 25th; e. Jan. 11, 1862, Sidney, Iowa.
447 Clemens, Clinton, P. Co. E, 25th; e. Jan. 16, 1862, Sidney, Iowa.
448 Clemens, Samuel M., P. Co. H, 25th; e. Oct. 6, 1861, Andrew Co., Mo.
449 Clevenger, Shubal V., P. Co. G, 25th; e. May 6, 1863, St. Louis, Mo.
450 Clevenger, Samuel, P. Cos. I, 25th, H and D, Eng.; e. March 17, 1863, Hamilton, Mo.
451 Cline, Charles, Sergt. Co. B, Eng.; e. Jan. 20, 1864; promoted Lieut. June 12, 1865.
452 Clinton, Edward, P. Co. G, 25th; e. June 12, 1861, Kansas City, Mo.
453 Clinton, Geo. W., P. Cos. A and E, Eng.; e. July 20, 1861, St. Louis, Mo.
454 Clinton, M. U., P. Co. B, Eng., e. July 28, 1861, Paris, Ill.
455 Close, Arthur, P. Co. A, 25th; e. Nov. 11, 1861, St. Joseph, Mo.
456 Clymo, Chas., Sergt. Co. C, 25th, e. July 20, 1861, St. Joseph, Mo.
457 Coad, James B., P. Co. K, Eng.; e. Oct. 3, 1861, New London, Iowa; ad. Las Animas, Colo.
458 Coder, Harrison, P. Co. E, 25th; e. Dec. 13, 1861, Atchison, Kas.
459 Coder, Robert, P. Co. E, 25th; e. Mar. 27, 1862, Rockport, Mo.
460 Cochran, Cyrus T., P. Cos. D and F, Eng.; e. Sept. 4, 1861, Flora, Ill.; a pensioner; ad. Xenia, Ill.
461 Cocklin, David, Sergt. Cos. C, 25th, A and B, Eng.; e. Oct. 26, 1861, St. Joseph, Mo.
462 Coffman, Herbert, P. Cos. F, 25th, H and D, Eng.; e. Dec. 16, 1861, North Salem, Mo.
463 Coffman, Pleasant, P. Cos. F, 25th, H and D, Eng.; e. July 22, 1861, North Salem, Mo.; ad. North Salem, Mo.
464 Coffey, John, P. Cos. G, 25th, L and E, Eng.; e. Jan. 6, 1862, Kansas City, Mo.
465 Cole, Tobias, P. Co. B, 25th; e. Nov. 1, 1861, St. Joseph, Mo.
466 Cole, Virgil, P. Co. K, 25th; e. Feb. 20, 1862.
467 Cole, Cornel, P. Co. A, 25th; e. June 25, 1861, St. Joseph, Mo.
468 Cole, Eli, P. Cos. I and C, Eng.; e. Oct. 12, 1861, McGregor, Iowa; ad. San Antonio, Tex.
469 Cole, Joseph, P. Co. C, Eng.; e. Sept. 6, 1861, Prairie City, Ill.; disch. dis. Jan. 13, 1862, St. Louis, Mo.
470 Coleman, Anthony P. Co. C, Eng.; e. Feb. 27, 1862.
471 **COLEMAN, BENJ. F.**, Capt. Cos. E, 25th, G and C, Eng.; e. Dec. 5, 1861, Forest City, Mo.; dead.

472 Coleman, John, P. Co. G, 25th; e. June 17, 1861, Kansas City, Mo.; ad. Soldiers' Home, Leavenworth, Kas.
473 Collary, Patrick, Cor. Cos. E, 25th, G and C, Eng; e. Jan. 4, 1862, Oregon, Mo.
474 Collamer, Philip, P. Co. B, 25th; e. June 13, 1861, St. Joseph, Mo.
475 Collins, B., P. Co. H, Eng.; not accounted for.
476 Collins, Daniel, P. Cos. I and C, Eng.; e. Oct. 8, 1861, McGregor, Iowa.
477 Combs, Geo. W., P. Co. I, 25th; e. Sept. 16, 1861, Gallatin, Mo.
478 Conant, —— P. Co. E, Eng.; e. Aug. 15, 1861, Adrian, Mich.
479 Cone, Augustus S., Cor. Cos. K and D, Eng.; e. Sept. 17, 1861, New London, Iowa; pensioner; ad. Yarmouth, Iowa.
480 Cone, Sam. R., P. Cos. K and D, Eng.; e. Sept. 30, 1861, New London, Iowa; ad. New London, Iowa.
481 Conklin, Joseph D., P. Cos. K and D, Eng.; e. Sept. 25, 1861, New London, Iowa.
482 Conklin, Chas. R. C. P., Sergt. Co. E, 25th; e. July 22, 1861, Forest City, Mo.; ad. Skidmore, Mo.
483 Conklin, Joseph S., Sergt. Cos. A and K, Eng.; e. July 20, 1861, St. Louis, Mo.; a pensioner; ad. Stockton, Kas.
484 Conley, Samuel, P. Cos. H, 25th, M and E, Eng.; e. May 25, 1863, Nodaway Co., Mo.; ad. Barnard, Mo.
485 CONNETT, WM. H., Lieut. Cos. E, K and G, Eng.; e. July 13, 1861, Adrian, Mich.; res. June 2, 1862.
486 Connor, Hugh, P. Co. G, 25th; e. June 13, 1861, Kansas City, Mo.
487 Connor, John, P. Co. K, 25th; e. June 18, 1863, St. Joseph, Mo.
488 Connor, Josiah, P. Co. H, 25th; e. June 25, 1863, Nodaway Co., Mo.
489 Conrad, Peter R., Sergt. Cos. G and I, Eng.; e. Sept. 13, 1861, Cape Girardeau, Mo.; ad. Dolles Mills, Mo.
490 Conroy, Richard, P. Co. G, 25th; e. June 18, 1861, Kansas City, Mo.
491 Conroy, Peter, P. Cos. I, H and D, Eng.; e. Sept. 17, 1861, McGregor, Iowa; deserted April, 1863, at Memphis, Tenn.
492 Cooke, Andrew J., P. Co. E, 25th; e. March 21, 1862, St. Joseph, Mo.
493 Cook, Homer C., P. Cos. I and C, Eng.; e. Sept. 24, 1861, McGregor, Iowa; died, Detroit, Minn., in 1887.
494 Cook, Wm., P. Co. G, 25th; e. June 27, 1861, Kansas City, Mo.
495 Cooley, Hiram, P. Cos. D, G and C, Eng.; e. Sept. 13, 1861, Cape Girardeau, Mo.
496 Cooper, Charles, P. Co. H, 25th; no record further.
497 Cooper, David, P. Cos. C and B, Eng.; e. Aug. 4, 1861, Prairie City, Ill.
498 Cooper, Geo., P. Co. E, 25th; e. Dec. 21, 1861, Holt Co., Mo.
499 Cooper, Jas., P. Co. G, Eng.; e. Sept. 13, 1861, Cape Girardeau, Mo.
500 Cooter, Geo. W., P. Cos. E, 25th, G and C, Eng.; e. Sept. 20, 1862, Leavenworth, Kas.; ad. Medora, Kas.
501 Copp, Chas. S., P. Cos. I and C, Eng.; e. Sept. 15, 1861, Denmark, Iowa; dead.
502 Copp, Henry H., P. Cos. I and C. Eng.; e. Sept. 15, 1861, Denmark, Iowa; ad. Brewster, Neb.
503 Corbet, Eugene, P. Co. C, 25th; e. Aug. 15, 1861, St. Joseph, Mo.
504 Cornell, Caleb, P. Cos. H, 25th, M and E, Eng.; e. March 27, 1863.
505 Cornell, Germain, P. Co. E, Eng.; e. Aug. 15, 1861, Adrian, Mich.
506 Cornell, Harvey, P. Co. E, Eng.; e. Aug. 15, 1861, Adrian, Mich.; dead.
507 CORNELL, JAMES, Lieut. Co. E, 25th; e. Jan. 13, 1862, St. Joseph, Mo.; disch. Dec. 7, 1863.
508 Coruell, Thos., mus. Co. G, 25th; e. Mar. 1, 1862, St. Joseph, Mo.
509 Cornwell, Wm. M., Cor. Cos. K and D, Eng.; e. Sept. 9, 1861, Burlington, Iowa; dead.
510 Cornwell, Wm., P. Co. A, 25th; e. June 17, 1861, St. Joseph, Mo.
511 Couchan, Wm., P. Co. K, 25th; e. June 12, 1862.
512 Court, Geo., P. Cos. K, 25th, M and E, Eng.; e. Feb. 1, 1862, Hawleyville, Iowa; dead.
513 Cowan, Pat., P. Co. G, 25th; e. June 27, 1861, Kansas City, Mo.
514 Cowick, Saml., P. Co. A, 25th; e. June 28, 1861, St. Joseph, Mo.
515 Cox, Fred H., P. Cos. H and D, Eng.; e. Nov. 21, 1861, St. Louis, Mo.
516 Cox, Isam, P. Cos. E, 25th, G and C, Eng.; e. Dec. 21, 1861, Holt Co., Mo.; ad. Shenandoah, Iowa.
517 Cox, Jas. W., P. Cos. E, 25th, G and C, Eng.; e. Dec. 15, 1861, Holt Co., Mo.

518 Cox, John, P. Co. E, 25th; e. Dec. 21, 1861, Holt Co., Mo.
519 Cox, Julius, P. Co. K, Eng.; e. Oct. 3, 1861, New London, Iowa; ad. Merrimack, Iowa.
520 Cox, Robert T., P. Cos. H and D, Eng.; e. Aug. 15, 1861, Flora, Ill.; died Waverly, Tenn., March 4, 1864.
521 Cox, Wm. H. H., P. Cos. D, 25rh, A and B, Eng.; e. Aug. 29, 1862, St. Joseph, Mo.; ad. Shenandoah, Iowa.
522 COY, L. W., Lieut. Cos. F, C and B, Eng.; e. Dec. 7, 1861; St. Louis, Mo.; disch. Oct. 29, 1865; was from New Hampshire; is a prosperous banker, and an officer in a Land and Lumber Co.; ad. Little Rock, Ark.
523 Craig, Alfred, P. Co. F, Eng.; e. Oct. 7, 1861; Cassville, Wis.; was wounded near Johnsonville, Tenn., while taking dispatches to the 16th Wis.; gunshot wound of head, shoulder and leg; has a pension; ad. Webster City, Iowa.
524 Craig, Edwin, Sergt. Cos. E, 25th, G and C, Eng.; e. July 22, 1861, Holt Co., Mo.
525 Craig, John, P. Cos. A and E, Eng.; e. July 20, 1861, St. Louis, Mo.
526 Craig, John W., P. Co. I, 25th; e. Feb. 12, 1862.
527 Craighead, Samuel F., P. Cos. G, 25th, L and E, Eng.; e. April 15, 1863, Harlan, Mo.
528 Craighead, John W., Cor. Co. G, 25th; e. July 28, 1861, Harlan, Mo.
529 Cottman, Wm. F., Sergt. Co. B, Eng.; e. July 28, 1861, Paris, Ill.
530 Crandall, Orrin, Cor. Cos. D and F, Eng.; e. Aug. 19, 1861, St. Louis, Mo.
531 Crawford, Allen, P. Co. C, 25th; e. July 28, 1861, St. Joseph, Mo.
532 Crawford, John, P. Co. A, 25th; e. June 14, 1861, St. Joseph, Mo.
533 Connor, Hugh, 2d, P. Cos. G, 25th, L and E, Eng.; e. Dec. 15, 1861, Kansas City, Mo.
534 Crawford, Joseph, Sergt. Co. E. 25th; e. —— Holt Co., Mo.
535 Crawford, Sam'l, P. Co. A. 25th; e. June 19, 1861, St. Joseph, Mo.
536 Criger, Alfred, P. Co. I, 25th; e. —— unknown.
537 Chilton, Sam'l, P. Co. I, 25th; e. July 25, 1861, Gallatin, Mo.
538 Crites, Harrison S., P. Cos. H, 25th, and M, Eng.; e. Dec. 21, 1861, St. Joseph, Mo.; ad. Durango. Colo.
539 Croll, Jeremiah B., P. Co. K, Eng.; e. Sept. 24, 1861, Wapello, Iowa; draws pension; ad. Wapello, Iowa.
540 Crook, Edwin, Cor. Cos. C and B, Eng.; e. Sept. 6. 1861, Prairie City, Ill.
541 Cross, Wm., P. Cos. A and E, Eng.; e. July 20, 1861, East St. Louis, Mo.; ad. 384 Main st., Memphis, Tenn.
542 Cross, John, P. Co. D, 25th; e. July 18, 1861, St. Joseph, Mo.
543 Crotts, Francis, P. Cos. B and E, Eng.; e. July 20, 1861, St. Louis, Mo.
544 Crouse, Albert, P. Cos. D, F and B, Eng.; e. Aug. 17, 1861; a pensioner; ad. Carlyle, Ill.
545 Crouse, Wm., Cor. Cos. D and F, Eng.; e. Aug. 17, 1861; ad. Carlyle, Ill.
546 Croy, James, P. Co. H, 25th; e. July 28, 1863, Nodaway Co., Mo.
547 Croy, Richard, Cor. Co. D. 25th; no further record.
548 Cuiney, Reuben, P. Cos. I and C, Eng.; e. Sept. 25, 1861, Burlington, Iowa; has pension: ad. Colfax, Wash. Ter.
549 Culner, Joel, P. Co. I, 25th; e. Sept. 21, 1861, Gallatin, Mo.
550 Culp, Melvin. P. Co. B. 25th; e. June 13, 1861, St. Joseph, Mo.
551 CUNNINGHAM, JOHN S., Lieut. Cos H and D, Eng.; e. Sept. 11, 1861, Oskaloosa, Iowa; is a book-keeper; ad. New Brighton. Pa.
552 Cunningham, Jas., P. Cos. A and E, Eng.; e. July 20, 1861, East St. Louis, Mo.
553 Currie, Jas., K., P Co. A, Eng.; e. July 20, 1861, St. Louis, Mo.; killed by Capt. Randolph at Vicksburg, 1863.
554 Curran, John, P. Cos. A and E, Eng.; e. July 20, 1861, East St. Louis, Mo.; ad. Wellsville, Ohio.
555 Curtis, Geo. H., P. Co. I, 25th; e. Aug 20, 1861, Gallatin, Mo.
556 Curtis, John, P. Co. E, 25th; e. July 22, 1861.
557 Curtis, Spencer, P. Co. F, 25th; e. Nov. 23, 1861, De Kalb Co., Mo.
558 Cutter, Wm. L., P. Cos. I and C, Eng.; e. Sept. 15, 1861, Denmark, Iowa; ad. Middle River, Iowa.
559 Cutter, Wm. H., P. Co. A, 25th; e. July 25, 1861. St. Joseph, Mo.
560 Coats, F. M., P. Cos. I and C. Eng., e. ——; ad. White Heath, Ill.
561 Copeland, Wm., P. Co. —, 25th; —— ad. Valisca, Iowa.
562 Daege, Joseph, P. Co. B, 25th; e. June 13, 1861, St. Joseph, Mo.

563 Dahn, James, P. Co. B, 25th; e. June 13, 1861, St. Joseph, Mo.
564 Daiu, Allen T., P. Co. I, 25th; e. March 3, 1862, Gallatin, Mo.
565 Daily, Daniel, P. Cos. A and E, Eng.; e. July 20, 1861, St. Louis, Mo.
566 Daily, John W., P. Co. D, 25th; e. July 16, 1861, St. Joseph, Mo.
567 Dakin, Chas. H., P. Cos. I and C, Eng.; e. Sept. 13, 1861, McGregor, Iowa.
568 Dalby, Henry, Cor. Cos. C, 25th, A and B, Eng.; e. Dec. 31, 1861, Stewartsville, Mo.; is pensioned; ad. Clarksdale, Mo.
569 Dalby, Philip, P. Co. C, 25th; e. Aug. 1, 1861, Stewartsville, Mo.
570 Dalby, Smith, P. Cos. C, 25th, A and B, Eng.; e. Dec. 6, 1861, Stewartsville, Mo.
571 Dalton, James, P. Co. K, 25th; e. Nov. 1, 1861, St. Joseph, Mo.
572 Damm, Casper, P. Cos. G and I, Eng.; e. Sept. 13, 1861, Cape Girardeau, Mo.; on pension roll; ad. Cape Girardeau, Mo.
573 Daniels, Moses, P. Cos., I, 25th, H and D, Eng.; e. Sept. 21, 1861, Gallatin, Mo.
574 Daniels, Azariah, P. Co. I, Eng.; e. Oct. 7, 1861, Burlington, Iowa; dead.
575 Daniels, Robert, P. Cos. H, 25th, M and E, Eng.; e. Sept. 21, 1862, Gallatin, Mo.; vet.
576 Daniels, Wm. S., P. Cos. H, 25th, M and E, Eng.; vet.
577 **DARBY, TIM.** Lieut. Co. D, 25th; e. Aug. 11, 1861, Clinton Co., Mo.; disch Jan. 1, 1864.
578 Daughinbaugh, Eli, P. Co. C, 25th; e. July 12, 1861, St. Joseph, Mo.
579 Daughinbaugh, John, P. Co. C, 25th; e. July, 12, 1861, St. Joseph, Mo.
580 Daugherty, Constantine, Sergt. Cos. K and D, Eng.; e. Sept. 20, 1861, Burlington, Iowa; is a hardware merchant and in good circumstances; a pensioner; ad. Ottumwa, Iowa.
581 **DAUGHERTY, FRANK.** Lieut. Co. A, Eng.; e. Aug. 2, 1861, St. Louis, Mo.; dismissed April 5, 1863.
582 Daugherty, John W., Sergt. Co. F, Eng., e. Sept. 23, 1861, Dubuque, Iowa.
583 Davidson, Chas. B., Sergt. Co. K, 25th; e. July 15, 1861, St. Joseph, Mo.
584 Davidson, C. H., P. Co. H, 25th; e. ——, Nodaway county, Mo.
585 Davidson, Fred W., P. Co. A, 25th; e. June 19, 1861, St. Joseph, Mo.
586 Davy, Atwood, P. Cos. B and C, Eng.; e. Aug. 4, 1861, Prairie City, Ill.
587 Davie, Sylvester, Sergt. Cos. C and B, Eng.; e. Aug. 12, 1861, Prairie City, Ill.
588 Davis, Andrew P., P. Co. C, Eng.; e. Oct. 4, 1864.
589 Davis, Geo. M., P. Cos. B, 25th, L and E, Eng.; e. June 13, 1861, St. Joseph, Mo.; ad. Savannah, Mo.
590 Davis, Jonathan, Sergt. Co. K, Eng.; e. Sept. 10, 1861, Burlington, Iowa.
591 Davis, Josiah P., P. Cos. F and B, Eng; e. Sept. 5, 1861, Monticello, Iowa.
592 Davis, Nathaniel L., P. Co. K, 25th; e. Dec. 15, 1861, Hawleyville, Iowa; ad. Hawleyville, Iowa.
593 Davis, Pleasant, P. Cos. C, 25th, A and B, Eng.; e. Oct. 26, 1861, Worth Co., Mo.
594 Davis, Robert P., P. Cos. B and K, Eng.; e. July 28, 1861, Paris, Ill.; ad. Terre Haute, Ind.
595 Davis, Russell, P. Cos. E, 25th, G and C, Eng.; e. Dec. 24, 1861, Holt Co., Mo.
596 Davis, Stephen, P. Cos. F, 25th, H and D, Eng.; e. March 1, 1862, Stewartsville, Mo.
597 Davis, Wm. L., P. Cos. C, 25th, A and B. Eng.; e. Oct. 26, 1861, Worth Co., Mo.; ad. Frankfort, Mo.
598 Davis, William, P. Cos. B and K, Eng.; e. Aug. 5, 1861, Paris, Ill.; ad. Terre Haute, Ind.
599 Dawson, Chas., P. Co. B, Eng.; e. Sept. 13, 1861, Paris, Ill.
600 Day, John, P. Co. I, 25th; e. Aug. 12, 1861, Grundy Co., Mo.
601 Deal, Stephen F., P. Co. F, 25th; e. Nov. 26, 1861, Island City, Mo.
602 Dean, Lycurgus L., P. Co. A, 25th; e. Dec. 17, 1861, Fremont, Iowa.
603 **DEAN, THADDEUS J.**, Capt. Co. I, Eng.; e. Sept. 13, 1861, West Point, Iowa; res. April 12, 1862; ad. Joseph, Union Co., Ore.
604 Deavers, Elisha, P. Cos. H and D, Eng.; e. Sept. 20, 1861, Paris, Ill.
605 De Bell, R., P. Co. A, 25th; e. June 19, 1861, Atchison, Kas.
606 Decker, Chas., P. Co. H, 25th; e. Aug. 14, 1861, Nodaway Co., Mo.
607 Decomb, Lewis, P. Co. E, Eng.; e. Jan. 4, 1864.
608 Deem, Robert B., P. Cos. B, K and A, Eng.; e. July 28, 1861, Paris, Ill.; has pension; ad. Washburn, Kas.
609 De Hass, Andrew J., P. Cos. C and B, Eng.; e. Sept. 24, 1863, Pocahontas, Tenn.

THE ROSTER. 197

610 Detrick, Jacob, P. Co. F, 25th; e. Dec. 31, 1861, North Salem, Mo.
611 Deaker, James, P. Co. H, 25th; e. Aug. 11, 1861, Nodaway Co., Mo.
612 Delambre, Henry, P. Cos. A and E, Eng.; e. July 20, 1861, St. Louis, Mo.
613 Delancy, John, P. Co. A, 25th; e. June 19, 1861, St. Joseph, Mo.
614 Dellers, Harvey, P. Co. B, 25th; e. June 13, 1861, St. Joseph, Mo
615 De Malloy, Fredk., P. Co. A, 25th; e. July 1, 1861, St. Joseph, Mo.
616 De Mier, Fredk., P. Co. G, Eng., e. Sept. 13, 1861, Cape Girardeau, Mo.
617 Denallen, Fred., P. Co. D, 25th; e. July 1, 1861, Andrew Co., Mo.
618 Dempsey, John, P. Co. B, 25th; e. June 13, 1861.
619 Denny, Joseph, P. Cos. H, 25th, M and E, Eng.; e. Dec. 12, 1861, Nodaway Co., Mo.
620 Dennis, Sanford, P. Co. H, 25th; e. Sept. 25, 1862, Iron Co., Mo.
621 Derrick, Wm., P. Co. F, Eng.; e. Sept. 20, 1861, Bloomington, Ill.; disch. dis. Feb., 1862, Otterville, Mo.; ad. Holden, Ill.
622 Deselms, Ellwood, P. Cos. D, F and B, Eng.; e. Aug. 15, 1861, Flora, Ill., draws a pension; ad. Aid, Wayne Co., Ill.
623 Deselms, John, P. Cos. D, F and B, Eng.; e. Sept. 14, 1861, Flora, Ill., dead.
624 Deskins, Geo. P., P. Co. F, 25th; e. Jan. 10, 1862, North Salem, Mo.
625 Detrick, Andrew, P. Co. F, Eng,; e. Sept. 26, 1861; Bloomington, Ill.; has a pension; ad. Herborn, Ill.
626 Detwiler, Michael, Sergt. Cos. K and D, Eng.; e. Sept. 20, 1861; Wapello, Iowa.
627 Devlin, Pat., P. Cos. K, 25th, G and C, Eng.; e. Nov. 15, 1861, Hawleyville, Iowa; ad. Topeka, Kas.
628 Dewein, John G., P. Cos. K and A, Eng.; e. Sept. 25, 1861; Burlington, Iowa.
629 Dexter, John, P. Co. K, Eng.; e. Sept. 21, 1861, Burlington, Iowa.
630 Dickinson, Albert P., P. Cos. C and B, Eng ; e. Aug. 4, 1861; Paris, Ill.; died Feb. 15, 1864, at Louisville, Ky.
631 Dickinson, Dayton, P. Cos. C and B, Eng., e; Aug. 12, 1861; Paris, Ill.
632 Dickson, Wm., P. Cos. I and C, Eng.; e. Sept. 26, 1861; Hardin, Iowa; ad. Salem, Ore.
633 Dickey, Joseph, P. Co. F, Eng.; e. Aug. 28, 1861; Dubuque, Iowa; is pensioned; disch. August, 1862; ad. Alton, Ill.
634 Dilgert, Adam, P. Co. B, 25th; e. June 13, 1861; St. Joseph, Mo.
635 Dilgert, Ferdinand, P. Co. B, 25th, e. Nov. 1, 1861; St. Joseph, Mo.
636 Dilgert, Martin, P. Co. B, 25th, e. Nov. 1, 1861; St. Joseph, Mo.
637 Dillon, Pat., P. Co. E, Eng ; e. Aug. 15, 1861; Adrian, Mich.
638 Dillman, John, P. Cos. D and F, Eng.; e. Oct. 3. 1861; Flora, Ill.
639 **DILL, HAMILTON, CAPT.** Co. H, 25th; Maj., Eng.; e. Aug. 14, 1861, Marysville, Mo.; disch. Oct 31, 1864 ; dead.
640 Dill, John B., P. Cos. B and K, Eng.; e. July 28, 1861, Paris, Ill.
641 Dilly, John W., Mus. Cos. C and B, Eng. ; e. Aug. 4, 1861, Prairie City, Ill.; disch. Aug. 22, 1862, Jackson, Tenn.
642 Dilly, Thos. A., Sergt. Cos C and B, Eng.; e. Aug. 4, 1861, Prairie City, Ill.; ad. Sterling, Kas.
643 Dilly, Wm. O., P. Cos. H and B, Eng.; e. Aug. 4, 1861, Prairie City, Ill.
644 Dipple, Peter, P. Co. D, Eng.; e. Aug. 17, 1861, Carlyle, Ill.; disch. dis. St. Louis, Mo., May 7, 1863, taken prisoner at Holly Springs, Miss., Dec. 20, 1862.
645 Dischbein, Geo., P. Cos. L, I and D, Eng.
646 Ditch, Daniel, P. Co. D, Eng.; e. Oct. 3, 1861, Flora, Ill.; deserted March 12, 1863, at Memphis, Tenn.
647 Ditmore, Wm., P. Cos. D, 25th, A and B, Eng.; e. Feb. 15, 1862, St. Joseph, Mo.
648 Divinia, Saml., P. Co. D, 25th; e. July 19, 1861, Caldwell, Mo.
650 Dixon, Wilson, P. Co E, 25th; e. Sept. 20, 1862, Independence, Mo.
651 Dolan, John, P. Co. G. 25th; e. Aug. 16, 1861, Kansas City, Mo.
652 Doll, Henry, P. Co. I, 25th; e. Aug. 12, 1861, Palmyra, Mo.
653 Doll, Saml. H., P. Co. A, 25th; e. July 23, 1861, St. Joseph, Mo.
654 Doman, John, P. Co. F, Eng.; e. Oct. 18, 1861, Bloomington, Ill.; ad. Marysville, Kas.
655 Donaldson, Wm. W., P. Co. H, 25th; e. July 29, 1862, St. Joseph, Mo.
656 Donaldson, John M., P. Cos. F, 25th, H and D, Eng.; e. Dec. 13, 1861, Rochester, Mo.; dead.

657 Donavan, Pat., P. Cos. A, 25th, M and E, Eng.; e. May 1, 1863, St. Joseph, Mo.
658 Dony, Saml. C., P. Cos. E, 25th, C and G, Eug.; e. July 22, 1861, White Cloud, Kas.; ad. White Cloud, Kas.
659 Donnell, Elwood O., P. Co. D, Eng.; e. Aug. 2, 1861, Keokuk, Iowa: disch. dis. July 26, 1863, Vicksburg, Miss.
660 **DONNELL, PAT.**, Lieut. Co. E, 25th; e. Sept. 27, 1862; commission revoked Oct. 24, 1862.
661 **DONNELLY, GEO. K.**, Capt. Co. I, 25th; e. July 25, 1861, Kidder, Mo.; resigned July 1, 1862.
662 Dobbins, Leonard, P. Co. I, 25th; e. Aug. 12, 1861, Palmyra, Mo.
663 Dobbins, Thomas, P. Co. E, 25th; e. July 22, 1861, Holt Co., Mo.
664 Dorkins, Andrew J., P. Co. D, 25th; e. July 12, 1861, St. Joseph, Mo.
665 Dodd, John H., P. Co. F, Eng.; e. Oct. 24, 1861, Bloomington, Ill.; dead, killed by accidental discharge of his gun at Holly Springs, Miss., Dec. 2 1862.
666 Doneke, August, P. Co. G, 25th; e., Dec. 27, 1861, Wyandotte, Kas.
667 Dort, John E., P. Co. K, Eng.; e. Sept. 21, 1861, Burlington, Iowa.
668 Doslin, Edw., P. Co. G, 25th; e. June 24, 1861, Kansas City, Mo.
669 Dover, Cyrus W., P. Co. K, Eng.; e. Sept. 23, 1861, New London, Iowa; ad. Dexter, Kas.
670 Downs, Chas. H., P. Co. F, 25th; e. Feb. 21, 1862, Stewartsville, Mo.
671 Downs, Thomas, P. Co. I, Eng.; e. Oct. 24, 1861, Monmouth, Ill.; dead.
672 Doyle, John, P. Cos. F, 25th, C and D, Eng.; e. Dec. 5, 1861, St. Joseph, Mo.
673 Doyle, James, P. Co. I, 25th; e. Feb 2, 1862. ——
674 Drns, Wm., P. Cos., B and K, Eng.; e. July 28, 1861, St. Louis, Mo.
675 Duck, John R., P. Co. C, Eng.; e. Oct. 5, 1864. ——
676 Deuel, Frank M., P. Cos. C and B, Eng.; e. Aug. 4, 1861, Prairie City, Ill.; ad. Keokuk, Iowa.
677 Duey, James, P. Co. E, 25th, G, Eng.; e. ——
678 Duffin, Geo., P. Co. H, 25th; e. ——
679 Dugan, John, P. Co. D, 25th; e. July 13, 1861, St. Joseph, Mo.
680 Duke, Mahlon, P. Cos. D and F. Eng.; e. Sept. 14, 1861, Flora, Ill.; ad. Rinard, Ill.; dis. July 26, 1863.
681 Dunbar, Nathan R., Sergt. Cos. B and K, Eng.; e. July 28, 1861, Paris, Ill.; draws a pension; ad. Paris, Ill.
682 Dunbar, J., P. Co. B, Eng.; e. July 28, 1861, Paris, Ill.; ad. same.
683 Duncan, John, P. Co. D, 25th; e. July 19, 1861, Caldwell Co., Mo.
684 Duncan, Josephus, P. Co. F, Eng.; e. Oct. 3, 1861, Cassville, Wis.; disch. Feb. 1863, at Memphis, Tenn., for injury to arms and right side, received in a railroad accident at Jackson, Tenn., Oct. 4, 1862 ; ad. Le Mars, Iowa.
685 Dunsford, Charles, Hospital Steward, Eng.; e. Feb. 15, 1861; died in Christman, Ill., 1878.
686 Dunlap, Albert, P. Co. A, 25th; e. June 14, 1861, St. Joseph, Mo.; ad. Kent, Iowa
687 **DUNLAP, THOS. A.**, Lieut. Co. D, 25th; e. July 26, 1861, St. Joseph, Mo.; dead, killed in battle of Shiloh April 6, 1862.
688 **DUNN, JAMES**, Capt. Cos. C, 25th and A, Eng.; e. July 22, 1861, St. Joseph, Mo.; ad. City Hall, St. Louis, Mo.
689 Dunn, Tim, P. Co. A, 25th; e. June 16, 1861, St. Joseph, Mo.
690 Dunn, Wm., P. Co. I, 25th, H and D, Eng.; e. Dec. 1, 1862, Pocahontas, Ark.
691 Dunn, Wm. R., P. Co. G, 25th; e. Feb 1, 1862, Omaha, Neb.
692 Dunning, Chas. W., P. Co. I, 25th; e. Jan. 2, 1862. ——
693 Durant, Washington, P. Co. C, 25th; e. July 1, 1861.
694 Durr, Pat., P. Co. H, Eng.; e. July 20, 1861, St. Louis, Mo.
695 Duval, Chas, Sergt. Co. C, 25th; e. July 5, 1861. ——
696 Duyer, Nicholas, P. Cos. A and E, Eng.; e. July 20, 1861, St. Louis, Mo.
697 Duyer, Wm., P. Co. G, 25th; e. June 15, 1861, Kansas City, Mo.
698 Drinker, Chas., Cor. Co. C, 25th; e. June 20, 1861, St. Joseph, Mo.
699 Devers, Wm., P. Cos. B, K and A, Eng.; e. July 28, 1861, Paris, Ill.; draws a pension; ad. Bement, Ill.
700 Dolin, Pat., P. Co. A, Eng.; e. July 20, 1861; ad. Topeka, Kas.
701 Doncy, James, P. Co. E, 25th; e. July 22, 1861, White Cloud, Kas.

702 Dotson, Wm., Corp. Cos. B and F, Eng.; e. July 28, 1861, Paris, Ill.; is a pensioner; ad. Columbia, Ill.
703 Eagan, Israel, P. Cos. A and E, Eng.; e. July 20, 1861, St. Louis, Mo.
704 Eagan, John, P. Co. G, 25th; e. Jan. 7, 1862. Omaha, Neb.
705 Eakley, Max, P. Cos. A, 25th, M and E, Eng.; e. June 28, 1861, St. Joseph, Mo.
706 Eastman, Albert, P. Co. D, Eng.; e. Oct. 26, 1861, Rushville, Ill.; died, Jackson, Tenn., Sept. 25, 1862, of consumption.
707 Eaton, John, P. Cos. F, 25th, H and D, Eng.; e. April 11, 1863, Independence, Mo.
708 Eaton, Newton, P. Cos. F, 25th, H and D, Eng.; e. Sept. 1, 1862, Independence, Mo.
709 Ebenbarger, Fredk., P. Cos. D and F, Eng.; e. Sept. 15, 1861, St. Louis, Mo.; is a pensioner; ad. Louisiana, Mo.
710 Eberle Henry, ——— e. June 13, 1861, St. Joseph, Mo.
711 Ebersoll, Silas, P. Co. I, 25th; e. Sept. 17, 1861, Pleasant View, Mo.
712 Ecord, Harrison, P. Cos. D, 25th, A and B, Eng.; e. July 21, 1862, Davis Co., Mo.
713 Echtle, Francis H., P. Co. B, 25th; e. June 13, 1861, St. Joseph, Mo.
714 Edinger, John H., P. Cos. D and F, Eng.; e. Aug. 17, 1861, Greenville, Ill.
715 **EDINGER, M. D.**, Lieut. Cos. E, D and F, Eng.; e. Aug. 15, 1861. ———
716 Edon, John, P. Cos. L and I, Eng; e. ———
717 Edwards, John, P. Co. C, 25th; e. July 21, 1861; ———
718 Eggeman, Henry, P. Cos. G, I and D, Eng.; e. Nov, 9, 1862; Cape Girardeau, Mo.; a pensioner; ad. Cape Girardeau, Mo.
719 Eggeman, John, P. Cos. I and G, Eng.; e. Sept. 13, 1861; Cape Girardeau, Mo.; ad. same.
720 **EGGLESTON, JOHN Q.**. Assist. Surg. 25th; e. Sept. 20, 1862; disch. Jan. 1, 1864; is a medical attendant at the Insane Asylum, Olathe, Kas.
721 Ellingsworth, Jas. R., P. Cos. F, 25th, H and D, Eng.; e. Feb. 20, 1862; Stewartsville, Mo.
722 Elliott, Jesse, P. Co. A, 25th, M and E, Eng.; e. Dec. 5, 1862; ad. Barnard, Mo.
723 Elliott, John, P. Cos. H and D, Eng.; e. Sept, 15, 1861; Annapolis, Ill.; draws a pension; ad. Annapolis, Ill.
724 Elliott, John, P. Co. H, 25th; e. Sept. 3, 1861; Nodaway Co., Mo.
725 Ellis, Jasper, P. Co. F, 25th; e. Feb. 16, 1862; Stewartsville, Mo.
726 Ellwood, Wm., P. Cos. C and B, Eng.; e. Aug. 4, 1861; Prairie City, Ill.; vet. Jan. 23, 1864.
727 Ellsworth, Henry, P. Cos. H, 25th, M and E; Eng.; e. July 19, 1861; St. Joseph, Mo.
728 English, Andrew J., P. Co. D, 25th; e. July 19, 1861; St. Joseph, Mo.
729 English, Henry, P. Co. G, 25th; e. Aug. 25, 1861; Harrisonville, Mo.
730 Ennis, Peter, P. Cos. A and E, Eng ; e. July 20, 1861; St. Louis, Mo.
731 Espinosa, Josie, P. Co. G, 25th; e. June 19, 1861, Santa Fe, N. M.
732 Esteps, Rudolph, P. Co. A, 25th; e. July 1, 1861, St. Joseph, Mo.
733 Estel, Martin A., P. Cos. D and F, Eng.; e. Aug. 15, 1861, St. Louis, Mo.
734 Estes, Henry, P. Cos. I, 25th, H and D, Eng.; e. Feb. 26, 1862, St. Joseph, Mo..
735 Estes, John T., P. Co. D, 25th; e. July 12, 1861, St. Joseph, Mo.
736 Euler, Mathias, Sergt. Co. B, 25th; e. June 13, 1861, St. Joseph, Mo.; killed in battle of Shiloh, April 6, 1862; color bearer.
737 Eulig, John, P. Co. B, 25th; e. June 13, 1861, St. Joseph, Mo.
738 Eustace, James, P. Co. K, 25th; e. Oct. 7, 1861, Kansas City, Mo.
739 Evans, James H., P. Co. A, 25th; e. June 20, 1861, St. Joseph, Mo.
740 Evans, John B., Cor. Cos. D and C, Eng.; e. Oct. 9, 1861, St. Louis, Mo.; ad. Evans, Weld Co., Col.
741 Evans, Joseph, P. Co. C, 25th; e. Nov. 4, 1862, Arkansas, Mo.
742 Evans, Levi, K., P. Co. F, Eng.; e. Sept. 12. 1861, Dubuque, Iowa.
743 **EVANS, SIMON S.**, Capt. Co. E, 25th; e. July 22, 1861, Oregon, Mo.; died Jan. 17, 1863.
744 Everett, Josiah, P. Co. K, Eng.; e. Sept. 16, 1861, Rushville, Ill.; died at Roseville, Ill., in 1887.
745 Everett, Wm., P. Cos. H and D, Eng.; e. Sept. 16, 1861, Shelbyville, Ill.; pensioned; ad. Millersville, Ill.

746 Eyles, John T., Sergt. Co. F, Eng.; e. Sept. 1, 1861, St. Louis, Mo.; dead.
747 Ewing, Andrew J., P. Cos. B, K and A, Eng.; e. July 28, 1861; vet. Jan., 1864; a pensioner; ad. Hutsonville, Ill.
748 Edwards, Samuel, P. Co. E, 25th; e. Dec. 21, 1861, Holt Co., Mo.
749 Faley, Patrick, P. Co. A, 25th; e. June 14, 1861, St. Joseph, Mo.
750 Fallon, Hugh, P. Co. G, 25th; e Feb. 9, 1862, St. Joseph, Mo.
751 Fanner, Andrew, P. Co. E, 25th; e. Jan. 5, 1862, Holt Co., Mo.
752 Fanner, Elijah, P. Co. E, 25th; e. Jan. 25, 1862, Forrest City, Mo.
753 Farmer, James II., P. Co. E, 25th; e. Feb. 16, 1862, Fremont, Iowa.
754 Farnsworth, Horace, P. Cos. I and C, Eng.; e. Sept. 16, 1861, Denmark, Iowa; died in 1887, in Nebraska.
755 Furris, Charles, P. Co. D, 25th; e. July 12, 1861, St. Joseph, Mo.
756 Fassold, John, P. Cos. G and I, Eng.; e. Sept. 13, 1861, Cape Girardeau, Mo.
757 Fay, George, P. Cos. I and C, Eng.; e. Sept. 16, 1861, McGregor, Iowa.
758 Ferrell, Frank, P. Cos. C and B, Eng.; e. Aug. 4, 1861, Prairie City, Ill.; ad. Monmouth, Ill.
759 Fesler, John, P. Co. A, Eng.; ———
760 Feuerbach, Henry, P. Cos. A and E, Eng.; e. July 20, 1861, St. Louis, Mo. He entered the service from patriotic motives, serving first in a three-months Missouri regiment, was taken prisoner, escaped, and returned as stated elsewhere in this History. He is a prosperous contractor and builder in good circumstances at 2550 Grand ave., St. Louis, Mo.
761 Fields, Alex., P. Cos. F, 25th; H and D, Eng.; e. May 1, 1863, Richmond, Mo.
762 Fields, Francis M., P. Co. F, 25th; e. Sept. 21, 1862, Richmond, Mo.
763 Fife, David, P. Cos. II., 25th; M and E; e. Dec. 1, 1862, St. Joseph, Mo.
764 Fife, David, Wagoner, Co. I, 25th; e. Dec. 10, 1862, Plattsmouth, Neb.
765 Fike, Isaac, Sergt. Co. D, 25th; e. Aug. 6, 1861, St. Joseph, Mo.; ad. Hopkins, Mo.
766 Finch, John, P. Co. E, Eng.; e. Aug. 15, 1861, Adrian, Mich.
767 Findese, Adam, P. Cos. L and I, Eng., e. ———
768 Findlay, J. W., P. Co. F, 25th; e. Aug. 26, 1862, Rochester, Mo.
769 Findlay, Henry D., P. Co. F, 25th; e. Jan. 4, 1862, Rochester, Mo.
770 Findlay, Saml. W., P. Co. A, 25th; e. July 28, 1861, Andrew Co., Mo.; ad. Browning, Linn Co., Mo.
771 Finn, Lewis H., P. Co. A, 25th; e. June 18, 1861, St. Joseph, Mo.
772 Fischer, John, P. Cos. L and I, Eng.; e. ———
773 Fisher, Daniel F., Sergt. Cos. I and C, Eng.; e. Sept. 16, 1861, Denmark, Iowa; ad. Fairfield, Neb.
774 Fisher, Geo., Cor. Cos. A and E, Eng.; e. Aug. 13, 1861, Cape Girardeau, Mo.; ad. the same.
775 Fisher, John, P. Cos. II, D and C, Eng.; e. Aug. 28, 1862, Sandford, Ind.
776 Fitzgerald, Edward, P. Co. G, 25th; e. Feb. 19, 1862, St. Joseph, Mo.
777 Fitzgerald, John, P. Co. D, Eng.; e. Sept. 2, 1861, St. Louis, Mo.; disch. dis. Aug. 22, 1862, St. Louis, Mo.
778 Fitzgerald, John, P. Co. G, 25th; e. July 13, 1861, Kansas City, Mo.
779 Fitzgerald, Wm., P. Cos. A and E, Eng; e. July 20, 1861, St. Louis, Mo.
780 Fitzhugh, Thomas, P. Cos. E, 25th, G and C, Eng.; e. Jan. 12, 1862, White Cloud, Kas.; ad. Kansas City, Mo.
781 Flaherty, John, P. Cos. F and B, Eng.; e. Sept. 17, 1861, Elkport, Iowa; vet. Dec. 30, 1863.
782 FLAD, HENRY, Capt. Co. B, Maj. Lt.-Col. and Col. Eng.; e. July 26, 1861, St. Louis, Mo. He was a civil engineer previous to the war; was employed by the Government as topographical engineer before he was appointed Captain of Co. B. Since the War he has been mostly engaged as Engineer of Public Works at St. Louis; was Chief Engineer and Director in building the great St. Louis steel bridge across the Mississippi River; is now Superintendent of Public Works for St. Louis; is in good circumstances; ad. City Hall, St. Louis, Mo.
783 Flanagan, Wm., P. Cos. C and B, Eng.; e. Sept, 6, 1861, Prairie City, Ill.; vet. Jan. 7, 1864.
784 Flatt, John, P. Co. II, 25th; e. Feb. 18, 1862, St. Joseph, Mo.
785 Fletcher, Thos., P. Co. E, 25th; e. ——— Forest City, Mo.
786 Flint, Nathaniel B., P. Co. A, Eng.; e. July 20, 1861, St. Louis, Mo.

THE ROSTER.   201

787 Flint, Thos. H., P. Cos. B and C, Eng.; e. July 28, 1861, Paris, Ill.; ad. Paris, Ill.
788 Flynn, Peter, P. Cos. G, 25th, and L, Eng.; e. Aug. 13, 1861, Kansas City, Mo.; ad. 324 Cherry st., Scranton, Pa.
789 Foley, Peter, P. Co. G, 25th; e. July 8, 1861, Weston, Mo.
790 **FOLSOM, DE WITT C.**, Capt. Co. C, Eng.; e. Aug. 4, 1861, Prairie City, Ill.; res. Jan. 4, 1862.
791 Folsom, Isaac Y., Sergt. Cos. C and D; e. Aug. 8, 1861, Prairie City, Ill.; courtmartialed and dishonorably disch. July, 1862.
792 Fool, James, P. Cos. B and K, Eng.; e. July 28, 1861, Paris, Ill.
793 Forbes, Daniel, P. Cos. A and I, Eng.; e, July 20, 1861, St. Louis, Mo.
794 Forbes, Milt., P. Co. F, 25th; e. Oct. 23, 1862, North Salem, Mo.
795 Foreacre, Andrew J., P. Cos. H, D and C, Eng.; e. Aug. 12, 1862, Sandford, Ind.; has a pension; ad. Sandford, Ind.
796 Forshea, John T., P. Cos. C and B. Eng.; e. Aug. 4, 1861, Avon, Ill.; pensioner; ad. Pekin, Ill.
797 Foster, Fenner, Cor. Cos. I and C, Eng.; e. Sept. 23, 1861, Toolsboro, Iowa; ad Cape Horn, Washington Ter.
798 Foster, Fred., P. Cos. L and I, Eng.; e. ———
799 Foster, John T., P. Co. H, 25th; e. Oct. 27, 1861, Nodaway Co., Mo.
800 Foster, James, P. Co. ———; ad. Sutton, Neb.
800 Fowler, Linden, Cor. Cos. A and E, Eng; e. July 20, 1861, Payson, Ill.
802 Fox, Martin H., P. Cos. H, 25th, M and E, Eng.; e. Aug. 2, 1862, Nodaway Co., Mo.
803 Fox, David, P. Co. H, 25th; e. Oct. 25, 1862, Nodaway Co., Mo.
804 Fox, Fountain, P. Cos. B, K and A, Eng.; e. July 28, 1861, Paris, Ill.; is a farmer in good circumstances; ad. Farmersburg, Ind.
805 Fox, Jared P., Co. H, 25th; e. Oct. 2, 1861, Nodaway Co., Mo.; ad. Hamilton, Mo.
806 Fox, Michael, P. Cos. F, 25th, H and D, Eng.; e. Nov. 30, 1861, St. Joseph, Mo.
807 Fox, Sam'l, P. Co. F, 25th; e. June 2, 1862, Bucklin, Mo.
808 Fagin, Milton, P. Cos. B and C, Eng.; e. July 28, 1861, Paris, Ill.
809 Frairy, Pat., P. Co. D, Eng., e. Aug.16, 1861, St. Louis, Mo.; died Nov.24,1862, in Hospital No. 3, Jackson, Tenn.
810 Franly, Pat., P. Co. H, 25th; e. ———, Nodaway Co., Mo.
811 **FRAUDE, MAX**, Lt. Co. L, Eng.; e. June 10, 1863, disch. Jan. 1, 1864 ; he had been with the Co. when it was in the 35th Missouri.
812 Frazier, McDaniel, P. Cos. A and E, Eng.; e. Aug. 5, 1861, St. Louis, Mo.
813 Frazier, Henry, P. Co. A, 25th; e. June 14, 1861, St. Joseph, Mo.
814 Frazier, Milt., P. Co. B, Eng.; e. July 28, 1861, Paris, Ill.; ad Ashmore, Ill.
815 Frazier, Wm. M., P. Cos. A and E, Eng.; e. July 20, 1861, St. Louis, Mo.; ad. 329 Ewing av. St. Louis, Mo.
816 Freeman, Milton, P. Co. C, 25th; e. ———
817 Frederick, Ephraim, P. Co. I. Eng.; e. Sept. 30, 1861, Burlington, Iowa; dead.
818 French, Jacob W., P. Co. F, Eng.; e. Sept. 23, 1861, Dubuque, Iowa.
819 Frich, Christian, P. Co. B, 25th; e. June 13, 1861, St. Joseph, Mo.
820 Fry, Henry, P. Co. B, 25th; e. June 13, 1861, St. Joseph, Mo.
821 Fry, L. W., P. Cos. B and K, Eng.; e. July 28, 1861, Paris, Ill.
822 Fudge, Henry, P. Co. H, Eng.; ———; died ———
823 Fudgetty, ———, P. Co. H, Eng.; e. Aug. 17, 1862, Vermillion, Ill.
824 Fuller, Francis, P. Cos. C, 25th, A and B, Eng.; e. Jan. 4, 1861, Savannah, Mo.
825 Fullerton, Calvin, P. Cos. C and B, Eng.; e. Sept. 6, 1862, Prairie City, Ill.
826 Fulton, Wm., P. Cos. H, D and C, Eng ; e. Aug. 25, 1862, Bloomfield, Ill.
827 Fuqua, Josiah, P. Cos. H, D and C, Eng.; e. Aug. 25, 1862, Sanford, Ind.
828 Fuqua, Marshal T., P. Cos. H, D and C, Eng.; e. Aug. 12, 1861, Sanford, Ind.; draws a pension; ad. Sanford, Ind.
829 Ferguson, Thos. J., P. Co. I, 25th; e. July 25, 1861, Gallatin, Mo.
830 Gallagher, Manus, P. Cos. H and D, Eng.; e. Sept. 18, 1861, Terre Haute, Ind.
831 Gallatine, Joseph, P. Cos. G and I, Eng., e. Sept. 13, 1861, Cape Girardeau, Mo.
832 Galpin, Joseph, P. Co. I, 25th; e. July 25, 1862, Gallatin, Mo.; ad. Soldiers' Home, Leavenworth, Kas.

833 Galpin, Newton, P. Co. I, 25th; e. Jan. 25, 1862. Gallatin, Mo.
834 Gamble, Jas., Wagoner Cos. F, 25th, H and D, Eng.; e. Jan. 23, 1862, Holland, Kas.; ad. St. Joseph, Mo.
836 Ganser, Richard, P. Cos. G, I and D, Eng.; e. Sept. 13, 1861; Cape Girardeau, Mo., vet.
837 Ganz, Wm., P. Co. K, Eng.; e. Sept. 17, 1861, Burlington, Iowa; dead.
838 Garber, John, P. Co. C, Eng.; e. Oct. 4, 1864, Brazil, Ind.; ad. Brazil, Ind.
839 Gardner, Geo K., P. Co. K, Eng.; e. Mar. 17, 1862, St. Joseph, Mo., pensioner; ad. Nodena, Ark.
840 Gardner, Louis B., P. Co. F, Eng.; e. Oct. 11, 1861, Dubuque, Iowa; ad. Rockville, Wis.
841 Gardner, Robert, P. Cos. A and E; e. July 20, 1861, St. Charles, Mo.
842 Garns, Gottfried, P. Cos. G and I, Eng.; e. Sept. 13, 1861, Cape Girardeau, Mo.; ad. same.
843 Garrity, Francis, P. Co. A, 25th; e. July 14, 1861; St. Joseph, Mo.
844 Gasper, Casper, P. Co. B, 25th; e. June 13, 1861, St. Joseph, Mo.
845 GAST, PAULUS, Lieut. Cos. G and I, Eng.; e. Sept. 13, 1861; St. Louis, Mo.; disch. Sept. 29, 1864. He is a prosperous and well-to-do merchant and winegrower; is Superintendent and Manager of the Gast Wine Co., northeast corner of Market and Third streets, (225 Market), St. Louis, Mo.
846 Gates, Fred, P. Cos. C, 25th, A and B, Eng.; e. July 15, 1861; St. Joseph, Mo.
847 Gates, Norman, P. Cos. C. 25th, A and B, Eng.; e. Oct. 26, 1861, St. Joseph, Mo.
848 Garrison, Levi B., P. Co. F, 25th; e. Oct. 23, 1862, Macon, Mo.
849 Gayhart, Peter, Mus. Co. D, 25th; A and B, Eng.; e. April 10, 1863.
850 Gehagan, Thos. H., P. Co. G, 25th; e. July 16, 1861, Leavenworth, Kas.
851 Gele, May, P. Co. B., 25th; e. March 19, 1862; ——— St. Joseph, Mo.
852 Gentles, Wm., P. Cos. G. 25th, H and E, Eng.; e. March 19, 1862; ———.
853 Gentry, Jas. H., P. Co. H, 25th; e. Sept. 3, 1862, Nodaway Co., Mo.
854 George, Henry D., P. Co. K, Eng.; e. Sept. 10, 1861, Burlington, Iowa.
855 George, James D., P. Co. A, 25th; e. Oct. 10, 1862, Patterson, Mo.
856 Gerschwiler, Anthony, P. Cos. G and I, Eng.; e. Sept. 13, 1861, Cape Girardeau, Mo.
857 Gerschwiler, Casper, P. Cos. G and I, Eng.; e. Oct. 10, 1861, Cape Girardeau, Mo.
858 Gerding, Geo., P. Co. B, 25th; e. June 13, 1861, St. Joseph, Mo.
859 Gibson, James, P. Cos. F, 25th, H and D, Eng.; e. June 13, 1861, Stewartsville, Mo.; ad. Clarinda, Iowa.
860 Gilbel, Henry, P. Co. I, 25th; ———.
861 Gilbert, Geo. L., P. Cos. I and C, Eng.; e. Sept. 16, 1861, McGregor, Iowa.
862 Gilbert, Henry R., P. Cos. H and D, Eng.; e. March 22, 1862, Grafton, Ill.; dead.
863 Gilbert, John W., P. Cos. H and D, Eng.; e. Oct. 21, 1861, St. Louis, Mo.; deserted.
864 Gilchrist, Lawrence, P. Co. G, 25th; L and E, Eng.; e. Jan. 11, 1862, Independence, Mo.
865 Gilchrist, Chas., Sergt. Co. E, 25th; e. July 22, 1861, Independence, Mo.
866 Gill, Wm., P. Co. G, 25th; e. June 17, 1861, Kansas City, Mo.
867 Gillen, John, Sergt. Cos. G, 25th; A and B, Eng.; e. Oct. 20, 1862, St. Louis, Mo.
868 Gillen, John, P. Co. C, 25th; e. June 20, 1861, Kansas City, Mo.
869 Gillen, Peter, P. Co, F, 25th; e. June 23, 1862, St. Joseph, Mo.
870 Gillespie, Chas., P. Cos. K and D, Eng.; e. Sept. 15, 1861, Burlington, Iowa;
871 Gilley, Michael, P. Cos. F and B, Eng.; e. Aug. 28, 1861, Gilbertville, Iowa; vet.; ad. Waterloo, Iowa.
872 Gillies, John, P. Cos. A and B, Eng.; e. Sept. 13, 1861, Cape Girardeau, Mo.
873 Gillett, Doc, P. Co. E, Eng.; e. Aug. 15, 1861, Adrian, Mich.
874 Gillett, Phillip, P. Co. A, 25th; e. June 28, 1861, St. Joseph, Mo.
875 GISEKE, HERMAN, Lt. Cos. B, 25th; L, Eng.; e. June 13, 1861, St. Joseph, Mo.; dead.
876 Gitten, John, P. Co. G, 25th; e. June 26, 1861, Kansas City, Mo.
877 Given, J. A., P. Cos. B and K, Eng.; e. July 28, 1861, Paris, Ill.

878 **GLENN, ADDISON N.**, Lt. Cos. H, 25th, and M, Eng.; e. Dec. 11, 1861, Whig Valley, Mo. *History*—Lieutenant Glenn was born in Gallia County, Ohio, September 16, 1839; enlisted as a private; was promoted to fifth Sergeant, September 1, 1862; to second Lieutenant, May 4, 1863; to first Lieutenant Company M, Engineers, January 1, 1864; was discharged when the Regiment was consolidated into five companies, October 31, 1864, at Atlanta, Ga.; was with the companies in all the duties and engagements up to his muster out; ad. Du Bois, Nebraska.
879 Glick, Fred, P. Co. B, 25th; e. June 13, 1861. St. Joseph, Mo.
880 Goddard, Curtis, P. Cos. C, 25th, A and B, Eng.; e. Aug. 1, 1861, St. Joseph, Mo.
881 Goerisch, Frank, P. Cos. B, 25th, and L, Eng.; e. June 13, 1861, St. Joseph, Mo.; ad. 1815 St. Joseph av., St. Joseph, Mo.
882 Goerish, John, P. Co. B, 25th; e. June 13. 1861, St. Joseph, Mo.
883 Goff, George, P. Co. C, 25th; e. Aug. 1, 1861.
884 Goforth, Adam, P. Co. H, 25th, and M, Eng.; e. Jan. 6, 1862, Nodaway Co., Mo.; ad. Barnard, Mo.
885 Goforth, Jas. D., Sergt. Cos. H, 25th, and M, Eng.; e. Dec. 10, 1861, Guilford, Mo.; ad. Barnard, Mo.
886 Goforth, John C., P. Co. H, 25; e. June 6, 1862, Nodaway Co., Mo.; ad. Arkoe, Mo.
887 Gollogly, Pat., P. Co. F, Eng.; e. Sept. 17, 1861, Cedar Falls, Iowa.
888 Golden, John B., P. Co. A, 25th; e. June 20, 1861, St. Joseph, Mo.
889 Golden, Wm. H., P. Cos. C and B, Eng.; e. Aug. 4, 1861, Prairie City, Ill.; vet. Jan. 4, 1864; a pensioner in very poor health from rheumatism; ad. Ravanna, Kas.
890 Goodbrooks. Isaac, P. Co. I, 25th; e. Jan. 25, 1861, Gallatin, Mo.
891 Goodman, Geo., P. Co. K, 25th; e. Dec. 15, 1861, Hawleyville, Iowa.
892 Goodman, Thos. M., Sergt. Cos. K 25th, G and C, Eng.; e. Oct. 1, 1862, Hawleyville, Iowa; was the sole survivor of the Centralia Massacre in Oct. 1864; died in Santa Barbara, Cal., in 1887.
893 **GOODRICH, SOLOMON**, Lieut. Cos. I, K and D; Eng. e. Sept. 15, 1861, McGregor, Iowa; he has been a traveling salesman since the close of the war; ad. Urbanna, Ill.
894 Goodwill, De Witt C., P. Cos. G, H and D, Eng.; e. Sept. 15, 1861, Cape Girardeau, Mo.
895 Gordley, John T., P. Co. G, 25th; e. Dec. 21, 1862, Omaha, Neb.
896 Gorman, John, P. Co. G, 25th; e. June 15, 1861, Kansas City, Mo.
897 Gordon. Theo., P. Co. H. 25th; e.———, Nodaway, Co., Mo.
898 Goss, August. P. Co. B, 25th; e. June 13, 1861, St. Joseph, Mo.
899 Grace, John, P. Co. E, Eng.; e. July 13, 1861, Adrian, Mich.
900 Grafenstien, Louis, Hosp. Stewd., 25th; e. June 13, 1861, St. Joseph, Mo.; died May 19, 1863.
901 Graham, A. B., P. Co. E, Eng.; e. August 15, 1861. Adrian, Mich.
902 Graham, Chas., P. Co. K, Eng.; e. Sept. 24, 1861, Burlington, Iowa.
903 Grammer, Fidelity, P. Co. B, 25th; e. June 13, 1861, St. Joseph, Mo.
904 Graves, Eli, P. Co. D, 25th; e. July 21, 1861, St. Joseph, Mo.
905 Graves, Daniel B., P. Co. K. Eng.; e. Sept. 14, 1861, Wapello, Iowa.
906 Graves, Henry, Sergt. Cos. H, 25th; M and E, Eng.; e. July 28, 1862.
907 Graves, Henry, P. Co. C, 25th; e. Dec. 19, 1861, St. Joseph, Mo.
908 Graves, Jas. M., Sergt. Co. D, 25th; e. July 12, 1861, St. Joseph, Mo.; ad. St. Joseph, Mo.
909 Graves, Joseph. P. Cos. I and C, Eng.; e.———.
910 Graves, Wm, Cor. Co. D, 25th; e. July 19, 1861, St. Joseph, Mo.
911 **GRAY, JAS. R.**, Lieut. Co. C, 25th; e. Dec. 1, 1862; promoted Capt. 7th Mo. Cav., April 7, 1863.
922 Gray, John, P. Cos D and C, Eng.; e. Aug. 15, 1861, St. Louis, Mo.
913 Grebe, Christian, P. Cos. I and C, Eng.; e. Sept. 26, 1861, Cape Girardeau, Mo.
914 Green, Augustus, P. Cos. F and B, Eng.; e. Sept. 9, 1861, Dubuque, Iowa; disch. Feb. 13, 1863, Memphis, Tenn., for injury to back, received between Holly Springs, Miss., and Lagrange, Tenn., Dec., 1862.
915 Green, Pat, P. Co. G, 25th; e. Jan. 20, 1861, Kansas City, Mo.

916 Greer, Benj. H., P. Cos. I and C, Eng.; e. Sept. 14, 1861; Rushville, Ill.; pensioned; ad. Altamont, Kas.
917 Greer, Henry, P. Co. H, 25th; e. March 1, 1862, St. Joseph, Mo.
918 Greer, Wm. McF., Mus. Cos. F, 25th, H and D, Eng.; e. Dec 30, 1861, Palermo, Kas.; ad. 400 Geary st., San Francisco, Cal.
919 Gordon, Henry T., P. Co. K, Eng.; e. Sept. 15, 1861, Roseville, Ill.
920 Gregg, John, P. Co. C, 25th; e. Aug. 10, 1861, Shenandoah, Iowa.
921 Gregg, Wm. A., P. Co. A, 25th; e. Oct. 21, 1861, Gallatin, Mo.
922 Gregory, Wm. B., Sergt. Co. A, 25th; e. June 14, 1861, St. Joseph, Mo.
923 Greslin, Wm., P. Co. D, 25th; e. July 21, 1861, St. Joseph, Mo.
924 Griffin, John, 1st, P. Co. G, 25th; e. July 8, 1861, Kansas City, Mo.
925 Griffin, John, 2d, P. Co. G, 25th; e. Aug. 9, 1862. St, Joseph, Mo.
926 Griffin, Martin M., P. Co C, 25th; e. July 12, 1861, St. Joseph, Mo.
927 Griffin, Thos., P. Cos. H, 25th; M and E, Eng.; e. Sept. 8, 1862, Nordway Co., Mo.; ad. Bolckow, Mo.
928 Griffith, Platt, P. Cos. A and E, Eng.; e. July 20, 1861, St. Louis, Mo.; a pensioner; ad. Media, Kas.; taken prisoner at Tuscumbia, June 1, 1862.
929 Green, William, P. Co. G, 25th; ad. San Francisco, Cal.
930 Griffith, Thomas, P. Co. D, 25th; e. July 15, 1861, Andrew Co., Mo.
931 Griffith, Wm, P. Cos. D, 25th; A and B, Eng.; e. July 18. 1861, St. Joseph, Mo.
932 Griswold, Henry B., P. Co. F, 25th; e. Jan. 23, 1862, Douglas Co , Mo.
933 Grodewohl, Lewis, P. Co. K, Eng.; e. Sept. 20, 1861, Wanello, Iowa.
934 Gro,an, James, P. Co. E, Eng.; e. July 13, 1861, Adrian, Mich.
935 Groom, John E., P. Co. E, Eng.; e. Aug. 21, 1861, Nodaway Co., Mo.
936 Groom, S. L., P. Co. H, 25th; e. Aug. 21, 1861, Nodaway Co., Mo.
937 Grous, Joseph, P. Cos. L and I, Eng; e. ———.
938 Grover, Sam'l, P. Co. F, Eng.; e. Oct. 7, 1861, Worthington, Iowa; disch. dis. 1862, Jackson, Tenn.
939 **GROW, ASA K.**, Lieut. and Sergt. Cos. C and B, Eng.; e. Aug. 4, 1861, Avon, Ill., res. Dec. 30, 1861; re-enlisted July 1, 1862; appointed Sergt. Co. C; ad. 1407 Farrar st., St. Louis, Mo.
940 Grow, Devilla, Cor. Cos. C and B, Eng.; e. Aug. 4, 1861, Prairie City, Ill.; vet. Jan. 18, 1864; ad. Geneseo, N. Y.
941 **GRUFF, CHAS. W.**, Adjt., 25th; e. May 10, 1861; died July 4, 1862.
942 Guthrie, ———, P. Co. H, 25th; e. ———.
943 Guyer, James, P. Cos. E, 25th; G and C, Eng.; e. Mar. 21, 1862, Oregon, Mo.; ad. same.
944 Gwinup, John, P. Co. K, Eng.; e. Sept. 11, 1861, Burlington, Iowa.
945 Grant, Ferdinand, P. Cos. G, 25th, and L, Eng ; e. ———.
946 Guyer, Lawrence, P. Cos. E, 25th; G and C, Eng.; e. Dec. 21, 1861, Holt Co., Mo.; ad. Oregon, Mo.
947 Guy, John, P. Cos. F 25th; H and D, Eng.; e. Dec. 11, 1861, Troy, Kas.
948 Guyer, Richard, P. Cos. E, 25th; G and C, Eng.; e. March 31, 1863, Holt, Co., Mo.; ad. Oregon, Mo.
949 Griffith, ———, Capt. Co. D, Eng.; e. Aug. 1861; vacated.
950 Haag, Daniel, P. Cos. I and C, Eng.; e. Sept. 31, 1861, Rushville, Ill.
951 Haende, Fred, P. Cos. G and I, Eng.; e. Sept. 13, 1861, Cape Girardeau, Mo.; pensioner; ad. Egypt Mills, Mo.
952 Haenze, Henry, P. Cos. G and I, Eng.; e. Sept. 13, 1861, Cape Girardeau, Mo.- ad. same; pensioned.
953 Haer, Gottlieb, P. Co. B, 25th; e. Nov. 1, 1861, St Joseph, Mo.
954 Hackaby, Joshua, Cor Cos. B and E. Eng.; e. July 28, 1861, Paris, Ill.
955 Hagan, A. N., P. Co. H, 25th; e. Dec. 10, 1861, Nodaway Co., Mo.
956 **HOGE, GEO. B.**, Capt Co. F, 25th; e. July 25, 1861, St. Joseph, Mo.; promoted Col. 113 Ill., Oct. 2, 1862.
957 Hagan, Henry, P. Co. C, 25th; e. July 28, 1861, St. Joseph, Mo.
958 Hagan, Pat., P. Co. G, 25; e. ———; ad. St. Joseph, Mo.
959 Hagadorn, Henry, 1st, P. Co. B, 25th; e. June, 13, 1861, St Joseph, Mo.
960 Hagadorn, Henry, 2d, P. Co. G, 25th, L and E, Eng ; e. Nov. 1, 1861, Plattsmouth, Neb.
961 Haggerty, Pat., P. Cos. D and F, Eng.; e. Sept. 14, 1861, Flora, Ill.
962 Hague, Alfred R., Sergt. Cos. C, 25th; A and B, Eng.; e. Jan. 2, 1862, De Kalb Co., Mo.; draws a pension; ad. Helena, Mo.

963 Hahn, Fred., P. Cos. G and I, Eng.; e. Sept. 13, 1861, Cape Girardeau, Mo.; has a pension; ad. Egypt Mills, Mo.
964 Hahn, Frederick, P. Co. B, 25th; e. June 6, 1861, St. Joseph, Mo.
965 Hahn, Geo., P. Co. B. 25th; e. June 6, 1861, St. Joseph, Mo.
966 Hahn, Jacob, P. Cos. G, I and D, Eng; e. Cape Girardeau, Mo.
967 **HAHN, WM. J.**, Lieut. Co. H, 25th; e. June 25, 1861, St. Louis, Mo.
968 Haight, Horace T., P. Co. E, Eng.; e. Aug. 13, 1861, Adrian, Mich.
969 Hall, Adolphus, P. Co. C, Eng.; e. Aug. 12, 1861, Prairie City, Ill.; drowned at Ashton, La., March 6, 1863, fell overboard from steamboat.
970 Hall, David, P. Cos. C, 25th, and A, Eng.; e. Sept. 26, 1862, St Joseph, Mo.; ad. Frazer, Mo.
971 Hall, Harvey C., Sergt. Co. K, 25th; e. Aug. 12, 1862, Page Co., Iowa.
972 Hall, James, P. Co. K, 25th; e. March 20, 1862, St. Joseph, Mo.
973 Hall, Lewis A., Sergt. Cos. C and B, Eng.; e. Aug. 4, 1861, Prairie City, Ill.; draws a pension; ad. Colorado Springs, Colo.
974 Hall, Samuel, P. Co. I, 25th; e. July 27, 1861, Kidder, Mo.
975 Hall, Thomas, P. Co. H, 25th; e. ———, Nodaway Co., Mo.
976 Halloran, A. J., P. Co. G, 25th; e. Dec. 31, 1861, Omaha, Neb.
977 Halpin, Michael, P. Co. G, 25th; e. July 13, 1861, Kansas City, Mo.
978 Ham, Wm., P. Cos. D, 25th, A and B, Eng.; e. Nov. 16, 1861, St. Joseph, Mo.
979 Halterman, Oliver, 1st Sergt. Cos. C and B, Eng.; e. May 10, 1862, Prairie City, Ill.; ad. Topeka, Kas.
980 Hamblin, Wilson D., P. Cos. H, D and C, Eng.; e. Nov. 17, 1863.
981 Hummell, Isaac, P. Co. K, Eng.; e. Oct. 1, 1861. New London, Iowa.
982 Hamilton, Benj. F., P. Cos. F and B, Eng.; e. Oct. 26, 1861, Grand Detour, Ill.; pensioned; ad. Haskell, Kas.
983 Hamilton, Samuel H., P. Cos. C and B, Eng; e. Aug. 4, 1861, Prairie City, Ill.
984 Hammer, James F., P. Co. D, 25th; e. Nov. 1, 1861, St. Joseph, Mo.
985 Hammon, John, P. Co. G, 25th; e. Dec. 21, 1861. Kansas City, Mo.
986 Hammond, George V., P. Co. D, 25th; e. July 29, 1862, St. Joseph, Mo.
987 Hammond, Robert, P. Co. G, 25th; e. Feb. 18, 1862, St. Joseph, Mo.
988 Hamp, Henry. P. Co. A, 25th; e. June 14, 1861, St. Joseph, Mo.
989 Hampton, J., P. Co. H, Eng.; e. ———.
990 Hampton, James V., P. Co. K, Eng.; e. Sept. 17, 1861, New London, Iowa; died at Iuka, Miss., of acute dysentery, Oct. 1863.
991 Hampton, Wm. H., P. Cos. K and D, Eng.; e. Sept. 17, 1861, New London, Iowa; ad. New London, Iowa.
992 Hampton, Michael, P. Cos. F, 25th, H and D, Eng.; e. April 15, 1863, Rochester, Mo.
993 Hand, John, P. Co. G, 25th; e. June 15, 1861, Kansas City, Mo.
994 Hanly, Jas., P. Co. G, 25th; e. June 15, 1861, Kansas City, Mo.
995 Hankins, Wm., P. Cos. E, 25th, G and C, Eng.; e. Nov. 11, 1861.
996 **HARDING, CHESTER**, Col. 25th; e. April 10, 1862, St. Louis, Mo. He was Adjutant-General of Missouri under Governor Gamble until appointed Colonel of the Twenty-fifth Regiment; was mustered out December 31, 1863, upon consolidation with the Engineer Regiment; afterward served as Colonel of the Forty-third Missouri Regiment, and served with that Regiment in Missouri until June 30, 1865, when that Regiment was mustered out. He afterward practiced law in St. Louis, Mo., and died there about ten years after the close of the war.
997 Hawley, Gustavus, P. Co. F, Eng.; e. Oct. 10, 1861, Shell Rock, Iowa, ad. the same place.
998 **HAWLEY, JAS. B.**, Lt. Co. B, 25th; e. July 25, 1861, St. Joseph, Mo., disch. Jan. 1, 1864; ad. St. Joseph, Mo.
999 Hawkins, James A., P. Co. F, 25th; e. Jan. 15, 1862, Rochester, Mo.
1000 Hawkins, John, P. Co. A, 25th; e. Jan. 3, 1862, Troy, Kas.; shot by guerrillas near Waverly, Tenn., July, 1864.
1001 Hawkins, Wm. 1st, P. Co. E. 25th; e. July 22, 1861, Oregon, Mo.
1002 Hawkins, Wm. 2d, P. Co. E. 25th; e. Nov. 26, 1861, Page Co., Iowa.
1003 Haupt, Chas. C., P. Cos. G, I and D, Eng.; e. Sept. 13, 1861, at Cape Girardeau, Mo; pensioned; ad. Kurreville, Mo.
1004 Haupt, Henry, P. Co B, 25 h; e. June 13, 1861, St. Joseph, Mo.
1005 Harden, Alex. C., P. Cos. E, 25th; G and C, Eng.; e. July 19, 1862, Holt Co., Mo.

1006 Harden, David C., P. Cos. C and B, Eng.; e. Sept. 16, 1861, Avon, Ill. He is at present an inmate of the Kansas Insane Asylum, the result of an accident while he was driving a mule team in the service; ad. 603 Locust st., Ottawa, Kas.
1007 Harding, Wm., P. Co. C, 25th; e. July 15, 1861, St. Joseph, Mo.
1008 Hardman, Samuel C., P. Cos. F and B, Eng.; e. Oct. 25, 1861, Dixon, Ill., vet.
1009 Hardway, Jacob C., P. Cos. F and B, Eng.; e. Oct. 23, 1861, Bloomington, Ill.; ad. same; vet.
1010 Hardway, John T., P. Cos. F and B, Eng.; e. Oct. 24, 1861, Bloomington, Ill.; vet.; ad. same.
1011 Hardwick, Ferdinand, Cor. Cos. A and E, Eng.; e. July 20, 1861, St. Louis, Mo.
1012 Harelson, Wm., P. Cos. B. 25th; L and E. Eng ; e. June 13, 1861, St. Joseph, Mo.
1013 Harlan, Gilbert, P. Co. A, 25th; e. Dec. 16, 1861, Fremont, Iowa.
1014 Harlow, Jas. H., P. Co. D, 25th; e. July 12, 1861, St. Joseph, Mo.
1015 Harmon, H. B., P. Cos. H and D, Eng.; e. Oct. 5, 1862.
1016 Harmer, Arthur, P. Co. B. Eng. ; e. Sept. 9, 1861.
1017 Harness, Abe, P. Co. A, 25th; e. March 1, 1862, St. Joseph, Mo.
1018 Harper, Silas, P. Co. B, 25th; e. Nov. 1, 1861, St. Jospeh, Mo.
1019 Harness, Seneca, P. Co. A, 25th ; e. Aug. 6, 1861, St Joseph, Mo.
1020 Harr, Geo., P Co. A. 25th ; e. June 14, 1861, St. Joseph, Mo.
1021 Harrington, Elisha, P. Co. E, Eng.; e. Aug. 15, 1861, Adrian Mich.; injured on board of boat Chickasaw Bayou, March, 1863.
1022 Harrigan, Jas., Sergt. Co. F, Eng.; e. Sept. 14, 1861, Cedar Falls, Iowa ; ad. Dubuque, Iowa.
1023 Harris, David C., P. Cos. K, 25th, G and C, Eng.; e. Sept. 23, 1862, Hawleyville, Iowa ; draws pension ; ad. same.
1024 Harris, Geo. H., P. Cos. F, 25th, H and D, Eng.; e. Sept. 22, 1862, St. Catharine, Mo. ; ad. Winigan, Mo.
1025 Harris, James, P. Co. G, 25th ; e. July 11, 1861, Kansas City Mo.
1026 Harris, James, P. Cos. H, 25th, M and E, Eng.; e. Dec. 16, 1861, Nodaway Co., Mo.; ad. Turkio, Mo.
1027 Harris, John, P. Co. H, 25th; e. March 19, 1861, Nodaway Co., Mo.
1028 Harris, Wm., P. Cos. I and C, Eng. ; e. Oct. 6, 1861, Hardin, Iowa.
1029 Harris, Henry, P. Cos. F, 25th, H and D, Eng. ; e. Sept. 22,1862, at Hawleyville, Iowa ; ad. same.
1030 Harris, Daniel, P. Cos. F, 25th, H and D, Eng.; e. Sept. 22, 1862, Hawleyville, Iowa ; ad. Clarinda, Iowa.
1031 Harrison, Robert J., P. Cos B and E, Eng.; e. Aug. 5, 1861, Paris, Ill.
1032 Harrison, Wm., P. Co. G, 25th; e. Nov. 1, 1861.
1033 Harrison, Wm. H., P. Co. B, 25th; e. Sept. 9, 1861.
1034 Hart, Frank, P. Cos. C and B, Eng.; e. Sept. 16, 1861, Prairie City, Ill.; ad. Smithfield, Ill.
1035 Hartman, Henry B., P. Cos. D and F, Eng.; e. Aug. 17, 1861, Carlyle, Ill.; died March, 1888.
1036 Hartman, Jacob, P. Co. G, Eng.; e. Sept. 13, 1861, Cape Girardeau, Mo.
1037 Hartung, Christian, Sergt. Cos. G and I, Eng.; e. Sept. 13, 1861, Cape Girardeau, Mo.; dead.
1038 Hasselpflug, C. G., P. Cos. A and E, Eng.; e July 20, 1861, St. Louis, Mo.
1039 HASIE, CHAS. R., Lt. Co. G, Eng.; e. Sept. 20, 1861, Cape Girardeau, Mo.; res. May 6, 1862; dead.
1040 HASIE, M. S., Maj. Eng.; e. Oct. 31, 1861, St. Louis, Mo.; res. Aug. 31, 1862, at Jackson, Tenn. Maj. Hasie is a prosperous merchant and capitalist in Kansas; ad. Arkansas City, Kas.
1041 Hascall, Chas., P. Co. E, Eng.; e. Aug. 13, 1861, Adrian, Mich.; died; widow, Emily E., resides in Cuba, N. Y.
1042 Hastings, Jackson, alias Jack Sanders—see Sanders, Jack.
1043 Hatfield, Joseph, P. Co. C. Eng.; e. Aug. 4, 1861, Avon, Ill.; deserted, Memphis, Tenn., Feb. 20, 1863.
1044 Hatfield, Wm. H., Cor. Co. C, Eng.; e. Aug. 4, 1861, Avon, Ill.; disch. March 23, 1863.
1045 Hatsch, Jacob, P. Co. B, 25th; e. Nov. 1, 1861, St. Joseph, Mo.

1046 Hatton, Willis, P. Co. E, Eng.; e. July 13, 1861, Adrian, Mich.; ad. Marshall, Ill.
1047 Hayman, John, P. Cos. D and F, Eng.; e. Oct. 3, 1861, Flora, Ill.; disch. dis. Oct. 18, 1863, St. Louis, Mo.
1048 Haynes, Daniel, P. Cos. E and D, Eng.; e. Aug. 13, 1861, Adrian, Mich.; is a pensioner; ad. Deerfield, Mich.
1049 Hanson, Wm., P. Co. K, 25th; e. ————; ad. Hamburg, Iowa.
1050 Haynes, Wm., P. Co C, Eng.; e. Feb. 22, 1862.
1051 Hayes, Geo. W., Sergt. Cos. H and D, Eng.; e. Sept. 6, 1861, Paris, Ill.; has a pension; ad. Lacona, Ill.
1052 Hays, Isaac R., P. Cos. E, 25th, G and C, Eng.; e. July 22, 1861, Holt Co., Mo.; ad. Fairport, Mo.
1053 Hays, Pat., P. Cos. A, 25th, M and E, Eng.; e. Dec. 7, 1861, Omaha, Neb.
1054 Hays, Roland, P. Cos. E, 25th; G and C, Eng.; e. Oregon, Mo.; ad. same.
1055 Hazard, John, P. Co. D, 25th; e. July 12, 1861, St. Joseph, Mo.; taken prisoner before Corinth, May, 1862; ad. Oregon, Mo.
1056 Hazie, Carl, P. Co. F, Eng.; e. Sept 26, 1861, Bloomington, Ill.
1057 Heald, Ira, P. Co. B, 25th; e. Sept. 1, 1862, St. Joseph, Mo.
1058 Hearn, Wm. H., P. Co. A, 25th; e. Oct. 16, 1862, De Kalb Co., Mo.
1059 Hebner, Geo., P. Cos. H and D, Eng.; e. Oct. 24, 1861, St. Louis, Mo.
1060 Heckenleible, Jacob, P. Co. B. 25th; e. June 13, 1861, St. Joseph, Mo.
1061 Hecker, Chas., P. Cos. D and C, Eng.; e. May 7, 1861, Carlyle, Ill.; ad. same.
1062 Heep, John, Cor. Cos. D and F, Eng.; e. Aug. 15, 1861, Flora, Ill.; dead.
1063 Hefferson, Wm., P. Co. G 25th; e. June 24, 1861, Kansas City, Mo.
1064 Heefner, Chas. W., P. Cos. B and C, Eng.; e. July 28, 1861, Paris, Ill.; has a pension; ad. Conlogue, Ill.
1065 Heefner, Levi, Mus. Cos. B and C, Eng.; e. July 28, 1861, Paris, Ill.
1066 Heggi, Frank, P. Cos. A, 25th, M and E, Eng.; e. Dec. 9, 1861, St. Joseph, Mo.
1067 Hein, John B., P. Co. G. 25th; e. Feb. 16, 1862, Omaha, Neb.
1068 Heins, John F., P Cos. K and B, Eng.; e. Sept. 28, 1861, Wapello, Iowa; is a pensioner; ad. Wapello, Iowa.
1069 Heins, Nicholas, P. Co. H, 25th; e.————.
1070 Hildreth, Isaac, P. Co. D, 25th, A and B, Eng.; e. July 28, 1862, St. Joseph, Mo.; ad. Griggsville, Ill.
1071 Helms, John C., Sergt. Cos. H and D, Eng.; e. Oct. 1, 1861, Vermillion, Ill.; dead.
1072 Hemsprauch, Bennie, P. Co. F, Eng.; e. Sept. 6, 1861, Dubuque, Iowa; died April 6, 1863, of small pox, Young's Point, La.
1073 Hencke, John, P. Cos. L and I, Eng.; e.————; died 1878.
1074 Hendershott, Frank, P. Co. E, Eng.; e, Aug. 13, 1861, Adrian, Mich.
1075 Henderson G. W., P. Co. H. Eng.; e.————,Paris, Ill.; died.
1076 HENDERSON, J. D., Lt. and A. Q. M., 25th; e. Nov. 1, 1861; disch. Jan 1, 1864.
1077 Henderson, Saml. P. Co. F, Eng.; e. Sept. 9, 1861, Mineral Point, Wis.; died Otterville, Mo., Feb. 26, 1862, of lung disease.
1078 Henderson, Washington, P Cos. H and D, Eng.; e. Oct. 1, 1861, Paris, Ill.
1079 Hennes, Wm., Sergt. Cos. G, I and D, Eng.; e. Sept. 13, 1861, Cape Girardeau, Mo.; vet.
1080 Hennessy, Jerry, P. Co. I, 25th; e. Dec. 11, 1861, Kansas City, Mo.
1081 Henning, Ernest, P. Co. G, Eng.; e. Sept. 13, 1861, Cape Girardeau, Mo.
1082 HENNINGS, HENRY, Lt. Co. L, Eng.; e. June 8, 1863; disch. Jan. 1, 1864.
1083 Henry, Albert G., P. Cos. C. and B, Eng.; e. Sept. 16, 1861, Prairie City, Ill.; ad. Pleasanton, Kas.
1084 Henry, Wm., P. Co. I, 25th; e. May 30, 1863, St. Joseph, Mo.
1085 Hensel, John, P. Co. B, 25th; e. June 13, 1861, St. Joseph, Mo.
1086 Hensler, John, Sergt. Cos. L, I and D. Eng.; e. Aug 15, 1862
1087 Hensley, Wm. H., Sergt. Cos. F and B, Eng.; e. Oct. 10, 1861, Albert Lea, Minn.; ad. Iowaville, Kas.
1088 Henze, Henry, P. Cos. G. and I, Eng.; e. Sept. 13, 1861, Cape Girardeau, Mo.; dead.
1089 HEQUAMBOURG, ALEX. G., Capt. Cos. G and E, Eng.; e. Oct. 31, 1861, St. Louis, Mo.; res. June 2, 1862; promoted to Colonel of 40th Mo. Inf.; ad. 1014 Dolman st., St. Louis, Mo.

1090 Herbst, Mich., Cor. Cos. G and I, Eng.; e. Sept. 13, 1861, Cape Girardeau, Mo.; draws a pension; ad. Cape Girardeau, Mo.
1091 Hermann, Frank, P. Co. K, Eng.; e. Sept. 23, 1861, Burlington, Iowa.
1092 Herring, Silas. P. Co. A, 25th; e. Feb. 17, 1862. St. Joseph, Mo.
1093 **HENION, TUNIS W.**, Capt. Co. E, Eng.; e. July 13, 1861, Adrian, Mich.; res. March 26, 1862; dead.
1094 Hiatt, Jesse,P. Cos. E, 25th, G and C, Eng.; e. Sept. 22, 1861, Atchison Co., Mo.; pensioner; ad. Independence, Kas.
1095 Hess, Henry, P. Cos. D, F and B, Eng.; e. Aug. 2, 1861, Keokuk, Iowa.
1096 **HENSLER, JOHN E.**, Capt. Co. I, 35th, and L, Eng.; res. June 7, 1863.
1097 Hibbard, Jas. A., P. Co. A, 25th; e. July 1, 1861, Troy, Kas.
1098 High, Charles, P. Cos. A, 25th, M and E, Eng.; e. Nov. 20, 1861, St. Joseph, Mo.
1099 **HIGHT, CHAS. E.**, Lt. Cos. A, 25th, M and E, Eng.; e. Dec. 26, 1861, Burlington, Iowa.
1100 Hildebiddle, Chas. T., Cor. Co. H, 25th; e. May 26, 1863, Guilford, Mo.; killed in the Centralia, Mo., massacre.
1101 **HILL, EBEN M.**, Capt. Co. D, Maj. and Lt.-Col. Eng.; e. Sept. 10, 1861; disch. July 22, 1865; is a hardware merchant at Hartland, Kas.
1102 Hill, Frederick, P. Cos. F and B, Eng.; e. Sept. 30, 1861, Cassville, Wis.; dead.
1103 Hill, George, P. Co. E. Eng.; e. March 26, 1863; ad. Burlington, Iowa.
1104 Hill, Geo., Sergt. Co. K, 25th, G, Eng.; e. Sept. 23, 1862, Hawleyville, Iowa.
1105 Hills, Henry, Cor. Cos. I and C, Eng.; e. Sept. 23, 1861, Denmark, Iowa; ad. Yarmouth, Iowa.
1106 Hill, Jackson, P. Cos. I, 25th, H and D, Eng.; e. March 17, 1863, Hamilton, Mo.
1107 Hill, Ichabod B., P. Co. E, 25th; e. Oct. 27, 1861, Holt Co., Mo.
1108 Hill, Perry P. Cos. I, D, F and B, Eng.; e. Sept. 23, 1861, Rushville, Ill.; vet.
1109 **HILL, WM.**, Capt. Cos. I and E, and Maj. Eng.; e. Sept. 6, 1861, Rushville, Ill.; dead.
1110 Hinds, Wm. H., P. Co. A, Eng.; e.———.
1111 Hines, Andrew, P. Cos. A and E, Eng.; e. July 20, 1861, St. Louis, Mo.
1112 Heinze, Peter, P. Co. B, 25th; e. Oct. 10, 1861, St. Joseph, Mo.
1113 Hobbs, Lyman S., P. Co. C; e.———.
1114 Hills, H. A., P. Co. K, 25th; e.———; ad. Elkhorn, Kas.
1115 Holbrecker, Thos. F., P. Cos. B, 25th, L and E, Eng.; e. Aug. 5, 1861, St. Louis, Mo; ad. St. Joseph, Mo.
1116 Hockett, Mahlon, Cor. Cos. H, D and C, Eng.; e. Aug. 12, 1862, Paris, Ill.; pensioner; ad. Paris, Ill.
1117 Hofer, John J., P. Cos. L, I and E, Eng.; e.———.
1118 Hoff, Adol., Sergt. Cos. G and I, Eng.; e. Sept. 13, 1861. Cape Girardeau, Mo.
1119 Hefferman, Chas., P. Co. A, 25th; e. June 20, 1861, St. Joseph, Mo.
1120 Hoffman, John M., Cor. Co. D, Eng.; e.———.
1121 Hoffman, Mathew, P. Co. B, 25th; e. June 13, 1861, St. Joseph, Mo.
1122 Hoffman, Saml., P. Cos. E, 25th, G and C, Eng; e. December 24, 1863, White Cloud, Kas.
1123 Hogan, Owen, P. Co. G, 25th; e. June 12, 1861, Kansas City, Mo.
1124 Hogan, Thos., P. Co. G, 25th; e. June 24, 1861, Kansas City, Mo.
1125 Holland, Miles H., P. Cos. K, 25th, G and C, Eng.; e. March 1, 1862, Hawleyville, Iowa; draws a pension; ad. Hawleyville, Iowa.
1126 Holcomb, Chestnut W., Sergt. Cos. F, 25th, H and D, Eng.; e. Sept. 11, 1861, Stewartsville, Mo.
1127 Holden, Samuel, P. Cos. H, D and C, Eng.; e. Aug. 25, 1861, Bloomfield, Ill.; ad. Cherry Point, Ill.
1128 Holes, Alby, P. Co. D, Eng.; e. Nov. 23, 1863.
1129 Hollenbeck, Jas. W., P. Cos. C and B, Eng.; e. Jan. 6, 1861, Prairie City, Ill.; vet. Jan. 16, 1864; ad. Alexis, Ill.
1130 Hollenbeck, Andrew J., Sergt. Cos. H, 25th, M and E, Eng.; e. Dec. 10, 1861, Guilford, Mo.
1131 Holliday, Linden, P. Cos. K, 25th, G and C, Eng.; e. Oct. 18, 1862, Hawleyville, Iowa; a Pensioner; ad. Memory, Iowa.
1132 Holliday, Moses H., P. Cos. D and C, Eng; e. Oct. 13, 1861, Middletown, Ill.; pensioned; ad. Carthage, Mo.

1133 Holliday, Robt., P. Co K, 25th; e. Jan. 11, 1862, Hawleyville, Iowa.
1134 Holliday, John S., P. Co. E, Eng.; e. July 13, 1861, disch. at St. Louis Gen. Hosp., April, 1863, died Tina, Mo., April 16, 1887.
1135 Hollister, Perry G., Cor. Cos. C and B, Eng.; e. Sept. 6, 1861, Prairie City, Ill.
1136 Holloway, Washt., P. Cos. I, C and A, Eng.; e. Nov. 6, 1862, Trenton, Iowa.
1137 Hollovoit, Edward, P. Co. G, 25th; e. Dec. 20, 1861, Kansas City, Mo.
1138 Holly, Jas. F., P. Cos. E, 25th; G and C, Eng.; e. Sept. 21, 1862, Atchison, Mo.
1139 Holton, Robt. C., P. Cos. D, 25th; A and B, Eng.; e. June 21, 1863, Livingston, Co., Mo.
1140 **HOOKER, HORACE B.**, Lt. Cos. I and C, Eng.; e. Oct. 27, 1862, disch. Jan. 1, 1864, is a proprietor of an extensive nursery near Rochester, N. Y.; ad. same. 112 West St. Paul St.
1141 **HOOKER, JAS. W.**, Lt. Co. A, Eng.; e. Nov. 1, 1862; res. July 11, 1863; dead
1142 Hopkins, ——, Cor. Co. E, Eng.; e. July 13, 1861, Adrian, Mich.; died March 3, 1864, Waverly, Tenn.
1143 Hoover, Benj. K., P. Cos. C and B, Eng.; e. Aug 4, 1861, Prairie City, Ill.; ad. New Sharon, Iowa.
1144 Horn, Jasper, P. Cos. A, 25th; M and E, Eng.; e. Nov. 18, 1862, St. Joseph, Mo.
1145 Homer, Arthur, P. Cos. C and B, Eng.; e. Sept 16, 1861, Dallas City, Ill.
1146 Howard, Chas., P. Co. K, Eng.; e. Sept. 20, 1861, Burlington, Iowa.
1147 Howell, David S., P. Cos. H, D and C, Eng ; e. Aug. 12, 1862, Sandford, Ind.; ad. same; has pension.
1148 Howell, —, P. Co. H, 25th; e.——.
1149 Hoy, Jas., P. Co. F, Eng.; e. Sept. 24, 1861, Bloomington, Ill.; died Aug. 1862, at Jackson, Miss.
1150 Hubbard, Alonzo, P Co. K, Eng.; e. Oct. 20, 1861, St. Louis, Mo.
1151 **HUDSON, H. E.**, Lt. and Capt. Co. E, Adjt. Eng.; e. Oct. 31, 1861, St. Louis, Mo.; disch. Oct. 31, 1864; died in Memphis, Tenn., about 1877.
1152 Hudson, Levi J., P. Co. B, Eng.; e. July 20, 1861, St. Louis, Mo.
1153 Hudson, Wm., Sergt. Co. E, 25th., e. July 22, 1861, Forrest City, Mo.
1154 Huff, —, P. Co. H, Eng.; e. ——; disch. dis. 1862.
1155 Hughbanks, Henry B., Cor. Cos. C and B, Eng.; e, Sept. 6, 1861, Prairie City, Ill.
      He was quite young when enlisted and scarcely of age when disch.; he is now a prosperous and well-to-do lawyer in Osage City, Kas.
1156 Hughs, Isaac, P. Cos. D and C, Eng.; e. Oct. 17, 1861, Mt. Sterling, Ill.; died in 1888, Alexandria, Mo.
1157 Hughes, John C., P. Cos. E, 25th, G and I, Eng.; e. Sept. 1, 1862, Atchison Co., Mo.; ad. Hamburg, Iowa.
1158 Hughes, Marshal, P. Cos. G, 25th, L and E, Eng.; e. Jan. 8, 1862, Omaha, Neb.
1159 Hughes, Mich. W., Cor. Co. D, 25th; e. July 18, 1861, St. Joseph, Mo.; died at Dorchester, Neb.
1160 Hughes, Wm., P. Co. E, 25th; e. Feb. 27, 1862, Sidney, Iowa; ad Hamburg, Iowa (or Savannah Mo.).
1161 Hulick, Joseph, P. Cos. I and C, Eng.; e. Sept. 28, 1861, Burlington, Iowa; died at Dorchester, Neb., in 1886.
1162 Hull, Mack, P. Co. D. Eng.; e. Sept. 14, 1861, Flora, Ill ; disch. dis. Otterville, Mo., Feb. 6, 1862.
1163 Humbolt, Chas., P. Cos. H, D and C, Eng.; e. Nov 15, 1861, Calhoun, Ill.; draws a pension; ad. Olivia, Minn.
1164 Humiston, Jas., Cor. Co. K, Eng.; e. Sept. 28, 1861, Wapello, Iowa
1165 Humiston, John, P. Co. K, Eng.; e. Sept. 28, 1861, Wapello, Iowa; ad. Wapello, Iowa.
1166 Hunter, Christopher, P. Cos. I and C. Eng.; e. Sept. 21, 1861, Columbus City, Iowa.
1167 Hunt, H. N., P. Co. E, Eng.; e. Aug. 13, 1861, Adrian, Mich ; has a pension; ad. Benedict, Neb.
1168 Hunter, John G., P. Co. H, 25th; e. Dec. 21, 1862, Nodaway, Co., Mo.
1169 Hunze, Aug., P. Cos. G and I, Eng.; e. Sept. 13, 1861, Cape Girardeau, Mo.; pensioned; ad. same.

1170 Hurst, Jackson, P. Cos. D. 25th, A and B, Eng.; e. Dec. 11, 1861, St. Joseph, Mo.
1171 Hurst, Jonas F., P. Co. E, 25th; e. July 22, 1861, White Cloud, Kas.
1172 HUNT, L. E., Chap., Eng.; e. July, 1863, Pocahontas, Tenn.; disch. Jan. 1, 1864.
1173 Hurst, St. Clair, Cor. Cos. D, 25th, A and B, Eng.; e. Nov. 20, 1861, St. Joseph, Mo.
1174 Hurley, Thos., P. Cos. A and E, Eng.; e. July 20, 1861, St. Louis, Mo.
1175 Hurst, Thomas, P. Co. H, 25th; e. Sept. 24, 1862, Iron Co., Mo.
1176 Hurst, Wm., P. Cos. H, 25th, M and E, Eng.; e. Sept. 23, 1862, Iron Co., Mo.
1177 Hurst, Wm. C., P. Co. K, 25th; e. Oct. 18, 1862, Hawleyville, Iowa.
1178 Huston, Thos., P. Co. I, 25th; e. Sept. 17, 1861, Plattsburg, Mo.
1179 Hutchings, Joseph, P. Co. D, 25th; e. Sept. 13, 1862, St. Louis, Mo.
1180 Hutchinson, Jas., P. Co. K, Eng.; e. Oct. 31, 1861, Bloomington, Ill.; died in 1862.
1181 Hutchinson, Jas. 2d, P. Co. K, Eng.; e. Oct. 31, 1861, Bloomington, Ill.
1182 Hutman, Jacob, P. Cos. L and I, Eng.; e. ———.
1183 Hutton, Henry, P. Co. E, Eng.; e. Aug. 13, 1861, Adrian, Mich.
1184 Hybarger, David H., P. Cos. B and K, Eng.; e. July 28, 1861, Paris, Ill.
1185 Hybarger, John C., P. Cos. B and K, Eng.; e. July 28, 1861, Paris, Ill.; ad. Paris, Ill.
1186 Ihm, John, P. Co. G, 25th; e. June 27, 1861, Kansas City, Mo.
1187 Imz, George, Sergt Co. B, 25th; e. June 13, 1861, St Joseph, Mo.
1188 Imz, Peter, P. Co. B, 25th; e. June 13, 1861, St. Joseph, Mo.
1189 Inskeep, Joseph H., P. Cos. H, 25th, M and E, Eng.; e. Oct. 2, 1862, Nodaway Co., Mo.
1190 Irwin, James, P. Cos. H, 25th, M and E, Eng.; e. Oct. 2, 1862, Nodaway Co., Mo.; pensioner.
1191 Irwin, Robt. C, P. Co. H, 25th; e. April 1, 1862. Nodaway Co, Mo.; ad. Maryville, Mo.
1192 Irwin, Hugh, P. Cos. E, 25th, G and C, Eng.; e. July 22, 1861, Holt Co., Mo.; pensioner; ad. Hays City, Kas
1193 Irwin, John, Cor. Cos. G, 25th, L and E, Eng.; e. July 21, 1861, St. Joseph, Mo.
1194 Irwin, John, Sergt. Cos. K, 25th, G and C, Eng.; e. Feb. 2, 1862, St. Joseph, Mo., has a pension; ad. South West City, McDonald Co., Mo.
1195 Ihle, May, P. Co. B, 25th, e. June 13, 1861, St. Joseph, Mo.
1196 Jacobs, Theoph., P. Cos. I and C, Eng.; e. Sept. 23, 1861, Burlington, Iowa.
1197 JACOBSON, AUGUSTUS, Adjt. and Capt. Co. E, Eng.; e. July 26, 1861; res. Sept. 7, 1862; promoted Col. 27th Mo. Inf. Sept. 27, 1862. Ad. Chicago, Ill.
1198 Jennings, Francis A., P. Co. C, Eng.; e. Sept. 6, 1861, Avon, Ill.; deserted Feb. 1, 1863, at Memphis, Tenn.; ad. Monmouth, Ill.
1199 Jerrold, Francis F., P. Cos. C and B, Eng.; e. Aug. 4, 1861, Prairie City, Ill.; died April 15, 1864. Gen. Hosp., Clarksville, Tenn.
1200 Jewell, Wm. P. Cos. B and K, Eng.; e. July 28, 1861, Paris, Ill.
1201 Jewett, Moses, Cor. Co. K, Eng.; e. Sept. 28, 1861, Wapello, Iowa; ad. New Boston, Ill.
1202 James, Geo., P. Co. E, 25th, e. July 22, 1861, Holt Co., Mo.
1203 James, Geo. B., P. Co. ——; e. March 2, 1862, Troy, Kas.
1204 James, Henry, P. Cos. H and D, Eng.; e. Sept. 21, 1861, Vermillion, Ill.; draws pension; ad. Soldiers' Home, Leavenworth, Kas.
1205 James, John W., P. Cos G, 25th, L and E, Eng.; e. Feb. 14, 1862, Gentry Co., Mo.
1206 James, Wm., P. Co. A, Eng.; e. Sept. 27, 1862, Weston. Mo.
1207 James, Wm. H., P. Co. F, 25th; e. Jan. 19, 1862, Troy, Kas.
1208 Jackson, Jasper, P. Co. B, 25th; e. Sept. 1, 1862, Kansas City Mo.
1209 Jackson, Jas. H., P. Cos. K, 25th, G and C, Eng.; e. July 15, 1863; Obion, Tenn.; pensioner; ad Omio, Jewell Co., Kas.
1210 Jackson, Wm., P. Cos. F, 25th, H and D Eng.; e. March 1, 1862, Chillicothe, Mo.
1211 Jared, Thos. N., P. Cos. H and D, Eng.; e. Jan. 3, 1863, Vermillion, Ill.
1212 Jarter, John A., P. Co. — 25th, — and E, Eng.; e. Feb. 8, 1862.
1213 John, Francis M., P. Cos. I and C, Eng.; e. Nov. 5, 1862, Augusta, Ill.

1214 Johus, Nathan H., Sergt. Cos. H and D, Eng.; e. Feb. 16, 1862, Vermillion, Ill.; dead
1215 Johns, Charles, P. Co. D, 25th; e. Aug. 6, 1861, Doniphan Co., Kas.
1216 Johnson, Andrew J., P. Cos. C and B, Eng.; e. Aug. 4, 1861, Prairie City, Ill.; ad. Friend, Neb.
1217 Johnson, Harley, P. Co. E. Eng.; e. Aug. 13, 1861, Adrian, Mich.; ad. Ottawa Lake Mich.
1218 Johnson, Henry, P. Co. B, 25th; e, June 13, 1861, St. Joseph, Mo.
1219 Johnson, Hiram, P. Co. E, Eng.; e. Aug. 13, 1861, Adrian, Mich.
1220 Johnson, Marion B., P. Co. I, 25th; e. Aug. 19, 1861, Pleasant View, Kas.
1221 Johnson, Thos. R., P. Co. C, Eng.; e. Aug. 4, 1861, Prairie City, Ill.; disch. dis. Dec. 31, 1861. St. Louis, Mo.
1222 Johnson, Wm. R., P. Cos. I and C, Eng.; e. Oct. 6, 1861, Hardin, Iowa.
1223 Johnson, Wm. B., P. Co. I, 25th; e. Aug. 9, 1861, Gallatin, Mo.
1224 Johnson, Seth H., P. Co. E, Eng.; e. Aug. 13. 1861, Adrian, Mich.; ad. Pere Cheney. Mich.
1225 Jones, Allen, P. Cos. H, D and C, Eng.; e. Aug. 12, 1862, Sandford, Ind.
1226 Jones, Amos K., Cor. Co. D, 25th; e. July 12, 1861, St. Joseph, Mo.
1227 Jones, Dwight, P. Cos. C and B, Eng.; e. Aug. 4, 1861, Prairie City, Ill.
1228 **JONES, E. L.**, Lt. Co. A, Eng.; e. Aug. 2, 1861, St. Louis, Mo.; res. March 2, 1862.
1229 Jones, George, P. Co. F, Eng.; e. Sept. 9, 1862, Manchester, Iowa; died at Washington a returned prisoner in 1862.
1230 Jones, James B., P. Co. K, Eng.; e.———; ad. Malvern, Iowa.
1231 Jones, James H., P. Cos. K, 25th, L and E, Eng ; e. Dec. 15, 1861, Glenwood, Iowa; ad. same.
1232 Jones, James W., P. Cos. H and D, Eng.; e. Sept. 27, 1861, Sandford, Ind.; a pensioner; ad. Sandford, Vigo Co., Ind.
1233 Jones, John F., P. Cos. I and C, Eng.; e. Oct. 10, 1861, Harding, Iowa.
1234 Jones, Josiah, P. Co. D, 25th; e. July 12, 1861, St. Joseph, Mo.
1235 Jones, Peter A., P. Co. D, 25th; e. July 29, 1861, St. Joseph, Mo.
1236 Jones, Samuel, Sergt. Co. E, Eng.; e. Aug. 13, 1861, Adrian. Mich.
1237 Jones, Wm., P. Cos. I, 25th, H and D, Eng.; e. June 25, 1861, Gallatin, Mo.
1238 Jones, Wm. H., P. Cos. D and H, Eng.; e. Sept. 27, 1861, Sandford, Ind.; ad. North Bend, (or Sand Creek,) Neb.
1239 Jones, Wm. H., P. Co. E, 25th; e. Sept. 21, 1862, Atchison Co., Mo.
1240 Jordan, Fred. W., P. Co. E, Eng.; e. Aug 13, 1861, Adrian, Mich; ad. same.
1241 Jordan, James, P. Co. I, 25th; e. Aug. 1, 1861, Gallatin, Mo.
1242 Jourdan, Robert H., P. Cos. B and K, Eng.; e. July 20, 1861, St. Louis, Mo.; ad. Clay City, Ind.
1243 Jordan, Sanford C., P. Cos. D and F, Eng.; e. Sept. 14, 1861, Flora, Ill.; ad. Rinard, Ill.
1244 Johnson, F. M., P. Cos. C and B, Eng.; e. Aug. 4, 1861, Avon, Ill.; ad. Augusta, Iowa.
1245 Johnson, J. R., P. Cos. I and C, Eng.; e. Aug. 4, 1861, Avon, Ill.; ad. Bushnell, Ill.
1246 Jones, Jared P., P. Co. E, Eng.; e. Aug. 13, 1861, Adrian, Mich.; ad. Soldiers' Home, Leavenworth. Kas.
1247 Judson, Lewis C., P. Co. E, Eng; e. Aug. 13, 1861, Adrian, Mich.; ad. Missouri Valley, Iowa.
1248 Julien, John, P. Co. B, 25th; e. June 13, 1861, St. Joseph, Mo.
1249 Julien, John, P. Co. G, 25th; e. Nov. 11, 1861, St. Joseph, Mo.
1250 Julien, Wm. E, P. Co. C, 25th; e. March 2, 1861, Independence, Mo.
1251 Kacherer, Lorenz, P. Cos. L, I and D, Eng.; e.———.
1252 Kaempfer, Wm., P. Co. G, Eng.; e. Sept. 13, 1861, Cape Girardeau, Mo.
1253 Kane, Jas., P. Co. F, 25th; e. Jan. 7, 1862, Third Fork, Mo.; ad. Soldiers' Home, Leavenworth. Kas.
1254 Kansch, Chas., P. Co. B 25th; e. June 13, 1861, St. Joseph, Mo.
1255 Karler, Gregory, P. Co B, 25th; e. June 13, 1861, St. Joseph, Mo.
1256 Kassell, Jno., P. Cos. G and I, Eng.; e. Sept. 13, 1861, Cape Girardeau, Mo.; has pension; ad. Egypt Mills, Mo.
1257 Karstner, Erastus, P. Cos. L and I, Eng.; e. ———.
1258 Kauth, Philip, P. Co. B, 25th; e. June 13, 1861, St. Joseph, Mo.

1259 Kearney, Nathaniel, Sergt. Cos. G, 25th, L and E, Eug.; e. Dec. 28, 1861, Wyandotte, Kas.
1260 Kearney, Stephen, Sergt. Cos. G, 25th, L and E, Eng.; e. June 26, 1861, Kansas City, Mo.; June 12, 1865, promoted Lt.
1261 Keating, John, Cor. Co. E, 25th; e. July 22, 1861, Forrest City, Mo.
1262 Keatly, Henry, P. Co. K, 25th, G and C, Eng.; e. Feb. 1, 1861, Oregon, Mo.
1263 Kelly, Daniel, P. Co. E, Eng.; e. Aug. 13, 1861, Adrian, Mich.; ad. Oceana, Mich.
1264 Kelly, Lawrence, P. Cos. H and D, Eng.; e. Sept. 30, 1861, St. Louis, Mo.
1265 Kelly, Pat., P. Co. G, 25th; e. June 13, 1861, Kansas City, Mo.
1266 Kelly, T. Jeff, Cor. Cos. C and B, Eng.; e. Sept 9, 1861, Avon, Ill.; ad. same.
1267 Kelly, Phil, P. Co. G, 25th; e. June 18, 1861, Independence, Mo.
1268 Kelly, Robert, P. Cos. C, 25th; A and B, Eng.; e. Dec. 19, 1861, St. Joseph, Mo.
1269 Kelly, Wm., P. Co. F, Eng.; e. Sept. 16, 1861, Dubuque, Iowa.
1270 Keller, Alfred, Cook (colored), Co. D, Eng.; e. April 1, 1861, Lake Providence, La.
1271 Kelsey, Lewis, P. Co. H, 25th; e. Aug. 14, 1861, Nodaway Co., Mo.
1272 Kennedy, Alvy, P. Co. D, 25th; e. Feb. 12, 1862, St. Joseph, Mo.
1273 Kennedy, Jerry, P. Cos. G, 25th; L and E, Eng.; e. December 30, 1861, Kansas City, Mo.
1274 Kenneday, M. L., P. Co. F, 25th; e. Nov. 28, 1861, Troy, Kas.
1275 Kennedy, Robert B., P. Cos. I and C, Eng.; e. Oct. 16, 1861, McGregor, Iowa.
1276 Kewin, Edwin, P. Cos. E, 25th, G and C, Eng.; e. Jan. 14, 1862, Oregon, Mo.; ad. Forrest City, Mo.
1277 Keys. Franklin, P. Co. F, 25th; e. Jan. 1, 1862, Bucklin, Mo.
1278 Keys, John, P. Co. F, Eng.; e. Oct. 26, 1861, Towanda, Ill ; ad. same.
1279 Kidd, John B., P. Cos. K, B and C, Eng.; e. Sept. 18, 1861, Prairie City, Ill.; a pensioner; ad. Smithfield, Ill.
1280 Keifer, John, P. Co. B, 25th; e. June 13, 1861, St. Joseph, Mo.
1281 Keith, Geo. J., P. Co. D, 25th; e. July 19, 1861, St. Joseph, Mo.
1282 Keith, Jas. P., P. Co. H, 25th; e. Sept. 26, 1862, Iron Co., Mo.
1283 Keith,———,P. Co.D, 25th; e. July 16, 1861, St. Joseph, Mo.
1284 Kilgour, John M., P. Co. D, 25th; e. Aug. 9, 1861, St. Joseph, Mo.
1285 Kill, Morritz, P. Co B, 25th; e. June 13, 1861, St. Joseph, Mo.
1286 KILP, ANTHONY, Lt. Co. G, Eng.; e. Aug. 17, 1861; dead.
1287 Kimball, David, P. Co. E, Eng.; e. Aug. 13, 1861, Adrian, Mich.
1288 Kimball, Henry H., P. Co. E. Eng.; e. Aug. 13, 1861, Adrian, Mich.
1289 King, Eben S., P. Co. F. Eng.; e. Sept. 25, 1861, Dubuque; Iowa.
1290 King, Enoch, P. Co. H. 25th; e. Sept. 29, 1862, Andrew Co., Mo.
1291 King, Wm. F., P. Co. H, 25th; e. Sept. 29, 1862, Andrew Co., Mo.
1292 Kinkel, Philip, P. Cos. L and I, Eng.; e.———.
1293 Kerby, Phelan, P. Co. A, 25th e. June 13, 1861, St. Joseph, Mo.
1294 Kipple, Fred, P. Co. B. 25th; e. June 13, 1861, St. Joseph. Mo.
1295 Kirk, Anton, Mus. Co. B, 25th; e. June 13, 1861, St. Joseph, Mo.
1296 Kirkham, Theo., P. Co. A, 25th; e. July 3, 1861, Easton, Mo.
1297 Kirchoff, Henry, P. Cos G, I and D, Eng.; e. Aug. 18, 1862, Cape Girardeau, Mo.; ad. same.
1298 Kirsch, Andrew, P. Co. A, 25th; e———; ad. Muscatine, Iowa.
1299 Kise, Danl., P. Cos. H and D, Eng.; e.———; ad. Cherry Point, Ill.
1300 Kishee, Geo., P. Co. D, Eng.; e. Aug. 15, 1861, St. Lous, Mo.
1301 Kitch, John, P. Co. E, Eng.; e. Nov. 1, 1861,———.
1302 Kitchen, John, P. Co. A, 25th; e. July 25. 1862, Maryville, Mo.
1303 Kitchen, Christian, P. Co A. 25th; e. July 3, 1861, St. Joseph, Mo.
1304 Klaunenberg, Wm. P. Cos. G and I, Eng.; e. Sept. 26, 1861, Cape Girardeau, Mo ; ad. Carlinville, Ill.
1305 Kleb, Christian, P. Cos. L, I and D; e. ———.
1306 KLINGLER, FRED., Lt. Co. B. 25th; e. Feb. 1, 1862, St. Joseph, Mo; wounded at battle of Shiloh, April 6, 1862; res Sept 7, 1862.
1307 Klingman, Martin, P. Cos. I and C, Eng.; e. Sept. 27, 1861, McGregor, Iowa; ad Highland Iowa.
1308 Klink. Jacob, P Co. B, 25th; e. Nov. 1, 1861, St. Joseph, Mo.
1309 KNAPPER, J. G., Lt. Co. B, Eng.; e. Mar. 25, 1863; res. May 9, 1863

1310 KNOWER, CHAS., Asst. Surg. Eng.; e. Oct. 1. 1861. St. Louis, Mo. Was a graduate of Maryland University School of Medicine; discharged October, 31, 1864; settled in St. Louis, Missouri, in the surgical instrument business; died about 1878.
1311 Knowles, Caleb, Sergt. Co. D, Eng.; e. ——.
1312 Knox, Wm., P. Co. I, 25th; e. Aug. 27, 1861, St. Joseph, Mo.
1313 Koch, Louis, P. Cos. L and I, Eng.; e. ——.
1314 Koch, John M., P. Cos. G and I, Eng.; e. Sept. 13, 1861, Cape Girardeau, Mo.; is pensioned; ad. Sheridan, Cal.
1315 Koho, Wm. A., Sergt. Cos. B and K, Eng.; e. Oct. 15, 1861, Kentucky, Ill.; draws a pension; ad. Vermillion, Ill.
1316 Koho, Benj., P. Cos. B and K, Eng ; e, Oct. 15, 1861, Kentucky, Ill.
1317 Koonts, F. M., P. Cos. H and D, Eug ; e. Oct. 15, 1861, Vermillion, Ill.; ad. Vermillion, Ill
1318 Kopper, Henry, P. Cos. G and I, Eng.; e. Sept. 13, 1861, Cape Girardeau, Mo.; ad. same; pensioner.
1319 **KORELL, VALENTINE**, Lt. Co. B, 25th, e. June 13, 1861, St. Joseph, Mo.; res. June 21, 1862; ad. Barnard, Mo.
1320 Kost, Geo. L., P. Co. F, 25th; e. Dec. 30, 1861, Stewartsville, Mo.; ad. Cameron, Mo.
1321 Kroll, Henry, P. Cos. G and I, Eng.; e. Sept, 13, 1861, Cape Girardeau, Mo.
1322 Kucher, Julius, P. Co. D, Eng.; e.——.
1324 Keubler, John, P. Cos. L and I, Eng.; e.——.
1325 Kuncie, Daniel, P. Co. A, 25th; e. June 14, 1861, St. Joseph Mo.
1326 Kunof, Chas., P. Co. B, 25th; e. June 14, 1861, St. Joseph, Mo.
1327 Kunzie, Fred. P. Cos. L and I, Eug.; e.——.
1328 Kurtz, Peter, P. Cos. H and D, Eng.; e. Nov. 8, 1861, St. Louis, Mo.; disch. dis. June 30, 1863, Jackson, Tenn.; draws a pension; ad. Maxville. Mo.
1329 Kusche, Julius, P. Cos L, I and D, Eng.; e.——.
1330 Kuykendall, Leonard E., P. Co. H. Eng.; e. Aug. 14, 1862. Sandford, Ind.
1331 **KREBS, JOHN**, Lt. Co. I 25th and L, Eng.; disch. Sept. 24, 1863.
1332 Labash, John, P. Cos. H, 25th, M and E, Eng.; e. April 4, 1863, Nodaway Co., Mo.
1333 La Baume, Fred, Sergt. Co. G, 25th; e. Jan. 4, 1862, St. Joseph, Mo.
1334 La Baume, Francis F., P. Co. A, 25th; e. June 14, 1861, St. Joseph, Mo.
1335 Lacy, L. R., P. Cos. G, 25th, L and E, Eng.; e. Feb. 12, 1862, Plattsburg, Mo.
1336 Laimon, John W., Sergt. Co. E, Eng.; e. July 13, 1861, Adrian, Mich.; ad. Sylvania, O.
1337 Lake, Seneca, P. Cos. C and B, Eng.; e. Sept. 16, 1861, Avon, Ill.; draws a pension ; ad. Salem, Kas.
1338 Lakey, James A., P. Cos. H. D and C, Eng.; e. Aug. 16, 1863, Pocahontas, Tenn.; is a pensioner; ad. Terre Haute, Ind.
1339 Lakey, John W., P. Cos. E, 25th, G and C. Eng.; e. Feb. 17, 1862, Fremont, Iowa; ad. Sidney, Iowa.
1340 Lakey, Pleasant H., P. Cos. H, D and C, Eng.; e. Aug. 12, 1863, Pocahontas, Tenn.
1341 Lakey, William, P. Cos. H. D and C, Eng.; e. Aug. 12, 1863, Pocahontas, Tenn.
1342 Lamb, Benjamin F., P. Cos. C and B, Eng.; e. Sept. 4, 1861, Prairie City, Ill.
1343 Lamb, Robert, P. Cos. G and E, Eng.; e. Sept. 13, 1861, Cape Girardeau, Mo.; a pensioner; ad Exeter, Ill.
1344 Laimon, William H., P. Co. A, 25th; e. June 18, 1861, Atchison, Kas.
1345 **LANCASTER, L. R.**, Lt. Cos. D, 25th and A. Eng.; e. Aug. 17, 1861, De Kalb Co., Mo ; is a prominent lawyer in St. Joseph, Mo.
1346 Lane, Edward, P. Co. K. Eng.; e. Sept. 25, 1861, Burlington, Iowa.
1347 Lane, Wm. J., P. Cos. H and D, Eng.; e. Aug. 12, 1862, Paris, Ill.
1348 Lainey, Edwin, P. Co. D, 25th; e. July 18, 1861, Andrew Co., Mo.
1349 Lanztine, Ernest, Sergt. Co. B, 25th; e. July 13. 1861, St. Joseph, Mo.
1350 Lape, Hiram T., Sergt. Cos. C and B, Eng.; e Aug. 4, 1861, Prairie City, Ill.; ad. Roseville, Ill.
1351 Larrimer, John P., Co. A, 25th; e. March 1, 1862, Nebraska City, Neb.
1352 Larrimer, Jas., P. Co. E, 25th; e. Sept. 20, 1861, Independence, Mo.

1353 Larrison, Martin, P. Co. D, 25th; e. July 12, 1861, St. Joseph, Mo.
1354 Laswell. Charnell, P. Cos. 1, 25th, H and D, Eng.; e. Dec. 17, 1861, Camden, Mo.
1355 Laswell, Lewis, P. Cos. I, 25th, H and D, Eng.;e. Dec. 16, 1861, Camden, Mo.
1356 Lauer, Henry, Cor. Co. B, 25th; e. June 13, 1861, St Joseph, Mo.
1357 Laur, Philip C., P. Co. B, 25th; e. Aug. 1, 1861, Linneus, Mo.
1358 Lavin, Edward, P. Co. G, 25th; e. June 22, 1861, Kansas City, Mo.
1359 Law, Chas., P. Co. D, Eng.; e. Aug. 25, 1861, St. Louis, Mo.; deserted March 5, 1862, St Louis.
1360 Lawrence, Henry, P. Co. A, 25th; e, June 25, 1861, St. Joseph, Mo.
1361 Layne, Richard, P. Cor. Cos. H. D and C, Eng.; e. Aug. 12, 1862, Paris, Ill.; died at Webster City, Iowa, about 1886.
1362 Layne, Samuel, P. Cos. H, D and C, Eng.; e. Aug. 12, 1862, Elbridge, Ill.
1363 Leach, Homer, P. Co. A, 25th; e. June 29, 1863, St. Joseph, Mo.
1364 Leach, N J., Sergt. Cos. I, 25th, H and D, Eng.; e. Dec. 14, 1861, Cameron, Mo.
1365 Lears, Frank G, P. Co. K, 25th, e. Nov. 7, 1861.
1366 Lears, John, P. Co. K, 25th, e. Nov. 7, 1861.
1367 Lee, Geo. W., P. Cos. B and K, Eng.; e. July 28, 1861. St. Louis, Mo.
1368 Leffler, Jas., P. Co. E, 25th, e. Feb. 17, 1862, Fremont, Iowa.
1369 Leffler, Samuel, P. Cos. E, 25th, G and C, Eng.; e. Feb. 17, 1862, Fremont, Iowa.
1370 Leigh, Amos H., P. Cos. C and B, Eng.; e. Sept. 6, 1861, Prairie City, Ill.
1371 Leintz, Warner, P. Cos. L and I, Eng.; e. ———.
1372 Leitch, William, P. Co. D, Eng.; e. Aug. 15, 1861, St. Louis, Mo.; disch. Feb. 6, 1862, Otterville, Mo.
1373 Lenscke, William, P. Co. G, Eng.; e. Sept. 13, 1861, Cape Girardeau, Mo.; dead.
1374 Lenk, Fred, P. Co. B, 25th, e. June 13, 1861, St. Joseph, Mo.
1375 Leonard, Joseph, P. Co. G, 25th, e. July 9, 1861, Kansas City, Mo.
1376 Leonard, Samuel, P. Cos. C and B, Eng.; e. Aug. 4, 1861, Prairie City, Ill.
1377 Leopold, H., P. Co. D, Eng.; e. Aug. 24, 1861. St. Louis, Mo ; deserted.
1378 Leigan, George, P. Co. D, 25th; e. July 19, 1861, St. Joseph, Mo.
1379 Levy, Joseph, P. Cos. K and D, Eng.; e. Sept. 18, 1861, Burlington, Iowa.
1380 Lewellen. Zadock, P. Co. K, 25th, e. Oct. 18. 1862, Hawleyville, Iowa.
1381 Leewin, Silas, P. Co. H, 25th, e. July 30, 1862, Holt Co., Mo.
1382 Lewis, Andrew J., P. Cos. E, 25th, G and C, Eng.; e. Sept. 21, 1862, Atchison Co., Mo.; ad. Independence, Kas.
1383 Lewis, George W., P. Co. A, 25th, e. June 20, 1861, St. Joseph, Mo.
1384 Lewis. Cyrus H., P. Co. E, Eng.; e. July 13, 1861, Adrian, Mich.; a pensioner; ad. Covert, Mich.
1385 Lewis, John, P. Co. A. Eng.; e. July 20, 1861, St. Louis, Mo.; killed in action Tuscumbia, Miss , June 1, 1862.
1386 Lewis, Wm. H., P. Cos. E, 25th, G and C, Eng.; e. June 6, 1863; Atchison Co., Mo.
1387 Libba, Elijah T., Cor. Co. D, Eng.; e. Aug. 14, 1861; Camden, Ill.; disch. dis. June 8, 1862, St. Louis, Mo.; pensioner; ad. Dawson, Neb.
1388 Linch, Stephen L., P. Cos. I and C, Eng.; e. Oct. 10, 1861: Dubuque, Iowa.
1389 Lincoln, David, P. Co. E, 25th; e. June 9, 1862, Andrew Co., Mo.
1390 Linder, Gottfried, P. Cos. L and I, Eng.; e. ———.
1391 Linderman, John H., P. Cos. K and B, Eng.; e. Sept. 28, 1861, Wapello, Iowa; has a pension; ad. Wapello, Iowa.
1392 Lindsley, Wm. M., P. Cos. E, 25th, G and I, Eng.; e. Sept. 30, 1861; Atchison Co., Mo.; ad. Watson (or Craig), Mo.
1393 Linderson, Elisha W., Sergt. Co. I, 25th; e. July 29, 1861, Gallatin, Mo.
1394 Lingg, Joseph, P. Co. F, Eng.; e. Oct. 31, 1861; Bloomington, Ill.; disch. dis. Otterville, Mo. Feb. 1862; dead.
1395 Linn, Chas., P. Cos. K and B, Eng.; e. Sept. 20, 1861, Burlington, Iowa; draws a pension; ad. Clyde, Kas.
1396 Linn, David, P. Cos. D and F, Eng.; e. Aug. 3, 1861, Flora, Ill.; has a pension; ad. Newton, Ill.
1397 Lindsay, Martin, P. Cos. E, 25th, G and C, Eng.; e. Sept. 30, 1861, Atchison Co., Mo.; ad. Lathrop, Mo.

1398 Lister, Francis, P. Cos. I, 25th, H and D, Eng.; e. Oct 6, 1862, Bloomington, Mo ; ad. Callisburg, Mo.
1399 Lister, Thos., P. Cos. I, 25th, H and D, Eng.; e. Oct. 6, 1862, Bloomington, Mo.
1400 Lister, Wm., P. Cos. I, 25th, H and D, Eng ; e. Oct. 6, 1861, Bloomington, Mo.; a pensioner; ad. Macon, Mo.
1401 Little, Francis, P. Cos. C, 25th, A and B, Eng.; e. Dec. 3, 1861, St. Joseph, Mo.
1402 Litchold, John, P. Co. B, 25th; e. June 13, 1861, St. Joseph, Mo.
1403 Livengood, Theo. F., P. Cos. E, 25th, G and C, Eng.; e. Dec 15, 1861, Holt Co., Mo.
1404 Livingston, Alf. H., P. Cos. E, 25th, G and C, Eng.; e. Dec. 13, 1861, Atchison Co., Mo.
1405 Livingston, Francis, P. Cos. A and B, Eng.; e. Dec. 17, 1861, Cape Girardeau, Mo.
1406 Lloyd, Richard, Cor. Cos. F, 25th, H and D, Eng.; e. Jan. 1, 1862 Chillicothe, Mo.; promoted 2d Lt., June 12, 1865.
1407 Lochard, Hugh A., P. Cos. E, 25th, G and C, Eng.; e. Dec. 30, 1861, Atchison Co., Mo.
1408 **LOCHBILER, CHRISTIAN**, Capt. Cos. L and I, Eng.; e. June 8, 1863, St. Louis, Mo.; disch Oct. 31, 1864, dead.
1409 Locke, Stephen, P. Co. C, 25th; e. June 4, 1862.
1410 Locke, Wm., P. Co D, 25th; e. July, 12, 1861.
1411 Loeffler, Bernhard, P. Co. B, 25th; e. June 13, 1861, St. Joseph, Mo.
1412 Laehr, Henry, P. Cos. B, 25th, L, Eng ; e. July 23, 1861, St. Joseph, Mo.; is a pensioner, ad. Alma, Kas; wounded in legs at Lexington.
1413 Loftus, John, P. Co. A, 25th; e. June 20, 1861, St. Joseph, Mo.
1414 Loftus, Michael, P. Cos. I, 25th, H and D, Eng.; e. Dec. 7, 1861, Cameron, Mo.; a pensioner.
1415 Logue, Erasmus, Cor. Co. I, Eng.; e. Sept. 15, 1861, Rushville, Ill.; died, Otterville, Mo.
1416 Lohkamp, Fredk., P. Co G. Eng.; e. Sept. 13, 1861, Cape Girardeau, Mo.
1417 Long, Abner G., P. Co. B, 25th; e. March 10, 1863, Andrew Co., Mo.
1418 Long, Hiram T., P. Co. B, 25th; e. March 10, 1863, Andrew Co., Mo.
1419 Long, Maurice, P. Co. E. Eng.; e. July 13, 1861, Adrian, Mich.; draws a pension; ad. Willow Springs, Mo.
1420 Long, Samuel, P. Co. A, Eng.
1421 Long, Wm., P. Co. G, 25th; e. June 27, 1861, Kansas City, Mo.
1422 Look, Henry, P. Co. G, Eng.; e. Sept. 13, 1861, Cape Girardeau, Mo.
1423 Lord, Geo. T., Cor. Co. H, 25th; e Dec. 31, 1861, Maryville, Mo.
1424 Lorenz, Geo., P. Co. B. 25th; e. June 13, 1861, Kansas City, Mo.
1425 Loudon, Lafayette, P. Co. E, Eng.; e. July 13, 1861, Adrian, Mich., ad. same.
1426 Louk, Emory G., P. Cos. C and B, Eng.; e. Sept. 16, 1861, Avon, Ill.; ad. Quenemo, Osage Co, Kas.
1427 Louth, Wm., P. Co. E, Eng.; e. July 13, 1861, Adrian, Mich.; ad. Morenci, Mich. Died June 17, 1889.
1428 Louther, James B., P. Co. A, 25th; e. June 17, 1861, St. Joseph, Mo.
1429 Loveland, Wm. H., P Cos. C and B, Eng.; e. Sept. 14, 1861, Prairie City, Ill.; vet. Jan. 21, 1864; ad. Ellisville, Ill.
1430 Low, David, P. Co. E, Eng.; e. July 13, 1861, Adrian, Mich.
1431 Lowe, Wm., P. Co. D, Eng.; e. Sept. 15, 1861; deserted.
1432 Lubernickle, John, P. Cos. L and I; e. ———.
1433 Ludlow, John, Sergt. Cos. A and E. Eng.; e. June 26, 1861, St. Louis, Mo.; ad. 1709 O'Fallon st , St. Louis, Mo.
1434 Ludlow, Wm., P. Cos. A and E, Eng ; e. June 26, 1861, St. Louis; Mo.
1435 Ludwig, Fredk., P. Co, B, 25th; e. June 13, 1861, St. Joseph, Mo.
1436 Luce, Alf., P. Cos. B and E, Eng.; e. July 20, 1861, St. Louis, Mo.
1437 Lucas, Geo. W., P. Cos. C and H; e. Aug 4, 1861, Prairie City, Ill.; deserted, Aug. 1863, supposed to the enemy.
1438 Lucas, Jas. W., P. Co. H, 25th; e. ———.
1439 **LUCAS, STEPHEN T.**, Lt. and Capt. Cos. H, 25th, M and E, Eng.; e. July 26, 1861; Forrest City, Mo.; has been sheriff of Holt Co., Mo.; ad. Forrest City, Mo.

1440 Lutz, Anthony, P. Cos. B and E, Eng.; e. Aug. 5, 1861, Paris, Ill.; pensioned.
1441 **LYLE, WM. K.**, Lt. Cos. B, 25th, L and E, Eng.; e. Dec. 9, 1861, St Joseph, Mo. *History*—He was born in Washington County, Pennsylvania, February 6, 1833, a grandson of Hon. Aaron Lyle, a soldier in the Revolutionary War and representative in Congress. In 1861 Lieutenant Lyle was a miner in Colorado, near Pike's Peak, where, upon the news of the firing on Fort Sumter every man took sides either for or against the Union. A secret organization was formed by the Union miners, in the fall of 1861. As the news from the States showed the need of more men from the North, he arranged to leave for the seat of war November 1, 1861, going toward Pennsylvania, but at Omaha, instead of going home first, enlisted under Lieutenant Bradshaw in the Twenty-fifth Missouri, Company A; was appointed Orderly Sergeant Company A, July 1, 1862; Second Lieutenant Company B, July 2, 1863; transferred to First Missouri Engineers and promoted to First Lieutenant Company L, December 31, 1863; transferred to Company E Consolidated Battalion First Missouri Engineers, October 31, 1864; promoted Captain, Company B Engineers, June 12, 1865; at dress parade, July 8, 1863, New Madrid, Missouri, he was presented by Sergeant Simmonds, on behalf of his comrades in Company A Twenty-Fifth, with a fine sword and belt in a neat speech by the Sergeant, setting forth the consideration in which he was held by his comrades. Shortly after the consolidation with the Engineer Regiment he was detailed Quartermaster of the Second Battalion, and at Nashville in August, 1864, Regimental Quartermaster. After the capture of Atlanta, he was detailed by order of Major-General Howard as Assistant Quartermaster, Engineers' Department of the Tennessee under Colonel C. B. Reese, Chief Engineer, and was ordered to return to Nashville, Tenn., and procure new material for a ponton train and engineer supplies, returning to Atlanta or the last train before the road was destroyed for the "March to the Sea." From Raleigh, North Carolina, he was sent under orders from General Howard to bring up reserve Headquarters, rejoining the Army at Alexandria near Washington, District Columbia. He is a prosperous and well-to-do merchant in the hardware business, South Burgettstown, Washington County, Pennsylvania.
1442 Lynch, Thos., P. Co. G, 25th; e. June 24, 1861, Kansas City, Mo.
1443 Lynch, John, P. Co. K, 25th; e. Aug. 16, 1861, Kansas City, Mo.
1444 Lytle, Gardner, P. Co. C, Eng.; e. Sept. 16, 1861, Prairie City, Ill.
1445 **LOOS, FRED.** Lt. Co. B, Van Horn's Battalion; e.———.
1446 Luding, Fred, P. Co. B 25th and L, Eng.; e.———, St. Joseph, Mo.
1447 Luullen, Zeel, P. Co. K, 25th; e.———.
1448 Madden, Pat., Sergt. Cos. G, 25th and L, Eng.; e. Dec. 1, 1861, Kansas City, Mo.
1449 Madden, Samuel G., P. Cos. G, 25th, L and B, Eng.; e, May 31, 1863.
1450 Mack, Martin, P. Co. I, Eng.; e. Sept. 24, 1861, Dubuque, Iowa; died, Oterville, Mo.; Dec. 1861.
1451 Mack, Robt., P. Cos. A and E, Eng.; e. July 20, 1861, St. Louis, Mo.
1452 Macklin, Patrick, P. Co. H, Eng ; e. Oct. 8, 1861, St. Louis, Mo.; disch. dis. Aug. 1863; ad. 2201 Madison av., St. Louis, Mo.
1453 **McLOON, HENRY P.**, Lt. Co. K, 25th; e. March 25, 1862, St. Joseph, Mo.; res. Sept. 17, 1862.
1454 McAlpin, Henry B., P. Cos. K, 25th and G, Eng.; e. Sept. 23, 1862, Hawleyville, Iowa; ad. same.
1455 McBee, Chas. P., Co. C, Eng.; e. Nov. 24, 1863.
1456 McBeth, Jas. B., P. Co. I, 25th; e. July 22, 1861, Gallatin, Mo.
1457 McBride, Jacob G., P. Cos. F and B, Eng.; e. Oct. 7, 1861, Cassville, Wis.; . dead.
1458 McBride, John, P. Co. D, Eng.; e. Sept. 25, 1861, Camden, Ill.; disch. dis. Feb 12, 1863, Memphis, Tenn.
1459 McBrien, John, P. Co. G, 25th; e. June 12, 1861, Kansas City, Mo.
1460 McBride, Wm., P. Cos. B and C, Eng.; e. Aug. 4, 1861, Paris, Ill.; a pensioner; ad. Sullivan, Ind.
1461 McBrier, James H., P. Co. C, Eng.; e. Oct. 4, 1862.
1462 McBryer, John F., P. Co. K, 25th; e. Sept. 23, 1862, Gallatin, Mo.
1463 McCabe, Peter, P. Co. A, 25th; e. June 14, 1861, St. Joseph, Mo.

1464 McCabe, Thomas, P. Co. G, 25th; e. June 25, 1861, Kansas City, Mo.
1465 McCune, William D., P. Co. A, 25th; June 17, 1861, St. Joseph, Mo.
1466 McCandless, John, P. Cos. K and D, Eng.; e. Sept. 25, 1861, Burlington, Iowa.
1467 McCarthy, Dennis, P. Cos. A and E, Eng.; e. July 20, 1861, St. Louis, Mo.
1468 McCartney, Benjamin E., P. Cos. F, 25th, H and D, Eng.; e. Dec. 30, 1861; Stewartsville, Mo.
1469 McCarty, Dan , P. Co. I, 25th; e. July 25, 1861, Gallatin, Mo.
1470 McCarty, Dan., P. Co. E, Eng.; e. July 13, 1861, Adrian, Mich.
1471 **McCARTY, EDWARD**, Lt. Co. G, 25th; e July 3, 1862; not accounted for; ad. 630 Charlotte st., Kansas City, Mo.
1472 McCarty, John. P. Co. G, 25th; e. Feb. 15, 1862, Troy, Kas
1473 McClary, Ralph B., Hosp. Stewd. and Co. C, Eng.; e. Aug. 4, 1861, Prairie City, Ill; is a practising physician at Monmouth, Ill.; draws a pension.
1474 McCash, Wm. F., Cor. Co. K, Eng.; e. Sept. 25th, 1861, Burlington, Iowa; ad. same.
1475 McClelland, Jas. A., P. Co. I, 25th; e. Aug. 29, 1861, Gallatin, Mo.
1476 McClelland, Wade C., P. Co I, 25th; e. Aug. 10, 1861, Gallatin, Mo.
1477 McClellan, John, P. Co. A, 25th; e. ——, 1862, Kansas City, Mo.; deserted.
1478 McClure, James, Sergt. Co. A, Eng.; e. July 20, 1861, St. Louis, Mo.; died in St. Louis, 1872.
1479 McClure. Joseph, P. Cos. H and D, Eng.; e, Aug. 16, 1862, Bloomfield, Ill.; ad. Vermillion, Ill
1480 McCormack, Dan., P. Cos. G, 25th, L and E, Eng.; e. Feb. 18, 1862, Kansas City, Mo.
1481 McCraven, Francis, Cor. Cos. D ard C, Eng.; e. Aug. 2, 1861, Keokuk, Iowa.
1482 McCullum, Amos. P Co. F, Eng.; e. Oct. 21, 1861, Decatur. Ill.; deserted.
1483 McCurry, John, P. Co. H, 25th; e. Aug. 14, 1861, Nodaway Co., Mo.
1484 McDade, John, Sergt. Co. F, Eng.; e. Sept. 14, 1861, Galena, Ill.; disch. dis. date not known.
1485 McDaniel, Samuel F., Cor. Cos. B and K, Eng.; e. July 28, 1861, Paris, Ill.
1486 McDonald, Alex, P. Co. D, Eng.; e. Aug. 16, 1861, St. Louis, Mo.; deserted March 5, 1862, St. Louis. Mo.
1487 McDonald, Edward, Sergt. Cos. H and D, Eng.; e. Nov. 14, 1861, St. Louis, Mo.; has a pensi n, is captain police second district, corner of Carr and 7th st.; ad. 1437 Wright st ; St. Louis, Mo.
1488 McDonald, James, P. Co. A. 25th; e. July 9, 1861, St. Joseph, Mo.
1489 McDonald, Jasper, P. Cos A and E, Eng.; e. July 20, 1861, St. Louis, Mo.
1490 McDonald, John, P. Co E, Eng ; e. July 13, 1861, Adrian, Mich.; ad. same.
1491 McDonald, Wm., P. Cos. B and E, Eng.; e. August 5, 1861, Paris, Ill.
1492 McElroy, Jas , P. Co. D, 25th; e. July 30, 1861, Andrew Co., Mo.
1493 McEwen, Leander, Cor. Co. D, Eng.; e. Sept. 11, 1861, St. Louis, Mo.; died Dec. 28, 1863, Cairo, Ill.
1494 McFadden, Robert, Cor. Co. G, Eng.; e. Sept. 13, 1861, Cape Girardeau, Mo.
1495 McFarland, Wm., P. Cos. K, 25th, G and C, Eng.; e. Feb. 1, 1862, Taylor Co., Iowa.
1496 McGarrell, Wm., P. Cos. A, 25th, M and E, Eng.; e. June 14, 1861, St. Joseph, Mo.; ad. San Bernardino, Cal.; pensioner.
1497 McGarvan, Wm., P. Co. B, Eng.; e. Jan. 12, 1864.
1498 McGarvin, Dennis, P. Co. I, 25th; e. July 25, 1861, Gallatin, Mo.
1499 McGrath, Roger, P. Cos. A and E, Eng.; e. July 20, 1861, East St. Louis, Ill.
1500 McGirr, David. P. Cos. A and E, Eng.; e. July 20, 1861, St. Louis, Mo.
1501 McGlashen, John, P. Co. D, Eng.; e. August 16, 1862, St. Louis, Mo.; dead.
1502 McGlancy, Jas , P. Cos. K, 25th, G and C, Eng.; e. Nov. 19, 1861, Hawleyville, Iowa.
1503 McGorry, Benedict. P. Co. F, Eng.; e. Oct. 1, 1861, Decatur, Ill.; is a Police Magistrate in Decatur, Ill.
1504 McGoffin, Marcus, P. Co. E, 25th; e. July 22, 1861, Oregon, Mo
1505 McGovern, Pat., P. Co. G, 25th; e. July 3, 1861, Kansas City, Mo.
1506 McGowan, Wm., P Co. A, 25th; e. Aug. 10, 1861, Kansas City, Mo.
1507 McGrail, John, Mus., Cos. A and E, Eng.; e. July 20, 1861, St. Louis, Mo.
1508 McGuire, Christopher M., Sergt. Cos. E, 25th, G and C, Eng.; e. Feb. 17, 1862. Sidney, Iowa; he is Sheriff (1888) of Phillips Co. Kas.; ad. Philipsburg, Kas.
1509 McHale, William, P. Cos. A and E, Eng.; e. July 20, 1861, St. Louis, Mo.

1510 McIntosh, Jesse, P. Co. C, 25th; e. Dec. 20, 1861.
1511 McIntyre, John D., P. Co. F, Eng.; e. Sept. 9, 1861, Manchester, Iowa.
1512 McIvor, Dan, P. Cos. F and B, Eng ; e. June 13, 1862, St. Louis, Mo.; he became blind in Gen. Hos., about 1864.
1513 McKain, Notley, P. Cos. D, F and A, Eng.; e. Aug. 15, 1861, Flora, Ill.; vet.; ad. Dunbar, Ohio.
1514 McKechner, John, P. Cos A and E, Eng.; e. July 20, 1861, St. Louis, Mo.
1515 McKee, Benj. F., P. Co. A, 25th; e. Dec. 20, 1861, St. Joseph, Mo.
1516 McKee, Lawrence, P. Co. G, 25th; e. June 17, 1861, Kansas City, Mo.
1517 McKenna, John, P. Cos. A and E, Eng.; e. July 20, 1861, St. Louis, Mo.
1518 McKenna, Pat., P. Co. G, 25th; e. June 26, 1861, Kansas City, Mo.
1519 McKenna, Peter, P. Co. G, 25th; e. June 24, 1861, Kansas City, Mo.
1520 McKinlay, John A., P. Cos. D, 25th, A and B, Eng.; e. July 16, 1861, St. Joseph, Mo.; ad. Grant City, Mo.
1521 McKinnis, Hiram, Sergt. Co. I, 25th; e. July 6, 1861, Cameron, Mo.
1522 McKnight, William, P. Co. D, 25th; e. July 19, 1861, Clinton, Mo.
1523 McLain, ——, P. Co. E, Eng.; e. July 13, 1861, Adrian, Mich.
1524 McLane, Joseph, P. Cos. H and D, Eng.; e. Aug. 12, 1862, Paris, Ill.
1525 **McLAREN, JOHN**, Lt. Cos. F, A and C, Eng.; e. Aug. 28, 1861, Dubuque, Iowa, disch. Dec. 20, 1864. He is a prosperous and wealthy wholesale lumber merchant at No. 2 Franklin St., Chicago, Ill.; ad. 339 S. Ashland av., Chicago, Ill.
1526 McLaughlin, Fred. W., P. Co. H, 25th; e Aug. 14, 1861, Nodaway Co., Mo.
1527 **McLELLAN, JOHN**, Lt. Co. A, 25th; e. May 16, 1862, cashiered Oct. 31, 1862.
1528 McLure, John, P. Cos. H and D, Eng.; e. Aug. 16, 1862, Bloomfield, Ill.
1529 McMahon, Mich., P. Co. G, 25th; e. June 26, 1861, Kansas City, Mo.
1530 McMeans, David, P. Cos. A and E, Eng.; e. July 20, 1861, St. Louis, Mo.
1531 McMeneman, Jas., P. Co. G, 25th; e. Aug. 1, 18 1, Kansas City, Mo.
1532 McMichael, Robt., P. Co. H, 25th; e. Aug. 14, 1861, Nodaway Co., Mo.
1533 McMillian, Geo., P. Co. C, 25th; e. July 12, 1861, Gentry Co., Mo.
1534 McMillian, Levi, P. Cos. H, D and C, Eng.; e. Aug. 30, 1861, St. Louis, Mo.
1535 McNair, R., P. Co. E, Eng.; e. July 13, 1861, Adrian, Mich.; died near Otterville, Mo., Oct., 1861.
1536 McNally, Richard, P Cos. I and C, Eng.; e. Oct. 12, 1861, McGregor, Iowa; ad. Wagner, Iowa.
1537 McNamara, Hugh, P. Cos. C, 25th, A and B, Eng. ; e. Dec. 31, 1861, Rushville, Mo.; vet. Jan. 20, 1864.
1538 McNeil, Elias, P. Cos. I and C, Eng.; e. Sept. 15, 1861, Denmark, Iowa; ad. same.
1539 McSperrin, Perry, P. Cos. C, 25th, A and B, Eng. ; e. Dec. 16, 1861, St. Joseph, Mo.; ad. Wathena Kas.
1540 McSweeney, Terrence, P. Co. G, 25th; e. June 20, 1861, Kansas City, Mo.
1541 McWaid, Samuel G., P. Co. F, 25th; e. Aug. 21, 1861, De Kalb Co., Mo.
1542 Magan, Charles W., P. Cos. H, 25th, M and E, Eng.; e Sept. 20, 1862, Nodaway Co., Mo.
1543 Magan, John W., P. Co. H, 25th; e. Sept. 20, 1862, Nodaway Co., Mo.; ad. St. Louis, Mo.
1544 Magg, Phil., P. Co. B, 25th, e. June 13, 1861, St. Joseph, Mo.
1545 Mainey, John, P Cos. A and E. Eng. ; e. July 20, 1861, St. Louis, Mo.
1546 Mallett, Adam. P. Co. B, 25th, e. Nov. 1, 1861, St. Joseph, Mo.
1547 Mallin, John, Cor. Cos. H, D, E and C, Eng ; e.——.
1548 Malinsky, Louis, P. Cos. A and E, Eng.; e. July 20, 1861, St. Louis, Mo.
1549 Mallory, Thomas, P. Co. G, 25th; e. June 17, 1861, Kansas City, Mo.
1550 Maloon, James, P. Co. G, 25th; e. June 24, 1861, Kansas City, Mo.
1551 Malony, Richard A., Sergt. Cos. C and B, Eng.; e. Aug. 4, 1861, Prairie City, Ill.; ad. Madison, Neb.
1552 Malony, Richard, P. Co. F, 25th; e. Feb. 22, 1862, St. Joseph, Mo.
1553 Manly, Harrison, P. Co. H, 25th; e. Mar. 25, 1863, Nodaway Co., Mo.
1554 Manly, Riley, P. Co. H, 25th; e. Aug. 14, 1861, Nodaway Co., Mo.
1555 Mann, Fred, P. Cos. D and F, Eng.; e. Aug. 15, 1861, St. Louis, Mo.; was badly injured in right arm in an accident near Johnsonville, Tenn., June 22, 1864.
1556 Mansfield, Edward, P. Co. G, 25th; e. June 20, 1861, Kansas City, Mo.

1557 Manuel, Lorenzo, P. Co. D, Eng.; e. Oct. 15, 1861, Camden, Ill.; died March 3, 1863; Gen. Hos., Memphis, Tenn.
1558 Maples, Richard, P. Cos. D, 25th, A and B, Eng.; e. Mar. 1, 1862, St. Joseph, Mo.; ad. Easton, Mo.
1559 Marcy, Stephen, P. Co. E, Eng.; e. July 13, 1861, Adrian, Mich.; is a pensioner; ad. 2122 Cummings St., Omaha, Neb.
1560 Markel, Jacob, P. Cos. A and E, Eng.; e. July 20, 1861, St. Louis, Mo.
1561 Markwell, John, P. Co. H, 25th; e. Aug. 4, 1861, ———; ad. Maryville, Mo.
1562 Marshall, John, Sergt. Cos. F, 25th, H and D, Eng.; e. Jan. 1, 1862, St. Catharines, Mo.; ad. North Salem, Mo.
1563 Martens, Henry, P. Co. G, Eng.; e. Sept. 13, 1861, Cape Girardeau, Mo.; disch. Oct. 1863, for injury, crushing both legs and ankles at Pocahontas, Tenn., in Sept. 1863; injured while unloading heavy bridge timbers from railroad cars; ad. Cape Girardeau, Mo.
1564 Martin, Almarine, P. Co. K, Eng.; e. Oct. 1, 1861, New London, Iowa; ad. Kirwin, Kas.
1565 Martin, Dennis, P. Cos. A and E, Eng.; e. July 20, 1861, St. Louis, Mo.
1566 Martin, John, P. Co. F, Eng.; e. Oct. 1, 1861, Bloomington, Ill.; died Apr., 1862, New Madrid, Mo.
1567 Martin, Jonathan J., P. Cos. E, 25th, G and C, Eng.; e. Jan. 2, 1862.
1568 Martin, Joseph A., Sergt. Cos. A and E, Eng.; e. July 20, 1861, St. Louis, Mo.
1569 Martin, Silas, P. Cos. A and E, Eng.; e. July 20, 1861, St. Louis, Mo.
1570 Marvin, J. J., Cor. Co. E, 25th; e. Jan. 3, 1862, Sonora, Mo.; ad. Falls City, Neb.
1571 Marx, Jacob, P. Cos. L and I, Eng.; e.———.
1572 Mason, Geo., P. Co. C, 25th; e. July 15, 1861.
1573 Mather, Peter, P. Co B, 25th; e. Nov. 1, 1861, St. Joseph, Mo.
1574 Mathews, Ezekiel, P. Co. D, 25th; e. July 17, 1861, St. Joseph, Mo.
1575 Mathews, Chas. D., P. Co. E, 25th; e. July 22, 1861, Brown Co., Kas.
1576 Mathews, Geo. W., P. Cos. B and K, Eng.; e. July 28, 1861, Paris, Ill.; dead.
1577 Mathews, Jas., P. Co. G, Eng.; e. Oct. 17, 1861, Cape Girardeau, Mo.
1578 Mathews, Jas. S., P. Co. E, 25th; e. July 22, 1861, Brown Co., Kas.
1579 Mathingly, John, P. Cos. G and J, Eng.; e. Sept. 13, 1861, Cape Girardeau, Mo.
1580 **MATTIS, SILAS W.**, Lt. Cos. K and F, Eng.; e. Sept., 1861, Burlington, Iowa.; died insane, at Nashville, Tenn.
1581 Maurer, Geo., P. Co. B, 25th; e. June 13, 1861, St. Joseph, Mo.
1582 Mavity, Jas. F., P. Cos. E, 25th, G and C, Eng.; e. Feb. 16, 1862, Sidney, Iowa.
1583 Mayenberg, John, P. Cos. L and I, Eng.; e.———.
1584 Mayer, Geo., P. Co. A, 25th; e. June 14, 1861, St. Joseph, Mo.
1585 Mays, James L., P. Cos. F, 25th, H and D, Eng.; e. Dec. 21, 1861, St. Catharines, Mo.; ad. Brookland, Ark.
1586 Maxwell, Jas. R., P. Co. H, 25th; e.———.
1587 Meacham, Ahira, P. Co. D, Eng.; e. Oct 1, 1861, Rushville, Ill.; disch. dis. Oct. 22, 1862, has pension; ad. Leon, Kas.
1588 Meacham, Arlin. P. Co. D, Eng.; e. Oct. 26, 1861, Rushville, Ill.; disch. dis. March 19, 1862, Otterville Mo.
1589 Meek, John, P. Cos. D and F. Eng.; e. Sept. 14, 1861, Flora, Ill.
1590 Mehoffy, Geo. W., P. Co C, 25th; e. July 27, 1861, Kansas City, Mo.
1591 Mehring, Fred, P. Cos. G and I, Eng.; e. Sept. 13, 1861, Cape Girardeau, Mo.; dead.
1592 Meier, August, P. Cos. G and I, Eng.; e. Sept. 13, 1861, Cape Girardeau, Mo.
1593 Meier, Fred, P. Co. G, Eng.; e Sept. 13, 1861, Cape Girardeau, Mo.
1594 Meisel, Henry, P. Co. B, 25th; e. June, 13, 1861, St. Joseph, Mo.
1595 Mellville, M. C., P. Co. A, 25th; e. June 15, 1861, St. Joseph, Mo.
1596 Mengoz, Eugene, Mus. Co. F, Eng.; e. Aug. 28, 1861, Gilbertville, Iowa; disch. dis. July, 1862, Jackson, Tenn.
1597 Mengoz, Francois, P. Co. F, Eng.; e. Sept. 20, 1861, Gilbertville, Iowa.
1598 Meredith, Mathias, P. Co. D, 25th; e. Feb. 20, 1862, St. Joseph, Mo.
1599 Merrick, Rufus P., P. Co. E, Eng.; e. July 13, 1861, Adrian, Mich.; is pensioned; ad. Charlotte, Mich.

1600 MERRITT, A. J., Capt. Co. K, Eng.; e. Sept. 1, 1861, Des Moines, Iowa; disch. Jan. 1, 1864; is a civil engineer and railroad contractor in good circumstances at 556 Drake Block, St. Paul, Minn.
1601 Merritt, Ancil L., P. Co. D, 25th; e. July 12, 1861, St. Joseph, Mo.
1602 Merritt, Franklin, P. Co. F, 25th; e. Nov. 27, 1862, St. Joseph, Mo.
1603 Merritt, Lewis, P. Co. D, 25th; e. July 12, 1861, St. Joseph, Mo.
1604 Merritt, Robert W., P. Co. D, 25th; e. July 12, 1861, St. Joseph, Mo
1605 Metcalfe, Francis M., P. Cos. F, 25th, H and D, Eng.; e. Dec. 31, 1861, Rochester, Mo.
1606 Merwin, Oscar, P. Co. F, Eng.; e. Oct. 19, 1861, Bloomington, Ill ; deserted.
1607 Meyer, Christian, P. Co. E, 25th; e. March 17, 1862, Atchison Co., Mo.
1608 Meyer, Frank, P. Cos. B, 25th, L and E, Eng.; e. Sept. 11, 1862, St. Joseph, Mo.
1609 Meyer, Henry, P. Cos. G and I, Eng.; e. Sept. 13, 1861, Cape Girardeau, Mo.; is a pensioner; ad. Cape Girardeau, Mo.
1610 Meyer, John E., Sergt. Co. B, 25th; e. June 13, 1861, St. Joseph, Mo.
1611 Meyforth, Frederick, P. Cos. L and I, Eng.; e. ——
1612 Michael, Shadrack, P. Cos. D, 25th, A and B, Eng.; e. Feb. 1, 1862, St. Joseph, Mo
1613 Michael, Zachariah, P. Cos. D, 25th, A and B, Eng.; e. Jan. 28, 1862, St. Joseph, Mo.
1614 Middleton, Robert D., Sergt. Cos. K and C, Eng.; e. Sept. 15, 1861, New London, Iowa; is a farmer in comfortable circumstances near Sedalia, Mo.
1615 Miles, Jesse R , P. Co. D, 25th; e. July 12, 1861, St. Joseph, Mo.
1616 Miles, John, P. Cos. I and C, Eng.; e. Oct. 5, 1862, Augusta, Iowa; ad. White Cloud, Kas.
1617 MILES, ALEX C., Lt. Co. E, 25th; e. July 22. 1861; res. Sept. 3, 1862.
1618 Miller, Andrew J., P. Co. A, Eng ; e. ——.
1619 Miller, August, P. Co. B, 25th; e. Nov. 11, 1861, St. Joseph, Mo.
1620 Miller, Charles, 1st, P. Co. B, 25th; e. Mar. 1, 1862, St. Joseph, Mo.
1621 Miller, Charles, 2d, P. Co. B, 25th; e. Nov. 1, 1861, St. Louis, Mo.
1622 Miller, F., P. Co. H, Eng.; e. ——.
1623 Miller, George W., Sergt. Cos A and E, Eng.; e. July 20, 1861, St. Louis, Mo.
1624 Miller, George W., P. Co. I, 25th; e. Aug. 12, 1861, De Kalb Co., Mo.
1625 Miller, John, P. Cos. H and D, Eng ; e. Oct. 18; 1861, Vermillion, Ill.
1626 MILLER, JOHN H., Lt. Co. G, 25th; e. July 17, 1861, Wyandotte, Kas.; res Mar. 14, 1863.
1627 Miller, John, P. Co. A, 25th; e. July 14, 1861, St. Joseph. Mo.
1628 Miller, Peter, P. Co. E, Eng.; e. July 13, 1861, Adrian, Mich.
1629 Miller, Peter, P. Co. B, 25th; e. June 13, 1861, St. Joseph, Mo.
1630 Miller, Robert A., P. Cos. K, 25th, G and C, Eng.; e. Nov. 13, 1862, Clarinda, Iowa; ad. same.
1631 MILLAR WM., Capt. Co. G, 25th; e. Jan. 21, 1861, Kansas City, Mo.; disch. Jan. 1, 1864.
1632 Miller, Wm., P. Co. B, 25th; e. Nov. 1, 1861, St. Joseph, Mo.
1633 Millican, Clark B., P. Cos. I and C, Eng.; e. Sept. 9, 1861, Rushville, Ill.; ad. St. Louis, Mo.
1634 Mills, Thomas, Sergt. Cos. D, 25th, A and B, Eng.; e. March 1, 1862.
1635 MILLS, ALEX. H., Lt. Co. E, 25th; e. July 22, 1861, Oregon, Mo.; res. Sept. 3, 1862; ad White Cloud, Kas.
1636 Marlatt, Wellington, P. Co. E, Eng.; e. July 13, 1861, Adrian, Mich.; a pensioner; ad. Hoskins, Dak.
1637 Mathews, Hiram T., P Cos. I and C, Eng.; e. Sept. 15, 1861, Toolsboro, Iowa; ad. same.
1638 Mathews, Homer O., P. Cos. I and C, Eng.; e. Sept. 15, 1861, Toolsboro, Iowa; draws a pension; ad. Toolsboro, Iowa.
1639 Millsap, Riley, P. Co. C, 25th; e. ——.
1640 Milton, Wm., P. Cos. ——, 25th —— and C, Eng.; e. June 13, 1862.
1641 Miner, Jas. F., Sergt. Co. F, Eng.; e. Aug. 28, 1861, Dubuque Iowa.
1642 Minhous, Herman, P. Cos. L, I and D, Eng.; e. ——.
1643 Misner, Wm., P. Cos. K, D and C Eng.; e. Sept. 25, 1861, Burlington, Iowa.
1644 Mitchell, John, P. Co. A, 25th; e. June 14, 1861, St. Joseph, Mo.
1645 Mitchell, John, P. Co. G, 25th; e. June 27, 1861, Kansas City, Mo.

1646 Mitchell, Winfield S., P. Co. F, 25th; e. Aug. 18, 1861, Oregon, Mo.
1647 Moberly, James, Cor. Cos. —, 25th, — and C, Eng.; e. Sept. 3, 1862.
1648 Montgomery, David, P. Co. D, Eng.; e. Aug. 14, 1861, Carlyle, Ill.; disch. for rheumatism, Jackson, Tenn., Oct. 23, 1862.
1649 Montgomery, John F., P. Co. K, Eng.; e. Sept. 17, 1861, New London, Iowa.
1650 Montgomery, Samuel, P. Cos. A and E, Eng.; e. July 20, 1861, St. Louis, Mo.
1651 Montgomery, Stephen, P. Co. D, 25th; e. July 17, 1861, St. Joseph, Mo.
1652 Moody, Albert J., P. Cos. L and I., Eng.; e. ———; ad. Shenendoah, Iowa.
1653 Moon, Enos, P. Co. C, 25th; e. July 12, 1861.
1654 Moon, Albert S., P. Cos. K, 25th, G and C, Eng.; e. Dec. 15, 1861, Hawleyville, Iowa,
1655 Moore, Dan. M., P. Co. K, Eng.; e. Sept. 1, 1861, Burlington, Iowa; is a pensioner; ad. Fairbury, Neb.
1656 Monfert, —, P. Co. —, Eng.; e. ———; ad. Burlington, Iowa.
1657 Moore, Henry, P. Co. G, 25th; e. Aug. 25, 1861, Kansas City, Mo.
1658 Moore, Isaac, P. Cos. F, 25th, H and D, Eng.; e. Sept. 19, 1862, Breckenridge, Mo.
1659 Moore, James R., P. Cos. H, 25th, G and C, Eng.; e. Sept. 22, 1862, Nodaway Co., Mo.
1660 Moore, Jas., 1st, P. Cos. F, 25th, H and D, Eng.; e. March 30, 1863, Breckenridge, Mo.
1661 Moore, James, 2d. P. Co. F, 25th; e. March 27, 1862, St. Joseph, Mo.
1662 Moore, John, Cor. Cos. H and D, Eng.; e. Aug. 12, 1862, Sandford, Ind.
1663 Moore, John N., P. Cos. ———, 25th, — and C, Eng.; e. Dec. 5, 1861.
1664 Moore, John, P. Cos. F, 25th, H and D, Eng.; e. Dec. 20, 1863, Breckenridge, Mo.
1665 Moore, Philip H., P. Cos. C and B, Eng.; e. Aug. 12, 1862, Bushnell, Ill.; disch. dis. May 19, 1864, Memphis, Tenn.; ad. Sunbury, Pa.
1666 Moore, Peter, P. Cos. C and B, Eng.; e. Aug. 12, 1862, Bushnell, Ill.
1667 Moore, Wm., P. Co. H, 25th; e. Sept. 8, 1862, Nodaway Co., Mo.
1668 Moore, Wm. S., P. Co. D, 25th; e. July 12, 1861, St. Joseph, Mo.
1669 Moran, Jas., P. Cos. I and C, Eng.; e. Sept. 13, 1861, West Point, Iowa.
1670 Morehead, Hugh, P. Co. A, 25th; e. June 15, 1861, St. Joseph, Mo.
1671 Morrell, Elbridge (Alias Wild Cat), P. Cos. I and C, Eng.; e. Sept. 3, 1861, Rushville, Ill.; ad. Bardolph, Ill.; pensioner.
1672 Morgan, David, Sergt. Cos. K, 25th, and G, Eng.; e. Dec. 1, 1861, Hawleyville, Iowa; ad. same; draws a pension.
1673 Morgan, Jas., P. Cos. D and C, Eng.; e. Oct. 26, 1861, Camp Point, Ill.
1674 Morgan, John, P. Co. K, 25th; e. Feb. 1, 1862, Hawleyville, Iowa.
1675 Morgan, Morgan, P. Cos. A and E, Eng.; e. July 20, 1861, St. Louis, Mo.
1676 Morgan, Stephen G., P. Co. K, 25th; e. Dec. 15, 1861, Hawleyville, Iowa.
1677 Morris, Jas. H., P. Co D, 25th; e. July 16, 1861, St. Joseph, Mo.
1678 Mosely, Sam., P. Co. K, 25th; e. Dec. 15, 1861, Hawleyville, Iowa.
1679 Morrison. Chas. W., Sergt. Cos. K, D and C, Eng.; e. March 11, 1862, St. Louis, Mo.; ad. Omaha, Neb.
1680 Morrison, Chas. W., Sergt. Co. D, Eng.; e. August 15, 1861, Olney, Ill.; died at Vicksburg, Miss., June 24, 1862.
1681 Morrison, Sanford W., P. Cos. D and F, Eng.; e. Sept. 14, 1861, Flora, Ill.; is pensioned; ad. Newton, Ill.
1682 Morris, John J., Cor. Co. H, 25th; e. Aug. 14, 1861, Nodaway Co., Mo.; ad. Falls City, Neb.
1683 Morton, Chas., P. Co. I, 25th; e. July 29, 1861, Gallatin, Mo.
1684 Morton, John N., P. Co. I, 25th; e. June 7, 1862, Gallatin, Mo.
1685 **MORTON, JOHN P.**, Capt. Cos. E, 25th, G and C, Eng.; e. Jan. 2, 1862, White Cloud, Kas.; was promoted to 2d Lt. Co. E, 25th, Dec. 8, 1863; 1st Lt. Co. G, Eng., Dec. 31, 1863; Capt. Co. C, Eng., Jan. 12, 1865; ad Prescott, Kas.
1686 **MORTON, MARCUS**, Lt. Co. I, 25th; e. July 29, 1861, Gallatin, Mo.; disch. Jan. 1, 1864; ad. Hamilton, Mo.
1687 **MORTON, WM. A.**, Lt. Cos. I, 25th, H and D, Eng.; e. July 7, 1861, Cameron, Mo.; disch. Feb. 28, 1865.; ad. Kingston, Mo.
1688 Mosher, G. W., P. Co. A, 25th; e. July 26, 1861, St. Joseph, Mo.
1689 Moniss Robert, P. Co. G, Eng.; e. Sept. 13, 1861, Cape Girardeau, Mo.
1690 Mulholland, Abner, P. Co. A, 25th; e. June 17, 1861, St. Joseph, Mo.

1691 Mulkey, Jos. F., P. Co. D, 25th; e. Jan. 18, 1862, St. Joseph, Mo.
1692 Mullett, John, P. Cos. G, 25th, L and E, Eng.; e. Feb. 24, 1862, Kansas City, Mo.
1693 Mullin, Wm. N , P. Co. F, Eng.; e. Oct. 4, 1861, Shell Rock, Iowa; disch. Jackson, Tenn., Oct., 1862.
1694 Mulvahill, Mich., Sergt. Co. G. 25th; e. June 13, 1861, St. Joseph, Mo.
1695 Mund, Louis, P. Cos. G and I, Eng.; e. Sept. 13, 1861, Cape Girardeau, Mo.
1696 Munch, Max, P. Co. B, 25th; e. June 13, 1861, St. Joseph, Mo.
1697 Munger, Richard L., Sergt. Cos. F, 25th, H and D, Eng.; e. Aug. 21, 1861, St. Joseph, Mo.; ad. Empire Prairie, Mo.
1698 Munger, Cyrus, Cor. Co. F. 25th; e. Aug. 12, 1861, Empire Prairie, Mo.
1699 Mungovan, Jas., P Co. G, 25th; e. June 17, 1861, Kansas City, Mo.
1700 Munroe, Jas., P. Cos. A and E, Eng.; e. July 20, 1861, St. Louis, Mo.
1701 Munson, Dan., P. Co. F, 25th; e. Aug. 18, 1861, Oregon, Mo.
1702 Murphy, Dennis, P. Co. G, 25th; e. June 26, 1861, Kansas City, Mo.
1703 Murphy, Chas., P. Cos. H, D and C, Eng.; e. Oct. 18, 1861, Elbridge, Ill.
1704 **MURPHY, JOHN E.**, Capt. Cos. B and K, Eng.; e. July 28, 1861, Paris, Ill.; disch. Oct. 31, 1864; is in business as a blacksmith at Paris, Ill.
1705 **MURPHY, JOHN**, Lt. Cos. G, 25th and L, Eng.; e. July 20, 1863, Kansas City, Mo.; disch. Oct. 31, 1864.
1706 Murphy, John, P. Cos. F and B, Eng.; e. Oct. 1, 1861, Bloomington, Ill.
1707 Murphy, John, P. Co. G, 25th; e. Dec. 30, 1861, Kansas City, Mo.
1708 Murray, Henry, P. Co. I. 25th; e. Jan. 2, 1862, Gallatin, Mo.
1709 Mutschler, Gottlieb, P. Cos. E and A, Eng.; e. July 13, 1861, Adrian, Mich.; has a pension; is a farmer in good circumstances near Clayton, Mich.
1710 Myers, Addison, P. Cos. H and D, Eng.; e. Aug. 25, 1862, Vermillion, Ill.
1711 **MARGASON, JOSEPH**, Lt. Co. I, 5th and 35th, and L, Eng.; e. Aug. 15, 1862; promoted Capt. Co. D, 35th Mo., Sept. 30, 1862.
1712 Nairn, Jas., P. Cos. A and E. Eng.; e. July 20, 1861, Booneville, Ind.
1713 Naile, Geo. L., P. Cos. H, D and C., Eng.; e. Aug. 12, 1862, Grandview, Ill.; ad. Grandview, Ill.
1714 Naile, Wm. H., P. Cos. H, D and C, Eng.; e. Aug. 12, 1862, Grandview, Ill.; pensioner; ad. Decatur, Ill.
1715 Nash, Wm. J., P. Cos. D, 25th, A and B, Eng.; e. July 28, 1862, St. Joseph, Mo.
1716 Naylor, Jas., P. Cos. B and K, Eng.; e July 28, 1861, St. Louis, Mo.
1717 Naylor, John W., Sergt. Cos. A and E, Eng.; e. July 20, 1861, St. Louis, Mo.
1718 Neff, Peter, P. Cos. H, 25th, M and E, Eng.; e. June 3, 1863, Nodaway Co. Mo.; ad. Savannah, Mo.
1719 Nelson, Geo. W., P. Cos. H, 25th, M and E, Eng.; e. March 25, 1863, Nodaway Co., Mo.
1720 Nevils, Pat., P. Co. G., 25th ; e. June 21, 1861, Kansas City, Mo.
1721 Nelson, H. H., P. Cos. H, 25th, M and E, Eng.; e. Jan. 3, 1863, Andrew Co., Mo.; ad Maryville, Mo.
1722 **NEAL, WM. A.**, Asst. Sur. Eng.; e. Oct. 5, 1861, New London, Iowa; was Hospital Steward from Oct. 15, 1861, to Feb. 4, 1864; Asst. Sur. from Feb. 6, 1864, to muster out of the Regiment July 28, 1865; is now engaged in the practice of medicine and surgery at No. 431 Main st., Elkhart, Ind.; is the author and compiler of this History.
1723 **NEWBERRY, OLIVER P.**, Capt. Co. I, 25th; e. July 25, 1862, Cameron, Mo.; was disch. and promoted Maj. of 5th Cavalry, Mo., March 28, 1863.
1724 **NEWHARD, JAMES M.**, Lt. Cos. E, 25th, G and C, Eng., e. July 22, 1861, White Cloud, Kas. He was Orderly Sergt. of Co. E, 25th, and at the consolidation was made 2d Lt. in Co. H, Eng.; May 12, 1865, promoted 1st Lt. Co. C; was detailed as Reg'l Adj. about Oct., 1864, and served as such the most of the time until muster out. Since the war he has lived in Maryville, Mo., and is now in very poor health from the effects of the railroad accident near Johnsonville, Tenn., June 22, 1864, where he was badly hurt; is living at No. 1258 Cypress Street, Oakland, Cal.
1725 Newman, Peter, P. Cos. I and C, Eng.; e. Sept. 22, 1861, McGregor, Iowa.
1726 Newton, Calvin, P. Cos. I and C, Eng.; e. Sept. 22, 1861, McGregor, Iowa.
1727 Nicol, Geo., P. Cos. H, D and C. Eng.; e. Nov. 23, 1861, St. Louis, Mo.
1728 Nicholas, Wm. N., P. Cos. D, F and B, Eng.; e. Oct. 3, 1861, Flora, Ill.; draws a pension; ad. West Liberty, Ill.

1729 **NICHOLS, FRED C.**, Capt. Co. A, 25th, Maj. Eng.; e. May 16, 1861; disch. Oct. 31, 1864; is or was in the Regular Army, Lt. 1st Art.
1730 **NICHOLSON, SAML. T.**, Capt. Co. E, Eng.; e. July 13, 1861, Adrian, Mich.; res. Dec. 3, 1861; is in business at Adrian, Mich.
1731 Noah, Uriah, P. Co. I, 25th; e. Aug. 12, 1861, Gallatin, Mo
1732 Nobles, Judson K., P. Cos. H, D and C, Eng.; e. Sept. 25, 1863, Pocahontas, Tenn.
1733 Nobles, Hezakiah G., P. Cos. H, D and C, Eng.; e. Oct. 1, 1863, Pocahontas, Tenn.
1734 Nobly, Jas C., Cor. Co. K, 25th; e. Sept. 23, 1862.
1735 **NOEL, CHAS. W.**, Lt. Co. K, 25th; e. Oct. 6, 1862; commissioned; vacated March 5, 1863.
1736 Noland, Jas., P. Co. A, 25th; e. July 23, 1861, St. Joseph, Mo.
1737 Noland, Wesley, P. Co. A, 25th; e July 9, 1861, St. Joseph, Mo.
1738 Noelle, John, P Cos. G and I, Eng.; e. Sept. 13, 1861, Cape Girardeau, Mo.
1739 Noll, John, P. Cos. L and I, Eng.; e. ——.
1740 **NORRIS, WM. H. P.**, Lt. Co. D, 25th; e. July 26, 1861, Ottumwa, Iowa; res. Sept. 7, 1863.
1741 Norton, Andrew J., P. Co. F, Eng.; e. Sept. 21, 1861, Monticello, Iowa.
1742 Norton, John, P. Co. G, 25th; e. July 9, 1861, Kansas City, Mo.
1743 Norton Oliver B., P. Cos. H and D, Eng.; e. Sept. 20, 1862, Tuscola, Ill.; ad. Decatur, Ill.
1744 Norton, Samuel, P. Co. H, Eng.; e. Oct. 12, 1861, Paris, Ill.; dead.
1745 Nunan, Jas., P. Co. C, Eng.; e. Aug. 4, 1861, Lafayette, Ind.; deserted.
1746 O'Brien, Thos., Cor. Co. F, Eng.; e. Sept. 9, 1861, Dubuque, Iowa.
1747 O'Brien, Dennis, Sergt. Co. G, 25th; e. June 22, 1861, Kansas City, Mo.
1748 O'Connell, Peter D., P. Cos A and E, Eng.; e. July 20, 1861, St. Louis, Mo.
1749 **ODENBAUGH, LISBON**, Capt. Co. H, Eng.; e. Oct. 1, 1861, Paris, Ill.; disch. dis. May 1, 1864; dead.
1750 Odin, Isaac N., P. Co. B, Eng.; e. Aug. 5, 1861, Paris, Ill.
1751 Odle, Henry, P. Cos. I and C, Eng.; e. Sept. 16, 1861, McGregor, Iowa.
1752 Oehl Fred., P. Co. G, Eng.; e. Sept. 13, 1861, Cape Girardeau, Mo.; a pensioner; ad. Arensburg, Mo.
1753 O'Flaherty, Corneil, P. Cos. 1 and C, Eng.; e. Sept. 21, 1861, Dubuque, Iowa.
1754 O'Flaherty, Dan., Cor. Co. G, 25th; e. June 12, 1861, Kansas City, Mo.
1755 O'Flaherty, Owen, P. Co. G, 25th; e. June 24, 1861, Kansas City, Mo.
1756 Ogden, Alf., P. Co. K, Eng.; e. Sept. 25, 1861; New London, Iowa; dead.
1757 Ogden, John, P. Co. E, 25th, e. July 25, 1861, Holt Co., Mo.
1758 Ogden, Joseph, P. Cos. D, 25th, A and B, Eng.; e. July 4, 1861, St. Joseph, Mo.; ad. Forrest City, Mo.
1759 Ogden, Martin, P. Co. C, 25th; e. July 4, 1861, Rushville, Mo.
1760 Ogden, Wm. T., P. Co. E, 25th; e. Aug. 22, 1862, Holt Co., Mo.
1761 Ogle, Elisha B, P. Cos. F, 25th, H. and D, Eng.; e. Sept. 11, 1862, Stewartsville, Mo.; ad. Maryville, Mo.
1762 O'Hara, Corneil, Sergt. Co. G, 25th; e. Jan. 13, 1861, Kansas City, Mo.
1763 O'Hara, John, P. Co. C, 25th; e. July 12, 1861, Kansas City, Mo.
1764 Ohler, Nicholas, P. Co. B, 25th; e. June 13, 1861, St. Joseph, Mo.
1765 Oldham, Wm., P. Co. I, 25th, e. Oct. 6, 1862, Gallatin, Mo.
1766 Omer, John W., P. Cos. K, 25th, C and B, Eng.; e. Feb. 20, 1862, Mt. Ayer, Iowa; ad. Tabor, Iowa.
1767 **O'NEIL, DAVID**, Lt. Co. B, Van Horn's, Battalion; e. June 12, 1861, Kansas City, Mo.; not officially accounted for.
1768 O'Neil, Dennis, P. Co. F, 25th; e. Aug. 21, 1861, De Kalb Co., Mo.
1769 O'Neil, John, P. Co. D, Eng.; e. Sept. 9, 1861, St. Louis, Mo.; disch. dis. Mar. 6, 1862. Otterville, Mo.
1770 Onstott, Benj., P Co C, 25th; e. July 13, 1861, St. Joseph, Mo.
1771 Onstott, Henry, P. Co. D, 25th; e. July 13, 1861, St. Joseph, Mo.
1772 O'Reiley, Pat., Sergt. Co. G, 25th; e. June 12, 1861, Kansas City, Mo.
1773 Orton, Wm. D., P. Cos. I and C, Eng.; e. Sept. 15, 1861, Denmark, Iowa.
1774 Osborn, David, P. Co. H, 25th; e. Aug. 14, 1861, Nodaway Co., Mo.
1775 Ostrander, Alf. B., Sergt. Cos. A and E, Eng.; e. July 1, 1861, St. Louis, Mo.

1776 Ostrander, Geo. W., 1st, P. Co. E, Eng.; e. July 13, 1861, Adrian, Mich.; ad. Ottawa Lake, Mich.
1777 Ostrander, Geo. W., 2d, P. Co. E, Eng.; e. July 13, 1861, Adrian, Mich.; ad. Elyria, Ohio
1778 O'Sullivan, Jas., P. Cos. C, 25th, A and B, Eng.; e. Jan. 1, 1862.
1778 Overholdt, G., P. Co. E, Eng.; e. July 13, 1861, Adrian, Mich.
1779 Overmill, Wm., P. Cos. B and E, Eng.; e. July 28, 1861, Paris, Ill.
1780 Overton, Isaac, P. Co. K, Eng.; e. Sept. 20, 1861, Burlington, Iowa.
1781 Owens, John, P. Cos. A, 25th, M and E, Eng.; e; June 14, 1861, St. Joseph, Mo.
1782 Owens, Squire T., P. Cos. H and D, Eng.; e. Sept. 15, 1861, Paris; Ill.
1783 PACE, L. C., Chap., 25th; e. Aug. 12, 1862, res. Nov. 1, 1862.
1784 Pace, Edward, P. Co. E, 25th; e. July 22, 1861, Page Co., Iowa.
1785 Page, Carey, P. Cos. C and B, Eng.; e. Aug. 4, 1861, Prairie City, Ill.; ad. Clyde Kns.; pensioner.
1786 Page, Chas. H., Cor. Co. H, 25th; e. Nov. 7, 1861, Amity, Iowa.
1787 Page, Isaac T., P. Cos. C and B, Eng.; e. Aug. 4, 1861, Prairie City, Iowa; ad. Perry, Iowa.
1788 Palmer, Jac., P. Cos. L and I, Eng.
1789 Palmer, Mathew H., P. Co. F, Eng ; e. Oct. 11, 1861, Albert Lea, Minn.; has a pension; disch. dis. Feb. 1862, at Otterville, Mo., ad. Mantorville, Dodge Co., Minn
1790 Palmer, Solon, P. Co. B, 25th; e. Aug 1, 1861, Linneus, Mo.
1791 Palmer, Wm. O., P. Co. I, 25th; e. July 13, 1861, Gallatin, Mo.
1792 Pangburn, Chas., P. Cos. F, K and B, Eng.; e. Oct. 7, 1861, Cassville, Wis.; is pensioned; ad. Charlotte, Mich.
1793 **PARKER, DANIEL G.**, Lt. Cos. F, B and G, Eng.; e. Nov. 1, 1861, Albert Lea, Minn.; is a pensioner, a merchant in good circumstances at Albert Lea, Minn.
1794 Parker, Chas., P. Cos. H and D, Eng.; e. Aug. 16, 1861, Bloomfield, Ill.
1795 Parker, Thos., P. Cos. H, 25th, M and E, Eng.; e. Sept. 9, 1862, Nodaway Co., Mo.; ad. Hopeville, Iowa.
1796 Parkhurst, Josiah, P. Cos. C and B, Eng.; e. Aug. 4, 1861, Prairie City, Ill.
1797 Parman, Wm., P. Cos. A, 25th, M and E, Eng ; e. Dec. 22, 1861, Fremont, Ia.
1798 Parnell, Isaac A., P. Co. D, 25th; e. Dec. 24, 1861, St. Joseph, Mo.
1799 Parnell, Wm. M., P. Cos. D, 25th, A and B, Eng.; e. Dec. 24, 1861, St. Joseph, Mo.
1800 Passenger, Chas. E., P. Co. G, 25th; e. Aug. 11, 1861, Kansas City, Mo.
1801 **PATTEN, W. G.**, Capt. Cos. C and B, Eng.; e. Aug. 4, 1861, Prairie City, Ill.; disch. Oct. 31, 1864; has served his country in the Kansas State Legislature since the war; is a prominent and influential citizen of Cottonwood Falls, Kas.
1802 Patten, John, P. Co. D, 25th; e. Nov. 4, 1861, Page Co., Iowa.
1803 Patten, John , P. Co. K, 25th; e. Aug. 2, 1861, Page Co., Iowa; ad. Lamoni, Mo.
1804 Patten, Samuel, P. Cos. I and C, Eng.; e. Sept. 30, 1861, Dubuque, Iowa.
1805 Patch, Henry, Cor. Cos. I, 25th, H and D, Eng.; e. March 18, 1862, Liberty, Mo.
1806 Paulin, Nathaniel, P. Co. A, 25th; e. June 14, 1861, St. Joseph, Mo.
1807 Paus, John, P. Co. B, 25th, L and E, Eng.; e. March 1, 1862, Linneus, Mo.; a pensioner; ad. St. Louis, Mo.
1808 Paus, William, P. Co. G, 25th; e. June 11, 1861, Kansas City, Mo.
1809 Payson, Louis B., P. Co. F, Eng.; e. Sept. 1, 1861, Waverly, Iowa; died at Gen. Hos. St. Louis, in 1862.
1810 Paxton Robert J., P. Co. K, Eng.; e. Sept. 24, 1861, Wapello, Iowa.
1811 Peabody, Everett, Col. 25th; e. Sept. 21, 1861, St. Louis Mo.; killed in battle of Shiloh, April 6, 1862. He was born in Massachusetts in 1830, graduated at Harvard College in 1850; the same year edited the *Literary Review;* soon after graduating he engaged in the business of civil engineering in the West. At the outbreak of the war he was resident engineer of the Hannibal & St. Joseph Railroad having previously been chief engineer of the Louisville & Nashville and the Memphis & Ohio Railroads.
1812 Peabody, Abraham, P. Co. D, 25th; e. July 12, 1861, St. Joseph, Mo.
1813 Peacock, Jas., P. Co. I, 25th; e. Dec. 25, 1861, Wyandotte, Kas.

1814 Pearcy, John M., P. Co. D, 25th; e. Dec. 5, 1861, St. Joseph, Mo.
1815 Pearcy, Levi A., P. Co. D, 25th; e. July 10, 1861, St. Joseph, Mo.
1816 Pearcy, Zimri, P. Co. D, 25th; e. July 10, 1861, St. Joseph, Mo.
1817 Pearman, Nathan, P. Co. D, 25th; e. Nov. 28, 1861, St. Joseph, Mo.
1818 Percy, John H., Cor. Co. F, Eng.; e. Sept. 16, 1861, Bloomington, Ill.; disch. Jackson, Tenn., Sept., 1862, for dis.
1819 Percy, Levi, P. Co. A, 25th; e. July 10, 1861, De Kalb Co., Mo.
1820 Percy, Roderick, P. Co. F, Eng ; e. Sept. 20, 1861, Bloomington, Ill.; disch. dis., Otterville, Mo., Feb., 1862.
1821 Peek, Jas. W., P. Co. H, 25th; e. Dec. 27, 1861, Quitman, Mo.
1822 Peek, Wilson, P. Co. H, 25th; e. Dec. 27, 1861, Quitman, Mo.
1823 Pelton, Saml., P. Co. E, Eng.; e. July 13, 1861, Adrian, Mich.
1824 Pelton, Wm. A., P. Co. E, 25th; e. Sept. 21, 1861, Atchison Co., Mo.
1825 Pell, Thos , P. Cos. G, 25th, L and E, Eng.; e. March 1, 1862, St. Joseph, Mo.
1826 Pans, Wm., P. Co. A, 25th; e.———; ad. 2835 Penna. av., St. Louis, Mo.
1827 Penny, Thos. D., P. Cos. E, 25th, G and C, Eng.; e. Jan. 11, 1862, Holt Co., Mo.
1828 Penny, John T., P. Co. F, Eng.; e. Sept. 20, 1861, Waverly, Iowa; disch. dis., Feb., 1863, Memphis, Tenn.; dead.
1829 Penny, Richard, P. Co. E, 25th; e. Jan. 11, 1862, Holt Co., Mo.; ad. Phelps City, Mo.
1830 Pennick, Jas. M., P. Cos. K, 25th, and M and E, Eng.; e. Dec. 10, 1861, Hawleyville, Iowa; died at Memory, Iowa.
1831 Peppelbaum, Henry, P. Cos. G, and I, Eng.; e. Sept. 13, 1861, Cape Girardeau, Mo.
1832 PENFIELD, S. M., Lt. Co. H, 25th; e. Aug. 14, 1861; killed in the battle of Shiloh, April 6, 1862.
1833 PERKINS, WM., Lt. Co. E, 25th; e. July 22, 1861, Holt Co., Mo.; res. Jan. 23, 1863.
1834 Permit, Mathew, P. Co. A, 25th; e. Oct. 16, 1862, De Kalb Co., Mo.
1835 Perry John, P. Co. C, 25th; e. July 15, 1861.
1836 Peters, Valentine, P Co. H, 25th; e. Aug. 21, 1861, Whig Valley, Mo.; killed in the Centralia massacre in October, 1865.
1837 Peters, Peter, P. Co. B, 25th; e. June 13, 1861, St. Joseph, Mo.
1838 Peterson, Andrew, P. Co. K, Eng.; e. Sept. 18, 1861, Wapello, Iowa.
1839 Petty, John C., P. Co. K, 25th; e. Feb. 18, 1862, Gentry Co., Mo.; ad. Neodosha, Kas.
1840 Phelps, John, P Co. H, 25th, M and E, Eng.; e. July 17, 1862, St. Joseph, Mo.
1841 Pherson, Wm., P. Cos. C and B, Eng.; e. Aug. 4, 1861, Prairie City, Ill.
1842 Phillips, Solon, Sergt. Cos. D and C, Eng.; e. Aug. 2, 1861, Keokuk, Iowa.
1843 Phillips, John, P. Cos. K, 25th, M and E, Eng.; e. Feb. 1, 1862, Quincy, Iowa.
1844 Phillips, Nathan S., P. Co. F, 25th; e. Sept. 11, 1862, Stewartsville, Mo.
1845 Pierman Nathan, P. Co. B, Eng , e. Nov. 28, 1861.
1846 Piper, Jas., Sergt. Cos. A and E, Eng. ; e. July 20, 1861, St. Louis, Mo., is a well respected influential citizen, and late Mayor of the city of his residence, Beaver Falls, Pa
1847 Piper, J W , P. Cos. B and K, Eng. ; e. July 28, 1861, Paris, Ill.; dead.
1848 Pitsch, John Peter, P. Co. B, 25th ; e Nov. 1, 1861, Linneus, Mo.
1849 Plaster, Saml. W., P. Cos. B and K, Eng.; e. July 28, 1861, Paris, Ill.
1850 Plunkett, Jas., P. Cos. A, 25th, M and E, Eng.; e. Dec. 26,1861,St.Louis,Mo.
1851 Plunkett, John, P. Co. A, 25th ; e. Sept. 16, 1862, St. Louis, Mo.
1852 Points, John A., Q. M. S. Eng.; e. Sept. 2, 1861, Camden, Ill ; draws a pension ; ad. Camden, Ill.
1853 Points, John B., P. Cos. I, D and C, Eng.; e. Oct. 14, 1861, Camden, Ill.; dead.
1854 Pollock, John, P. Co. F, Eng.; e. Oct. 30, 1861, Lancaster, Wis.; has a pension ; ad. Lancaster, Wis.
1855 Pollock, Jas., P. Co. E, 25th ; e. Feb. 1, 1862, Holt Co., Mo.
1856 Poland, Enoch, P. Co. A, 25th ; e. June 15, 1861, St. Joseph, Mo.
1857 Poole, John F., P. Cos. H and D, Eng.; e. March 3, 1863, Tuscola, Ill.; is pensioned ; ad. Tuscola, Ill.
1858 Poore, Geo. W., P. Cos. I, 25th, H and D,Eng.; e. Feb 26,1862,St.Joseph,Mo.
1859 Porter, John W., P. Cos. H, 25th, M and E, Eng.; e. Dec. 31, 1862, Nodaway Co., Mo.; ad. Barnard, Mo.

1860 Pottstock, Henry, P. Cos. G and I, Eug.; e. Sept. 13, 1861, Cape Girardeau, Mo.; a pensioner; ad. 1233 De Soto av., St. Louis, Mo.
1861 POWELL, JAS. E., Maj. 25th; e. March 24, 1862, St. Joseph, Mo.; killed in the battle of Shiloh April 6, 1862; was a brave, capable officer, universally liked by the officers and men.
1862 Powell, Gabriel, P. Cos. F, 25th, H and D, Eng.; e. June 1, 1862, Empire Prairie, Mo.
1863 Powell, George, Cook (colored) Cos. H and D, Eug.; e. April 3, 1863, Lake Providence, La.
1864 Powell, George W., P. Co. I, 25th; e. Aug. 19, 1861, Gallatin, Mo.
1865 Powell, Jonathan, P. Co. I, 25th; e. Jan. 1, 1862, Gallatin, Mo.
1866 Powell, Kaller, P. Co. I, 25th; e. July 25, 1861, Gallatin, Mo.
1867 Powell, Wm., P. Cos. B. K and A, Eug.; e. July 28, 1861, Paris, Ill.; died Terre Haute, Ind., 1878.
1868 Powell, Wm. P. Co. D, 25th; e. Nov. 29, 1861, De Kalb Co., Mo.
1869 Powell, Wm. C., P. Co. I, 25th; e. Aug. 19, 1861, Gallatin Mo.
1870 Powell, Wm. S., P. Co. D, Eng.; e. Oct. 14, 1861, Camp Point, Ill.; died Milliken Bend, Miss., June 24, 1863.
1871 Power, Pierce M., Cor. Co. G, Eug.; e. Sept. 13, 1861, Cape Girardeau, Mo.
1872 Powers, John G., P. Co. D, Eng.; e. Aug. 15, 1861, Flora, Ill.; disch. dis., St. Louis, Mo., Oct. 26, 1861; dead.
1873 Powers, Mack, P. Co. D, Eng.; e. Oct. 24, 1861, Mt. Sterling, Ill.; disch.dis., Memphis, Tenn., April 26, 1863; dead.
1874 Powers, Lawrence, P. Cos. A and E, Eug.; e. July 20, 1861, St. Louis, Mo.
1875 Powers, Pat., P. Co. G, 25th; e. June 17, 1861, Kansas City, Mo.
1876 PRESCOTT, ALVAH R., Lt. Cos. F and I, Eng.; e. Sept. 23, 1861, McGregor, Ill.; disch. Nov. 2, 1864. He assisted in raising the men for Co. F, in 1861; served for a time as a Sergt., and as Commissary Sergt. Since the war he has been a prominent and respected citizen and for many years Postmaster at Postville, Iowa.
1877 Priedham, P. Cos. A and E, Eng.; e. July 20, 1861, St. Louis, Mo.
1878 Purcell, John, P. Co. G, 25th; e. June 13, 1861, Kansas City, Mo.
1879 Purkett, John, P. Co. E, 25th; e. July 22, 1861, St. Joseph, Mo.
1880 Purtle, Jas. J., P. Co. F, Eug.; e. Sept. 30, 1861, Cassville, Wis.
1881 Pyles, Vincent, P. Co. F, 25th; e. June 13, 1862, Troy, Kas.
1882 Quick, Paul P., P. Co. F, Eug.; e. Oct. 6, 1861, Cedar Rapids, Iowa.
1883 Quick, Thomas, P. Co. G, 25th; e. June 18, 1861, Kansas City, Mo.
1884 Quinn, John, P. Cos. C and B, Eng.; e. Aug. 4, 1861, Prairie City, Ill.; ad., Avon, Ill.; pensioner.
1885 Quinn, Maurice, P. Co. G, 25th; e. Dec. 28, 1861, Kansas City, Mo.
1886 Quinn, Neil, P. Cos. A, 25th, M and E, Eng.; e. July 25, 1862, St. Joseph, Mo.
1887 Quist, F. M., P. Co. B, —; e. July 20, 1861, St. Louis, Mo.
1888 Rabick, Henry, P. Cos. G and I, Eng.; e. Sept. 13, 1861, Cape Girardeau, Mo.; is pensioned; ad. Cape Girardeau, Mo.
1889 Rackney, L. G., P. Co. B, Eng.; e. July 28, 1861, Paris, Ill.
1890 Raglan, John, P. Co. A, Eng.; e. June 27, 1862, Cape Girardeau, Mo.
1891 Rainer, John, P. Co. H, Eug.; e. Oct. 27, 1861, St. Louis, Mo.
1892 Ralston, Jas. P. Cos. D, 25th, A and B, Eng.; e. Aug. 29, 1862, St. Joseph, Mo.; is a pensioner; ad. Denver, Mo.
1893 Ralston, Josiah, P. Cos. D, 25th, A and B, Eng.; e. Aug. 29, 1861, St. Joseph, Mo.
1894 Ralston, Wm., P. Cos. D, 25th, A and B, Eng.; e. July 28, 1861, St. Joseph, Mo.
1895 Ramsey, Dan., P. Co. E, Eng.; e. July 13, 1861, Adrian, Mich.
1896 Ramsey, Thos., P. Co. E, 25th; e. June 5, 1862, Holt Co., Mo.
1897 RANDOLPH MAHLON, Capt. Cos. A and F, Eng.; e. Dec. 30, 1861, St. Louis, Mo., disch. special order, Dec. 25, 1833; ad. room 14, No. 245, Broadway, New York City.
1898 Randolph, Mich., P. Co. E, 25th; e. July 22, 1861, Holt Co., Mo.
1899 Ransom, Shores, P. Co. I, 25th; e. July 25, 1861, Grundy Co., Mo.
1900 Rapp, Benj., P. Co. B, 25th; e. Nov. 1, 1861, St. Joseph, Mo.
1901 Rarick, Henry, P. Cos. H and D, Eng.; e. Sept. 15, 1861, Paris, Ill.; is pensioned; ad. Paris, Ill.

THE ROSTER. 227

1902 Rasco, Jas. H., P. Cos. K, 25th, G and C, Eng.; e. Feb. 11, 1862, Littsville, Mo.; ad. Sidney, Iowa.
1903 Rasco, Logan, P. Cos. K, 25th, G and C, Eng.; e. April 10, 1863, Nodaway Co., Mo.; ad. Sidney, Iowa.
1904 Raspberry, Jas., P. Cos. A and E, Eng.; e Feb. 7, 1862, Cape Girardeau, Mo.
1904½ Rathburn, Lewis, P. Co. H, Eng.; e. Oct. 25, 1861, St. Louis, Mo.; disch. dis. St. Louis, July 2, 1862.
1905 Ray, Dan. B., P. Co. E, 25th; e. June 11, 1862, Holt Co., Mo.; ad. Tecumseh, Neb.
1906 Raybourne, John H., P. Co. C, Eng.; e. Sept. 16, 1861, Roseville, Ill.; drowned Jackson, Tenn., July 2, 1862, while trying to save a drowning comrade.
1907 Reardon, Jas., P. Cos. K, 25th, G and C, Eng.; e. March 1, 1862.
1908 Rease, Fredk., P. Co. B, 25th; e. June 13, 1861, St. Joseph, Mo.
1909 Reed, Eugene L., P. Cos. C and B, Eng.; e. Aug. 4, 1861, Prairie City, Ill.; disch. Jefferson Barracks, Mo., Nov. 24, 1862.
1910 Reed, Sam. B., Mus. Cos. K, 25th, G and C, Eng.; e. Oct. 7, 1862, Arcadia, Mo.; ad Piedmont, Mo.
1911 Reed, Thomas B., P. Cos. H, D and C, Eng.; e. Aug 13, 1862, Sandford, Ind.; pensioner; ad. Bowie, Tex.
1912 Reed, Thomas H., P. Cos. H, 25th, M and E, Eng.; e. June 1, 1862, Nodaway Co., Mo.
1913 Reed. Wm. S., P. Cos. K, 25th, G and C, Eng.; e. Oct. 7, 1862, Arcadia, Mo.; ad. Hogan, Iron Co., Mo.
1914 Reidy, Jas., Sergt. Cos. G, 25th, L and E, Eng.; e. Jan. 3, 1862, Kansas City, Mo.; ad. same.
1915 Regot, Henry, P. Co. A, 25th; e. Sept. 1, 1861, Kansas City, Mo.
1916 Reidel, Chas., P. Cos. B, 25th, L and E, Eng.; e. March 1, 1863, Kansas City, Mo.
1917 Reiner, Casper, P. Co. B, 25th and L, Eng.; e. Nov. 1, 1861, St. Joseph, Mo.
1918 Reiner, John, P. Co B, 25th; e. June 13, 1861, St. Joseph, Mo.
1919 Reiner. Louis, P. Cos. G and I, Eng.; e. Sept. 13, 1861, Cape Girardeau, Mo.; ad. same; has a pension.
1920 Reineka, Henry, P. Cos. G, I and D, Eng.; e. Aug. 18, 1862, Cape Girardeau, Mo.; dead.
1921 Rehmann, Henry, P. Co. G, Eng.; e. Sept. 13, 1861, Cape Girardeau, Mo.
1922 Remyer, J., P. Cos. H and D, Eng.; e. ———.
1923 Renz, Martin, P. Co. B, 25th and L, Eng.; e. Nov. 1, 1861, St. Joseph, Mo.
1924 Resmeyer, Fred. Cor. Co. B, 25th; e. June 13, 1861, St. Joseph, Mo.
1925 Ressler, Phil., Sergt. Co. B, Eng.; e. Sept. 15, 1862.
1926 Resplandin, Otto. P. Cos. B, 25th, L and E, Eng.; e. June 13, 1862, St. Joseph, Mo.
1927 Reuter, Chas., P. Co. F, Eng.; e. Sept. 28, 1861, Bloomington, Iowa; died of pernicious remittent fever, near Young's Point, La., about March 25, 1863.
1928 Reuter, Jas., P. Co. B, 25th; e. Nov. 1, 1861, St. Joseph, Mo.
1929 Reuter. Joseph, P. Co. G, 25th ; e Nov. 1, 1861, St. Joseph, Mo.
1930 Reynolds, Chas., P. Cos. A and E, Eng.; e. July 20, 1861, St. Louis. Mo.
1931 Reynolds, Howard, P. Cos. H, 25th, M and E, Eng.; e. Nov. 5, 1861, Nodaway Co., Mo.; ad. Wilcox, Mo.
1932 Reynolds, John, Cor. Cos. G, 25th, L and E, Eng.; e, May 23, 1863, Harlem, Mo.
1933 Rhodes, Alb't, P. Co. E, Eng.; e. July 13, 1861, Adrian, Mich.; draws a pension ; ad. St. Charles, Mich.
1934 Rhodes, Noah, P. Cos. D, F and B. Eng.; e. Sept. 14, 1861, Flora, Ill.
1935 Rhodes, Peter, P. Co. I, 25th; e. March 27, 1861, St. Joseph, Mo.; ad. De Kalb, Mo.
1936 Rhodes, Wm. C., P. Co. H, 25th; e. Aug. 14, 1861, Guilford, Mo.
1937 Rhoads, David, P. Co. H, 25th ; e. Sept. 3 1862, Nodaway Co., Mo.
1938 Rhoads, Jas. M., P. Co. H, 25th; e. Sept. 3, 1862, Nodaway Co., Mo.
1939 Rhae, John A., Cor. Cos. I and C, Eng.; e. Sept. 27, 1861, McGregor, Iowa.
1940 Rice, Alex. F., P. Co. K, Eng.; e. Sept. 15, 1861, New London, Iowa.
1941 Rice, Geo. W., P. Co. F, 25th; e. Jan. 2, 1862, North Salem, Mo.
1942 Rice, John, P. Co. E, 25th, G and C, Eng.; e. Sept. 2, 1863.

1943 Rice, Sarency, P. Cos. H, D and C, Eng.; e. Aug. 26, 1862, Sandford, Ind.; disch. dis. Washington, D. C., May 30, 1865; ad. Sandford, Ind.
1944 Ricedorf, Geo. W., Cor. Cos. E, 25th, G and C, Eng.; e. July,22, 1861, Doniphan, Kas.
1945 Rich, Wm. J., P. Co. H, 25th; e. Sept. 26, 1862, Iron Co., Mo.
1946 Richard, Jacob, P. Cos. L, I and D, Eng.; e. ——; ad. Fredonia, Kas.
1947 Richards, Geo., P. Co. H, 25th; e. Aug. 19, 1861, Nodaway Co., Mo.
1948 Richards, Jas. H., P. Co. H, 25th; e. Aug. 14, 1861, Nodaway Co., Mo.
1949 Richardson, John, P. Co. A, 25th; e. July 14, 1861, St. Joseph, Mo.
1950 Richardson, Leroy, Cor. Cos. C and B, Eng.; e. Aug. 4, 1861, Prairie City, Ill.
1951 Richardson, Wm. C., P. Co. E, 25th; e. July 22, 1861, Holt Co., Mo,
1952 Richardson, Wm. B., P. Co. C, Eng.; e. Aug. 4, 1861, Prairie City, Ill.; died Nov. 24, 1862, at Jackson, Tenn.
1953 Ricketts, Jno. S., P. Cos. H and D, Eng.; e. Oct. 11, 1861, Jefferson City, Mo.; disch. dis., in 1863.
1954 **RICKETTS, JOSHUA**, Lt. Cos. B and C,Eng.;e. July 28, 1861, at Paris, Ill.; res. Feb. 16, 1863. He is an editor and proprietor of a newspaper at Ashmore, Ill.
1955 Ricketts, T. S. S., P. Co. H, 25th; e. Aug. 14, 1861, Maryville, Mo.
1956 Reidel, Chas., Cor. Co. G, 25th and L, Eng.; e. Feb. 1, 1862, Kansas City, Mo.
1957 Riley, Jas., P. Cos. L, I and D, Eng.; e. July 3, 1862.
1958 Riley, John, P. Cos. A. 25th, M and E, Eng.; e. Nov. 5, 1862, Andrew Co., Mo.
1959 Riley, John W., P. Cos. G, 25th, L and E, Eng.; e. May 25, 1863, Clay Co., Mo.
1960 Rippetoe, John, P. Co. F, Eng.; e. Oct. 14, 1861, Bloomington, Ill.
1961 Rister, Hugh, P. Cos. D and C, Eng.; e. Sept. 14, 1861, Flora, Ill.; a pensioner; ad. Homer, Ill.
1962 Ritgarot, Christ., P. Cos. G and I, Eng.; e. Sept. 13, 1861, Cape Girardeau, Mo.; ad. same; has a pension.
1963 Roach, John, P. Cos. A and E, Eng.; e. July 20, 1861, St. Louis, Mo.; dead.
1964 Roark, Lewis, P. Co. D, 25th; e. July 12, 1861, St. Joseph, Mo.
1965 Roberts, David, P. Co. D, 25th; e. July 12, 1861, St. Joseph, Mo.
1966 Roberts, Flavius J., P. Co. A, 25th; e. Nov. 2, 1861, Rockport, Mo.
1967 Roberts, Jesse, P. Cos. C. 25th, A and B, Eng.; e. Dec. 19, 1861, Belmont, Mo.; ad. St. Joseph, Mo.
1968 Roberts, John, P. Co. D, 25th; e. July 12, 1861, Andrew Co., Mo.
1969 Roberts, Lewis F., P. Cos. H and D, Eng.; e. Aug. 24, 1861, Vermillion, Ill.; dead.
1970 Roberts, Thos. B., P. Cos. H and D, Eng.; e, Sept. 18, 1861, Vermillion, Ill.
1971 Robertson, Wm., P. Co. D, 25th; e. July 13, 1861, St. Joseph, Mo.
1972 Robbins, Joseph, Sergt. Cos. K, 25th, G and C. Eng.; e. Feb. 1, 1862, Hawleyville, Iowa; draws a pension; ad. Elk City, Kas.
1973 Robbins, Wm., P. Co. K, 25th; e. Feb. 1. 1862, Hawleyville, Iowa.
1974 Robinson, Jas., P. Co. F, Eng.; e. Aug. 28, 1861, Dubuque, Iowa.
1975 Robinson, Jas., P. Cos. H, 25th, M and E. Eng.; e. July 21, 1863, Nodaway Co., Mo.; killed in the Centralia massacre, Sept. 27, 1864.
1976 Robinson, Jerome B., Cor. Co. G. 25th; e. Feb. 3, 1862, Omaha, Neb.
1977 Robinson, Geo., P. Cos. I and C, Eng.; e. Sept. 30, 1861, Dubuque, Iowa.
1978 Robinson, Henry M., P. Co. C, 25th; e. July 6, 1861, St. Joseph, Mo.
1979 Robinson, Saml. M., P. Cos. H, 25th, M and E, Eng.; e. July 21, 1863, Nodaway Co., Mo.
1980 **ROBINSON J. W.**, Capt. Co. C, 25th; e. July 12, 1861, St. Joseph, Mo.; not accounted for after March, 1862.
1981 Roby, Wm., Sergt. Cos. B, K and A, Eng.; e. Aug. 5, 1861 Paris, Ill.; promoted 2d Lt., June 12, 1865.
1982 Rodebaugh, Danl., P. Cos. C and B, Eng.; e. Aug. 4, 1861, Prairie City, Ill.
1983 Roderick, Lewis A., P. Co. K, 25th; e. July 22, 1861, Forest City, Mo.
1984 Roderick, Lewis, P. Co. E, 25th; e. July—,1861, Holt Co., Mo.
1985 Rogers, B., P. Co. H, Eng.; e.——; dead.
1986 Roede, John, P. Co. B, 25th; e. June 13, 1861, St. Joseph, Mo.
1987 Roesler, Philip H., P. Co. B, 25th; e.——

1988 Rogers, Benj., P. Cos. H and D, Eng.; e. Oct. 12, 1861, Kentucky, Ill.
1989 Rogers, Jas., P. Co. C, 25th ; e. July 23, 1861, Stewartsville, Mo.
1990 Rogers, Saml., P. Co. C, 25th ; e. Aug. 1, 1861, Stewartsville, Mo.
1991 Roher, Benj. E., P. Cos. B and E, Eng.; e. July 20, 1861, St. Louis, Mo.
1992 Rohsicher, Edward, P. Co. B, 25th ; e. April 19, 1863, St. Joseph, Mo.
1993 Romaine, Amos, P. Cos. C, 25th, A and B, Eng.; e. Dec. 22, 1861,St.Joseph, Mo.
1994 Roman, Olaf P., P. Co. K, Eng.; e. Sept. 28, 1861, Burlington, Iowa.
1995 Romande, Joseph, P. Co. B, 25th, e. June 13, 1861, St. Joseph, Mo.
1996 Roney, Patrick, P. Co. K, Eng.; e. Oct, 25, 1861, Bloomington, Ill.
1997 Rose, Caswell, P. Cos. K, 25th, G and C, Eng.; e. Nov. 5, 1862, Page Co., Iowa; killed in Centralia massacre Sept. 27, 1864.
1998 Rose, Lewis, Cor. Cos. B, 25th, L and E, Eng.; e. March 20, 1863, St. Joseph, Mo.
1999 Rosebaugh, A. J., P. Cos. H and D, Eng.; e. Aug. 12, 1861, Paris, Ill.
2000 Ross, Alf. D., P. Cos. I and C, Eng.; e. Sept. 23, 1861, Burlington, Iowa.
2001 Ross, Christopher, P. Cos. C and B, Eng.; e. March 10, 1863 ; dead.
2002 Ross, Isaac W., P. Cos. B, K and A. Eng.; e. July 28, 1861, Paris, Ill. ; vet.; draws a pension ; ad. Vermillion, Ill
2003 Rostock, Ferdin., Mus., Cos. E, 25th, G and C, Eng.; e. Dec. 15, 1861, Oregon, Mo.; ad. same.
2004 Rothe, Carl, P. Cos. L and I, Eng.; e. ——.
2005 Rothmel, Wm., P. Cos. F and B, Eng.; e. Sept. 28, 1861, Bloomington, Ill.; has a pension; ad. Paoli, Kas.
2005½ Rouse, John, P. Co. C, 25th; e. July 5, 1861.
2006 Rouse, Marion, P. Co. C, 25th; e. July 23, 1861.
2007 Rowe, Jas., P. Co. A, 25th; e. July 25, 1862, St. Joseph, Mo.
2008 **ROWELL, CHAS. T.**, Capt. Co. B, Eng.; e. July 21, 1861, Paris, Ill.; served until Aug. 5, 1861, and refused to muster; dead.
2009 **ROWLEY, JOHN D.**, Lt. Co. F, Eng.; e. Sept. 9, 1861; res. July 14, 1862; ad. Holden, Ill.
2010 Rowley, John B., P. Co. K, Eng.; e. Oct. 15, 1861, St. Louis, Mo.
2011 Rubel, Jac., P. Cos. G and I, Eng.; e. Sept. 13, 1861, Cape Girardeau, Mo.; is a pensioner; ad. Cape Girardeau.
2012 Reddick, John, P. Co. G, Eng.; e. July 13, 1861, Cape Girardeau, Mo.
2013 Rudolph, Victor, Sergt. Co. B, 25th and L. Eng.; e. June 13, 1861, St. Joseph, Mo.
2014 **RUMBAUGH, GEO. W.**, Capt. Co. K, 25th; e. Feb. 1, 1862, Hawleyville, Iowa; res. Sept. 2, 1862.
2015 Rummell, David, P. Cos. D and C, Eng.; e. Oct. 27, 1861, Mereditia, Ill.
2016 Ruof, John, P. Co. B, 25th; e. June 13, 1862, St. Joseph, Mo.
2017 Rusmisel, Geo. M., P. Cos C, 25th, and A, Eng.; e. ——.
2018 Rusmisel, John H., P. Cos. C. 25th, and A, Eng.; e. ——.
2019 Russell, Soloman, P. Co. D, 25th; e. Aug. 7, 1861, St. Joseph, Mo.
2020 Ryan, Andrew, P. Co. G, 25th; e. Aug. 9, 1861, Kansas City, Mo.
2021 Ryan, Richard A., 1st Sergt. Co. A, Eng.; e. July 20, 1861, St. Louis, Mo.; killed in action near Farmington, Miss., during the siege of Corinth, May 29, 1862; he was a very capable and well-liked soldier, and had just been recommended for promotion.
2022 Ryan, Thomas, P. Co A, Eng.; e. July 20, 1861, St. Louis, Mo.
2023 Ryan, Wm., P. Cos. F, 25th, H and D, Eng.; e. Feb. 2, 1862, St. Joseph, Mo.
2024 Reinhold, Joseph, P. Co. A, 25th, M and E, Eng.; e. Jan. 1, 1862, Wyandotte, Kas.
2025 Randall, Theo. P., P. Co. G, Eng.; e.—; died Young's Point, La., April, 1863.
2026 Rupert, Levi, P. Cos. A and E. Eng., e. July 20, 1861, St. Louis, Mo.; dead; died Burlington, Iowa, about 1878, of chronic diarrhœa.
2027 Sadner, John, P. Co. I, 25th; e. Nov. 1, 1861.
2028 Salisbury, Henry M., P. Co. A, 25th; e. Dec 18, 1861, Elwood, Kas.
2029 Salvage, Rudolph, P. Co. F, 25th; e. Aug. 26, 1861, Stewartsville, Mo.
2030 **SALSMAN, GUSTAVUS**, Lt. Co K, 25th, and G, Eng.; e. Feb. 1, 1862, Forrest City, Mo.; disch. Oct. 31, 1864.
2031 Sampson, Benj. F., P. Co. D, 25th; e. July 12, 1861, St. Joseph, Mo.
2032 Sampson, Dennis, P. Co. C, 25th, M and E, Eng.; e. Sept. 27, 1862.

THE FIRST MISSOURI ENGINEERS.

2033 Sampson, Josiah, P. Co. D, 25th; e. July 12, 1861, St. Joseph, Mo.
2034 Sanders, Geo. A., P. Cos. II, D and C, Eng.; e. Aug. 15, 1862, Paris, Ill.
2035 Sanders, Jack (alias Jack Hastings), P. Co. E, Eng.; e. July 13, 1861, Adrian, Mich.; dead.
2036 Sanders, Joseph, P. Co. D, 25th; e. June 27, 1861, Kansas City, Mo.
2037 Sandusky, Andrew, Cor. Co. C, 25th, A and B, Eng.; e. Mar. 4, 1862, Andrew Co., Mo.; ad. Cosby, Mo.
2038 Sanford, Fred., P. Co. G, Eng.; e. Sept. 13, 1861, Cape Girardeau, Mo.
2039 SANFORD, NATHAN. Capt. Co. H, Eng ; e. Sept. 15, 1861, Camden, Ill.; after raising Co. H he failed to muster.
2040 Sanford, Nathan, P. Cos. D and C, Eng.; e. Aug. 15, 1861, Camden, Ill.
2041 Saraman, Jas., P. Cos. K, 25th, G and C, Eng.; e. Aug. 12, 1862.
2042 Sarine, Henry, P. Co. H, 25th; e. Sept. 13, 1861, Maryville, Mo.
2043 Savage, Abial, P. Cos. C and B, Eng.; e. Sept. 16, 1861, Ft. Madison, Iowa.
2044 Savage, Chester, P. Co. E, Eng.; e. July 13, 1861, Adrian, Mich.; died about 1883, at Medina, Mich.
2045 Savage, John, P. Co. A, Eng.; e. July 20, 1861, St. Louis, Mo.
2046 Scanlan, Pat., P. Co. G, 25th; e. June 26, 1861, Kansas City, Mo.
2047 Sanger, Thomas, P. Co. H, 25th; e. ———; ad. Breckenridge, Mo.
2048 Scarff, Wm. T., P. Co. A, 25th; e. Jan. 18, 1862, St. Joseph, Mo.
2049 Scarlett, Nelson H., P. Co. E, 25th; e. July 22, 1861, Forest City, Mo.
2050 Schaffer, John, P. Co. B, 25th; e. Feb. 28, 1862, St. Joseph, Mo.
2051 Schaltenhand, Edward, P. Co. B, 25th; e. June 13, 1861, St Joseph, Mo.
2052 Schoup, Fred, P. Co. B, 25th; e. June 13, 1861, St. Joseph, Mo.
2053 Scheele, John O., P. Co. D, Eng.; e. Aug. 15, 1861, St. Louis, Mo.; deserted Oct. 17, 1862.
2053¼ Schill, Martin, P. Cos. L, I and D, Eng.; e. ———; ad. Soldiers' Home, Leavenworth, Kas.
2053½ Scheiding, Frank, P. Cos. B, 25th and L, Eng.; e. July 3, 1861, St. Joseph, Mo.
2054 Schleip, Fred, P. Co. B, 25th and L, Eng.; e. Aug. 1, 1861, Laclede, Mo.
2055 Schmidt, Fred, P. Cos. G and I, Eng.; e. Sept 13, 1861, Cape Girardeau, Mo.; ad. Appleton, Mo.
2056 Schmidt, Henry, P. Co. G, Eng.; e. Sept. 26, 1861, Cape Girardeau, Mo.
2057 SCHMITZ, JOSEPH, Capt. Co. B, 25th; e. May 16, 1861.
2058 Schmumacher, Geo., Sergt. Co. B, 25th and L, Eng.; e. June 13, 1861, St. Joseph, Mo.
2059 Schnuble, Michael, P. Cos. L, I and D, Eng.; e. ———.
2060 Schnittens, Jac., P. Cos. H, 25th; M and E, Eng.; e. Oct. 27, 1861, Andrew Co., Mo.
2061 Schneider, John B., P. Co. G, 25th and L, Eng.; e. March 9, 1863, St. Joseph, Mo.
2062 Schneider, Emil, P. Cos. G, I and D, Eng.; e. Sept. 13, 1861, Cape Girardeau, Mo.; ad. same; a pensioner.
2063 Schoen, Henry, P. Cos. G and I, Eng.; e. Sept. 13, 1861, Cape Girardeau, Mo.; ad. same; is pensioned.
2064 Schofield, Jns., Sergt. Co. F, 25th; e. Aug 21, 1861, St. Joseph, Mo.
2065 Scholl, Henry, P. Cos. G, I and D, Eng.; e. Sept. 13, 1861, Cape Girardeau, Mo.
2066 SCHONSCHEN, JAS., Lt. Co. B, 25th; e. June 13, 1861, St. Joseph, Mo.
2067 Schrader, Christoph., P. Cos. G and I. Eng.; e. Oct. 10, 1861, Cape Girardeau, Mo.; pensioned.
2068 Schrader, Fred., P. Cos. G and I, Eng.; e. Sept. 13, 1861, Cape Girardeau, Mo.; ad. same; is a pensioner.
2069 Schroeder, Fred., P. Cos. G and I. Eng.; e. Sept. 13, 1861, Cape Girardeau; ad. same; is pensioned.
2070 Schubert, Herman, Sergt. Cos. G, 25th, L and E, Eng.; e. June 27, 1861, Wyandotte, Kas.
2071 Schiffelt, F. M., P. Co. A, 25th; e. June 15, 1861, St. Joseph, Mo.
2072 Schottman, Wm., P. Cos. G and I, Eng.; e. Sept. 13, 1861, Cape Girardeau, Mo.; ad. same; has a pension.
2073 Schifflett, J. M., P. Co. A, 25th; e. July 8, 1861, St. Joseph, Mo.
2074 Shultz, Jac., P Co A, 25th; e. June 20, 1861, St. Joseph, Mo.
2075 Schumacher, Christian, P. Co. B, 25th; e. June 13, 1861, St. Joseph, Mo.

THE ROSTER. 231

2076 Schurner, John, Cor. Cos. G and I, Eng.; e. Sept. 13, 1861, Cape Girardeau, Mo.
2077 Scott, Jeremiah, P. Co. C, Eng.; e. Oct. 5, 1864, Sandford, Ind.; draws a pension; ad. Fountainett, Ind.
2078 Scoville, Asa C., P. Co. 1, 25th; e. Aug. 4, 1861, Maryville, Mo.
2079 **SCOVILLE, ELBERT E.**, Lieut. Cos. I, 25th, H and D, Eng.; e. Nov. 27, 1861, Victoria, Mo.; ad. Hamilton, Mo.
2080 Scroop, John, P. Co. B, Eng.; e. Aug. 5, 1861, Paris, Ill.
2081 **SCUPHAM, JOHN R.**, Lt. Co. B, Eng.——; e.——.
2082 Seiberts, Ferdinand, Sergt. Co. E, Eng.; e. July 13, 1861, Adrian, Mich.
2083 Seiferd, Geo., P. Co. K, Eng.; e. Sept. 26, 1861, Burlington, Iowa.
2084 Seiler, Mich., P. Cos. G and I, Eng.; e. Sept. 13, 1861, Cape Girardeau, Mo.
2085 Seeman, Fred., Cor. Cos. B, 25th and L, Eng.; e. June 13, 1861, St. Joseph, Mo.
2085½ Seeman, Geo., P. Cos. B, 25th and L, Eng; e. Nov. 1, 1861, St. Joseph, Mo.
2086 Sellers, Marcus D., P. Co. C, Eng.; e. Oct. 5, 1864.
2087 Senor, M. D. L., P. Co. F, 25th; e. Jan. 13, 1862, Troy, Kas.
2088 Senor, Thos. P., P. Co. F, 25th; e. Jan. 15, 1862, Troy, Kas.
2089 Senthouse, John, P. Cos H and D, Eng.; e. Nov. 11, 1861, Belleville, Ill.; has a pension: ad. Soldiers' Home, Leavenworth, Kas.
2090 Serber, Eliel, P. Co. C, 25th; e. Aug. 28, 1861.
2091 Sexton, Michael, P. Co. G, 25th; e. July 5, 1861, Kansas City, Mo.
2092 Shackelford, Saml. N., P. Co. K, Eng.; e. Mar. 28, 1862, St Joseph, Mo.; pensioned; ad. Soldiers' Home, Leavenworth, Kas.
2093 Shafer, Geo. R., P. Co. B. 25th; e. Aug. 1, 1861, Linneus, Mo.
2094 Shaffer, Fred, Sergt. Co. B, 25th; e. June 13, 1861, St. Joseph, Mo.
2095 Sanborn, Francis, P. Co. A, 25th; e. July 23, 1861, St. Joseph, Mo.
2096 Shandy, Henry H., P. Cos. E, 25th, G and C, Eng.; e. Nov. 25, 1861, Atchison Co., Mo.; ad. Phelps City, Mo.
2097 Shandy, Thos. H., P. Cos. E, 25th, G and C, Eng.; e. Nov. 25, 1861, Atchison Co., Mo.; ad. 606 Delaware St., Leavenworth, Kas.
2098 Shank, Lemuel, P. Co. H, Eng.; e. Aug. 15, 1862, Paris, Ill.; disch. dis. Aug. 15, 1862, Jackson, Tenn.; ad. New Goshen, Ind.
2099 Shanklin, Jas., P. Co. H, 25th; e.——, Nodaway Co., Mo.
2100 Shanley, Danl. L., P. Co. B, 25th, L, and E, Eng.; e. Feb. 16, 1862, St. Joseph, Mo.
2101 Shannon, Lawrence, P. Co. G, 25th; e. June 12, 1861, Kansas City, Mo.
2102 Shannon, Wm., P. Co. C, 25th; e. Aug. 15, 1861, Kansas City, Mo.
2103 Sharkey, Thos., P. Co. K, 25th; e. June 21, 1861, Kansas City, Mo.
2104 Shawcross, Morris F., P. Cos. C and B, Eng.; e. Aug. 4, 1861, Prairie City, Ill.; ad. Avon, Ill.
2105 Shedd, Chas. F., P. Cos. I and C, Eng.; e. Sept. 15, 1861, Denmark, Iowa; ad. Fairfield, Neb.
2106 Shedd, Jas. A., Sergt. Cos I and C, Eng ; e. Sept. 15, 1861, Denmark, Iowa; dead.
2107 Sheely, Fred, P. Co. A, Eng.; e. July 20, 1861, St. Louis, Mo.
2108 Shelby, Calvin, P. Co. —, 25th and A, Eng.; e.——.
2109 **SHELTON, CHAS. S.**, Sur. Eng.; e. Aug. 11, 1861, St. Louis, Mo.; res. July 30, 1863; died, Jersey City, N. J., about 1869.
2110 Shelton, Thomas, P., Cos. H, D and C, Eng.; e. Aug. 23, 1863, Pocahontas, Tenn.
2111 Sherrard, Saml., P. Cos. B, 25th and L, Eng.; e. June 15, 1861, St. Joseph, Mo.; ad. Fairport, Mo.
2112 Sheilds, David, P. Co. H, 25th; e.——.
2113 **SHERWOOD, DANIEL B**, Lt. Cos. C and I, Eng.; e. Aug. 4, 1861, Prairie City, Ill.; died Jefferson Barracks, Mo., Aug. 8, 1863.
2114 Shesley, Aaron, P. Cos. I and C, Eng.; e. Aug. 30, 1862, Littleton, Ill.; ad. same.
2115 Shesley, Josiah M., P. Cos. I and C, Eng.; e. Aug. 30, 1862, Littleton, Ill.
2116 Shewell, Zach., P. Co. D, Eng.; e. Aug. 17, 1861, Carlyle, Ill.; died St. Louis, Mo., Oct. 31, 1861.
2117 Schilling, Bertholdi, P. Co. G, 25th ; e. Feb. 1, 1862, Kansas City, Mo.
2118 **SHINN, GEO. W.**, Lt. Co. B, 25th ; e. July 25, 1862; disch. Jan. 1, 1864.
2119 Shintal, Christoph, P. Co. F, Eng.; e. Sept. 23, 1861, Dubuque, Iowa.

2120 Shopers, Henry, P. Co. B, 25th ; e. June 13, 1861, St. Joseph, Mo.
2121 Short, Phil., Cor. Cos. B and K, Eng.; e. July 20, 1861, St. Louis, Mo.
2122 Shrieves, Washt., P. Cos. I and D, Eng.; e. Sept. 23, 1861, Rushville, Ill.; deserted at Memphis, Tenn., Feb. 12, 1863.
2123 Shults, John, P. Co. D, 25th ; e. July 12, 1861, St. Joseph, Mo.
2124 **SHUMAN, GEO. W.**, Lt., Co. B, Eng.; e. June 13, 1861, St. Joseph, Mo.
2125 **SHURTLEFF, NATHANIEL**, Capt. Co. K, 25th ; e. Feb. 1, 1862, Forest City, Mo., res. Jan. 23, 1863.
2126 Sigler, Valentine, P. Co. C, 25th ; e. ———.
2127 Sigler, Adolph, P. Cos. C, 25th, A and B, Eng.; e. Dec. 15, 1863, St. Joseph, Mo.
2128 Sheard, Samuel, P. Cos. B, 25th ; and L. Eng.; e ———.
2129 Shell, Jas. F., P. Co. I, 25th; e ———; ad Maryville, Mo.
2130 Sillick, Asher, P. Cos. I and C, Eng.; e. Sept. 21, 1861, Burlington, Iowa.
2131 Silvers, Francis M., P. Cos. G, 25th, L and E, Eng.; e. Feb. 15, 1862, St. Joseph, Mo.
2132 Simerly, Andrew, P. Co. E, 25th; e. July 19, 1862, Andrew Co., Mo.
2133 Simms, Isaac, P. Cos. H, 25th, M and E, Eng.; e. July 30, 1861, Oxford, Mo.
2134 Simmonds, Geo. F., Sergt. Co. A, 25th; e. July 17, 1862, Color Sergt. of 25th.
2135 Simmons, Jas. B., P. Cos. I and C, Eng.; e. Sept. 16, 1861, Denmark, Iowa; ad. Scott City, Kas.
2136 Simon, Francis, P. Co. A, Eng.; e. July 20, 1861, St. Louis, Mo.
2137 Simpkins, Thos. D., P. Co. K, Eng.; e. Sept. 26, 1861, Burlington, Iowa.
2138 Sine, Lorenzo D., P. Co. H, 25th; e. Dec. 15, 1861, Nodaway Co., Mo.
2139 Singleton, Henry, Sergt. Co. I, 25th; e. July 29, 1861, Gallatin, Mo.
2140 **SINGLETON, JOHN W.**, Lt., Co. I, 25th; e Nov. 1, 1861, Gallatin, Mo.; ad. Parsons, Kas.; res. March 18, 1863
2141 Singleton, Julius F., P. Cos. I, 25th, H and D, Eng.; e. March 17, 1863, Gallatin, Mo.
2142 Singleton, Wm. O., P. Cos. I, 25th, H and D, Eng.; e. March 17, 1863, Gallatin, Mo.
2143 Sirmers, Jas., P Co. C. Eng.; e. Oct. 5, 1864.
2144 Sligo, F. M., P. Co. A, 25th; e. Aug. 7, 1861, Weston, Mo.
2145 Shinn, Saml., P. Co. A, 25th; e. June 17. 1861, St. Joseph, Mo.
2146 Sloan, Jas., P. Co. H, 25th; e. Aug. 20, 1861, Nodaway Co., Mo.
2147 Slocum, John, P. Co. H. 25th; e. Aug. 4, 1861.
2148 Skidmore, Newton, P. Co. I, 25th; e. Sept. 17. 1861, Pleasant View, Mo.
2149 Skirvin, Wm., P. Cos. H, D and C, Eng.; e. Sept. 13, 1861, Schuyler Co., Ill.
2150 Smiley, John G., P. Co. G. 25th; Jan. 18. 1861, Independence, Mo.
2151 Smith, Ashel, P. Co. A, 25th; e. June 14, 1861, St. Joseph, Mo.
2152 Smith, Chas. D., P. Co. E, 25th; e. Jan. 2. 1862, White Cloud, Kas.
2153 Smith, Donnelly, Cor. Co. F, Eng.; e. Sept. 9, 1861, Manchester, Iowa.
2154 Smith, Daniel F., P. Co. E, Eng.; e. July 13, 1861, Adrian, Mich.
2155 Smith, Franklin, P. Co. E, Eng.; e. July 13, 1861, Adrian, Mich.
2156 Smith, Geo. W., P. Co. E Eng.; e. July 13, 1861, Adrian, Mich.
2157 Smith, Francis, P. Cos. I, C and A, Eng.; e. Sept. 9, 1861, Rushville, Ill.; vet. Feb. 4, 1864; pensioned; ad. Neosho, Mo.
2158 Smith, Francis M., P. Co. E. 25th; e. Jan. 10, 1862, Holt Co., Mo.
2159 Smith, Hamilton D, P. Co. D, Eng.; e. Oct. 1, 1861; ad. Terre Haute, Ind.; is a pensioner.
2160 Smith, Henry H., P. Cos. D and C, Eng.; e. Aug. 15, 1861, Flora, Ill.
2161 Smith, Jacob, P. Co. F, Eng.; e. Oct. 1, 1861, Grand Detour, Ill.; died St. Louis, Mo., Feb. 1862.
2162 Smith, Jas., P. Co. F, Eng.; e. Oct. 11, 1861, Dubuque, Iowa; died Gen. Hos. Cincinnati, Ohio, June, 1862.
2163 Smith, Jas B., P. Cos. F, 25th, H and D, Eng.; e. Oct. 1, 1862, Bucklin, Mo.; ad. Dunlap, Kas.
2164 Smith, John, P. Co. E. Eng.; e. July 13, 1861, Adrian, Mich.
2165 Smith, John, P. Cos. H and D, Eng.; e. Oct. 17, 1861, Paris, Ill.
2166 Smith, John, P. Co. A, 25th; e. June 20, 1861, St. Joseph, Mo.
2167 Smith, John, P. Co. F, 25th; e. Aug. 15, 1861, Douglas Co., Mo.
2168 Smith, John S., P. Cos. B and K, Eng.; e. July 28, 1861, Paris, Ill.; has a pension; ad. Tuscola, Ill.

2169 Smith, Joseph, P. Cos. I and C, Eng.; e. Sept. 13, 1861, Rushville, Ill.; ad. same.
2170 Smith, Littleton A., P. Cos. II, D and C, Eng.; Nov. 12, 1861; Pleasant Hill, Ill.
2171 Smith. Montillion, P. Cos. I and C, Eng.; e. Sept. 30, 1861, Dubuque, Iowa.
2172 Smith, Peter, P. Co. Drum Major, 25th; e. ——; ad. Malvern. Iowa.
2173 Smith, Richard, P. Co. G, 25th; e. June 27, 1861, Kansas City, Mo.
2174 **SMITH, ROBERT G.**, Lt. Cos. A and F, Eng.; e. July 20, 1861, St. Louis, Mo.; res. Feb. 16, 1863.
2175 Smith, Wm., P. Co. A, 25th; e. June 20, 1861, St. Joseph, Mo.
2176 Smith, Wm., P. Co. G, 25th; e. Dec. 21, 1861, Kansas City, Mo.
2177 Smith, Wm. G., P. Co. E, Eng.; e. July 13, 1861, Adrian, Mich.
2178 Smith, Wm. J., P. Co. B, Eng ; e. July 28, 1861. St. Louis, Mo.
2179 Smith, Thos. J., P. Co. H, 25th; e. July 28, 1862, Andrew Co., Mo.
2180 Smith, Thos. P., P. Co. F, 25th; e. Jan. 15, 1862, Troy, Kas.
2181 Smith, Walter E., P. Cos. C and B, Eng.; e. Aug 4, 1861, Prairie City, Ill.
2182 Smitzon, Henry, P. Cos. F, 25th, H and D, Eng.; e. Sept. 20, 1862, Independence, Mo.
2183 Snider, Geo., P. Cos. D, 25th, A and B, Eng.; e. Feb. 10, 1862, St. Joseph, Mo.
2184 Snider, Jas. A., Prin. Mus., Eng. and Sergt. Cos. C and B, Eng.; e. Aug. 4, 1861, Prairie City, Ill.
2185 Snooks, Geo. E., P. Cos. A, 25th, and M and E, Eng.; e. June 20, 1861, Rushville, Mo.
2186 Snorf, Milton C., P. Cos. H, D and C, Eng.; e. Aug. 12, 1862, New Goshen, Ind.; ad. Brainard, Kas.
2187 Snow, Edwin A., P. Co. A. 25th; e. June 3, 1863, St. Joseph Mo.; ad. Ottawa, Kas.
2188 Snow, Edwin H., P. Co. A, 25th; e. June 20, 1861, St. Joseph, Mo.
2189 Snyder, Dexter, P. Cos. A, 25th, M and E, Eng.; e. Sept. 20, 1862, De Kalb Co., Mo.
2190 Snyder, John B., P. Cos. A, 25th, M and E, Eng.; e. Dec. 24, 1861, De Kalb Co., Mo.
2191 Saleman, Herman, P. Cos. L and I, e. ——.
2192 Soper, Joseph, P. Co. E, Eng.; e. July 13, 1861, Adrian, Mich.
2193 Sovereign, Gabe, P. Cos. C and B, Eng.; e. Aug. 4, 1861, Prairie City, Ill.
2194 Spears, Sanford, P. Co. B, Eng.; e. Dec. 15, 1863.
2195 **SPAULDING, E. T.**, Lt. Co. C, 25th; e. March 25, 1862; died June 1, 1862.
2196 **SPEARS, HENRY**, Lt. Van Horn's Battalion; e. June 28, 1861.
2197 Specht, Alois, P. Cos. L and I, Eng.; e. ——; ad. Cincinnati, Grant Co., Kas.
2198 Speir, John, P. Co. F, Eng.; e. Nov. 5, 1861, Dixon, Ill.
2199 Spencer, Geo. Cor. Cos. D and H, Eng.; e. Sept. 14, 1861, Flora, Ill.; dead.
2200 Spencer, John, P. Co. F, Eng.; e Oct. 1, 1861, Grand Detour, Ill.; dead.
2201 Sperry, Lucius, P. Cos. I and C, Eng.; e. Sept. 15, 1861, Denmark, Iowa; dead.
2202 Spicer, Henry, P. Cos. H, D and C, Eng.; e. Aug. 14, 1862, Sandford, Ind.
2203 Splenner, Wm. J., P. Co. I, 25th; e. Aug. 6, 1861, Grundy Co., Mo.
2204 Spoon, Geo., P. Co. F, Eng.; e. Sept. 14, 1861, Janesville, Wis.
2205 Sprinkler, John, P. Co. C, 25th; e. Aug. 15, 1861.
2206 Sprous, John H., P. Cos. I, C and B, Eng.; e. Sept. 30, 1861, Toolsboro, Iowa; ad. same.
2207 Sprous, Sidney, P. Cos. I, C and B, Eng., e. Oct. 25, 1861, Burlington, Iowa.
2208 Spunagle, Danl., P. Cos. C and B, Eng.; e. Aug. 4, 1861, Prairie City, Ill.; ad. Clarinda, Iowa.
2209 Spunagle, Jacob, P. Cos. C and B, Eng.; e. Dec. 12, 1861, Prairie City, Ill.
2210 Spunagle, Wm., P. Cos. C and B, Eng.; e. Aug. 4, 1861, Prairie City, Ill.; ad. Clarinda, Iowa.
2211 Stafford, David, P. Co. C, 25th; e. Dec. 28, 1861.
2212 Stagner, Thos. J., P. Cos. F, 25th, H and D, Eng.; e. Jan. 17, 1862, Stewartsville, Mo.; ad. Breckenridge, Mo.
2213 Stailey, Solomon, P. Cos. II, D and C, Eng.; e. Aug. 2, 1862, Sandford, Ind.; ad. Hume, Edgar Co., Ill.
2213½ Stahl, Gabriel, P. Cos. B, 25th and L, Eng.; e. June 13, 1861, St. Joseph, Mo.

2214 Stalcup, David, P. Cos. C and B, Eng.; e. Aug. 4, 1861, Prairie City, Ill.; ad. Laurel, Iowa.
2215 Standeclaus, A., P. Co. H, Eng.; prom. Lt. C. T.
2216 Standeford, —, P. Co. K, Eng.; e. Sept. 16, 1861, Roseville, Ill.
2217 Stanley, Danl. L., P. Co. G, 25th.; e. Feb. 15, 1862, St. Joseph, Mo.
2218 Stanley, Jas. T., P. Cos. F, 25th, H and D, Eng.; e. Jan. 17, 1863, Independence, Mo.; pensioner; ad. Tekama, Burt Co., Neb.
2219 Stanley, Jos. W., P. Co. E, 25th; e. Dec. 17, 1861, St. Joseph, Mo.
2220 Stanly, Thos., Co. E, 25th; e. Dec. 18, 1861, St. Joseph, Mo ; ad. same.
2221 Stanley, John T., P. Cos. F, 25th, H and D, Eng.; e. ——; ad. Mexico, Mo.
2222 Stanton, Ed., P. Co. E, 25th; e. Dec. 19, 1861, Holt Co., Mo.; ad. Veteran's Home, Napa Co., Cal.
2223 Stanton, Jas. S., Cor. Cos. I and C, Eng.; e. Sept. 16, 1861, Denmark, Iowa; a pensioner; ad. Garner, Iowa; disch. dis. 1863.
2224 Stansberry, Eph. B., P. Co. A, 25th; e. June 14, 1861, St. Joseph, Mo.
2225 Starr, John S., Hos. Stewd., Eng.; e. Sept. 16, 1861, Denmark, Iowa; died Atlanta, Ga., of dysentery, Oct., 1864.
2226 Statelan, Erastus, P. Co. C, 25th; e. June 10, 1862.
2227 Staube, Geo., P. Co. A, 25th; e. June 14, 1861, St. Joseph, Mo.
2228 Steagle, Joseph, P. Cos. A and K, Eng.; e. Aug. 5, 1861, St. Louis, Mo.
2229 Steinberg, Fred, P. Cos. G and I, Eng.; e. Sept. 13, 1861, Cape Girardeau, Mo.; ad. Jackson, Mo.
2230 Steineman, Adolph, P. Cos. G and I, Eng.; e. Sept. 13, 1861, Cape Girardeau, Mo.
2230½ Steinforth, Henry, P. Cos. B, D and L, Eng.; e. Nov. 1, 1861, St Joseph, Mo.
2231 Steinhoff, Ernest, P. Cos. G and I, Eng.; e. July 13, 1861, Cape Girardeau, Mo.
2232 Steuihoff, Wm , Cor. Cos. G and I, Eng.; e. July 13, 1861, Cape Girardeau, Mo.; pensioner; ad. Cambridgeboro. Pa.
2233 Stember, John T., P. Co. G, 25th; e. Nov. 1, 1861, St. Joseph, Mo.
2234 Stephens, Jas., P. Cos. H, 25th, M and E, Eng.; e. Sept. 6, 1862, Nodaway Co., Mo.
2235 Stephens, John, P. Cos. C and B, Eng.; e. Aug. 4, 1861, Prairie City, Ill.; died, Otterville, Mo., March 25, 1862, typoid fever.
2236 Stephens, Isaac, P. Co. G, 25th and L. Eng.; e. March 1, 1862, St. Joseph, Mo.
2237 Stephens, John O., P. Cos. E, 25th, G and E, Eng.; e. Sept. 6, 1862, Nodaway Co., Mo.; ad. St. Joseph. Mo.
2238 Stephens, Pete, P. Co. G, 25th; e. Jan. 18, 1861, St. Joseph, Mo.
2239 Sternberg, Fred, P. Cos. G, I and D, Eng.; e. Sept. 13, 1861, Cape Girardeau, Mo.
2240 Stewart, Alex, P. Co. G, 25th; e. Feb, 22, 1862, St. Joseph, Mo.
2241 Stewart, Z. P., P. Co. K, Eng.; e. Sept. 26, 1861, New London, Iowa.
2242 Stewart, Henry, P. Co. A, 25th; e. June 15, 1861, Elmwood, Ill.
2243 Stewart, Jas., P. Co. B, Eng.; e. July 25, 1861, Paris, Ill.; ad. same.
2244 Stewart, John L., Cor. Co. F, Eng.; e. Sept. 23, 1861, Bloomington, Ill.; has a pension; ad. Shell Rock, Iowa.
2245 Stewart, John, P. Co. F, Eng.; e. Oct. 1, 1861, Decatur, Ill.; ad. same; draws a pension.
2246 Stewart, Marion, P. Co. B, Eng.; e. July 28, 1861, Paris, Ill.; ad. Brocton, Ill.; is a well-to-do farmer and stockbroker.
2247 Stewart, Thos. C., P. Cos. I and C, Eng.; e. Sept. 24, 1861, McGregor, Iowa; ad. Petersburg, Ind.; pensioner.
2248 Stewart, Wm. H., P. Co. H, 25th; e. Aug. 14, 1861, Nodaway Co., Mo.; ad. Baldwin City, Kas.
2249 Stewart, Wm. W., Sergt. Cos. C and B, Eng.; e. Aug. 4, 1861, Prairie City, Ill.; ad. Greeley, Iowa (or Vineland, Mo.).
2250 Stiff, Isaac C., P. Cos. C and B, Eng.; e. Aug. 4, 1861, Prairie City, Ill.; vet. Jan. 18, 1864.
2151 Stillions, Danl. M., Cor. Cos. K, 25th, M and E, Eng.; e. Dec. 15, 1861, Hawleyville, Iowa.
2252 Stillwell, Francis M., P. Cos. G, 25th, L and E, Eng.; e. July 20, 1861, Lexington, Mo.

2253 Stinson, Richard P., P. Cos. C and B, Eng.; e. Aug. 4, 1861, Prairie City, Ill.
2254 Steeckler, Daniel, P. Cos. L and I, Eng.; e.———.
2255 Stoelzer, Wm., P. Cos. L and I, Eng.; e.———.
2256 Stoddard, Wm. B., P. Cos. C and B, Eng.; e. Sept. 6, 1861, Avon, Ill.
2257 Stockwell, Jas., P. Co. I, 25th; e. Aug. 25, 1861, Pleasant View, Mo.
2258 Stokes, Joseph, P. Cos. H and D, Eng.; e. Nov. 9, 1861, St. Louis, Mo.; deserted March, 1862.
2259 Stoneking, John G., P. Co. C, Eng; e. Aug. 4, 1861, Birmingham, Ill.; disch. dis. St. Louis, Mo., March 31, 1862.
2260 Stoll, Jacob, P. Co. B, 25th; e. July 20, 1861, St. Joseph, Mo.
2261 Stolte, Christoph, P. Cos. G and I, Eng.; e.———; pensioner, Cape Girardeau, Mo.
2262 **STORY, OSCAR F.**, Capt., Cos. F, 25th, M and E, Eng.; e. Aug. 2, 1861; disch. Jan. 4, 1865, at Bucklin, Mo.; died.
2263 Stotts, David C., P. Cos D, 25th and A, Eng.; e. July 30, 1861, Andrew Co., Mo.; ad. Savannah, Mo.
2264 Stotts, Jac., P. Cos. B and K, Eng.; e. July 28, 1861, Paris, Ill.; a pensioner, ad. Vermillion, Ill.
2265 Stotts, Wm., P. Cos. B, K and A, Eng.; e. Aug. 12, 1862, Vermillion, Ill.; ad. same; is pensioned.
2266 Stout, Wm. S., P. Co. F, 25th; e. Aug. 21, 1861, Civil Bend, Mo.
2267 Strange, Robt., P. Co. F, 25th; e. March 7, 1862, St. Joseph, Mo.
2268 Strasser, Wm., P. Cos. L, I and D. Eng.; e. ———.
2269 Striblin, Jordan, P. Co. D, 25th; e. July 20, 1861, St. Joseph, Mo.
2270 Strickland, Wes. C., P. Co. B, Eng.; e. July 28, 1861, Paris, Ill.
2271 Stringer, Jas., P. Cos. H, D and C, Eng.; e. Nov. 15, 1861, St. Louis, Mo.
2272 Strong, Rufus C., P. Co. K, Eng ; e. Oct. 31, 1861, Bloomington, Ill.
2273 Strotsteffen. John, P. Cos. I and C, Eng.; e. Sept. 13, 1861, West Point, Iowa; has a pension; ad. Lincoln, Neb.
2273½ Stuber, John, P. Cos. B. 25th and L, Eng.; e. Nov. 1, 1861, St. Joseph, Mo.
2274 Studa, Lucas, P. Co. B, Eng.; e. June 20, 1861, St. Joseph, Mo.
2275 Stufflebean, Geo., P. Co F, 25th; e. Dec. 21, 1861, North Salem, Mo.
2276 Stufflebean, John, P. Co. F, 25th; e. May 2, 1862, North Salem, Mo.
2277 Stump, Joseph, P. Cos. H, D and C, Eng.; e. Aug. 12, 1861, Vermillion, Ill.; dead.
2278 Stevens; John, P. Co. F, 25th; e. Jan. 10, 1862, Iowa Point, Kas.
2279 Stephenson, John, P. Co. D, 25th; e. July 19, 1861, Clinton, Mo.
2280 Sutor, Lewis, P. Co. A, 25th; e. March 7, 1862, Clinton, Mo.
2281 Suler, Mich., P. Cos. G, I and D, Eng.; e. June 23, 1862, Cape Girardeau, Mo.
2282 Sullivan, Daniel, P. Co. G, 25th; e. June 22. 1861, Kansas City, Mo.
2283 Sullivan, Florence, P. Cos. G, 25th, L and E, Eng.; e. March 8, 1862, St. Joseph, Mo.
2284 Sullivan, John, P. Co. F, Eng.; e. Sept. 25, 1861, Dubuque, Iowa; deserted Commerce, Mo., March 5, 1862.
2285 Sullivan, Thomas, P. Co. G, 25th; e. June 22, 1861, Kansas City, Mo.
2286 **SUMNER, H. M.**, Lt. Cos. A, D and E, Eng.; e. Dec. 31, 1861, St. Louis, Mo.; promoted Capt. June 12, 1865; died about 1880.
2287 Surm, Lorenzo D., P. Cos. G, 25th, I and E, Eng.; e. Dec. 16, 1861.
2288 Sutton, George, P. Co. F, Eng.; e. Sept. 2, 1861, Cassville, Wis.; draws a pension; ad. Boscobel, Wis.
2289 Sutton, Robert, P. Cos. D, F and B, Eng.; e. Aug. 15, 1861, St. Louis, Mo.
2290 Swank, John, P. Cos. I and C, Eng.; e. Sept. 19, 1861, Burlington, Iowa; is pensioned; ad. Pomeroy, Wash. T.
2291 Swank, William H. H., P. Cos. I and C, Eng.; e. Sept. 19, 1861, Burlington, Iowa; was Hos. Cook over two years, owing to his inability for active duty; is a pensioner; ad. Eugene, Iowa.
2292 Swansen, Irwin, P. Co. A, Eng.; e. July 20, 1861, St. Louis, Mo.
2293 Swansen, Swan, P. Cos. K and D, Eng.; e. Sept. 20, 1861, Burlington, Iowa; is pensioned; ad. York, Neb.
2294 Swartwout Jas., P. Cos. E, 25th, G and C, Eng.; e. Dec. 31, 1861, Oregon, Mo.
2295 Sweeney, Jas., P. Co. H, 25th; e. Sept. 20, 1861, Nodaway Co., Mo.
2296 Sweeney, Hugh, P. Cos. D and F, Eng.; e. Aug. 15, 1861, St. Louis, Mo.

2297 Sweeney, Thos., P. Co. D, 25th, A and B, Eng.; e. Jan. 14, 1862, Hamilton, Mo.
2298 Sweet, Spencer, P. Co. D, Eng.; e. August 15, 1861, St. Louis, Mo.; disch. dis. June 25, 1863, Milliken Bend, Miss.
2299 Swimmer, Henry, P. Co. A, 25th; e. July, 15, 1861, Maryville, Mo.
2300 Swettman, Wm., P. Cos. G and I, Eng.; e. Sept. 13, 1861, Cape Girardeau, Mo.
2301 Sylvester, John W., P. Cos. I and C, Eng.; e. Sept. 28, 1861, Burlington, Iowa.
2302 **STAPLES, C. A.**, Chap. Eng.; e. Oct. 31, 1861; res. June 6, 1862.
2303 Seeman, John, P. Co. E, Eng.; e. July 18, 1861, Adrian, Mich.; is a pensioner; ad. Ottawa Lake, Mich.
2304 Shatzle, Chas., P. Cos. C, 25th, and A, Eng.; e. ———.
2305 Tabler, Benj. F., Sergt. Cos. H and D, Eng.; e. Sept. 15, 1861, Vermillion, Ill.; is pensioned; ad. Albany, Oreg.
2306 Talbot, Thos., P. Co. D, 25th; e. July 12, 1862, St. Joseph, Mo.
2307 Talcott, Dean, P. Co. F, Eng.; e. Sept. 9, 1861, Manchester, Iowa; has a pension; ad. Maynard, Iowa.
2308 Tally, Elihu G., P. Cos. C and B, Eng.; e. Sept. 24, 1863, Pocahontas, Tenn.; draws a pension; ad. Abingdon, Ill.
2309 **TANNER, BENJ. R.**, Lt. and Capt. Cos. K, 25th, G and D, Eng.; e. Dec. 1, 1861, Hawleyville, Iowa; pensioned; ad. Brown P. O., Montrose Co., Colo.
2310 Tanner, John P., Sergt. Co. B, 25th; e. June 13, 1861, Kansas City, Mo.
2311 Taylor, Geo. L., Cor. Cos. I and C, Eng.; e. Sept. 15, 1861, Denmark, Iowa; ad. Aurora, Ill.
2312 Taylor, John T., P. Cos. D, 25th, A and E, Eng.; e. March 1, 1862, St. Joseph, Mo.
2313 Taylor, Wm. L., P. Co. D, Eng.; e. Oct. 26, 1861, Rushville, Ill.; died in hospital, Cairo, Ill., Aug. 9, 1862.
2314 Taus, Alex., P. Cos. H, 25th, M and E, Eng.; e. June 26, 1861, Nodaway Co., Mo.
2315 Tearney, John, P. Co. A, 25th; e. June 26, 1861, St. Joseph, Mo.
2316 Tebbins, Herman, P. Cos. L, I and D, Eng.; e. ———.
2317 Templer, John, P. Co. F, 25th; e. Aug. 19, 1861, Douglas Co., Mo.
2318 Templeton, Thos. G., Sergt. Co. E, Eng.; e. July 13, 1861, Adrian, Mich.; prom. 1st Lt. 1st Mich. Eng.; dead.
2319 Terry, Enos A., P. Co. I, 25th; e. Sept. 21, 1861, Davies Co., Mo.
2320 **TETER LOUIS**, Lt. Co. C, 25th; e. Nov. 1, 1861, St. Joseph, Mo.; cashiered March 11, 1862.
2321 Tetrick, John H., P. Cos. D and F, Eng.; e. Sept. 14, 1861, Flora, Ill.
2322 Tice, Chas. L., P. Co. E, 25th; e. Aug. 30, 1861, St. Joseph, Mo.
2323 Tice, David, P. Co. E, 25th; e. Dec. 27, 1861, Holt Co., Mo.
2324 Tilden, David, P. Cos. E, 25th, G and C, Eng.; e. July 22, 1861, Holt Co., Mo.
2325 Timmins, Jas., P. Cos. H and D, Eng.; e. Oct. 19, 1861, Rushville, Ill.
2326 Tiser, Andrew, P. Co. K, Eng.; e. Sept. 20, 1861, Wapello, Iowa; a pensioner; ad. Union, Hardin Co., Iowa.
2327 Theinert, Joseph, P. Cos. L and I, Eng.; e. ———.
2328 Theis, Nicholas, P. Cos. L, I and D, Eng.; e. ———; ad. St. Louis, Mo.
2329 **THOMAS, ENNIS C.**, Capt. Co. D, 25th, e. July 25, 1861, De Kalb Co., Mo.; res. Dec. 1, 1863; ad. Plattsburg, Mo.
2330 Thomas, Jacob, P. Co. B, 25th and L, Eng.; e. June 13, 1861, St. Joseph, Mo.
2331 Thomas, Jas. B., P. Cos. K, 25th, G and C, Eng.; e. Oct. 18, 1862, Hawleyville, Iowa; dead.
2332 Thomas, Joseph Mc., P. Cos. K, 25th, G and C, Eng.; e. Oct. 18, 1862, Hawleyville, Iowa; ad. same; has a pension.
2333 Thomas, Jas. W., P. Co. D, 25th, A and B, Eng.; e. Aug. 29, 1862, St. Joseph, Mo.; killed in Centralia massacre, Sept. 27, 1864.
2334 Thomas, John, Mus., Co. I, 25th; e. Nov. 28, 1862, Platt Co., Mo.
2335 Thomas, John B., P. Co. G, 25th; e. June 27, 1861, Kansas City, Mo.
2336 Thomas, Josiah, P. Cos. F, 25th, H and D, Eng.; e. Jan. 5, 1862, Rochester, Mo.
2337 Thomas, Lewis, P. Co. G, 25th; e. March 15, 1863, Clinton, Co., Mo.

THE ROSTER. 237

2338 Thomas, Shelton, P. Cos. H. D and C, Eng.; et Aug. 23, 1863, Pocahontas, Tenn.
2339 Thomas, W. P., P. Cos. F, 25th, H and D, Eng.; e. Sept. 11, 1862, Rochester Mo.; ad. Stewartsville (or Clarksdale), Mo.
2340 **THOMPSON, CHAS. R.**, Lt. Cos. D and E, Eng ; e. Oct. 31, 1861; promoted Capt. Gen. Rosecrans' Staff, March 7, 1863, promoted Colonel 12th U. S. C. T. in 1863; ad. San Diego, Cal.
2341 Thompson, Claiborne, P. Cos. G, 25th, L and E, Eng.; e. Feb. 5, 1862, Clinton, Mo.
2342 Thompson, David, P. Co. D, 25th; e. March 2, 1862, St. Joseph, Mo.
2343 Thompson, David, P. Cos. C and B, Eng.; e. Aug. 4, 1861, Prairie City, Ill.
2344 Thompson, Geo. W., P. Cos. H and D, Eng.; e. Sept. 18, 1861, Vermillion, Ill.; dead.
2345 Thompson, John W., P. Cos. H and D, Eng.; e. March 3, 1863, Vermillion, Ill.
2346 **THOMPSON, JOSEPH**, Lt. Co. A and Capt. Co. I, 25th; e. June 16, 1861, St. Joseph, Mo.; ad. St. Joseph, Mo.
2347 Thompson, Joseph, Co. I, 25th; e. June 14. 1861, St. Joseph, Mo.
2348 Thompson, Jacob E., Sergt. Cos. D, 25th, A and B, Eng.; e. Feb. 13, 1863; wounded before Columbia, S. C., Feb. 14, 1865, by a spent and unexploded 6th shell; hit in right shoulder.
2348½ Thompson, Louis, P. Cos. B; 25th and L, Eng.; e. March 15, 1863, St. Joseph, Mo.
2349 Thompson, Wm. H., P. Cos. K, 25th, H and D, Eng.; e. Feb. 13, 1863, St. Joseph, Mo ; ad. Smith Center, Kas.
2350 Thompson, Wm., P. Co. H, Eng.; died Nov. 1861.
2351 Thornburg, John H., P. Cos. B and K, Eng.; e. ———; disch. dis. ———; dead.
2352 Thornburg, Leonard C., P. Cos. B and K, Eng.; e. July 28, 1861, Paris, Ill.; draws a pension; ad. Vermillion, Ill.
2353 **THORNE, JOSHUA**, Sur. Van Horn's Battalion; e. June 24, 1861.
2354 Thresher, Geo., P. Co. A, Eng.
2355 Thrager, Fred., P. Cos. L and I, Eng.; e.———; ad. Pekin, Ill.
2356 Tobin, Jas., P. Cos. H and D, Eng.; e. Sept. 18, 1861, Paris, Ill.
2357 Todd, Jas. A., P. Co B, Eng.; e. Sept. 13, 1862.
2358 Todd, Lewis, P. Cos. D and C, Eng.; e. Sept. 10, 1861, Flora, Ill.
2359 Toler, Wm , P. Co. K, Eng.; e. Sept. 18, 1861, Prairie City, Ill.
2360 Tombertin, Lacy, P. Cos. I and C, Eng.; e. Sept. 16, 1861, Rushville, Ill.; a pensioner; ad. Industry, Ill.
2361 Tomlinson, Wm., Sergt. Co. D, 25th; e. July 12, 1861, St. Joseph, Mo.
2362 Toolin, Andrew, P. Co. E, 25th; e. Feb. 17, 1862, Atchison Co., Mo.
2363 Tracy, Jasper, P. Co. H, 25th; e. Nov. 27, 1861, St. Joseph, Mo.
2364 Tracy, Joseph C., Cor. Co. G, 25th, L and E, Eng.; e. Nov 20. 1861.
2365 Tracy, Thos., P. Co. D, 25th; e. June 25, 1862, Atchison Co., Mo.
2366 Trail, Martin, P. Cos. G, 25th and L, Eng.; e. May 23, 1863. Harlem, Mo.
2367 Tangott, Chas., P. Co. C. 25th; e. March 5, 1863, Liberty, Mo.
2368 Trape, Chas., P. Cos. G, 25th, L and E, Eng.; e. May 20, 1863, Harlem, Mo.
2369 Traube, Wm., Cor. Co. G, Eng.; e. Sept. 13, 1861, Cape Girardeau, Mo.
2370 Travis, Absalom, P. Cos. I and C. Eng.; e. Sept. 23, 1861, Rushville, Ill.; dead.
2371 Trimborn, Peter, P. Co. A, Eng.; e. July 20, 1861, Louisiana, Mo.
2372 Tritt, Burgoyne, P. Cos. H, D and C, Eng.; e. Sept. 21, 1862, Sandford,Ind.; ad. same ; pensioner.
2373 Tritt, Morgan, P. Co. H ; e.———: ad Sandford, Ind.
2374 Trogden, Isaac R., P. Cos. H, D and C, Eng.; e. May 12, 1862, Vermillion, Ill.; has pension ; ad. Sandford, Ind.
2375 Truax, John, P. Cos. I, 25th, H and D, Eng.; e. July 23, 1862, Maryville, Mo.
2376 Truitt, Wm., P. Co. I. 25th; e. Sept. 21, 1861, Kidder, Mo.
2377 Tubbs, Frank, P. Co. E, Eng.; e. July 13, 1861, Adrian, Mich.; ad. Ottawa Lake, Mich.
2378 Tucker, Hiram, P. Cos. A, 25th, M and E, Eng.; e. Sept. 16, 1862, New Madrid. Mo.
2379 Tucker, Stephen, P. Cos. K and D, Eng.; e. Sept. 24, 1861, Burlington, Iowa.

2380 Tuckerman, Geo., P. Co. F, 25th; e. Jan. 1, 1862, St. Joseph, Mo.
2381 Tullner, Julius, Cor. Cos. G and I, Eng.; e. Sept. 13, 1861, Cape Girardeau, Mo.; ad. same; pensioned.
2382 **TUNICA, FRANCIS**, Lieut. Cos. K and A, Eng.; e. Nov. 21, 1861, St. Louis, Mo.; disch. Dec. 8, 1864.
2383 Turner, David, P. Cos. C, 25th, A and B, Eng.; e. Feb. 16, 1862, St. Joseph, Mo.; ad same.
2384 Turner, Ira. Sergt. Co. A, Eng.; e. July 20, 1861, St. Louis, Mo.
2385 Turner, Phil. P. Co. A, Eng.; e. Oct. 23, 1862, St. Louis, Mo.
2386 Turner, Wm., P. Cos. C, 25th, A and B, Eng.; e. Feb. 10, 1862, St. Joseph, Mo.
2387 Turney, Wm. M., P. Cos. E, 25th, G and D, Eng.; e. Sept. 1, 1861, St. Joseph, Mo.
2388 **TWEEDDALE, WM.**, Capt. Co. F, Eng., Maj. Eng., Lt.-Col. Eng.; e. Sept. 14, 1861, Dubuque, Iowa; disch. May 31, 1865; was a civil engineer and contractor before the war; since has been Supt. public works and public buildings for the State of Kansas and built the Kansas State House; ad. Topeka, Kas.
2389 Tweedy, Wm. S., P. Co. H, Eng.; e.; dead.
2390 Tyler, Jas. H., P. Co. D, 25th; e. June 25, 1862, St. Joseph, Mo.
2391 Tyler, John, P. Co. D, 25th; e. July 17, 1861, St. Joseph, Mo.
2392 Tyrrell, John, P. Co. G, 25th; e. June 6, 1861, Kansas City, Mo.
2393 Tool, Simuel, P. Cos. B and K, Eng.; e. July 28, 1861, Paris, Ill.; draws a pension; ad. Connersville, Ind.
2394 Ulrich, Ernest, Sergt. Co. G, Eng.; e. Sept. 13, 1861, Cape Girardeau, Mo.; disch.
2395 Ulrich, Christian, P. Cos. G and I, Eng.; e. —; pensioner; ad. Advance, Mo.
2396 Ulsh, Francis M., P. Co. E, 25th; e. June 14, 1861, Doniphan, Kas.
2397 Ulstchi, John, P. Co. G, 25th; e. Nov. 1, 1861, St. Joseph, Mo.
2397½ Ultschi, Jacob, P. Cos. G, 25th and L, Eng.; e. June 13, 1861, St. Joseph, Mo.
2398 Underwood, Horace, P. Cos. H and D, Eng.; e. Nov. 12, 1861, Vermillion, Ill.; a pensioner; ad. Center Valley, Ind.
2399 Underwood, Thomas, P. Co. D, 25th; e. July 12, 1861, St. Joseph, Mo.; ad. Colwich, Kas.
2400 Underwood, Wm., Cor. Cos. H, 25th, M and E, Eng.; e. Nov. 26, 1861.
2401 Unkefer, William H., P. Cos. A, 25th, M and E, Eng.; e. June 18, 1861, St. Joseph, Mo.
2402 Unzer, Charles, P. Co. C, 25th; e. July 28, 1861.
2403 Updegraff, George, P. Cos. A and K, Eng.; e. July 20, 1861, St. Louis, Mo.
2404 Uthe, Christoph, P. Co. A. Eng.; e. July 20, 1861, St. Louis, Mo.
2405 Valaster, Mathias, P. Cos. L and I, Eng.; e. ———.
2406 Volk, Otto, Co. B, 25th; e. Oct. 6, 1861, St. Joseph, Mo.
2407 Valley, Joseph D., P. Co. D, Eng.; e. Aug. 24, 1861, St. Louis, Mo.; disch. dis. Jackson, Tenn., Oct. 22, 1862.
2408 Vance, Andrew J., P. Cos. H, 25th, M and E, Eng.; e. May 16, 1863, Nodaway Co., Mo.; ad. New Market, Iowa.
2409 Vance, Conrad, P. Co. H, 25th; e. Sept. 22, 1862, Nodaway, Co., Mo.
2410 Vanderhoof, Orange, P. Co. H, 25th; e. Aug. 14, 1861, Andrew Co., Mo.; ad. Maryville, Mo.
2411 Vaudin, John, P. Co. B, Eng.; e. Aug. 5, 1861, Paris, Ill.; ad. Wichita, Kas.
2412 Vanhoutin, J. J., Cor. Cos. H and D, Eng.; e. Sept. 16, 1861, Vermillion, Ill.; pensioned; ad. Vermillion, Ill.
2413 **VON DAUN**, Capt. Co B, Van Horn's Battalion; e. June 11, 1861.
2414 **VAN HORN, ROBERT T.**, Lt.-Col. 25th, Mo.; e. June 24, 1861. Col. Van Horn is editor and chief manager of the *Kansas City Daily and Weekly Journal*, and is as he always was a stanch Republican in politics. Before the war he was the leading Unionist of his section and raised the Van Horn Battalion in the vicinity of Kansas City; was elected to the State Senate of Missouri in 1862; the duties of which office required so much of his time that he was not much with his Regiment after the battle of Shiloh. He has served one or more terms as representative in Congress from his district since 1864. There is no editor of more influence or whose writing carries more weight in the country. His address is, Journal Office, Kansas City, Mo.

2415 Vanguudy, Jas., P. Cos. II, 25th, M and E, Eng.; e.———.
2416 Vannice, Jas. S., P. Cos. C and B, Eng.; e. Aug. 12, 1862, Bushnell, Ill.
2417 Van Norman, F. A., P. Co. B, Eng.; e. July 28, 1861, St. Joseph, Mo.
2418 Vansickle, Andrew, P. Co. H, 25th; e.———, Nodaway, Co., Mo.
2419 Vansickle Perry, P. Co II, 25th; e.———, Nodaway Co., Mo.
2420 Vaught, Geo. W., P. Co. D, 25th; e. Feb. 25, 1862, Andrew Co., Mo.
2421 Vaught, Wm. A., P. Co. D, 25th; e. Aug. 6, 1861, Andrew Co., Mo.
2422 Veach, Hollan, P. Cos. D, 25th, A and B, Eng.; e. Jan. 1, 1862, St. Joseph, Mo.
2423 Vedder, Jefferson W., Mus. Co. F, Eng.; e. Oct. 11, 1861, Cassville, Wis. is pensioned; ad. Henry, Dak.
2424 Vermillion, Reason C., P. Cos. II, D and C, Eng.; e. Oct. 5, 1863, Sandford, Ind.; pensioned; ad. St. Mary's, Ind.
2425 Vermillion, Wm., Cor. Cos. B and K, Eng.; e. July 28, 1861, Paris, Ill.
2426 Vest, Chas., P. Co. E, 25th; e. Dec. 25, 1861, Oregon, Mo.
2427 Vice, Milton. P. Cos. D and F, Eng.; e. Aug. 15, 1861, St. Louis, Mo.
2428 Vichmann, Louis, Sergt. Cos. L and I, Eng.; e.———; ad. 4622 Easton av St. Louis, Mo.
2429 Vinyard, John, P. Co. D, 25th; e. July 25, 1861, St. Joseph, Mo.
2430 Vinson, Wm., P. Co. D, Eng.; e. Aug. 17, 1861, Carlyle, Ill.; died, Jackson Tenn., Aug. 8, 1862.
2431 Vinson, Jas., P. Co. H, 25th; e. Aug. 14, 1861, Andrew Co., Mo.
2432 Vogel, Wm., Sergt. Co. G, Eng.; e. Sept. 13, 1861, Cape Girardeau, Mo killed himself with his musket, Nashville, Tenn., Feb. 4, 1864.
2433 Vornkuhl, Conrad, P. Cos. G, I and D, Eng.; e. Aug. 18, 1862, Cape Girardeau, Mo.; ad. same; pensioner.
2434 Vornkuhl, Henry, P. Cos. A and E, Eng.; e. Dec. 17, 1861, St. Louis, Mo.
2435 **VREELAND, JACOB H.**, Capt. Co. A, Eng.; e. Aug. 2, 1861, St. Louis, Mo.; dismissed, court martial, March 11, 1862.
2436 **VOERSTER, J. D.**, Capt. Cos. L and I, Eng., while in the 5th and 35th, Mo.; res. Jan. 17, 1862.
2437 Vortz, Bartholomew, P. Cos. B, 25th and L, Eng.; e. June 13, 1861, St. Joseph, Mo.
2438 **WADE, CHAS. A.**, Capt. Co. C, 25th; e. July 29, 1861, St. Joseph, Mo.; killed in battle of Shiloh, April 6, 1862.
2439 Wagner, Christoph., P. Cos. II, D and C, Eng.; e. Nov. 29, 1861, St. Louis, Mo.
2440 Wagner, E. R., P. Co. II, 25th; e.———.
2441 Wagner, Ferdinand, P. Cos. F, C and B, Eng.; e. Feb. 16, 1862, Dubuque, Iowa; died Atlanta, Ga., Oct., 1864.
2442 Wakefield, Jas., Cor. Cos. A, 25th, M and E, Eng.; e. March 23, 1862, St. Joseph, Mo.
2443 Wallbridge, Henry, P. Co. A, 25th; e. Sept. 16, 1861, Maryville, Mo.
2444 Walden, Louis, P. Co. A, Eng.; e. Aug 13, 1861, Cape Girardeau, Mo.
2445 Walders, Fredk., P. Cos. G and I, Eng.; e. Sept. 13, 1861, Cape Girardeau, Mo.; dead.
2346 Waldron, John, P. Cos. C and B, Eng.; e. Sept. 16, 1861, Prairie City, Ill.
2449 Waldron, Jasper, P. Cos. C and B, Eng.; e. Aug. 4, 1861, Prairie City, Ill.; ad. Wayne, Kas.
2448 Walker, Chas., Cor. Cos. C, and B, Eng.; e. Aug. 4, 1861, Prairie City, Ill.
2447 Walker, Ferdinand, P. Co. C, 25th; e. July, 25, 1861, St. Joseph, Mo.
2450 Walker, Geo. W., P. Co. G, 25th; e. Jan. 14. 1862, Gentry Co., Mo.
2451 Walker, Laf., P. Co. D, 25th; e. July 12, 1861, St. Joseph, Mo.
2452 Walker, Wm., Cor. Co. G, 25th; e. Feb. 14, 1862; Gentry Co., Mo.
2453 Walker, Wm. V. N., Sergt. Cos. G, 25th, L and E, Eng.; e. Feb. 14, 1862, St. Joseph, Mo.; ad. Darlington, Mo.
2454 Wallace, John, P. Cos. E, 25th, G and C, Eng.; e. March 13, 1862; St. Joseph, Mo.
2455 Wallace, Jos., P. Co. G, 25th; e. Feb. 15, 1862, Clinton, Mo.
2456 Wallace, Wm., P. Cso. G, 25th and L, Eng.; e. Feb. 15, 1862, Clinton, Mo.
2457 Wallage, David F., P. Cos. H, D and C, Eng.; e. Aug. 23, 1862, Vermillion, Ill.; has a pension; ad. Horace, Ill.
2458 Waller, Jeff. C., P. Cos. H and D, Eng.; e. Sept. 15, 1861, Paris, Ill.; pension; ad. Dennison, Ill.

2459 Wallage, B. F., P. Co. B, Eng.; e. July 28, 1861, Paris, Ill.
2460 Waller, Wm. R., P. Cos. C, 25th, A and E, Eng.; e. Sept. 10, 1862, St. Joseph, Mo.; ad. same.
2461 Walsh, John J., P. Co. A, Eng.; e. July 20, 1861, St. Louis, Mo.
2462 Walsh, Joseph, P. Co. A, 25th; e. Dec. 26, 1861, St. Joseph, Mo.
2463 Walsh, Mich., P. Co. G, 25th; e. June 17, 1861, Kansas City, Mo.
2464 Walsh, Wm., P. Co. G, 25th; e. June 26, 1861, Kansas City, Mo.
2465 Walters, Vincent, P. Co. E, 25th; e. July 22, 1861, St. Joseph, Mo.
2466 Wardlaw, Joseph, P. Cos. F, D and B, Eng.; e. Aug. 15, 1861, St. Louis, Mo.; dead.
2467 Ward, Peter, P. Co. G, 25th; e. June 24, 1861, Kansas City, Mo.
2468 Ward, Benj. W., P. Cos. I and C, Eng.; e. Oct. 10, 1861, Burlington, Iowa; ad. Yarmouth, Iowa.
2469 Ward, Wm. H., Co. D and Q.M.S., Eng.; e. Sept. 16, 1861; ad. Greenup, Ill.; pensioned.
2470 Warner, Jas., P. Co. A, 25th; e. Dec. 18, 1861, St. Joseph, Mo.
2471 Wash, Geo. T., P. Co. E, 25th; e. Jan. 10, 1862, Oregon, Mo.
2472 Washburn, Gus, P. Co. E, Eng.; e. July 13, 1861, Adrian, Mich.
2473 Washburn, Roswell G., P. Co. E, Eng., e. July 13, 1861, Adrian, Mich.
2474 Watkins, Amaziah, P. Cos. B and K, Eng.; e. July 28, 1861, Paris, Ill.
2475 Watkins, E. L., P. Co. F, Eng., e. ——.
2476 Watkins, Henry H., P. Cos. D and C, Eng.; e. Aug. 17, 1861, Carlyle, Ill.
2477 Watson, Chas. H., P. Co. G, 25th.; e. Dec. 18, 1861, Kansas City, Mo.
2478 Watson, Thos., Cor. Co. A, Eng.; e. July 20, 1861, St. Louis, Mo.; killed in skirmish at Tuscumbia River June 1, 1862.
2479 Watson, Thos., P. Co. E, 25th; e. July 22, 1861, Holt Co., Mo.
2480 Watts, Sinclair, P. Co. I, 25th; e. July 31, 1861, Davies Co., Mo.
2481 Webber, Jas. W., Sergt. Cos. A, 25th, M and E, Eng.; e. July 17, 1863, St. Joseph, Mo.; promoted Lt. June 12, 1865.
2482 Watkins, Samuel G., P. Co. D, Eng.; e. Aug. 17, 1861, Carlyle, Ill.; disch. dis. Otterville, Mo., Feb. 6, 1862.
2483 Watkins, Thos., P. Cos. A, 25th, M and E, Eng.; e. Oct. 2, 1862, Pilot Knob, Mo.
2484 Way, Nathan J., P. Cos. I and C, Eng.; e. Nov. 6, 1862, Trenton, Iowa.
2485 Way, Wm. B., P. Cos. D and F, Eng.; e. Aug. 15, 1861, Flora, Ill.; is pensioned; ad. Olivet, Dak.
2486 Wayt, Nathaniel, P. Co. C, 25th; e. July 7, 1861, St. Joseph, Mo.
2487 Weatherman, M. F., P. Cos. H, 25th, M and E, Eng.; e. Sept. 3, 1862, Nodaway Co., Mo.; is a pensioner; ad. Conception, Mo.
2488 Weaver, Barnett, P. Cos. C, 25th, A and B, Eng.; e. Oct. 26, 1861, St. Joseph, Mo.
2489 Webber, Eugene, P. Co. E, Eng.; e. July 13, 1861, Adrian, Mich.
2490 Webber, John, P. Co. E, Eng.; e. July 13, 1861, Adrian, Mich.
2491 Webber, Louis, P. Co. F, Eng.; e. May 26, 1862, Dubuque, Iowa.
2492 Webster, Milo B., P.Co.K, Eng.; e. Sept. 16, 1861, Burlington, Iowa; ad. same.
2493 Weddell, Aaron M., P. Co. A, 25th; e. June 18, 1861, St. Joseph, Mo.
2494 Weekley, John, P. Co. D, 25th; e. July 12, 1861, St. Joseph, Mo.
2495 Weekley, Wm., P. Co. D, 25th; e. July 12, 1861, St. Joseph, Mo.
2496 Weightman, Thomas, P. Cos. I and C, Eng.; e. Sept. 12, 1861, Rushville, Ill.; a pensioner; ad. Oskaloosa, Kas.
2497 Weighl, Joseph, Sergt. Co. B. 25th; e. June 13, 1861, St. Joseph, Mo.
2498 Weihl, Charles, P. Cos. B, 25th, and L, Eng.; e. June 13, 1861, St. Joseph, Mo.; ad. 1120 S. 16th st., St. Joseph, Mo.
2499 Weitkam. Aug., P. Cos. L and I, Eng.; e. ——.
2500 Wertle, Joseph, P. Cos. L and I, Eng.; e. ——.
2501 Weller, John, P. Co. H, 25th, e. Aug. 14, 1861, Nodaway Co., Mo.
2502 Wellner, Fred., P. Co. A, Eng.; e. July 20, 1861, St. Louis, Mo.
2503 Welsh, Martin V., P. Cos. B, and K, Eng.; e. July 20, 1861, St. Louis, Mo.; ad. Forrest Home, Mo.
2504 Weltire, John, P. Co. I, 25th; e. Nov. 1, 1861, St. Joseph, Mo.
2505 Wender, Arnold, Sergt. Cos. B, 25th and L, Eng.; e. June 13, 1861, St. Joseph, Mo.; ad. Arvilla, Mo.
2505½ Werner, Geo., P. Cos. B, 25th and L, Eng.; e. June 13, 1861, Kansas City; Mo.

2506 **WERTH, G. LOUIS,** Capt. Co. G, Eng.; e. Sept. 9, 1861, Cape Girardeau, Mo.; disch. Dec. 31, 1863. After leaving the Regiment he was for a time a boot and shoe merchant in Nashville, Tenn. He is now, and has been for several years, a well-to-do dealer in musical instruments at Montgomery, Ala.
2507 Wessell, Aug., P. Cos. G, I and D, Eng.; e. Nov. 2, 1862, Cape Girardeau, Mo.; a pensioner; disch. Washington, D. C., July 18, 1865, has been in the Missouri Hospital for the insane.
2508 Wessell, Henry, P. Cos. G, and I, Eng.; e. Sept. 13, 1861, Cape Girardeau, Mo.; has a pension; ad. Gordonville, Mo.
2509 West, Benj. F., P. Cos. D, 25th, A and B, Eng.; e. June 24, 1862, St. Joseph, Mo.
2510 West, John W., P. Co. D, 25th; e. Dec. 24, 1861, St. Joseph, Mo.
2511 West, Sam. G., P. Co. D, 25th; e. July 12, 1861, St. Joseph, Mo.
2512 West, Stephen H., Sergt. Cos. I and C, Eng.; e. Sept. 27, 1861, McGregor, Iowa; ad. Lewiston, Me.
2513 West, Thos. W., P. Co. D, 25th; e. June 24, 1862, St. Joseph, Mo.
2514 Westfall, Wm. W., P. Cos. I and C, Eng.; e. Sept. 19, 1861, Burlington, Iowa; has a pension; ad. Beloit, Wis.
2515 Westfall, Geo., P. Cos. I and C, Eng.; e. Sept. 19, 1861, Burlington, Iowa; ad. Columbus Junction, Iowa.
2516 Weston, Chas., Sergt. Co. G, 25th; e. Dec. 18, 1861, Kansas City, Mo.
2517 Whalen, Hiram, P. Cos. D, 25th, A and B, Eng.; e. Feb. 13, 1862, St. Joseph, Mo.
2518 Whalen, Pat., P. Cos. G, 25th, L and E, Eng.; e. June 18, 1861, Kansas City, Mo.
2519 Wheeler, Geo. W., P. Cos. I and C, Eng.; e. Oct. 6, 1861, Hardin, Iowa.
2520 Wheeler, Wm. R., P. Cos. D, 25th, A and B, Eng.; e. July 25, 1862, Atchison, Kas.
2521 Whipple, Dan. J., P. Co. E, 25th; e. Dec. 26, 1861, Oregon, Mo.
2522 Whipple, Harlow, P. Co. E, 25th; e. Feb. 3, 1862, Oregon, Mo.
2523 Whipple, Sam. W., P. Cos. E, 25th, G and C, Eng.; e. Dec. 24, 1861, Oregon, Mo.; ad. same.
2524 Whipple, Stephen J., P. Co. E, 25th; e. Dec. 24, 1861, Oregon, Mo.; ad. Forest City, Mo.
2525 Whipple, Virgil, P. Co. E, 25th; e. Jan. 1, 1861, Oregon, Mo.
2526 Whiskerson, Peter, P. Co. D, 25th; e. July, 19, 1861, St. Joseph, Mo.
2527 Whisler, Adam, P. Co. K, Eng.; e. Oct. 7, 1861, Wapello, Iowa.
2528 **WHITCOMB, ASHEL D.,** Sergt. Co. K, Lt. Cos. C, D and I, Capt. Co. E, Eng.; e. Sept. 5, 1861, Burlington, Iowa. He is in poor health; draws a pension; has been a wagon-maker since the war in Wapello, Iowa.
2529 White, Geo. A., P. Co. H, 25th; e. Sept. 27, ——, Iron Co., Mo.
2530 White, John, P. Co. A, 25th; e. June 19, 1861, St. Joseph, Mo.
2531 White, Joseph H., P. Cos. C and B, Eng.; e. Sept. 6, 1861, Prairie City, Ill.
2532 White, Marcus L., P. Co. C, Eng.; e. Aug. 4, 1861, Prairie City, Ill.; deserted, Memphis, Tenn., Feb. 10, 1863.
2533 White, Peter (alias), P. Co. F, Eng.; e. Aug. 20, 1861, Dubuque, Iowa; suicided by shooting with his musket, Sedalia, Mo., Nov., 1861.
2534 White, Thomas, P. Cos. D and C, Eng.; e. Aug. 15, 1861, St. Louis, Mo.; ad. Soldiers' Home, Leavenworth, Kas.
2535 White, S., P. Co. ——, 25th; ad. Dawson, Neb.
2536 Whitmack, Solomon, P. Co. E, 25th; e. July 2, 1862, St. Joseph, Mo.; ad. Lebanon, Iowa (or Mo.).
2537 Whitmarsh, Tim. F., Mus. Cos. I and C, Eng.; e. Sept. 15, 1861, Denmark, Iowa; ad. same; pensioned.
2538 Whitsel, Dan. H., P. Cos. H and D, Eng.; e. Aug. 12, 1862, New Goshen, Ind.; disch. dis. 1863.
2539 Whitten, Albt., P. Co. H, 25th; e. Aug. 14, 1861, Atchison Co., Mo.
2540 Whitten, Caswell, P. Co. H, 25th; e. Dec. 16, 1861, Nodaway Co., Mo.
2541 Whitten, Jas., P. Cos. H, 25th, M and E, Eng.; e. Sept. 6, 1862; dead.
2542 Wickham, Henry, P. Co. A, Eng.; e. July 20, 1861, St. Louis, Mo.
2543 Wiggins, Sam., P. Co. C, Eng.; e. Aug. 4, 1861, Prairie City, Ill.; died St. Louis, Mo., Sept. 14, 1861.

THE FIRST MISSOURI ENGINEERS.

544 Wilcox, Absalom, Sergt. Cos. E, 25th, M and E, Eng.; e. Feb. 27, 1862; ad. Yankton, Dak.
2545 **WILCOX, NATHAN W.,** Lt. Cos. K and G, Capt. Co. D, Eng.; e. Aug. 13, 1861, New London, Iowa; disch. Dec. 25, 1863.
2546 Wild, John, P. Cos. L, I and D, Eng.; e.———.
2547 Wildberger, Adam, Mus. Cos. B, 25th and L, Eng.; e. June 13, 1861, St. Joseph, Mo.; ad. No. 1305 Sylvania st.; same.
2548 Wildberger, John, P. Cos. B, L, 25th; e. July 13, 1861, St. Joseph, Mo.; ad. same.
2549 Wiley, Andrew F., P. Cos. I and C, Eng.; e. Oct. 8, 1861, Dubuque, Iowa; ad. Slate Hill, York Co., Pa.
2550 Wilks, Elijah, P. Cos. A and E, Eng.; e. Aug. 3, 1861, Cape Girardeau, Mo.
2551 Wilkins, Wm. J., P. Cos. H and D, Eng.; e. Sept. 20, 1861, Paris, Ill.
2552 Wilkison, Henry, P. Co. E, 25th; e. Jan. 11, 1862, Oregon, Mo.
2553 Wilson, Andrew J., P. Co. D, 25th; e. July 19, 1861, St. Joseph, Mo.
2554 Wilson, Benj. F., P. Cos. K and B, Eng.; e. Sept. 18, 1861, New London, Iowa; pensioned; ad. Neligh, Neb.
2555 Wilson, Dan., P. Co. D, 25th; e. July 25, 1862, St. Joseph, Mo.
2556 Wilson, Geo. W., P. Cos. F, C and B, Eng.; e. Sept. 12, 1861, Elkport, Iowa.
2557 Wilson, Harrison, P. Co. D, 25th, e. July 12, 1861, St. Joseph, Mo.
2558 Wilson, Henry J., P. Cos. E, 25th, G and C, Eng.; e. July 22, 1861, Holt Co., Mo.
2559 Wilson, Hiram, P. Cos. D, 25th and A, Eng.; e. July 12, 1861, St. Joseph, Mo.; ad. Hall's Station, Mo.
2560 Wilson, Jas., P. Co. E, Eng.; e. July 13, 1861, Adrian, Mich.
2561 Wilson, John, P. Cos. D, 25th, H and D, Eng.; e. Jan. 27, 1862, St. Joseph, Mo.
2562 Wilson, Josiah, P. Cos. D, 25th, A and B, Eng.; e. Dec. 31, 1861, St. Joseph, Mo.
2563 Wilson, Joseph, P. Co. A, 25th; e. June 14, 1861, St. Joseph, Mo.
2564 Wilson, Wm., P. Cos. D, 25th and A, Eng.; e. July 18, 1861, Andrew Co., Mo.; ad. Oakley, Kas.
2565 Willand, Henry, P. Co. G, 25th; e. June 27, 1861, Kansas City, Mo.
2566 Willard, Murray J., P. Co. D, 25th; e. Aug. 2, 1861, St. Joseph, Mo.
2567 Wille, Henry, P. Cos. B, 25th and L, Eng.; e. July 13, 1861, St. Joseph, Mo.; ad. same, 707 Richardson st.
2568 Willicke, Wm., P. Cos. A and K, Eng.; e. Aug. 13, 1861, Cape Girardeau, Mo.; ad. same.
2569 Williams, Chas. H., P. Cos. F, 25th, H and D, Eng.; e. Apr. 11, 1863, Independence, Mo.; ad. same; pensioner.
2570 Williams, Dennis, P. Cos. K and D, Eng.; e. Sept. 28, 1861, Wapello, Iowa.
2571 Wiliams, Edward, Sergt. Co. B, 25th; e. June 13, 1861, St. Joseph, Mo.
2572 Williams, Elijah, P. Cos. I and C, Eng.; e. Sept. 23, 1861, Dubuque, Iowa.
2573 Williams, Jas., Cor. Cos. F and B, Eng.; e. Sept. 11, 1861, Dubuque, Iowa, dead.
2574 Williams, Jas. T., P. Cos. F, 25th, H and D, Eng.; e. Jan. 11, 1863, Independence, Mo.
2575 Williams, George, P. Cos. E, 25th, G and C, Eng.; e. Jan. 10, 1862, Oregon, Mo.
2576 Williams, Lemuel, P. Cos. A, 25th and M and E, Eng.; e. June 10, 1863, Clay Co., Mo.
2577 Willis, John F., P. Cos. A, 25th, M and E, Eng.; e. March 6, 1862, St. Louis, Mo.
2578 Willis, Thomas, P. Co. D, 25th; e. March 8, 1862, St. Joseph, Mo.
2579 **WINEGAR, ELI,** Lt. Cos. K, I and C, Eng.; e. Oct. 3, 1861; disch. Oct. 31, 1864; dead; supposed to have been killed in Tennessee by guerrillas in 1865.
2580 Winegar, Samuel, P. Cos. L and I, Eng.; e. ———; dead.
2581 Winegardner, Peter, P. Co. A, Eng.; e. July 20, 1861, St. Louis, Mo.
2582 Winn, David, P. Cos. C, 25th, A and B, Eng.; e. Dec. 15, 1861, Gentry Co., Mo.
2583 Winn, Ruel L., P. Co. C, 25th; e. Dec. 15, 1861, Gentry Co., Mo.

2584 Wise, Daniel L., Sergt. Cos. II, D and C, Eng.; e. Aug. 25, 1862, Bloomfield, Ill.; ad. Cherry Point, Ill.
2585 Witkam, Aug., P. Cos. L, I and D, Eng.;e. June 3, 1862.
2586 Witzel, Wm., P. Cos. G and I, Eng.; e. Sept. 26, 1861, Cape Girardeau, Mo.
2587 Wolfe, Jacob A., P. Cos. II and D, Eng.; e. Sept. 15, 1861, Vermillion, Ill.; ad. Sandford, Ind.
2588 Wolfe, Josiah W. D., P. Cos. II, D and C, Eng.; e. Sept. 12, 1862, Sandford, Ind.; ad. same; a pensioner.
2589 Wolfe, Simon, P.Cos. II, D and C, Eng.; e. Aug.12, 1862, Sandford,Ind.;dead.
2590 Wolfkuhl, Henry, P. Cos. G and I, Eng.; e. Sept. 13, 1861, Cape Girardeau, Mo.
2591 Wollestadt, Carl, P. Cos. L and I, Eng.; e. ———.
2592 Woodeach, Thos. D., P. Co. —, 25th and B, Eng.; e. July 15, 1862.
2593 Woodcock, Thos., P. Co. D, 25th; e. Jan. 13, 1862, Andrew Co., Mo.
2594 Wood, Aaron, P. Cos. E, 25th, G and C, Eng.; e. Dec. 12, 1861; ad. Westbro, Mo.; pensioner.
2595 **WOOD, CHAS. C.**, Lt. Co. I, Eng.; e. Nov. 7, 1862.
2596 Wood, Benj. G., P. Cos. II and D, Eng.; e. Aug. 12, 1862, New Goshen, Ind.
2597 Wood, Wm., P. Co. D, 25th; e. July 19, 1861, St. Joseph, Mo.
2598 Woods, Albt. J., P. Cos. C and B, Eng.; e. Sept. 16, 1861, Prairie City, Ill.; ad. Vineland, Kas.
2599 Woods, Ira M., P. Cos. C and B, Eng.; e. Sept. 16, 1861, Avon, Ill.; ad. same.
2600 Woods, Isaac, P. Cos. C and B, Eng.; e. Aug. 4, 1861, Avon, Ill.; ad. Vineland, Kas.
2601 Woods, Isaac W., P. Cos. C and B, Eng.; e. Sept. 16, 1861, Prairie City, Ill.; ad. Lawrence, Kas.; is pensioned.
2602 Woods, Wm. C., P. Cos. C and B, Eng.; e. Sept. 16, 1861, Prairie City, Ill.
2603 Woodruff, Allen D., P. Cos. K, 25th, G and C, Eng.; e. Feb. 4, 1862, Hammond, N. Y.
2604 Woodruff, Wm. H., P. Cos. B and K, Eng.; e. July 28, 1861, Paris, Ill. draws a pension; ad. Nevins, Ill.
2605 Woody, Geo. W., P. Co. K, Eng.; e. Sept. 10, 1861, Prairie City, Ill.; a pensioner; ad. Galesburg, Ill.
2606 Woody, —, P. Co. II, 25th; e. Dec. 21, 1861, Nodaway Co., Mo.
2607 Worden, Luther B., P. Co. F, Eng.; e. Oct. 18, 1861, Bloomington, Ill.; died Jackson, Tenn., July, 1862.
2608 Worley, Wm., P. Co. B, Eng.; e. July 28, 1861, Paris, Ill.
2609 Winkler, Chas., Mus. Co. B. 25th; e. June 13, 1861, St. Joseph, Mo.
2610 Winkler, Gottleib, P. Co. G, Eng.; e. Sept. 13, 1861, Cape Girardeau, Mo.
2611 Wright, John W., P. Cos. II and D, Eng.; e. Aug. 7, 1861, St. Louis, Mo.
2612 Wright, Woodford, P. Cos. B, K and A, Eng.; e. July 28, 1861, Paris, Ill.; is a pensioner; ad. Quaker City, Ohio.
2613 Wykoff, Norman L., Sergt. Cos. A, 25th, M and E, Eng.; e. July 11, 1861, Macon Co., Mo.; promoted Lt.. June 12, 1865; ad. Howland, Mo.
2614 Wyman, Francis M., P. Co. D, 25th; e. July 12, 1862, Doniphan Co., Kas.
2615 **WARD, J. D.**, Lt. R. Q. M., Eng.; e. Sept. 15, 1861, St. Louis, Mo.; res. Jan. 13, 1862.
2616 **WRIGHT, ALPHA**, Chap., 25th; e. Dec. 31, 1862; disch. Jan. 1, 1864.
2617 Whitson, —, Cor. Co. A, Eng.; e. July 20, 1861, St. Louis, Mo.; killed in skirmish at Tuscumbia River, June 1, 1862.
2618 Yard, Marion H., P. Cos. A, 25th, M and E, Eng.; e. vet., Jan. 28, 1864; ad. Norborne, Mo.
2619 Yarnall, John S., Cor. Cos. D and C, Eng.; e. Aug. 15, 1861, Flora, Ill.; draws a pension; ad. Exeter, Barry Co., Mo.
2620 Yeakley, Mich. W., P. Co. D, 25th; e. March 1, 1862, St. Joseph, Mo.; ad. same.
2621 Yocum, Jewett, P. Co. C, 25th; e. Nov. 20, 1861.
2622 Yocum, Miner, P. Co. C, 25th; e. Nov. 20, 1861.
2623 York, Jas. A., P. Co. D, 25th; e. July 12, 1861, St. Joseph, Mo.; ad. Rockport (or Lathrop), Mo.
2624 Young, Andrew J., Cor. Cos. E, 25th, G and C, Eng.; e. Sept. 21, 1862, Atchison Co., Mo.; ad. Phelps City, Kas.
2625 Young, August, P. Co. B, 25th; e. June 13, 1861, St. Joseph, Mo.

2626 Young, Chas., P. Co. D, 25th; e. March 1, 1862, Doniphan Co., Kas
2627 Young, Fenton, P. Co. K, Eng.; e. April 12, 1861, Burlington, Iowa.
2628 Young, Chas. A., P. Co. A, 25th; e. Jan. 30, 1862, San Francisco, Cal.
2629 Young, Henry, P. Co. A, 25th; e. June 14, 1861, St. Joseph, Mo.
2630 Young, Lewis, Sergt. Co. A, Eng.; e. July 20, 1861, St. Louis, Mo.; promoted Lt. Colored Troops in 1863.
2631 Young, Robert, P. Co. A, 25th; e. Jan. 8, 1862, St. Joseph, Mo.
2632 Young, Thomas E., P. Cos. B and K, Eng.; e. July 28, 1861, Paris, Ill.
2633 Zink, Jacob, P. Cos. C, 25th, A and B, Eng.; e. Feb. 10, 1862, St. Joseph, Mo.
2634 Zones, John W., P. Co. D, 25th; e. Aug. 2, 1861, De Kalb Co., Mo.
2635 Zweig, Fred., P. Cos. L, I and D, Eng.; ad. Columbia, Ill.
2636 Zenner, John, Sergt. Cos. B, 25th and L, Eng.; e. June 13, 1861, St. Joseph, Mo.

ADDENDA.

WHAT OTHER PARTS OF THE ARMY WERE DOING.

TO give a better understanding of the part taken by the Missouri Engineer Regiment in the late war we add from descriptions published, orders and diaries written during the war; the operations and achievements of the armies as a whole with whom we served; omitting entirely operations where we were not present.

A GENERAL DESCRIPTION OF THE BATTLE OF SHILOH.

The battle of Pittsburg Landing, or Shiloh, was one of the most desperate conflicts ever known in history, and the most severe and hardest fought battle of the Rebellion, as well as, up to that time, the most decisive of the war. With overwhelming numbers opposing them, and surprised as they were by the enemy, it was only by the bravest and most stubborn fighting, that the Union troops gained this most splendid victory. And, although the tide seemed turned against them during the early part of the battle, everything seemed to favor them on the second day; and after two days' fighting they had regained all they had lost, and driven back and conquered the Rebels.

The troops engaged in this battle were the Divisions of Prentiss, Sherman and McClernand, who were in advance, and Hurlbut's and Smith's, the latter under command of General W. H. L. Wallace. Hurlbut's and Wallace's Divisions were stationed between the Tennessee River and the others. On the second day, these were joined by the Divisions of Generals Lewis Wallace, Nelson, Crittenden and McCook.

On the evening of the fourth of April, the enemy made a reconnoissance with two of their regiments, and, after a slight skirmish, retired, as their forces under Price and Van Dorn had not yet arrived. Although the Generals commanding the Rebel army had fixed upon the fifth of April for the day of attack, they resolved to wait one day longer, until their re-enforcements should arrive. This gave General Buell time to reach Grant, and, without doubt, saved the country from a terrible disaster which must have been the result, had his re-enforcements failed to arrive. Johnson and Beauregard were aware that Buell was advancing from Nashville, to join Grant, and for this reason at first resolved to attack him before Buell should arrive.

Just at break of day, on Sunday morning, the 6th of April, the pickets of Prentiss and Sherman were driven in by the enemy, and the Rebels were almost instantly in our camp. They found the troops entirely unprepared for anything like an attack. The officers and men were scattered about, some still in their beds, some dressing, and some eating their breakfast,—and none in readiness for their early and unexpected visitors.

The five Divisions stationed at this point were hurriedly drawn up in line of battle, and, without a moment's preparation, met the enemy. Many of the regiments were new troops, their officers inexperienced, and many of them became panic-stricken. General Prentiss, and the greater part of his Division, were at this time taken prisoners. Sherman used all his energies to rally his men. Riding along the lines, encouraging them, and exposing his own life, he did much to save the Division from utter destruction. Although our forces returned their fire most vigorously, our men were driven back from their camp. The enemy, bringing up a fresh force, opened fire upon our left wing, under General McClernand. Along the whole line, for a distance of over four miles, this fire was returned with terrible effect, by both Infantry and Artillery.

General Hurlbut's division was then brought forward, and a most desperate conflict ensued. The Rebels were first driven back with great loss of life, but rallied, and in turn, drove our men back.

The Rebel forces, commanded by able generals, were handled with a skill that drew admiration from all, and although repulsed again and again, they continued sending fresh troops to the front, and again bent their energies to the work.

Late in the afternoon, the most desperate fighting that had occurred during the entire day, took place. The Rebels undoubtedly thought that if they failed in defeating us on that day, that their chances for success would be doubtful, as a part of General Buell's army had arrived on the opposite side of the river. The Rebels could see the reënforcements from the river bank, and to this place they directed their attention. The Union troops were, indeed, contending against fearful odds, their army numbering about thirty-eight thousand men, while that of the Rebels exceeded sixty thousand.

Many of the panic-stricken, and the skulkers, were gathered near the river, and no appeals from their officers could rally them.

General Lewis Wallace's Division, which was at Crump's Landing, was ordered up in the morning, but being led by a circuitous route, failed to reach the scene of action until night.

About 5 o'clock P. M., the Rebels occupied about two-thirds of the Union camps, and were constantly driving them towards the river. Toward evening the gunboats Lexington and Tylor, which had lain idle spectators during the day's fearful contest, seeking in vain for an opportunity to bring their guns to bear upon the enemy, commenced raining shells upon the rebel hordes. The boats fired rapidly and well; and with the incessant clash of guns, on land, and the crash and roar of shells from the boats, that Sabbath evening wore away.

The men lay on their arms during the night in line of battle. Buell and Lew Wallace would be there, and ready to assist them in the morning, for all through the night Buell's men were marching up from Savannah, and were being ferried across, or were coming upon transports; and Wallace's Division had arrived in the evening, and would be in readiness ere the morning dawned. A heavy thunder storm came up about midnight, drenching the two armies, but proving a most excellent dressing for the wounds of the many who were suffering on that bloody field.

At daylight on the morning of the 7th of April, the two divisions of Nelson and Crittenden advanced upon the enemy. Lew Wallace's Division commenced the battle by an artillery fire upon a battery of the enemy, causing them to retreat. Nelson's troops were in the advance, and the fighting was most desperate, continually driving back the Rebels. The fire soon became general along the whole line,—Crittenden following close to Nelson, and next to him McCook. Generals Sherman's, McClernand's and Hurlbut's men, although terribly jaded from the previous day's fighting, came up, and gallantly added new laurels to those already won.

But the Rebels resisted at every point; they felt that all depended upon a most desperate effort on their part, and their generals urged them on, thinking to flank us on the right, and thus gain the day.

Success seemed theirs for a time, but our left under Nelson, was dividing them, and by eleven o'clock, General Buell's forces had succeeded in flanking them, and capturing their batteries. The Rebels again rallied, but some regiments from Wood's and Thomas' coming in just then, were sent to General Buell, who again drove the enemy back. About three o'clock in the afternoon, General Grant, at the head of five regiments of Cavalry, ordered a charge across the field, himself commanding. The men followed with a shout, and the Rebels fled in dismay, and did not make another stand. The retreating Rebels were followed by Buell, and by half-past five, their whole army was retreating toward Corinth.

The main army, well nigh worn out with hard fighting, gladly welcomed the close of this victorious day. On the following morning, General Sherman started forward with the remainder of his Division, in pursuit. He met the enemy's Cavalry on the road to Corinth, where a sharp skirmish ensued, and he drove them from the field with the loss of several killed and wounded.

General Grant, in his official report of the battle of Pittsburg Landing, says: "I feel it a duty to a gallant and able officer, Brigadier General W. T. Sherman, to make special mention. He not only was with his command during the entire two days of the action, but displayed great judgment and skill in the management of his men; although severely wounded in the hand, on the first day, his place was never vacant. He was again wounded, and had three horses killed under him. General Prentiss was taken prisoner on the first day's battle, and General W. H. L. Wallace was mortally wounded."

From General Sherman's report we learn, that on Friday, the 4th instant, the enemy's Cavalry drove in his pickets, posted about a mile and a-half in advance of his center, on the main Corinth Road, capturing one lieutenant, and seven men; that he ordered a pursuit by the Cavalry of his Division, driving them back about five miles, and killing many. On Saturday, the enemy's Cavalry was again very bold, coming well down to their front, yet it was thought that he designed nothing but a strong demonstration. On Sunday morning, early, the 6th instant, the enemy drove our advance guard back on the main body, when General Sherman ordered under arms, all his Division, and sent word to General McClernand, asking him to support his left; to General Prentiss, giving him notice that the enemy was in our front, in force, and to General Hurlbut, asking him to support General Prentiss. At this time, seven A. M., Sherman's Division was arranged as follows:

CAPTAIN B. F. BUZARD, CO. K, 25TH H. AND D. ENGINEERS.

LIEUTENANT PAULUS GAST, COS. G AND I.

First Brigade, composed of the Sixth Iowa, Colonel J. A. McDowell; Fortieth Illinois, Colonel Hicks; Forty-sixth Ohio, Colonel Worthington; and the Norton Battery, Captain Behr, on the extreme left, guarding the bridge on the Purdy Road, over Owl Creek.

Second Brigade, composed of the Fifty-fifth Illinois, Colonel D. Stuart; Fifty-fourth Ohio, Colonel T. Kilby Smith; and the Seventy-first Ohio, Colonel Mason, on the extreme left, guarding the ford over Lick Creek.

Third Brigade, composed of the Seventy-seventh Ohio, Colonel Hildebrand; Fifty-third Ohio, Colonel Appler; and the Fifty-seventh Ohio, Colonel Mungen, on the left of the Corinth Road, its right resting on Shiloh Meeting-house.

Fourth Brigade, composed of the Seventy-second Ohio, Colonel Buckland; Forty-eighth Ohio, Colonel Sullivan; and the Seventeenth Ohio, Colonel Cockerill, on the right of the Corinth Road, its left resting on Shiloh Meeting-house.

Two batteries of Artillery, Taylor's and Waterhouse's, were posted, the former at Shiloh, and the latter on a ridge to the left, with a front fire over open ground between Mungen's and Appler's Regiments. The Cavalry, eight companies of the Fourth Illinois, under Colonel Dickey, were posted in a large open field to the left and rear of Shiloh Meeting-house, which Sherman regarded as the centre of his position. Shortly after seven A. M., with his entire staff, Sherman rode along a portion of our front, and when in the open field before Appler's Regiment, the enemy's pickets opened a brisk fire on his party, killing his orderly, Thomas D. Hollister, of Company H, Second Illinois Cavalry. The fire came from the bushes which line a small stream that rose in the field in front of Appler's camp, and flows to the north along the whole front of the place where this Division was located. This valley afforded the enemy cover, but our men were so posted as to have a good fire at him as he crossed the valley and ascended the rising ground on our side.

About eight A. M. the glistening bayonets of heavy masses of Rebel Infantry could be seen to our left front, in the woods beyond the small stream alluded to, and Sherman became satisfied for the first time that the enemy designed a determined attack on our whole camp. All the regiments in his Division were then in line of battle, at their proper posts. Sherman rode to Colonel Appler, and ordered him to hold his ground at all hazards, as he held the left flank of our first line of battle, and he had a good battery on his right and strong support in his rear. General McClernand had promptly and energetically responded to Sherman's request, and had sent him three regiments, which were posted to protect Waterhouse's battery and the left flank of Sherman's line. The battle began by the enemy opening battery in the woods to our front, and throwing shell into our camp.

Taylor's and Waterhouse's batteries promptly responded, and the heavy battalions of Infantry could be seen passing obliquely to the left across the open field in Appler's front; also other columns advancing directly upon Sherman's Division. The Union infantry and Artillery opened fire along the whole line, and the battle became general. Other heavy masses of the enemy's forces kept passing across the field to their left, and directing their course on General Prentiss. Sherman saw at once that the enemy designed to pass his left flank, and fall upon Generals McClernand and Prentiss, whose line of camps was almost parallel with the Tennessee River, and about two miles back from it. Very soon the sound of musketry and artillery announced that General Prentiss was engaged, and about 9 A. M. he began to fall back. About this time Appler's Regiment broke in disorder; Mungen's Regiment followed, and the enemy pressed forward on Waterhouse's battery thereby exposed. The three Illinois Regiments in immediate support of this battery, stood for some time, but the enemy's advance was vigorous, and the fire so severe that when Colonel Raith, of the Forty-third Illinois received a severe wound, and fell from his horse, his regiment and the others manifested disorder and the enemy got possession of three guns of this (Waterhouse's) battery. Although our left was thus turned, and the enemy was pressing our whole line, Sherman deemed Shiloh so important that he remained by it, and renewed his orders to Colonels McDowell and Buckland to hold their ground; and these positions were held until 10 o'clock A. M., when the enemy had got his Artillery to the rear of our left flank, and some change became absolutely necessary. Two regiments of Hildebrand's Brigade (Appler's and Mungen's) had already disappeared to the rear, and Hildebrand's own Regiment was in disorder. Sherman, therefore, gave orders for Taylor's battery, still at Shiloh, to fall back as far as the Purdy and Hamburg Road, and for McDowell and Buckland to adopt that road as their new line. He rode across the angle and met Behr's battery at the cross roads, and ordered it immediately to come into battery, action right. Captain Behr gave the order, but was almost instantly shot from his horse, when drivers and gunners fled in dismay, carrying off the caissons, and abandoning five out of six guns without firing a shot. The enemy pressed on, gaining this battery, and the Union troops were again forced to choose a line of defense. Hildebrand's Brigade had substantially disappeared from the field, though he himself bravely remained. McDowell's and Buckland's Brigades maintained their organization, and were conducted by Sherman's aids so as to join on McClernand's right, thus abandoning the original camps and line of Sherman.

This was about 10 o'clock A. M., at which time the enemy made a furious attack on General McClernand's whole front. He struggled most desperately, but finding him pressed, McDowell's Brigade was moved directly against the left flank of the enemy, forcing him back some distance, and the men were directed to avail themselves of every cover—trees, fallen timber, and a wooded valley to our right. This position they held for four long hours, sometimes gaining and at other times losing ground, Generals McClernand and Sherman acting in perfect concert and struggling to maintain this line. While they were so hard pressed two Iowa Regiments approached from the rear, but could not be brought up to the severe fire that was raging in our front. At 4 P. M. it was evident that Hurlbut's line had been driven back to the river, and knowing that General Wallace was coming with reënforcements from Crump's Landing, Sherman and McClernand, on consultation, selected a new line of defense, with its right wing covering a bridge by which General Wallace had to approach.

The Union troops fell back as well as they could, gathering, in addition to their own, such scattered forces as they could find, and formed the new line. During this change the enemy charged them, but were handsomely repulsed by an Illinois Regiment.

The Fifth Ohio Cavalry, which had come up, rendered good service in holding the enemy in check for some time, and Major Taylor also came up with a new battery, and got into position just in time to get a good flank fire upon the enemy's column as he pressed on General Mc'Clernand's right, checking his advance, when General McClernand's Division made a fine charge on the enemy, and drove him back into the ravines to our front and right. Sherman had a clear field about two hundred yards wide in his immediate front, and contented himself with keeping the enemy's Infantry at that distance during the day. In this position his army rested for the night. His command had become decidedly of a mixed character. Buckland's

Brigade was the only one that retained organization. Colonel Hildebrand was personally there, but his Brigade was not. Colonel McDowell had been severely injured by a fall from his horse, and had gone to the river, and the three regiments of his Brigade were not in line.

The Thirteenth Missouri, Colonel Crafts J. Wright, had reported to Sherman on the field, and fought well, retaining its regimental organization, and formed a part of his line during Sunday night and all day Monday. Other fragments of regiments and companies had also fallen into his Division, and acted with it during the remainder of the battle.

Generals Grant and Buell visited Sherman in his bivouac that evening, and from them he learned the situation in the other parts of the field. General Wallace arrived from Crump's Landing shortly after dark, and formed his line to the right and rear of Sherman. It rained hard during the night, but our men were in good spirits, and lay on their arms, being satisfied with such bread and meat as could be gathered at the neighboring camps, and determined to redeem on Monday the losses of Sunday.

At daybreak of Monday Sherman received General Grant's orders to advance and recapture their original camps. He dispatched several members of his staff to bring up all the men they could find, and especially the Brigade of Colonel Stuart, which had been separated from the Division the day before; and at the appointed time the Division, or what remained of it, with the Thirteenth Missouri and other fragments of regiments, moved forward and occupied the ground on the extreme right of General McClernand's camp, where they attracted the fire of a Rebel battery near Colonel McDowell's former headquarters. Here Sherman remained awaiting for the sound of General Buell's advance upon the main Corinth Road. About 10 o'clock A. M. the firing in this direction, and its steady approach, satisfied him; and General Wallace being on his right, flanked with his well-conducted Division, Sherman led the head of his column to General McClernand's right, formed in line of battle facing south, with Buckland's Brigade directly across the ridge, and Stuart's Brigade on its right, in the woods, and thus advanced steadily and slowly, under a heavy fire of musketry and artillery. Taylor had just come up from the rear, where he had gone for ammunition, and brought up three guns, which Sherman ordered into position to advance by hand-firing. These guns belonged to Company A, Chicago Light Artillery, commanded by Lieutenant P. P.

Wood, and did most excellent service. Under cover of their fire, the troops advanced until they reached the point where the Corinth Road crosses the line of General McClernand's camp; and here was seen the well-ordered and compact Kentucky forces of General Buell, whose soldierly movement alone gave confidence to our new and less disciplined forces, Willich's regiment advancing upon a point of water oaks and thicket, behind which the enemy was in great strength, and entered it in beautiful style. Then arose some of the most severe musketry firing ever heard, lasting twenty minutes, when this splendid regiment had to fall back. This green point of timber is about five hundred yards east of Shiloh Meeting-house, and it was evident that there was to be the struggle. The enemy could also be seen forming his line to the south. General McClernand sending to Sherman for Artillery, he detached to him the three guns of Wood's battery, with which he speedily drove them back; and seeing some others in the rear, Sherman sent one of his staff to bring them forward, when, by almost Providential decree, they proved to be two twenty-four pounder Howitzers, belonging to McAllister's Battery, and served as well as guns ever could be. This was about 2 p. m. The enemy had one Battery close by Shiloh, and another near the Hamburg Road, both pouring grape and cannister upon any column of troops that advanced upon the green point of water oaks. Willich's Regiment had been repulsed; but a whole Brigade of McCook's Division advanced, beautifully deployed, and entered this dreaded wood. Sherman ordered his Second Brigade, then commanded by Colonel Kilby Smith (Colonel Stuart being wounded), to form on its right, and his Fourth Brigade, Colonel Buckland, on its right—all to advance with the Kentucky Brigade before mentioned (Rousseau's Brigade of McCook's Division). He gave personal direction to the twenty-four pounder guns, whose well-directed fire silenced the enemy's guns to the left, and afterward at the Shiloh Meeting-house. Rousseau's Brigade moved in splendid order steadily to the front, sweeping everything before it, and at 4 p. m. the Union troops stood upon the ground of their original front line, and the enemy was in full retreat. Sherman directed his several Brigades to resume at once their original camp.

General McCook's splendid Division from Kentucky drove back the enemy along the Corinth Road, which was the great center of the field of battle, and where Beauregard commanded in person, supported by Bragg's, Polk's and Breckinridge's Divisions. Johnson was killed by exposing himself in front of his troops at the time of their attack on Buckland's Brigade on Sunday morning.

Sherman's Division was made up of regiments perfectly new, all having received their muskets for the first time at Paducah. None of them had ever been under fire, and to expect the coolness and steadiness of older troops would be wrong. They knew not the value of combination and organization. When individual fear seized them, the first impulse was to get away. His third Brigade broke much sooner than it should have done. Colonel Hildebrand, its commander, was as cool as man could be, and no one could have made stronger efforts to hold his men to their places than he did. He kept his own Regiment, with individual exceptions, in hand an hour after Appler's and Mungen's Regiments had left their proper field of action. Colonel Buckland managed his Brigade well. General Sherman commended him to General Grant as a cool, intelligent and judicious man, who needed only confidence and experience to make a good commander. His subordinates, Colonels Sullivan and Cockerill, behaved with great gallantry, the former receiving a severe wound on Sunday, and yet commanding and holding his Regiment well in hand all day, and on Monday until his right arm was broken by a shot. Cockerill held a larger proportion of his men than any Colonel in Sherman's Division, and was with him from first to last. Colonel J. H. McDowell, commanding the First Brigade, held his ground on Sunday until ordered to fall back, which he did in line of battle, and when ordered he conducted the attack on the enemy's left in good style. In falling back to the next position he was thrown from his horse and injured, and his Brigade was not in position on Monday morning. His subordinates, Colonels Hicks and Worthington, displayed great personal courage. Colonel Hicks led his Regiment in the attack on Sunday, and received a severe wound. Lieutenant-Colonel Walcutt, of the Ohio Forty-sixth, was severely wounded on Sunday. Sherman's Second Brigade, Colonel Stuart, was detached nearly two miles from head-quarters. He had to fight his own battle on Sunday against superior numbers, as the enemy interposed between him and General Prentiss early in the day. Colonel Stuart was wounded severely, and yet reported for duty on Monday morning. He was compelled to leave during the day, when the command devolved on Colonel Kilby Smith, who was always in the thickest of the fight, and led the Brigade handsomely. Lieutenant-Colonel Kyle, of the Seventy-first, was mortally wounded on Sunday.

A GENERAL DESCRIPTION OF THE BATTLE OF SHILOH.

Several times during the battle cartridges gave out, but General Grant had thoughtfully kept a supply coming from the rear. General Sherman commended the Fortieth Illinois and Thirteenth Missouri for steadfastly holding their ground under heavy fire, although their cartridge-boxes were empty.

At the time of recovering their camps, the men were so fatigued that they could not follow the retreating masses of the enemy, but on the next day Sherman followed them up for six miles.

The Cavalry kept to the rear, and took little part in the action, but it would have been madness to have exposed horses to the musketry fire, under which they were compelled to remain from Sunday at 8 A. M. till Monday at 4 P. M.

General Buell, Colonel Fry, and others of General Buell's staff, rode up to General Sherman about sunset, about the time General Grant was leaving. General Buell asked many questions, and got a small map, and said that by daylight he could have 18,000 fresh men, which would settle the matter.

I understood Grant's forces were to advance on the right of the Corinth Road and Buell's on the left, and accordingly at daylight I advanced my Division by the flank, the resistance being trivial, up to the very spot where the day before the battle had been most severe, and then waited till near noon for Buell's troops to get up abreast, when the entire line advanced and recovered all the ground we had ever held. I know that, with the exception of one or two severe struggles, the fighting of April 7th was easy, as compared with that of April 6th.

I never was disposed, nor am I now, to question anything done by General Buell and his army, and know that, approaching our field of battle from the rear, he encountered that sickening crowd of laggards and fugitives that excited his contempt and that of his army, who never gave full credit to those in the front line, who did fight hard, and who had, at 4 P. M., checked the enemy, and were preparing the next day to assume the offensive. I remember the fact better from General Grant's anecdote of his Donelson battle, which he told me then for the first time—that, at a certain period of the battle, he saw that either was ready to give way if the other showed a bold front, and he determined to do that very thing, to advance on the enemy when, as he prognosticated, the enemy surrendered. At 4 P. M. of April 6th he thought the appearance the same, and he judged, with Lew Wallace's fresh Division and such of our startled troops as had recovered their equilibrium, he would be justified in dropping the defensive and assuming the offensive in the morning. And I repeat, I received such orders before I knew General Buell's troops were at the river. I admit that I was glad that Buell was there, because I knew his troops were older than ours, and better systematized and drilled, and his arrival made that certain which before was uncertain. I have heard this question much discussed, and must say that the officers of Buell's army dwelt too much on the stampede of some of our raw troops, and gave us too little credit for the fact that for one whole day, weakened as we were by the absence of Buell's army, long expected; of Lew Wallace's Division, only four miles off, and of the fugitives from our ranks, we had beaten off our assailants for the time. At the same time our Army of the Tennessee have indulged in severe criticism at the slow approach of that army which knew the danger that threatened us from the concentrated armies of Johnson, Beauregard and Bragg that lay at Corinth. In a war like this, where opportunities of personal prowess are as plenty as blackberries to those who seek them at the front, all such criminations should be frowned down; and were it not for the military character of your journal I would not venture to offer a correction of a very popular error.

Another very common mistake is in attributing to General Grant the selection of that battlefield. It was chosen by that veteran soldier, Major-General Charles F. Smith, who ordered Sherman's Division to disembark there and strike for the Charleston Railroad. This order was subsequently modified by his ordering Hurlbut's Division to disembark there, and Sherman's higher up the Tennessee to the mouth of Yellow Creek, to strike the railroad at Burnsville. But floods prevented our reaching the railroad, when General Smith ordered Sherman in person also to disembark at Pittsburg, and take posts well out, so as to make plenty of room, with Snake and Lick Creeks the flanks of a camp for the Grand Army of Invasion.

It was General Smith who selected that field of battle, and it was well chosen. On any other we surely would have been overwhelmed, as both Lick and Snake Creeks forced the enemy to confine his movements to a direct front attack, which new troops are better qualified to resist than where flanks are exposed to a real or chimerical danger. Even the Divisions of that Army were arranged in that camp by General Smith's orders, Sherman's Division forming, as it were, the outlying picket, whilst McClernand's and Prentiss' were the real line of battle, with W. H. L. Wallace in support of the right wing, and Hurlbut of the left—Lew Wallace's Division being detached. All these subordinate dispositions were made by the order of General Smith before General Grant succeeded him to the command of all the forces up the Tennessee—headquarters, Savannah. If there was any error in puting that army on the west side of the Tennessee, exposed to the superior force of the enemy also assembling at Corinth, the mistake was not General Grant's—but there was no mistake. It was neccessary that a combat, fierce and bitter, to test the manhood of the two armies, should come off, and that was as good a place as any. It was not then a question of military skill and strategy, but of courage and pluck. Every life lost to us that day was necessary, for otherwise, at Corinth, at Memphis, at Vicksburg, we would have found harder resistance had we not shown our enemies that, rude and untutored as we then were, we could fight as well as they.

Nearly all the new troops that at Shiloh drew from General Sherman official censure have more than redeemed their good name.

THE GRAND MOVEMENT BY THE RIGHT FLANK TO JONESBORO'.

Sherman became satisfied that, to reach the Macon Road, and thereby control the supplies for Atlanta, he would be compelled to move the whole army. Before beginning this movement, he ordered from Chattanooga, four 4½-inch rifled guns, to try their effect on the city of Atlanta. These guns arrived on the 10th, and were put to work day and night, and did execution on the city, causing frequent fires, and creating confusion; yet the enemy seemed determined to hold his forts, even if the city was destroyed. On the 16th of August, Sherman issued his orders, prescribing the mode and manner of executing the grand movement by the right flank, to begin on the 18th.

This movement contemplated the withdrawal of the Twentieth Corps, General Williams, to the intrenched position at Chattahoochee Bridge, and the march of the main army to the West Point Railroad, near Fairburn, and afterward to the Macon Road, at or near Jonesboro', with wagons loaded with provisions for fifteen days. About the time of the publication of the orders referred to above, Sherman learned that Wheeler, with a large mounted force, variously estimated from 6,000 to 10,000 men, had passed around by the east and north, and had made his appearance on our lines of communication near Adairsville, and had succeeded in capturing 200 of our beef cattle, and had made a break in the railroad near Calhoun. This was just such a movement as Sherman desired. He had made ample preparations for such a contingency, and this movement left him superior to the enemy in Cavalry. Sherman suspended the execution of his orders for the time being, and ordered General Kilpatrick to make up a well-appointed force of about 5,000 Cavalry, and move from his camp about Sandtown, during the night of the 18th, to the West Point Road. This force started as ordered, and pushed on to Fairburn, on the West Point Railroad, where it met the enemy and drove him from the ground. Kilpatrick then moved on to Jonesboro', where he did considerable damage, and then rested his force for the night near Lovejoy's. He succeeded in destroying about three miles of the Macon Railroad and one train of cars. The enemy attempted to surround his force and capture them, but they succeeded in cutting their way through their ranks, and moved onward. They crossed the Cotton River on the morning of the 21st, and reached Lithonia, on the Georgia Railroad, east of Atlanta, in the evening of the same day. After resting for the night, the expedition joined the main army on the following morning.

After an interview with General Kilpatrick, Sherman was satisfied that whatever damage he had done would not produce the result desired. He therefore renewed his orders for the movement of the whole army. This, of course, involved the necessity of raising the siege of Atlanta, taking the field with our main force, and using it against its intrenchments. All the army commanders were at once notified to send their surplus wagons, incumbrances of all kinds, and sick, back to the intrenched position at the bridge, and that the movement would begin on the night of the 25th.

Accordingly, all things being ready, the Fourth Corps, General Stanley, drew out of its lines on the extreme left, and marched to a position below Proctor's Creek. The Twentieth Corps, General Williams, moved back to the Chattahoochee. This movement was made without loss, save a few things left in camp by thoughtless officers or men. On the night of the 26th, the Army of the Tennessee drew out and moved rapidly by a circuit well toward Sandtown, and across Camp Creek. The Army of the Cumberland, moved below Utoy Creek, and General Schofield remained in position. This movement was effected with the loss of but a single man in the Army of the Tennessee. He was wounded by a shell from the enemy. The third move brought the Army of the Tennessee on the West Point Railroad, above Fairburn, the Army of the Cumberland about Red Oak, and General Schofield closed in near Digs and Mims. Sherman then ordered one day's work to be expended in destroying the road and it was done with a will. Twelve and one-half miles were destroyed, the ties burned, and the rails heated and tortured by the utmost ingenuity of old hands at the work. Several cuts were filled up with the trunks of trees, with logs, rocks, and earth intermingled with loaded shell, prepared with torpedoes, to explode in case of an attempt to clear them out. Sherman, in person, inspected this work; and, satisfied with the execution, he ordered the army to move next day eastward, by several roads—General Howard on the right, toward Jonesboro'; General Thomas in the centre, by Shoal Creek Church to Couch's, on the Decatur and Fayetteville road; and General Schofield on the left, about Morrow's Mills.

On the 31st of August, the enemy came out of his works at Jonesboro', and attacked General Howard. Howard was admirably situated to receive him, and thoroughly repulsed the attack. The attacking party was composed of Lee's and Hardee's Corps; and after a contest of more than two hours, withdrew, leaving on the field over 400 dead, and his wounded, of which about 300 were left in Jonesboro'. His losses could not have been much less than 2,500. Hearing the sound of battle at Jonesboro' about noon, orders were renewed to push the other movements on the left and centre; and about 4 o'clock, P. M., the reports arrived simultaneously that General Howard had repulsed the enemy at Jonesboro'; that General Schofield had reached the railroad a mile below Rough-and-Ready, and was working up the road, breaking it as he went; that General Stanley, of General Thomas' army, had taken possession of the road below General Schofield, and was destroying its working south; and that General Bird, of General Davis' Corps, had struck it still lower down, within four miles of Jonesboro'.

Orders were at once given for all the army to turn on Jonesboro', and Howard was ordered to keep the Rebels busy, while Thomas should move down from the north, with General Schofield on his left. Sherman also ordered the troops, as they moved down, to continue the thorough destruction of the railroad, because it was then in his hands, and he did not know but that events might divert attention from it. General Garrard's Cavalry was directed to watch the roads in the rear, and to the north of the army. General Kilpatrick was sent south, down the west bank of the Flint River, with instructions to attack or threaten the railroad below Jonesboro'. Sherman expected the whole army would close down on Jonesboro' by noon of the 1st of September. General Davis' Corps, having a shorter distance to travel, was on time and deployed, facing the south, his right in connection with General Howard, and his left on the railroad. General Stanley and General Schofield were then moving down along the Rough-and-Ready Road, and along the railroad, breaking it as they moved. When General Davis joined General Howard, General Blair's Corps, on Howard's left, was thrown in reserve, and was immediately sent well to the right, below Jonesboro', to act against that flank, along with General Kilpatrick's Cavalry. About 4 o'clock P. M. General Davis was all ready, and commenced the assault on the lines across open fields, carrying them very handsomely, and taking, as prisoners, the greater part of Govan's brigade, including its Commander, with two four-gun batteries. The next morning the enemy was gone. He had retreated south.

Rumors began to reach Sherman, through prisoners, that Atlanta had been abandoned during the night of September 1st; that Hood had blown up his ammunition trains, which accounted for the sounds so plainly heard in the direction of Atlanta, but which, as yet, had not been explained; that Stewart's Corps was then retreating toward McDonough, and that the militia had gone off toward Covington. It was then too late for Sherman to interfere and attempt to prevent their escape, and besides he was well satisfied with the substantial victory already gained. Accordingly, he ordered the work of destroying the railroad to cease, and the troops to be held in hand, ready for any movement that further information from Atlanta might warrant.

General Davis' Corps had been left above Jonesboro', and General Garrard's Cavalry was still further back, and the latter was ordered to send to Atlanta and ascertain the exact truth, and the real situation of affairs. But the same night (September 4th), a courier arrived from General Slocum, reporting the fact that the enemy had evacuated Atlanta, blown up seven trains of cars, and had retreated on the McDonough Road. General Slocum had entered and taken possession on the 2d of September.

The object of the movement against the railroad was, therefore, already reached and concluded. As it was idle to pursue the enemy in that wooded country with a view to his capture, Sherman gave orders, on the 4th, to prepare to move back slowly to Atlanta. On the 5th his forces moved to Jonesboro, five miles, where they remained a day. On the 7th they moved to Rough and Ready, seven miles, and the next day to the camps selected. The Army of the Cumberland were grouped round about Atlanta, the Army of the Tennessee about East Point, and that of the Ohio at Decatur, where the troops occupied clean and healthful camps.

Thus Sherman again accomplished, by wise and honorable strategy, what he could not have otherwise done without the sacrifice of his noble army. Whoever will consider the extent and strength of the fortifications of Atlanta, as represented by the enemy, will not doubt the truth of this statement.

An eye witness of the bombardment of Atlanta, who was within the fortifications at the time, thus speaks of their strength, and the comparative security of the citizens:

"The trenches are impregnable. It might be possible for a heavy massed column to penetrate them, but not without immense loss, and then not to be held. The works, which were admirably located at first, have been materially strengthened, and the assaults of the enemy (Sherman's forces) have only developed our most commanding positions, and demonstrated where the engineer's skill and the miner's labor could be employed to the best advantage.

"In front of the great circular line of entrenchments, for many rods, the fields are broken and irregular, dotted with stumps, and strewn with a complete tangle of tree-tops and branches, forming a barrier against approach. In front of the batteries, blind pitfalls, miniature stockades, palisades and *chevaux-de-frise* in all directions, and make a *net work out of whose entanglement a wild fox could barely escape*. By the time a charging line could pass these barriers, under a tornado of grapeshot, shell and minnie, the line would be so broken and reduced as to be totally ineffectual.

"The works are almost invulnerable, and every day adds something to their strength, and the soil is unfavorable to mining operations.

"There are also excavations in the soil, roofed with heavy logs, over which is heaped the loose earth to the height of a young Ararat. These little mounds may be seen all over the city. The garden to almost every house which does not boast a cellar is supplied with its artificial bomb-proof. They are perfectly secure against the metal storm, and many of them are quite comfortably furnished with beds and chairs and other furniture. Women and children are huddled together in them for hours at a time, and when the city is furiously shelled at night, the whole community may be said to be under ground. Especially is this the case when the moon is unusually bright, and the approach of the shells cannot be marked by their fiery trail."

HEADQUARTERS MILITARY DIVISION OF THE MISSISSIPPI,
IN THE FIELD, ATLANTA, GA.,
THURSDAY, September 8, 1864.

SPECIAL FIELD ORDERS, No. 68.

The officers and soldiers of the Armies of the Cumberland, Ohio and Tennessee have already received the thanks of the Nation, through its President and Commander-in-Chief; and it now remains only for him who has been with you from the beginning, and who intends to stay all the time, to thank the officers and men for their intelligence, fidelity and courage displayed in the campaign of Atlanta.

On the 1st of May our armies were lying in garrison, seemingly quiet, from Knoxville to Huntsville, and our enemy lay behind his rocky-faced barrier at Dalton, proud, defiant and exulting. He had had time since Christmas to recover from his discomfiture on the Mission Ridge, with his ranks filled, and a new commander-in-chief second to none of the Confederacy in reputation for skill, sagacity and extreme popularity. All at once our armies assumed life and action, and appeared before Dalton; threatening Rocky Face, we threw ourselves upon Resaca, and the Rebel army only escaped by the rapidity of his retreat, aided by the numerous roads with which he was familiar, and which were strange to us. Again he took post in Altoona, but we gave him no rest, and by a circuit toward Dallas, and subsequent movement to Ackworth, we gained the Altoona Pass. Then followed the eventful battles of Kenesaw, and the escape of the enemy across the Chattahoochee River.

The crossing of the Chattahoochee and breaking of the Augusta Road was most handsomely executed by us, and will be studied as an example in the art of war. At this stage of our game, our enemies became dissatisfied with their old and skillful commander, and selected one more bold and rash. New tactics were adopted. Hood first boldly and rapidly, on the 20th of July, fell on our right at Peach Tree Creek, and lost; again, on the 22d, he struck our extreme left, and was severely punished, and finally again, on the 28th, he repeated the attempt on our right, and that time must have been satisfied, for since that date he has remained on the defensive. We slowly and gradually drew our lines about Atlanta, feeling for the railroads which supplied the Rebel army and made Atlanta a place of importance. We must concede to our enemy that he met these efforts patiently and skillfully, but at last he made the mistake we had waited for so long, and sent his Cavalry to our rear, far beyond the reach of recall. Instantly our Cavalry was on his only remaining road, and we followed quickly with our principal army, and Atlanta fell into our possession as the fruit of all concerted measures backed by a brave and competent army. This completed the grand task which had been assigned us by our government, and your General again repeats his personal and official thanks to all the officers and men composing this army, for the indomitable courage and perseverance which alone could give success.

We have beaten our enemy on every ground he has chosen, and have wrested from him his own Gate City, where were located his foundries, arsenals and workshops, deemed secure on account of their distance from our base, and the seemingly impregnable obstacles intervening. *Nothing* is impossible to an army like this, determined to vindicate a government which has rights wherever our flag has once floated, and is resolved to maintain them at any and all costs.

In our campaign many, yes, very many, of our noble and gallant comrades have preceded us to our common destination, the grave; but they have left the memory of deeds on which a nation can build a proud history. McPherson, Harker, McCook, and others dear to us all, are now the binding links in our minds that should attach more closely together the living, who have to complete the task which still lays before us in the dim future. I ask all to continue as they have so well begun, the cultivation of the soldierly virtues that have ennobled our own and other countries. Courage, patience, obedience to the laws and constituted authorities of our government, fidelity to our trusts and good feeling among each other, each trying to excel the other in the practice of those high qualities, and it will then require no prophet to foretell that our country will in time emerge from this war, purified by the fires of war, and worthy of its great founder, "Washington."

W. T. SHERMAN, *Major-General Commanding.*

Official: L. W. DAYTON, *Aid-de-Camp.*

The operations of General Sherman's army, which resulted in the capture of Atlanta, make some of the most wonderful pages in the history of war. The army endured long marches, great hardships and bloody battles, seemingly without a murmur of complaint. The artifices to mislead the enemy were so successful, Sherman's marches were so well guarded, his army so well fed, his battles so well fought and won, that both officers and soldiers deserve the highest credit and praise. The Southern people were made to believe that, so far as Johnson and Hood were concerned, they had succeeded in "drawing Sherman on"; that they had accomplished the very thing they had intended from the start, and now that they had him "just where they wished," they would break up his long line of communications, compel him to evacuate Atlanta, and then fall upon him and destroy his army. The people of the North, and the army, regarded the campaign as one of the greatest, most successful and decisive of the war. Even foreign nations and foreign papers—some of which were not particularly friendly to our Government or army, and which have from the beginning of the war predicted the downfall of the great Republic—were constrained to admit that Sherman's campaign was a great success.

As soon as Sherman had occupied Atlanta, he began to strengthen and protect his communications with Chattanooga and the North, well knowing that the enemy would attempt to destroy them and thus compel the evacuation of Atlanta. He also somewhat strengthened the fortifications of Atlanta, and that his plan might be kept from the enemy, he issued an order compelling all citizens to leave the place, giving them the choice of going South or North. This was denounced by the enemy and their friends, in the North and in England, as an unheard of cruelty. In this order, the wisdom of which is not now doubted, General Sherman said: "Citizens are requested to leave Atlanta and proceed either North or South. The Government will furnish transportation, South as far as Rough and Ready; North as far as Chattanooga. All citizens may take their movable property with them. Transportation will be furnished for all movables. Negroes who wish to do so may go with their masters, other male negroes will be put in Government employ, and the women and children sent outside the lines."

That this order might be carried out, an agreement was entered into between Sherman and Hood for a truce to last ten days.

It was generally believed that Sherman intended to hold Atlanta permanently, as a base of future operations. But whoever will consider the various lines of communication, and their total length, will see at a glance that he never could have entertained such an idea for a moment. The distance from Louisville, Ky., on the Ohio River, to Nashville, is 185 miles; from Nashville to Chattanooga, 151 miles; and from Chattanooga to Atlanta, 136 miles. Total distance, 472 miles. Over this long route supplies were carried to Atlanta. Thus it was evident that it would take a very large force to guard and keep open this line of communications. The enemy, however, supposed this was Sherman's purpose, and at once set to work with their Cavalry on the lines of communication.

A strong force, under command of General Forrest, appeared in Northern Alabama, where they compelled the garrison at Athens, Ala., under command of Colonel Campbell, after a fight of two hours' duration, to surrender. The garrison consisted of 500 men of the Sixth and Eighth Indiana Cavalry. A detachment of 300 men, sent from Decatur, Ala., to reinforce the garrison at Athens, were, after a most obstinate engagement, captured. Forrest then destroyed several miles of the Tennessee & Alabama Railroad between Decatur and Athens, and all the bridges on the road. He then advanced towards Pulaski, Tenn., a village seventy-five miles south of Nashville. General L. H. Rousseau advanced to meet Forrest with the force of Infantry and Cavalry under his command. He was hard pressed by the enemy, and was compelled to fall back slowly. Rousseau subsequently readvanced and maintained his position. While Rousseau was engaged with Forrest near Pulaski, a detachment from the Rebel forces passed around Pulaski, and severed the communication between that place and Nashville In the meantime, guerrillas in Kentucky captured two trains of cars on the route from Louisville to Nashville. They burned nineteen cars.

On the 29th of October, three days after Rousseau met Forrest at Pulaski, Wheeler and Roddy were north of Decatur, Ala., making their way toward the railroad between that place and Chattanooga, for the purpose of destroying the railroad between Huntsville and Stevenson, and then effect a junction with Forrest at Tullahoma, Tenn. General Rousseau changed his operations to the Chattanooga Railroad, at Tullahoma.

But we can not stop to notice all the efforts of the enemy to interrupt the communications of Sherman. These, undoubtedly, were the forerunners of Hood's great movement North. The Richmond papers threw out dark, mysterious hints of some grand event that was about to be enacted that would compel Sherman to evacuate Atlanta and retreat back to Chattanooga, or else his army would be annihilated. So confident were the enemy of the success of their new scheme that their President, Jeff. Davis, in a public speech made at Macon, Georgia, on Sabbath, September 25th, announced the determination of Hood to march into Tennessee to sever the wonderfully attenuated lines of communications held by Sherman.

General Sherman had anticipated this movement, and made all necessary arrangements to carry out his plans—the grandest movement of the war. He sent detachments under various commanders at different points along the railroad between Atlanta and Chattanooga, and all his spare forces to General Thomas.

About the time that Davis made his famous speech at Macon, General Hood transferred his army from Lovejoy's Station, in the region of Jonesboro', twenty miles South of Atlanta, on the Macon Railroad, to the West Point Railroad, near Newman. On the 29th and 30th of September the enemy crossed the Chattahoochee, threw himself on the railroad running from Chattanooga to Atlanta, occupied Dallas, and threatened Rome and Kingston. On the 5th of

October Hood struck at the important post of Altoona. His General, S. G. French, in command of the advance Division of Stewart's Corps, made the assault, and was handsomely repulsed by our forces under the command of the gallant General Corse, a most skillful and intrepid officer.

In the meantime, Sherman had left Atlanta in possession of the Twentieth Corps, General Slocum commanding, impregnably fortified and with abundant supplies, and with two corps he moved North after Hood. He followed him closely like a pursuing foe. When Hood's general was assaulting Altoona, General Sherman was at Kenesaw Mountain, from the summit of which he signaled to General Corse at Altoona, over the heads of Hood's troops, to hold out until he relieved him.

On the 12th of October, Hood, with one Corps of his army, invested Dalton, and the two other Corps were engaged in tearing up the railroad obstructing Snake Creek Gap, in order to delay Sherman, who was rapidly pursuing. Threatening Chattanooga for a moment, Hood suddenly broke away and marched westerly to Lafayette, and southwesterly to Gadsden. Thus in the campaign of a month's duration, Hood had succeeded in severing the railroad between Chattanooga and Atlanta. At the end of the month, however, Sherman's forces, by great industry and skill, re-opened the road.

Anticipating Hood's movement to cross the Tennessee, troops were placed at Bridgeport and other points along the river. With the remainder of the army, Sherman moved to Galesville in pursuit of the enemy, at which place he remained for several days. This place, it will be remembered, is in Northern Alabama, near the Georgia line. Hood remained for more than a week at Gadsden, where he threw up fortifications. While in this position, it is said, upon pretty good authority, that Hood's army had a "*happy time.*" Beauregard had brought reënforcements to Hood. Whereupon the chief officers, Generals Hood, Beauregard, S. D. Lee, Cheatham, Clayton, Cleburn, and Bate, made speeches, promising to "*wipe Sherman out from the list of Yankee officers.*"

On the 23d of October Hood began to move his forces northwesterly through Lookout Mountain toward Gunter's Landing and Decatur, on the Tennessee River. In the meantime, the army of General Dick Taylor had quickly moved up the Mobile and Ohio Railroad from Eastern Louisiana to Corinth, and thence to Tuscumbia.

About the 1st of November portions of Hood's army crossed the river at Muscle Shoals, between Florence and Decatur, and at other points along the river. His forces were attacked at various points. The Union gunboats took part in these engagements, and in some instances succeeded in repulsing the enemy, and for the time defeated their efforts to cross the river. The gunboat Undine and transports Venus and Cheseman were captured at Fort Herman, on the river, after a hard fight with the enemy's shore batteries. Most of the crew were killed or wounded. At Johnsonville, eight steamboats, loaded with government stores, were burned by the Union forces, to prevent them from falling into the hands of the enemy. The place was evacuated, and soon occupied by Forrest, who captured two of our gunboats that were left to defend the town.

Here Sherman and Hood parted, and forever. The enemy and the people of the entire country seemed to be unable to comprehend Sherman's movements, and were greatly perplexed. Sherman said of Hood: "*Let him go North; our business is down South. If he will cross the river and march North, I will give him his rations.*"

General Thomas was appointed to the command of all the troops in Tennessee and Kentucky, and had a force large enough to meet the enemy and manage him.

About the time that Hood was crossing the Tennessee, Sherman sent the following characteristic telegram:

"Hood has crossed the Tennessee. Thomas will take care of him and Nashville, while Schofield will not let him into Chattanooga or Knoxville. Georgia and South Carolina are at my mercy, and I shall strike. Do not be anxious about me. I am all right."

While Sherman was engaged in the pursuit of Hood north, the enemy that were south of Atlanta, supposing that place abandoned, started with a grand flourish of trumpets to recapture what they had lost. They approached at two points, and after an engagement, which lasted about thirty minutes, they were disappointed and chagrined, and compelled to march back in greater haste than they advanced, leaving on the field upwards of twenty of their number killed and wounded.

Hood continued his march north until he reached Franklin, within about twenty miles of Nashville, where his columns were terribly shattered by the troops of General Schofield in the battle at that place. From thence he marched to and invested Nashville, from which position he was subsequently driven by the forces of that noble old soldier, General Thomas, after losing a large part of his army and most of his Artillery. Thus ended the inglorious campaign of Hood to Sherman's rear.

While Hood was on the banks of the Tennessee, preparing for the invasion and conquest of the middle portions of that State, Sherman, to the astonishment of the enemy and the whole country, was marching back towards Atlanta.

Sherman announced his plans, in part, to his friend Captain Pennock of the United States Navy, in the following letter:

KINGSTON, GEORGIA, November 3d, 1864.

Captain Pennock, United States Navy, Mound City:

In a few days I will be off for salt water, and hope to meet my old friend D. D. Porter again. Will you be kind enough to write and tell him to look out for me about Christmas, from Hilton Head to Savannah?

W. T. SHERMAN, *Major-General.*

At the time this letter was written Sherman was making every preparation for his great triumphal march through Georgia. All valuable property was removed to Chattanooga. The bridge across the Chattahoochee was burned, the railroad was torn up for miles and the rails heated and twisted so as to be unfit for future use, and large quantities of them were sent to Chattanooga.

Sherman issued the order for his march at Kingston, Georgia, November 9th, 1864, from which we learn that the army was to be divided into two wings; the right commanded by Major-General O. O. Howard; the left by Major-General H. W. Slocum. The right wing was composed of the Fifteenth and Seventeenth Corps; the left of the Fourteenth and Twentieth Corps. In addition to these forces there was, also, a large body of Cavalry, commanded by General Kilpatrick, and a Brigade of Artillery for each Corps, and one Battery of Horse Artillery for the Cavalry. The Fourteenth Corps was commanded by Brevet Major-General Jeff C. Davis, the Fifteenth by Brevet Major-General Osterhaus, the Seventeenth by Major-General Blair, and the Twentieth by Brigadier-General Williams.

The whole army, estimated by the enemy at thirty-five thousand actually numbered nearly sixty thousand well equipped soldiers, accustomed to long marches, fierce battles and glorious victories. They marched without tents or a general train of supplies. They were ordered to supply themselves from the country through which they marched. The frequent orders and exhortations of the Rebel authorities compelling the Southern people to cease the culture of cotton, their late king, and raise breadstuffs, was an assurance to Sherman and his soldiers that they would find bread on the route.

We here subjoin the order of Generals Sherman and Slocum, documents well worth reading and preserving. They shed light on all of this grand movement:

SHERMAN'S ORDERS FOR HIS MARCH.

HEADQUARTERS MILITARY DIVISION OF THE MISSISSIPPI, }
IN THE FIELD, KINGSTON, GEORGIA, November 9, 1864. }

SPECIAL FIELD ORDERS, No. 120.

1. For the purpose of military operations this army is divided into two wings, viz: The right wing, Major-General O. O. Howard commanding, the Fifteenth and Seventeenth Corps; the left wing, Major-General H. W. Slocum commanding, the Fourteenth and Twentieth Corps.

2. The habitual order of march will be, whenever practicable, by four roads, as nearly parallel as possible, and converging at points hereafter to be indicated in orders. The Cavalry, Brigadier-General Kilpatrick commanding, will receive special orders from the Commander-in-Chief.

3. There will be no general trains of supplies, but each corps will have its ammunition and provision train distributed habitually as follows: Behind each Regiment should follow one wagon and one ambulance; behind each Brigade should follow a due proportion of ammunition wagons, provision wagons and ambulances. In case of danger, each Army Corps should change this order of march by having its advance and rear Brigade unincumbered by wheels. The separate column will start habitually at 7 A. M., and make about fifteen miles per day, unless otherwise fixed in orders.

4. The army will forage liberally on the country during the march. To this end, each Brigade Commander will organize a good and sufficient foraging party, under the command of one or more discreet officers, who will gather, near the route traveled, corn or forage of any kind, meat of any kind, vegetables, corn corn meal, or whatever is needed by the command; aiming at all times to keep in the wagon trains at least ten days' provisions for the command, and three days' forage. Soldiers must not enter the dwellings of the inhabitants or commit any trespass; during the halt or a camp they may be permitted to gather turnips, potatoes and other vegetables, and drive in stock in front of their camps. To regular foraging parties must be entrusted the gathering of provisions and forage at any distance from the road traveled.

5. To Army Corps Commanders is entrusted the power to destroy mills, houses, cotton gins, etc., and for them this general principle is laid down: In districts and neighborhoods where the army is unmolested, no destruction of such property should be permitted; but should guerrillas or bushwhackers molest our march, or should the inhabitants burn bridges, obstruct roads, or otherwise manifest local hostility, then Army Corps Commanders should order and enforce a devastation more or less relentless, according to the measure of such hostility.

6. As for horses, mules, wagons, etc., belonging to the inhabitants, the Cavalry and Artillery may appropriate freely and without limit; discriminating, however, between the rich, who are usually hostile, and the poor or industrious, usually neutral or friendly. Foraging parties may also take mules or horses to replace the jaded animals of their trains, or to serve as pack-mules for the Regiments or Brigades. In all foraging, of whatever kind, the parties

engaged will refrain from abusive and threatening language, and may, when the officer in command thinks proper, give written certificates of the facts, but not receipts; and they will endeavor to leave with each family a reasonable portion for their maintenance.

7. Negroes who are able-bodied, and can be of service to the several columns, may be taken along; but each Army Commander will bear in mind that the question of supplies is a very important one, and that his first duty is to see to those who bear arms.

8. The organization at once of a good Pioneer Battalion for each Corps, composed, if possible, of negroes, should be attended to. This Battalion should follow the Advance Guard, should repair roads, and double them if possible, so that the columns will not be delayed after reaching bad places. Also, Army Commanders should study the habit of giving the Artillery and wagons the road, and marching their troops on one side; and, also, instruct the troops to assist wagons at steep hills or bad crossings of streams.

9. Captain O. M. Poe, Chief Engineer, will assign to each wing of the army a ponton train, fully equipped and organized, and the commander thereof will see to its being properly protected at all times.

By order of MAJOR-GENERAL W. T. SHERMAN.

L. M. DAYTON, *Aid-de-Camp.*

GENERAL SLOCUM'S ORDER TO HIS WING OF THE ARMY.

HEADQUARTERS TWENTIETH CORPS, }
ATLANTA, GA., Nov. 7, 1864. }

CIRCULAR.

When the troops leave camp on the march about to commence, they will carry, in haversack, two days' rations salt meat, two days' hard bread, ten days' coffee and salt, and five days' sugar. Each Infantry soldier will carry sixty rounds of ammunition on his person. Every effort should be made, by officers and men, to save rations and ammunition ; not a round of ammunition should be lost or unnecessarily expended. It is expected that the command will be supplied with subsistence and forage mainly from the country. All foraging will be done by parties detailed for the purpose by Brigade Commanders, under such rules as may be prescribed by Brigade and Division Commanders. Pillaging, marauding, and every act of cruelty or abuse of citizens will be very severely punished. Each Brigade Commander will have a strong rear guard on every march, and will order the arrest of all stragglers. The danger of straggling on this march should be impressed upon the mind of every officer and man of the command. Not only the reputation of the Corps, but the personal safety of every man will be dependent, in a great measure, upon the rigid enforcement of discipline and care taken of the rations and ammunition.

By command of MAJOR-GENERAL SLOCUM.

H. W. PERKINS, *A. A. G.*

The troops were all concentrated in and near Atlanta. The city was set on fire in order to destroy everything that might be of use to the enemy.

An eye witness of the burning of Atlanta, on the day and night of the 15th of November, thus describes that scene:

"Atlanta is entirely deserted of human beings, excepting a few soldiers here and there. The houses are vacant; there is no trade or traffic of any kind; the streets are empty. Beautiful roses bloom in the gardens of fine houses, but a terrible stillness and solitude cover it all, depressing the hearts even of those who are glad to destroy it. In your peaceful homes at the North you cannot conceive how these people have suffered for their crimes.

"A grand and awful spectacle is presented to the beholder in this beautiful city, now in flames. By order, the Chief Engineer had destroyed, by powder and fire, all the storehouses, depot buildings and machine shops. The heaven is one expanse of lurid fire; the air is filled with flying, burning cinders; buildings covering over two hundred acres are in ruins or in flames; every instant there is the sharp detonation or the smothered burning sound of exploding shells and powder concealed in the buildings, and then the sparks and flame shoot away up into the dark red roof, scattering the cinders far and wide.

"These are the machine shops where have been forged and cast Rebel cannon, shot and shell, that have carried death to many a brave defender of our Nation's honor. These warehouses have been the receptacle of munitions of war, stored, to be used for our destruction. The city which, next to Richmond, has furnished more material for prosecuting the war than any other in the South, exists no more as a means for the enemies of the Union.

"A brigade of Massachusetts soldiers are the only troops now left in the town. They will be the last to leave it. To-night I heard the really fine band of the Thirty-third Massachusetts playing 'John Brown's soul goes marching on,' by the light of the burning buildings. I have never heard that noble anthem when it was so grand, so solemn, so inspiring."

On the 14th and 15th, the march began in earnest. As Cortez burned his ships behind him, and thus cut off all possibility of a retreat, so Sherman broke up his communications; cut loose from all support and marched, relying upon his noble soldiery and his own genius for a successful issue of the campaign.

For days and weeks he was not heard from except through the enemy's channels. The General, his brave army and their movements were covered with a dark cloud from the view of their friends. No one seemed to know where they were or whither they were marching, or what had befallen them. All over the North, men daily, and almost hourly inquired, where is Sherman? His bold movement, imperfectly comprehended, was regarded as full of peril and hazardous in the extreme. Nevertheless not a few believed most confidently, that he would make a successful march either to the Gulf or to the Atlantic coast.

This movement was as incomprehensible to the enemy as to us, and far more perplexing to them. They regarded it as a retreat, and not as the deliberate plan of a great military genius. Their views, as expressed by their public presses, are curious, and should be preserved, as a record of the times, and the manner in which they were either deceived or undertook to deceive the public in regard to Sherman's movements.

We here insert a few extracts from the enemy's press, as a monument of Sherman's great achievement, and their amazing folly.

EXTRACTS FROM THE REBEL PRESS

[From the Augusta Constitutionalist, November 20th.]

We must retard, harass, starve, destroy the army of Sherman. The opportunity is ours. The hand of God is in it. The blow, if we can give it as it should be given, may end the war. We urge our friends in the track of the advance to remove all forage and provisions, horses, mules, negroes, and stock, and burn the balance. Let the invader find the desolation he would leave behind him staring him in the face. You must do it yourself, or the enemy will do it.

It is fully believed that General Sherman, finding his way north entirely closed, and a bold and defiant army confronting him, has determined upon making a bold retreat to the rear, where no army of consequence could impede his movement.

In our judgment it is the Anabasis of Sherman. It is plain his only object can be the making of a certain and secure base. He must move fast and obtain his object speedily, or he is lost.

His movement is occasioned by the fact that Forrest has destroyed his stores at Johnsonville, and cut his communication on the north.

Sherman has many weary miles to march in obtaining his object. It is absurdity to talk about his making a winter campaign with no communication with his Government. He is retreating—simply retreating. He will destroy as he goes, but that makes it none the less so.

[From the Savannah *News*, November 22d, 1864.]

A few days, however, will develop his designs, when, if our united efforts are properly directed, he will reap the reward of his reckless temerity in utter annihilation. We have only to arouse our whole arms-bearing people—hover on his front, his flanks and rear—remove from his reach or destroy everything that will subsist man or beast—retard his progress by every means in our power, and when the proper time comes, fall upon him with the relentless vengeance of an insulted and outraged people, and there need be no doubt of the result. As the great Napoleon found his Moscow, so will the brutal Sherman find his Atlanta.

Meanwhile the left wing of the army, Slocum's column, passed through Decatur, Covington and Madison, and having destroyed everything that could be of advantage to the enemy, marched on toward Milledgeville, the capital. Before reaching the latter place, it is said that Sherman camped on one of the plantations of Howell Cobb. Said one who was with the army at the time: "We found his granaries well filled with corn and wheat, part of which was distributed and eaten by our animals and men. A large supply of syrup made from sorghum, which we found at nearly every plantation on the march, was stored in an outhouse. This was also disposed of to the soldiers and the poor decrepit negroes, which this humane, liberty-loving Major-General left to die in this place a few months after. Becoming alarmed, Cobb removed all the able-bodied mules, horses, cows and slaves. He left behind some fifty old men,—cripples, and women and children—with scarcely enough clothing to cover their nakedness, with little or no food, and without means of procuring any. We found them cowering over the fire-places of their miserable huts, where the wind whirled through the crevices between the logs, frightened at the approach of the Yankees, who, they had been told, would kill them. A more forlorn, neglected set of human beings I never saw."

General Sherman distributed provisions among them, and assured them that we were their friends, and not their foes.

Slocum, with the Twentieth Corps, on the 22d of November, entered Milledgeville.

As a general rule, our soldiers were not permitted to enter private houses, or disturb the property of private families. They were allowed to help themselves freely to the productions of the country, such as sweet potatoes, chickens, turkeys, ducks, beef, and whatever might be necessary for the comfort of the "inner man." Few of the "boys in blue" made the march on empty stomachs.

Keeping the general direction of the two railroads, as heretofore indicated, the two wings of the army moved on, overcoming the obstacles in their way without much difficulty and without any very serious fighting. The enemy learned, when it was too late, that Sherman would not delay his columns for the sake of capturing the city of Macon, where they had a strong force concentrated behind breastworks and fortifications. Nor could the enemy tell as the army moved east, whether Sherman aimed at Augusta and Charleston or Savannah. The deception was kept up until the whole army was concentrated at Millen, with the exception of the Cavalry, a portion of which, under Kilpatrick, occupied Waynesboro, between Millen and Augusta, for the purpose of keeping up the deception. The army then turned south and marched down the peninsula between the Savannah and Ogeechee Rivers. On the afternoon of the 8th of December, the signal guns of the navy, in Ossabaw Sound, were distinctly heard, which sent a thrill of gladness through the hearts of our brave soldiers.

On the evening of December the 9th, General Howard sent Captain Duncan and two scouts to open up communications with General Foster and Admiral Dahlgren. The captain descended the Ogeechee river in a small boat on the 12th, and delivered the following dispatch to Admiral Dahlgren:

HEADQUARTERS, ARMY OF THE TENNESSEE,
NEAR SAVANNAH CANAL, Dec. 9, 1864.
To the Commander of the United States Naval Forces in the vicinity of Savannah, Georgia:

SIR—We have met with perfect success thus far. The troops are in fine spirits and near by.

Respectfully,
O. O. HOWARD, *Major-General*,
Commanding Right Wing of the Army.

On Tuesday, December 13th, the Second Division of the Fifteenth Corps captured Fort McAllister. This work is situated on the Ogeechee River fifteen miles from Savannah, at the point where the river is crossed by the Savannah, Albany and Gulf Railroad, and about six miles from Ossabaw Sound. The capture of this fort opened complete communications between the army and the navy.

Sherman sent to the War Department the following dispatch, announcing the capture of Fort McAllister and the success of his march to the sea:

"To-day, at 5 p. m., General Hazen's Division, of the Fifteenth Corps, carried Fort McAllister by assault, capturing its entire garrison and stores. This opened to us the Ossabaw Sound, and I passed down on a gun-boat to communicate with the fleet. Before opening the communication we had completely destroyed all railroads leading into Savannah, and invested the city. The left is on the Savannah River, ten miles above this city, and the right on the Ogeechee, at King's Bridge.

"The army is in splendid order, the weather fine, and supplies abundant. Our march was most agreeable, and not molested by guerrillas. We reached Savannah three days ago, but owing to Fort McAllister we could not communicate; but now we have Fort McAllister, we can go ahead. We have captured two boats on Savannah River, and prevented their gunboats from coming down. The estimated population of Savannah is twenty-five thousand, and the garrison fifteen thousand. General Hardee commands.

"We have not lost a wagon on the trip, but have gathered in a large supply of negroes, mules and horses. Our teams are in better condition than when we started. My first duty will be to clear the army of superfluous negroes, mules and horses.

"I have utterly destroyed over two hundred miles of rail, and consumed all stores and provisions that were essential to the armies of Lee and Hood.

"The quick work made with McAllister, and the opening of communication with our fleet, and consequent independence for supplies, dissipates all their boasted threats to head me off and starve the army.

"*I regard Savannah as already gained.*
                        "Yours truly,
(Signed,)   "W. T. SHERMAN,
                              "*Major-General.*"

In this connection, the reader will be pleased with the following extracts from the journal of one who accompanied the grand triumphal march of Sherman, from which he will be able to gather a history of the more important events and incidents of the march not heretofore recorded in these pages:

SUPPLIES ABUNDANT.

Vegetables of all kinds, and in unlimited quantities, were at hand, and the soldiers gave thanks as soldiers may, and were merry as soldiers can be. In truth, so far as the gratification of the stomach goes, the troops are pursuing a continuous thanksgiving.

In addition to fowls, vegetables and meats, many obtain a delicious syrup made from sorghum, which is cultivated on all the plantations, and stored away in large troughs and hogsheads. The mills here and there furnish fresh supplies of flour and meal, and we hear little or nothing of "hard-tack," that terror to weak mastication. Over the sections of country lately traversed I find very little cultivation of cotton. The commands of Davis appear to have been obeyed; and our large droves of cattle are turned nightly into the immense fields of ungathered corn to eat their fill, while the granaries are crowded to overflowing with both oats and corn.

We have also reached the sand regions, so that the fall of rain has no terrors; the roads are excellent, and would become firmer from a liberal wetting. The rise of the river will not bother us much, for each Army Corps has its pontons, and the launching of its boats is the matter of an hour.

The country people all through this section were found to be extremely ignorant. Rich men there are, whose plantations line the roads for miles; men and women who own, or did own, hundreds of slaves, and raised every year their thousand bales of cotton; but their ignorance is only equaled by that twin sister of ignorance, intolerance. I can understand, as I never did before, why it was that a few persons, who every year represented the South in Congress, were able to wield that influence as a unit. Many of the people claim to have been Unionists from the beginning of the war. It seems hard, sometimes, to strip such men as clear of all eatables as do our troops, who have the art cultivated to the most eminent degree; but, as General Sherman often says to them: "If it is true that you are Unionists, you should not have permitted Jeff Davis to dragoon you until you are as much his slaves as once the niggers were yours."

General Sherman invites all able-bodied negroes (others could not make the march) to join the column, and he takes especial pleasure when they join the procession, on some occasions telling them they are free; that Massa Lincoln has given them their liberty, and that they can go where they please; that if they earn their freedom they should have it: but that Massa Lincoln has given it to them anyhow. Thousands of negro women join the column, some carrying household truck; others, and many of them there are, who bear the heavy burden of children in their arms, while older boys and girls plod by their sides. All these women and children are ordered back, heartrending though it may be to refuse them liberty.

But the majority accept the advent of the Yankees as the fulfillment of the millennial prophecies. The "day of jubilee," the hope and prayer of a lifetime, has come. They cannot be made to understand that they must remain behind, and they are satisfied only when General Sherman tells them—as he does every day—that we shall come back for them some time, and that they must be patient until the proper hour of deliverance comes.

THE PASSAGE OF THE OGEECHEE.

We have had very little difficulty in crossing the Ogeechee. The Twentieth Corps moved down the railroad, destroying it to the bridge. The Seventeenth Corps covered the river at this point, where a light bridge was only partially destroyed. It was easily repaired, so that the Infantry and Cavalry could pass over it, while the wagons and Artillery used the pontons. The Ogeechee is about sixty yards in width at this point. It is approached on the northern or western side through swamps, which would be impassable were it not for the sandy soil which packs solid when the water covers the roads, although in places there are treacherous quicksands which we are obliged to corduroy.

This evening I walked down to the river. A novel and vivid sight was it to see the fires of pitch pine flaring up into the mist and darkness, the figures of men and horses looming out of the dense shadows in gigantic proportions. Torchlights are blinking and flashing away off in the forests, while the still air echoed and reëchoed with the cries of the teamsters and the wild shouts of the soldiers. A long line of the troops marched across the front bridge, each soldier bearing a torch; their light reflected in quivering lines in the swift-running stream.

IN A FOG.

Soon a fog, which settles like a blanket over the swamps and forests of the river bottoms, shut down upon the scene, and so dense and dark was it, that torches were of but little use, and men were directed here and there by the voice.

CAPTURE OF FORT McALLISTER.

DECEMBER 13TH.

At Fort McAllister. To day I have been a spectator of one of those glorious sights where the actors, passing through the most fearful ordeal of fire which befalls the soldier, come out successful, and are always after heroes.

The Second Division of the Fifteenth Corps have marched to-day fifteen miles; and, without the assistance of Artillery, have crossed an open space of six hundred yards, under a fierce fire of twenty-one heavy guns, crawling through a thick abatis, crossed a ditch of great depth, at whose bottom were driven thick palisades, torn them away, surmounted the crest and palisades, shot and bayoneted the gunners, who refused to surrender, at their posts, and planted the Stars and Stripes upon the work in triumph. The assault was made with a single line, which approached the fort from all sides but that of the river, at the same instant, never for an instant wavering, no man lurking shelter, but facing the fire manfully.

The explosion of torpedoes at this point did not deter them. General Sherman's old Division and Corps had been told that he had said, "Carry the place by assault to-night, if possible." They resolved to fulfill their old commander's wish, and they did it. Perhaps in the history of this war there has not been a more striking example of the evidence of quick, determined action. Had we waited, put up intrenchments, shelled the place, and made the usual approaches, we should have lost many more lives, and time was invaluable. As it is, our entire loss is not more than ninety men killed and wounded, and we have gained a necessity — a base of supplies. Our whole army are eager to emulate such a glorious example, and this *esprit du corps* has been raised to the grandest height.

General Sherman did not feel that his march to the sea was completed until Savannah was captured. That city fell, as Jericho of old did, without resistance. Its gates were opened, and the conqueror marched in.

After the capture of Fort McAllister, Sherman began the systematic investment of the city. The enemy made the best use of every natural advantage against us. The rice fields below the city were flooded by means of the canals, rendering an advance from that quarter difficult. The swamps north and west were perplexing barriers. These difficulties were only in the way of an assault. Our lines, however, were greatly annoyed in the gradual approach by torpedoes, which the enemy had ingeniously disposed. They were so perfectly covered as to be almost unnoticable, and so arranged that the slightest pressure of the foot upon the small plug sufficed to explode them.

This danger Sherman overcome, by ordering the Rebel prisoners in his hands to go before our advancing lines, find the torpedoes, and dig them up—dig up the death-traps which perhaps their own hands had planted.

The investment of the city was as complete as it could be made by the 20th of December. Every outlet of the city was completely in our possession, except the causeway just below Hutchinson's Island, and every effort was made to secure that.

On the morning of the 20th of December, Sherman sent by flag of truce his demand for the surrender of the city, closing his dispatch with the words of General Hood in his demand for the surrender of Dalton and the negro troops: "If this demand is not complied with, I shall take no prisoners." Of course this was intended as irony on the part of Sherman.

General Hardee, in his reply, boasted that he had men and supplies enough to hold the city, and that he would not surrender.

Arrangements were completed for the assault and bombardment. Even the guns of the enemy, which had been captured with the surrounding forts, had been removed and placed in position to aid in the attack.

General Hardee anticipated the assault, and on the night of the 20th evacuated, passing over the Union Causeway under the protection of his iron-clads and the batteries of the lower end of Hutchinson's Island. The rear guard of the fugitives fired the navy-yard, and the iron-clads were blown up.

On the following morning, December 21, 1864, the beautiful city of Savannah was surrendered by the Mayor and Council of the City, with the request that private property and the rights of citizens should be respected.

Thus ended the most remarkable march in the annals of history. European journals, and among these the London *Times*, admit that the march of Sherman from Chattanooga to Savannah is absolutely without a parallel. "As the Pilgrims landed and sent liberty and a glorious form of nationality Westward, along their northern lines of march, so the West sounded back to the ocean again that sublime hymn of universal freedom which our fathers sung on Plymouth Rock when they dedicated this continent to God."

This wonderful march, and those who took part in it, will be remembered. The pen of the historian and the lays of the minstrel will keep this great event fresh in the memory of men. Even now, and thus beautifully, has this story been woven into verse:

SHERMAN'S MARCH TO THE SEA.

Our camp-fires shone bright on the mountain
  That frowned on the river below,
While we stood by our guns in the morning,
  And eagerly watched for the foe,
When a rider came out from the darkness,
  That hung over mountain and tree,
And shouted, "Boys, up and be ready,
  For Sherman will march to the sea."

When cheer upon cheer for bold Sherman
  Went up from each valley and glen,
And the bugle re-echoed the music
  That came from the lips of the men;
For we know that the stars on our banner
  More bright in their splendor would be,
And that blessing from North-land would greet us
  As Sherman marched down to the sea.

Then forward, boys, forward, to battle,
  We marched on our wearisome way,
And we strewed the wild hills of Resaca—
  God bless those who fell on that day.
Then Kenesaw, dark in its glory,
  Frowned down on the flag of the free;
But the East and the West bore our standard
  As Sherman marched down to the sea.

Still onward we pressed till our banner
  Swept out from Atlanta's grim walls,
And the blood of the patriot dampened
  The soil where the traitor's flag falls.
But we paused not to weep for the fallen
  Who slept by each river and tree;
Yet we twined them wreaths of the laurel
  As Sherman marched down to the sea.

GENERAL JOHN POPE.

GENERAL JOHN A. LOGAN.

MAJOR-GENERAL W. T. SHERMAN.

MAJOR GENERAL O. O. HOWARD.

CAPTURE OF FORT McALLISTER.

> Proud, proud was our army that morning,
> That stood by the cypress and pine,
> When Sherman said: "Boys, you are weary;
> This day fair Savannah is thine."
> Then sang we a song for our chieftain
> That echoed o'er river and lea,
> And the stars on our banner shone brighter
> When Sherman marched down to the sea.

After the escape of General Hardee with his 13,000 troops, and the surrender by the Mayor of the City, our army marched in, to the evident delight of the citizens. In numerous instances men and women looked upon the old flag and wept, and some hailed it with lively demonstrations of joy.

The fruits of the capture were as follows: The city; all its fortifications intact, with the adjoining rivers and harbors; about 1,200 prisoners; 152 guns; 38,000 bales of cotton; large quantities of ammunition and rice; 13 locomotives and 200 railroad cars. The forts captured were McAllister, on the Ogeechee; Lawton and Lee, on the Savannah River, near the city, and Jackson, on the river, two miles below the city.

THE CAMPAIGN IN THE CAROLINAS.

This campaign may be called the climax of this colossal war. The movement of Sherman, which commenced on the 1st day of May, 1864, and ended with the surrender of Johnston's army and all the Confederate forces from the Chattahoochee to the Potomac on the 26th day of April, 1865, extending through almost an entire year, was but one campaign; was but the carrying out of the plan of Sherman when he marched from Chattanooga—a campaign that has no parallel in the annals of history.

Less than one month was consumed at Savannah in making proper dispositions of captured property and other local matters, and in preparations for the march North through the "sacred soil of South Carolina."

By the 15th of January, 1865, Sherman and his splendid army were ready for the march. Preliminary to this, General Howard, commanding the right wing, was ordered to embark his forces at Thunderbolt, transport them to Beaufort, and thence, by the 15th of January, make a lodgment on the Charleston Railroad at Pocotaligo. This was accomplished punctually, at little cost, by the

Seventeenth Corps, Major-General Blair, and a depot for supplies was established near the mouth of Pocotaligo Creek, with easy water communications back to Hilton Head. As our troops advanced toward the Charleston Railroad they met the enemy, who fell back after a short skirmish. The next day an attempt was made to flank the enemy's position, but they hastily evacuated their works, leaving three guns behind them. This position was gained with the loss of about ten men killed and wounded. The attempt of General Foster to carry this same position, about a month previously, cost him twelve or fifteen hundred men.

THE LEFT WING.

The left wing, commanded by Major-General Slocum, and the Cavalry, commanded by Major-General Kilpatrick, were ordered, in the meantime, to rendezvous near Robertsville and Coosawachie, South Carolina, with a depot of supplies at Pureysburg, or Sister's Ferry, on the Savannah River. General Slocum had a good ponton bridge constructed opposite the city, and the "Union Causeway," leading through the low rice fields opposite Savannah, was repaired and corduroyed, but before the time appointed to start the heavy rains of January had swollen the river, broken the pontoon bridge and overflowed the whole bottom, so that the causeway was four feet under water, and Slocum was compelled to look higher up for a passage over the Savannah River. He moved up to Sister's Ferry, but even there the river, with its overflowed bottoms, was nearly three miles wide, so that he did not succeed in getting his whole wing across until the first week in February.

In the meantime General Grant had sent to Sherman Grover's Division of the Nineteenth Corps, to garrison Savannah, and had drawn the Twenty-third Corps, Major-General Schofield's command, from Tennessee and sent it to reënforce the commands of Major-Generals Terry and Palmer, operating on the coast of North Carolina, to prepare the way for the march of Sherman.

On the 18th of January Sherman transferred the forts and city of Savannah to Major-General Foster, commanding the Department of the South. Sherman then imparted to Foster his plans of operations and instructed him how to follow his movements inland by occupying, in succession, the city of Charleston and such other points along the sea-coast as would be of any value to us.

The combined naval and land forces under Admiral Porter and General Terry had, on the 16th of January, captured Fort Fisher and the Rebel forts at the mouth of Cape Fear River, and thus gave to Sherman another point of security on the sea-coast.

Sherman had already resolved, in his own mind, and had advised General Grant that he would undertake, "at one stride," to make Goldsboro', and open communications with the sea by the Newbern Railroad. He ordered Colonel W. W. Wright, Superintendent of Military Railroads, to proceed, in advance, to Newbern, and to be prepared to extend the railroad out from Newbern to Goldsboro' by the 15th of March. On the 19th of January all preparations were finished and the orders for the march given. The Chief Quartermaster and Commissary, Generals Easton and Beckwith, were ordered to complete the supplies at Sister's Ferry and Pocotaligo, and then follow the movements of the army coastwise, looking for its arrival at Goldsboro', North Carolina, about the 15th of March, where they were to open communications with Sherman from Morehead City.

On the 22d of January General Sherman in person embarked at Savannah for Hilton Head, where he held a conference with Admiral Dahlgren of the United States Navy, and Major-General Foster, commanding the Department of the South, and the next day proceeded to Beaufort, riding out thence on the 24th to Pocotaligo, where the Seventeenth Corps, Major-General Blair, was encamped. At that time the Fifteenth Corps was somewhat scattered. Wood's and Hazen's Divisions were at Beaufort. John E. Smith's was marching from Savannah by the coastward, and Corse was still at Savannah, cut off by storms and the freshet in the river.

On the 25th a demonstration was made against the Combahee Ferry and the Railroad Bridge across the Salkehatchie, merely to amuse the enemy, who had evidently adopted that river as his defensive line against our supposed *objective point*—the City of Charleston. General Sherman reconnoitered the line in person, and saw that the heavy rains had swollen the river so that water stood in the swamps for a breadth of more than one mile, at a depth of from one to twenty feet. Not having the remotest intention of approaching Charleston, a comparatively small force was able, by seeming preparations to cross over, to keep in their front a considerable force of the enemy who seemed disposed to contest our supposed advance on Charleston.

On the 27th General Sherman rode to the camp of General Hatch's Division of Foster's command, on the Tullafuiney and Coosawatchie Rivers, and directed those places to be evacuated, as no longer of any use to us. That Division was then moved to Pocotaligo to keep up the feints already begun, until we should, with the right wing, move higher up and across the Salkehatchie about River's or Broxton's Bridge.

On the 29th Sherman learned that the roads back of Savannah, had at last become sufficiently clear of the flood to admit of General Slocum putting his wing in motion, and that he was already approaching Sister's Ferry, whither a gun-boat, the Pontiac, Captain Luce, kindly furnished by Admiral Dahlgren, had preceded him to cover the crossing. In the meantime three Divisions of the Fifteenth Corps had closed up at Pocotaligo, and the right wing had loaded its wagons and was ready to start. Sherman, therefore, directed General Howard to move one Corps, the Seventeenth, along the Salkehatchie as high up as River's Bridge, and the other, the Fifteenth, by Hickory Hill, Bosser's Cross-Roads, Anglesey Post Office and Beaufort's Bridge. Hatch's Division was ordered to remain at Pocotaligo, feinting at the Salkehatchie Railroad Bridge and Ferry until our movement turned the enemy's position and forced him to fall behind the Edisto.

The Seventeenth and Fifteenth Corps drew out of camp on the 31st of January, but the real march began on the 1st of February. All the roads northward had for weeks been held by Wheeler's Cavalry, who had, by details of negro laborers, felled trees, burned bridges and made obstructions to impede our march. But so well organized were the Pioneer Battalions, and so strong and intelligent our men, that obstructions seemed only to quicken their progress. Felled trees were removed and bridges rebuilt by the heads of columns before the rear could close up. On the 2d of February the Fifteenth Corps reached Toper's Cross Roads, and the Seventeenth was at River's Bridge. From Toper's Cross Roads Sherman communicated with General Slocum, still struggling with the floods of the Savannah River at Sister's Ferry. He had two Divisions of the Twentieth Corps, General Williams, on the east bank, and was enabled to cross over on his pontons the Cavalry of Kilpatrick. General Williams was ordered to Beaufort Bridge by way of Lawtonville and Allendale, Kilpatrick to Blackville by way of Barnwell, and General Slocum was ordered to hurry the crossing at Sister's Ferry as much as possible and overtake the right wing on the South Carolina Railroad. General Howard, with the right wing, was directed to cross the Salkehatchie and push rapidly for the South Carolina Railroad, at or near Midway. The enemy held the line of the Salkehatchie in force, having Infantry and Artillery intrenched at River's and Beaufort's Bridges. The Seventeenth Corps was ordered to carry River's Bridge, and the Fifteenth Corps Beaufort's Bridge. The former position was carried promptly and skillfully by Mower's and Giles A. Smith's Divisions of the Seventeenth Corps. on the 3d of February, by crossing the swamp, nearly three miles wide. with water varying from knee deep to shoulder deep. The weather was bitter cold, and Generals Mower and Smith led their Divisions in person, on foot, waded the swamps, made a lodgment below the bridge, and turned on the Rebel Brigade which guarded it, driving it in disorder and confusion towards Branchville. Our casualties were one officer and seventeen men killed, and seventy wounded, who were sent to Pocotaligo.

For this success great credit should be given to Generals Mower and Smith, who promptly carried out General Sherman's orders in the face of great difficulties. To march a whole day, and that, too, a bitter, cold day in mid-winter, through water up to the arm-pits, in places, required endurance, such as none but brave and true soldiers could or would endure. Such men can not well fail of success.

A correspondent, who examined the position abandoned by the enemy, speaks of it as follows:

"FEBRUARY 5TH.

"I have examined the works at Beaufort Bridge to-day, which were evacuated by the rebels as soon as we made the crossing at River's Bridge. It is a place of remarkable strength, both in its natural advantages and the strong line of works which defend the passage. A Brigade with a single section of Artillery could have held an army at bay. So it would seem, at least, when one wades and stumbles over the narrow road which leads for half a mile through the swamp. When you come out of the dense jungle, and before crossing the main branch of the stream, you see before you, upon its border, a line of well-built works extending for a quarter of a mile on either side. Here are three embrasures, which were pierced for heavy guns, while the parapet is surmounted by the protecting head-log. If the enemy had not been flanked below, and could have held this place, it would have cost us hundreds of lives. As it is, we gained the peninsula formed by the Salkehatchie and Edisto Rivers. We have the choice of going to Augusta or Charleston.

The latter place we can capture with less trouble than Savannah gave us, supposing we made a direct attack, for we can make an excellent base at Bull's Bay. I know that the General expects to capture Charleston by operating a hundred miles away from its walls—a strategy which has not always been practiced in this war.

"General Williams is up with two of the Divisions of the Twentieth Corps. Kilpatrick and his cavalry are at Allandale, and the balance of the left wing have crossed the Savannah. The army here has made a short move to-day, and we are within a single day's march of the Charleston & Augusta Railroad. We hear that the Rebels intend defending it at several points, but they cannot protect the whole line, and we will flank them somewhere."

After the line of the enemy on the Salkehatchie was broken, they retreated hastily behind the Edisto River, at Branchville, and our whole army was pushed rapidly to the South Carolina Railroad, at Midway, Bamberg, or Lowry's Station and Graham's Station. The Seventeenth Corps, by threatening Branchville, forced the enemy to burn the Railroad Bridge, and Walker's Bridge below, across the Edisto. All hands were at once set to work to destroy the railroad track. From the 7th to the 10th of February this work was thoroughly prosecuted by the Seventeenth Corps from Edisto up to Bamberg, and by the Fifteenth Corps from Bamberg up to Blackville. In the meantime General Kilpatrick had brought his Cavalry rapidly by Barnwell to Blackville, and had turned toward Aiken, with orders to threaten Augusta, but not to be drawn needlessly into serious battle. This he skillfully accomplished, skirmishing heavily with Wheeler's Cavalry, first at Blackville and afterwards at Williston and Aiken. General Williams, with two Divisions of the Twentieth Corps, marched to the South Carolina Railroad, at Graham's Station, on the 8th, and General Slocum arrived at Blackville on the 12th of the month. The destruction of the railroad was continued by the left wing from Blackville up to Windsor. By the 11th of February all the army was on the railroad from Midway to Johnson's Station, thereby dividing the enemy's forces, which still remained at Branchville and Charleston on the one hand and at Aiken and Augusta on the other.

For a clear and satisfactory account of the rest of the campaign, we refer to the official report of General Sherman, which we here insert word for word:

GENERAL SHERMAN'S OFFICIAL REPORT.

"We then began the movement on Orangeburg. The Seventeenth Corps crossed the south fork of the Edisto River at Binnaker's Bridge, and moved straight for Orangeburg, while the Fifteenth Corps crossed at Holman's Bridge, and moved to Poplar Springs in support. The left wing and Cavalry were still at work on the railroad, with orders to cross the South Edisto at New and Guignard's Bridges, move to the Orangeburg and Edgefield Road, and there await the result of the attack on Orangeburg. On the 12th the Seventeenth Corps found the enemy entrenched in front of the Orangeburg Bridge, but swept him away by a dash, and followed him, forcing him across the bridge, which was partially burned. Behind the bridge was a Battery in position, covered by a cotton and earth parapet, with wings as far as could be seen. General Blair held one Division (Giles A. Smith's) close up to the Edisto, and moved the other two to a point about two miles below, where he crossed Force's Division by a ponton bridge, holding Mower's in support. As soon as Force emerged from the swamp, the enemy gave ground, and Giles A. Smith's division gained the bridge, crossed over, and occupied the enemy's parapet. He soon repaired the bridge, and by four in the afternoon the whole Corps was in Orangeburg, and had begun the work of destruction on the railroad. Blair was ordered to destroy this railroad effectually up to Lewisville, and to push the enemy across the Congaree, and force him to burn the bridges, which he did on the 14th; and without wasting time or labor on Branchville or Charleston, which I knew the enemy could no longer hold, I turned all the columns straight on Columbia. The Seventeenth Corps followed the State Road, and the Fifteenth Corps crossed the North Edisto from Poplar Springs, at Schilling's Bridge, above the mouth of "Cawcaw Swamp" Creek, and took a country road, which came into the State Road at Zeigtor's. On the 15th the Fifteenth Corps found the enemy in a strong position at Little Congaree Bridge (across Congaree Creek), with a *tete-de-pont* on the south side, and a well-constructed fort on the north side, commanding the bridge with Artillery. The ground in front was very bad, level and clear, with a fresh deposit of mud from a recent overflow. General Charles R. Woods, who commanded the leading Division, succeeded, however, in turning the flank of the *tete-de-pont* by sending Stone's Brigade through a cypress swamp to the left; and, following up the retreating enemy promptly, he got possession of the bridge and fort beyond. The bridge had been partially damaged by fire, and had to be repaired for the passage of artillery, so that night closed in before the head of the column could reach the bridge across the Congaree River, in front of Columbia. That night the enemy shelled our camps from a Battery on the east side of the Congaree, above Granby. Early next morning (February 16) the head of the column reached the bank of the Congaree, opposite Columbia, but too late to save the fine bridge which spanned the river at that point. It was burned by the enemy. While waiting for the pontons to come to the front, we could see the people running about the streets of Columbia, and occasionally small bodies of Cavalry, but no masses. A single gun of Captain De Grass' Battery was firing at their Cavalry squads, but I checked his firing, limiting him to a few shots at the unfinished State House walls, and a few shells at the railroad depot, to scatter the people who were seen carrying away sacks of corn and meal that we needed. There was no white flag or manifestations of surrender. I directed General Howard not to cross directly in front of Columbia, but to cross the Saluda at the Factory, three miles above, and afterward Broad River, so as to approach Columbia from the north. Within an hour of the arrival of General Howard's head of column at the river opposite Columbia, the head of column of the left wing also appeared, and I directed General Slocum to cross the Saluda at Zion Church, and thence to take roads direct for Winnsboro', breaking up *en route* the railroads and bridges about Alston.

"General Howard effected a crossing of the Saluda near the Factory on the 16th, skirmishing with Cavalry, and the same night made a flying bridge across Broad River, about three miles above Columbia, by which he crossed over Stone's Brigade, of Wood's Division, Fifteenth Corps. Under cover of this Brigade, a ponton bridge was laid on the morning of the 17th. I was in person at this bridge, and at 11 o'clock in the forenoon learned that the Mayor of Columbia had come out in a carriage and made a formal surrender of the city to Colonel Stone, Twenty-fifth Iowa Infantry, commanding Third Brigade, First Division, Fifteenth Corps. About the same time a small party of the Seventeenth Corps had crossed the Congaree in a skiff, and entered Columbia from a point immediately west. In anticipation of the occupation of the city, I had made written orders to General Howard touching the conduct of the troops. These were to destroy absolutely all arsenals and public property not needed for our own use, as well as all railroads, depots, and machinery useful in war to an enemy, but to spare all dwellings, colleges, schools, asylums and harmless private property. I was the first to cross the ponton bridge, and in company with General Howard, rode into the city. The day was clear, but a perfect tempest of wind was raging. The Brigade of Colonel Stone was already in the city, and was properly posted. Citizens and soldiers were on the streets, and general good order prevailed. General Wade Hampton, who commanded the Confederate Rear Guard, had, in anticipation of our capture of Columbia, ordered that all cotton, public and private, should be moved into the streets and fired, to prevent our making use of it. Bales were piled everywhere, the rope and bagging cut, and tufts of cotton were blown about in the wind, lodged in the trees and against houses, so as to resemble a snowstorm. Some of these piles of cotton were burning, especially one in the very heart of the city, near the Court House, but the fire was partially subdued by the labor of our soldiers. During the day the Fifteenth Corps passed through Columbia, and out on the Camden Road. The Seventeenth did not enter the town at all; and as I have before stated, the left wing and Cavalry did not come within two miles of the town.

"Before one single public building had been fired by order, the smoldering fires set by Hampton's order were rekindled by the wind, and communicated with the buildings around. About dark they began to spread, and got beyond the control of the Brigade within the city. The whole of Wood's Division was brought in, but it was found impossible to check the flames, which, by midnight, had become unmanageable, and raged until about 4 o'clock in the morning, when, the wind subsiding, they were got under control. I was up nearly all night, and saw Generals Howard, Logan, Wood and others laboring to save houses and protect families thus suddenly deprived of shelter, and of bedding and wearing apparel. I disclaim, on the part of my army, any agency in this fire; but, on the contrary, claim that we saved what of Columbia remained unconsumed. And, without hesitation, I charge General Wade Hampton with having burned his own city of Columbia, not with a malicious intent, or as the manifestation of a silly " Roman stoicism," but from folly and want of sense, in filling it with lint, cotton and tinder. Our officers and men on duty worked well to extinguish the flames, but others, not on duty, including the officers who had long been imprisoned there, rescued by us, may have assisted in spreading the fire after it had once begun, and may have indulged in unconcealed joy to see the ruin of the capital of South Carolina. During the 18th and 19th the arsenal, railroad depots, machine shops, foundries and other buildings were properly destroyed by detailed working parties, and the railroad track torn up and destroyed down to Kingsville and the Wateree Bridge, and up in the direction of Winnsboro'.

"At the same time the left wing and Cavalry had crossed the Saluda and Broad Rivers, breaking up the railroad about Alston, and as high up as the bridge across Broad River on the Spartanburg Road, the main body moving straight for Winnsboro', which General Slocum reached on the 21st of February. He caused the railroad to be destroyed up to Blackstakes Depot, and then turned to Rocky Mount, on the Catawba River. The Twentieth Corps reached Rocky Mount on the 22d, laid a ponton bridge, and crossed over during the 23d. Kilpatrick's Cavalry followed, and crossed over in a terrible rainstorm during the night of the 23d, and moved up to Lancaster, with orders to keep up the delusion of a general movement on Charlotte, N. C., to which General Beauregard and all the Cavalry of the enemy had retreated from Columbia. I was also aware that Cheatham's Corps, of Hood's old army, was aiming to make a junction with Beauregard at Charlotte, having been cut off by our rapid movement on Columbia and Winnsboro'. From the 23d to the 26th we had heavy rains, swelling the rivers, and making the roads almost impassable. The Twentieth Corps reached Hamburg Rock on the 26th, and waited there for the Thirteenth Corps to get across the Catawba. The heavy rains had so swollen the river that the ponton bridge broke, and General Davis had very hard work to restore it, and get his command across. At last he succeeded, and the left wing was all put in motion for Cheraw. In the meantime the right wing had broken up the railroad to Winnsboro, and thence turned for Pea's Ferry, where it was crossed over the Catawba before the heavy rains set in, the Seventeenth Corps moving straight on Cheraw via Young's Bridge, and the Fifteenth Corps by Tiller's and Kelly's Bridges. From this latter Corps detachments were sent into Camden to burn the bridge over the Wateree, with the railroad depot, stores, etc. A small force of mounted men, under Captain Duncan, was also dispatched to make a dash and interrupt the railroad from Charleston to Florence, but it met Butler's Division of Cavalry, and, after a sharp night skirmish on Mount Elon, was compelled to return unsuccessful. Much bad road was encountered at Lynch's Creek, which delayed the right wing about the same length of time as the left wing had been at the Catawba. On the 2d of March the leading Division of the Twentieth Corps entered Chesterfield, skirmishing with Butler's Division of Cavalry, and the next day, about noon, the Seventeenth Corps entered Cheraw, the enemy retreating across the Pedee, and burning the bridge at that point. At Cheraw we found much ammunition and many guns, which had been brought from Charleston on the evacuation of that city. These were destroyed, as also the railroad trestles and bridges down as far as Darlington. An expedition of mounted Infantry was also sent down to Florence, but it encountered both Cavalry and Artillery, and returned, having only broken up in part the branch road from Florence to Cheraw.

"Without unnecessary delay, the columns were again put in motion, directed on Fayetteville, N. C., the right wing crossing the Pedee at Cheraw, and the left wing and Cavalry at Sneedsboro'. General Kilpatrick was ordered to keep well on the left flank, and the Fourteenth Corps, moving by Love's Bridge, was given the right to enter and occupy Fayetteville first. The weather continued unfavorable and roads bad, but the Fourteenth and Seventeenth Corps reached Fayetteville on the 11th of March, skirmishing with Wade Hampton's Cavalry, that covered the rear of Hardee's retreating arm, which, as usual, had crossed Cape Fear River, burning the bridge. During the march from the Pedee, General Kilpatrick had kept his Cavalry well on the left and exposed flank. During the night of the 9th of March his three Brigades were divided to picket the roads. General Hampton detecting this, rushed in at daylight and gained possession of the camp of Colonel Spencer's Brigade, and the house in which General Kilpatrick and Colonel Spencer had their quarters. The surprise was complete, but General Kilpatrick quickly succeeded in rallying his men, on foot, in a swamp near by, and by a prompt attack, well followed up, regained his artillery, horses, camp and everything, save some prisoners, whom the enemy carried off, leaving their dead on the ground.

"The 12th, 13th and 14th were passed at Fayetteville, destroying absolutely the United States arsenal and the vast amount of machinery which had formerly belonged to the old Harper's Ferry United States arsenal. Every building was knocked down and burned, and every piece of machinery utterly broken up and ruined, by the First Regiment Michigan Engineers, under the immediate supervision of Colonel O. M. Poe, Chief Engineer. Much valuable property, of great use to the enemy, was here destroyed or cast into the river.

"Up to this period I had perfectly succeeded in interposing my superior army between the scattered parts of the enemy. But I was then aware that the fragments that had left Columbia under Beauregard had been reinforced by Cheatham's corps from the West, and the garrison of Augusta, and that ample time had been given to move them to my front and flank about Raleigh. Hardee had also succeeded in getting across Cape Fear River ahead of me, and could, therefore, complete the junction with the armies of Johnston and Hoke in North Carolina. And the whole, under the command of the skillful and experienced Joe Johnston, made up an army superior to me in Cavalry, and formidable enough in Artillery and Infantry to justify me in extreme caution in making the last step necessary to complete the march I had undertaken. Previous to reaching Fayetteville, I had dispatched to Wilmington, from Laurel Hill Church, two of our best scouts, with intelligence of our position, and my general plans. Both of these messengers reached Wilmington, and on the morning of the 12th of March, the Army Tug Davidson, Captain Ainsworth, reached Fayetteville from Wilmington, bringing me full intelligence of the outside world. On the same day this tug carried back to General Terry, at Wilmington, and General Schofield, at Newbern, my dispatches to the effect that, on Wednesday, the 15th, we would move for Goldsboro', feigning on Raleigh, and ordering them to march straight for Goldsboro', which I expected to reach about the 20th. The same day the gunboat Eolus, Captain Young, United States navy, also reached Fayetteville, and through her I continued to have communication with Wilmington until the day of our actual departure. While the work of destruction was going on at Fayetteville, two ponton bridges were laid across Cape Fear River, one opposite the town and the other three miles below.

"General Kilpatrick was ordered to move up the plank road, to and beyond Averysboro'. He was to be followed by four Divisions of the left wing, with as few wagons as possible; the rest of the train, under escort of the two remaining Divisions of that wing, to take a shorter and more direct road to Goldsboro'. In like manner, General Howard was ordered to send his trains, under good escort, well to the right, toward Faison's Depot and Goldsboro', and to hold four Divisions light, ready to go to the aid of the left wing if attacked while in motion. The weather continued very bad, and the roads had become mere quagmire. Almost every foot of it had to be corduroyed to admit the passage of wheels. Still, time was so important, that punctually, according to order, the columns moved out from Cape Fear river, on Wednesday, the 16th March. I accompanied General Slocum, who, preceded by Kilpatrick's Cavalry, moved up the river, or plank road, that day, to Kyle's Landing, Kilpatrick skirmishing heavily with the enemy's rear guard, about three miles beyond Taylor's Hole Creek. At General Kilpatrick's request, General Slocum sent forward a Brigade of Infantry to hold a line of baricades.

"Next morning the column advanced in the same order, and developed the enemy, with Artillery, Infantry and Cavalry, in an intrenched position in front of the point where the road branches off toward Goldsboro' through Bentonville. On an inspection of the map it was manifest that Hardee, in retreating from Fayetteville, had halted in the narrow, swampy neck between Cape Fear and South Rivers in hopes to hold me to save time for concentration of Johnston's armies at some point to his rear, namely, Raleigh, Smithfield or Goldsboro'. Hardee's forces were estimated at twenty thousand men. It was necessary to dislodge him that we might have the use of the Goldsboro' Road, so as to keep the feint on Raleigh as long as possible. General Slocum was, therefore, ordered to press and carry the position, only difficult by reason of the nature of the ground, which was so soft that horses would sink everywhere, and even men could hardly make their way over the common pine barrens.

"The Twentieth Corps, General Williams, had the lead, and Ward's Division the advance. This was deployed, and the skirmish line developed the position of a Brigade of Charleston heavy Artillery, armed as Infantry (Rhett's), posted across the road behind a light parapet, with a battery of guns enfilading the approach across a cleared field. General Williams sent a Brigade (Casey's) by a circuit to the left and turned this line, and, by a quick charge, broke the Brigade which rapidly retreated back to a second line, better built, and more strongly held. A Battery of Artillery (Winninger's) well posted, under the immediate directions of Major Reynolds, Chief of Artillery of the Twentieth Corps, did good execution on the retreating Brigade, and, on advancing Ward's Division over the ground, General Williams captured three guns and two hundred and seventeen prisoners, of which sixty-eight were wounded, and left in a house near by with a Rebel officer, four men and five days' rations. One hundred and eight Rebel dead were buried by us. As Ward's Division advanced he developed a second and stronger line, when Jackson's Division was deployed forward on the right of Ward, and two Divisions of Jeff. C. Davis' (Fourteenth) Corps on the left, well toward Cape Fear. At the same time, Kilpatrick, who was acting in concert with General Williams, was ordered to draw back his Cavalry and mass it on the extreme right, and in concert with Jackson's right to feel forward for the Goldsboro' Road. He got a Brigade on the road, but it was attacked by McLaws' Rebel Division furiously, and, though it fought well and hard, the Brigade drew back to the flank of the Infantry. The whole line advanced late in the afternoon, drove the enemy well within its intrenched line, and pressed him so hard that next morning he was gone, having retreated in a miserable, stormy night over the worst of roads. Ward's Division of Infantry followed, too, and through Averysboro', developing the fact that Hardee had retreated, not on Raleigh, but on Smithfield. I had, the night before, directed Kilpatrick to cross South River at a milldam to our right rear, and move up on the east side toward Elevation. General Slocum reports his aggregate loss in the affair known as that of Averysboro', at twelve officers and sixty-five men killed, and four hundred and seventy-seven wounded. We lost no prisoners. The enemy's loss can be inferred from his dead (one hundred and eight), left for us to bury. Leaving Ward's Division to keep up a show of pursuit, Slocum's column was turned to the right, built a bridge across the swollen South River, and took the Goldsboro' Road, Kilpatrick crossing to the north, in the direction of Elevation, with orders to move eastward, watching that flank. In the meantime the wagon trains and guards, as also Howard's column, were wallowing along the miry roads towards Bentonville and Goldsboro'. The enemy's Infantry, as before stated, had retreated across our front in the same direction, burning the bridges across Mill Creek. I continued with the head of Slocum's column, and encamped the night of the 18th with him on the Goldsboro' Road, twenty-seven miles from Goldsboro', about five miles from Bentonville, and where the road from Clinton to Smithfield crosses the Goldsboro' Road. Howard was at Lee's store' only two miles south, and both columns had pickets three miles forward to where the two roads came together, and became common to Goldsboro'.

"All the signs induced me to believe that the enemy would make no further opposition to our progress, and would not attempt to strike us in flank while in motion. I, therefore, directed Howard to move his right wing by the new Goldsboro' Road, which goes by way of

Falling Creek Church. I also left Slocum, and joined Howard's column, with a view to open communication with General Schofield, coming up from Newbern and Terry, from Wilmington. I found General Howard's column well strung out, owing to the very bad roads, and did not overtake him in person until he had reached Falling Creek Church, with one regiment forward to the cross-roads, near Cox's Bridge, across the Neuse. I had gone from General Slocum about six miles, when I heard artillery in his direction, but was soon made easy by one of his staff officers overtaking me, explaining that his leading Division (Carlin's) had encountered a Division of Rebel Cavalry (Dibbrell's), which he was driving easily. But soon other staff officers came up, reporting that he had developed near Bentonville the whole of the Rebel Army under General Johnston himself. I sent him orders to call up the two Divisions guarding his wagon trains, and Hazen's Division of the Fifteenth Corps, still back near Lee's store, to fight defensively until I could draw up Blair's Corps, then near Mount Olive Station, and, with the remaining three Divisions of the Corps, come up on Johnston's left rear from the direction of Cox's Bridge. In the meantime, while on the road, I received couriers from both Generals Schofield and Terry. The former reported himself in possession of Kinston, delayed somewhat by want of provisions, but able to march so as to make Goldsboro' on the 21st; and Terry was at or near Faison's Depot. Orders were at once dispatched to Schofield to push for Goldsboro', and to make dispositions to cross Little River in the direction of Smithfield as far as Millard; to General Terry to move to Cox's Bridge, lay a ponton bridge, and establish a crossing; and to Blair to make a night march to Falling Creek Church; and at daylight the right wing, General Howard, less the necessary wagon guards, was put in rapid motion on Bentonville. By subsequent reports I learned that General Slocum's head of column had advanced from its camp of March 18th, and first encountered Dibbrell's Cavalry, but soon found his progress impeded by Infantry and Artillery. The enemy attacked his head of column, gaining temporary advantage, and took three guns and caissons of General Carlin's Division, driving the two leading Brigades back on the main body. As soon as General Slocum realized that he had in his front the whole Confederate Army, he promptly deployed the two Divisions of the Twentieth Corps, General Williams. These he arranged on the defensive, and hastily prepared a line of barricades. General Kilpatrick also came up at the sound of Artillery, and massed on the left. In this position, the left received six distinct assaults, by the combined forces of Hoke, Hardee and Cheatham, under the immediate command of General Johnston himself, without giving an inch of ground, and did good execution on the enemy's ranks, especially with our Artillery, the enemy having little or none.

"Johnston had moved by night from Smithfield with great rapidity, and without unnecessary wheels, intending to overwhelm my left flank before it could be relieved by its coöperating columns. But he "reckoned without his host." I had expected just such a movement all the way from Fayetteville, and was prepared for it. During the night of the 19th General Slocum got up his wagon train, with its guard of two Divisions, and Hazen's Division of the Fifteenth Corps, which reenforcements enabled him to make his position impregnable. The right wing found Rebel Cavalry watching its approach, but unable to offer any serious opposition, until our head of column encountered a considerable body behind a barricade at the forks of the road near Bentonville, about three miles east of the battle field of the day before. On moving forward the Fifteenth Corps, General Logan found that the enemy had thrown back his left flank, and had constructed a line of parapet connecting with that toward General Slocum, in the form of a bastion, its salient on the main Goldsboro' road, interposing between General Slocum on the west, and General Howard on the east, while the flanks rested on Mill Creek, covering the road back to Smithfield. General Howard was instructed to proceed with due caution until he had made strong connection on his left with General Slocum. This he soon accomplished, and at 4 o'clock on the afternoon of the 29th a complete and strong line of battle confronted the enemy in his intrenched position, and General Johnston, instead of catching us in detail, was on the defensive, with Mill Creek and a single bridge in his rear. Nevertheless, we had no object to accomplish by a battle, unless at an advantage, and therefore my general instructions were to press steadily with skirmishers alone, to use Artillery pretty freely on the wooded space held by the enemy, and to feel pretty strongly the flanks of his position, which were, as usual, covered with the endless swamps of this region of country. I also ordered all empty wagons to be sent at once to Kinston for supplies, and other impediments to be grouped near the Neuse, south of Goldsboro', holding the real army in close contact with the enemy, ready to fight him if he ventured outside of his parapets and swamp obstructions. Thus matters stood about Bentonville on the 21st of

March. On the same day General Schofield entered Goldsboro' with little or no opposition, and General Terry had got possession of the Neuse River, at Cox's Bridge, ten miles above, with a ponton bridge laid and Brigade across, so that the three armies were in actual connection, and the great object of the campaign was accomplished.

"On the 21st a steady rain prevailed, during which General Mower's Division of the Seventeenth Corps, on the extreme right, had worked well to the right around the enemy's flank, and had nearly reached the bridge across Mill Creek, the only line of retreat open to the enemy. Of course there was extreme danger that the enemy would turn on him all his reserves, and, it might be, let go his parapets to overwhelm Mower. Accordingly, I ordered at once a general attack by our skirmish line, from left to right. Quite a noisy battle ensued, during which General Mower was enabled to regain his connection with his own Corps, by moving to his left rear. Still he had developed a weakness in the enemy's position of which advantage might have been taken; but that night the enemy retreated on Smithfield, leaving his pickets to fall into our hands, with many dead unburied, and wounded in his field hospitals. At daybreak on the 22d pursuit was made two miles beyond Mill Creek, but checked by my order. General Johnston had utterly failed in his attempt, and we remained in full possession of the field of battle.

"General Slocum reports the losses of the left wing, about Bentonville, at nine officers and one hundred and forty-five men killed, fifty-one officers and eight hundred and sixteen men wounded, and three officers and two hundred and twenty-three missing, taken prisoners by the enemy; total, one thousand two hundred and forty-seven. He buried on the field one hundred and sixty-seven Rebel dead, and took three hundred and thirty-eight prisioners. General Howard reports the losses of the right wing as two officers and thirty-five men killed, twelve officers and two hundred and thirty-nine men wounded, and one officer and sixty men missing; total three hundred and ninety-nine. He also buried one hundred Rebel dead, and took one thousand two hundred and eighty-seven prisoners. The Cavalry of Kilpatrick was held in reserve, and lost but few, if any, of which I have no report as yet. Our aggregate loss at Bentonville was one thousand six hundred and forty-six. I am well satisfied that the enemy lost heavily, especially in his assault on the left wing, during the afternoon of the 19th; but as I have no data save his dead and wounded left in our hands, I prefer to make no comparison. Thus, as I have endeavored to explain, we had completed our march on the 21st, and had full possession of Goldsboro', the real 'objective,' with its two railroads back to the seaports of Wilmington and Beaufort, North Carolina. These were being rapidly repaired by strong working parties, directed by Colonel W. W. Wright, of the Railroad Department. A large number of supplies had already been brought forward to Kinston, to which place our wagons had been sent to receive them. I therefore directed General Howard and the Cavalry to remain at Bentonville during the 22d, to bury the dead and remove the wounded, and on the following day all the armies to move to the camps assigned them about Goldsboro', there to rest and receive the clothing and supplies of which they stood in need. In person I went on the 22d to Cox's Brigade to meet General Terry, whom I met for the first time, and on the following day rode into Goldsboro', where I found General Schofield and his army. The left wing came in during the same day and next morning, and the Cavalry moved to Mount Olive Station, and General Terry back to Faison's. On the 25th the Newbern Railroad was finished, and the first train of cars came in, thus giving us the means of bringing from the depot at Morehead City full supplies to the army.

"It was all important that I should have an interview with the General-in-Chief, and presuming that he could not at this time leave City Point, I left General Schofield in chief command and proceeded with all expedition by rail to Morehead City, and thence by steamer to City Point, reaching General Grant's headquarters on the evening of the 27th of March. I had the good fortune to meet General Grant, the President, Generals Meade, Ord, and others, of the Army of the Potomac, and soon learned the general state of the military world, from which I had been, in a great measure, cut off since January. Having completed all necessary business, I reëmbarked on the navy steamer Bat, Captain Barnes, which Admiral Porter placed at my command, and returned via Hatteras Inlet and Newbern, reaching my own headquarters, in Goldsboro', during the night of the 30th. During my absence full supplies of clothing and food had been brought to camp, and all things were working well. I have thus rapidly sketched the progress of our columns from Savannah to Goldsboro', but for minute details must refer to the reports of subordinate commanders and of staff officers, which are not yet ready, but will in due season be forwarded and filed with this report. I can not, even with any degree of precision, recapitulate the vast amount of injury done to the enemy, or the quantity of guns and materials of war captured and destroyed. In general terms, we have traversed the country from Savannah to Goldsboro', with an average breadth of forty miles, consuming all the forage, cattle, hogs, sheep, poultry, cured meats, corn meal, etc. The public enemy, instead of drawing supplies from that region to feed his armies, will be compelled to send provisions from other quarters to feed the inhabitants. A map herewith prepared by my Chief Engineer, Colonel Poe, with the routes of the four Corps and Cavalry, will show, at a glance, the country traversed. Of course, the abandonment to us by the enemy of the whole sea-coast, from Savannah to Newbern, N. C., with its forts, dock-yards, gunboats, etc., was a necessary incident to our occupation and destruction of the inland routes of travel and supply. But the real object of this march was to place this army in a position of supply, whence it could take an appropriate part in the spring and summer campaign of 1865. This was completely accomplished on March 21st, by the junction of the three armies and occupation of Goldsboro'.

"In conclusion, I beg to express, in the most emphatic manner, my entire satisfaction with the tone and temperament of the whole army. Nothing seems to dampen their energy, zeal or cheerfulness. It is impossible to conceive a march involving more labor and exposure; yet I cannot recall an instance of bad temper by the way, or hearing an expression of doubt as to our perfect success in the end. I believe that this cheerfulness and harmony of action reflects upon all concerned quite as much honor and fame as 'battles gained' or 'cities won,' and I therefore commend all, generals, staff officers, and men, for these high qualities, in addition to the more soldierly ones of obedience to orders and the alacrity they have always manifested when danger summoned them 'to the front.'"

The grand march of Sherman's army from Savannah to Goldsboro', North Carolina, secured to us the entire sea-coast as far north as Newbern. The capture of Branchville and Columbia secured the fall of Charleston, the cradle of secession and the "hot bed of treason." For long months our naval forces had been thundering away at that stronghold, but without succeeding in its capture. It fell by the strategy of Sherman without the firing of a single gun.

Early in the evening of February 17, 1865, Brigadier General Schimmelpfenning, Commander of the Northern District of the Department of the South, discovered some indications which led him to believe that the enemy were about to evacuate Charleston and its defenses. He ordered his pickets and picket boats to keep a sharp lookout, and report immediately any movement on the part of the enemy. In the night a terrific explosion took place in Charleston, which shook every ship in the harbor and off the bar, and was heard for many miles around. Immediately after the explosion flames broke out in various parts of the city. The first explosion, which was at the railroad depot, was the means of firing the houses in the vicinity, from which the flames rapidly spread until the conflagration became general in that part of the city. A large number of women and children were killed by the explosion.

About 6 o'clock on the morning of the 18th, General Schimmelpfenning moved his forces and occupied the city and its defenses. The formidable earthworks on James Island were found abandoned, and the guns spiked.

At 8 o'clock a detachment was sent to take possession of Fort Sumter, and raise the flag which floated over Sumter when General Anderson surrendered the fort, nearly four years previously. At 8 o'clock the old flag was raised over Sumter, amid deafening cheers.

As fast as our foes could be thrown into the city, they were set to work to put out the fires. Thus, whatever remains of Charleston, was saved from being consumed to ashes by Federal soldiers' Union hands. Thousands of bales of cotton were burned by the enemy.

REFUGEES AND LOYALISTS.

One of the most significant features of our journey through the South has been the frequent prayer and entreaty of the people that they might be permitted to join our column and march with us to the sea, or wherever we might go, so that they could leave the region of despotism, anywhere out of the South, and toward the pure air of freedom again. One is a mechanic, who was born and reared in the old Granite State. He came here four years ago as master mechanic in a railroad machine-shop. He has been able to avoid service in the Rebel Army, because his services were necessary in the shop. He is taken along for his services and can be made of good use.

Here is a daughter and mother, whose son is in the Federal army. Their little means have long since been exhausted, and they wish to go to Connecticut, where relatives will gladly care for them and where they can get news of their son and brother. Another is a poor Irish woman, whose husband has been conscripted into the Rebel Army, and is now a prisoner, sick in a Northern hospital.

At Columbia there were several families of wealth and position, who had always been suspected of loyal proclivities. Upon our occupation of that city it became known to the Rebel inhabitants that these people had always assisted our prisoners, and previous to our approach, had secreted a great many at imminent peril. It would be impossible to reject these generous, self-sacrificing friends. The fire had not spared their houses, and they were homeless, but we well knew that to remain after our visit would be certain death. Up to this time the want of means of transportation had necessitated a refusal of these requests. But some of the wagons were now empty; then there were a number of vehicles captured from the enemy; horses and mules we bring in every day, and, again, not a few of the families asking our protection are able to furnish their own transportation.

General Howard was in command of the troops at Columbia, and these unfortunates did not appeal in vain to his generous, sympathetic heart, which never refuses to sympathize with those in distress.

With the approbation of General Sherman, General Howard at once organized an emigrant train, which was placed under guard of the escaped prisoners belonging to other commands. This train has been separated, and apportioned to each Division of the Fifteenth and Seventeenth Corps. They are getting along famously. Ladies who have been always accustomed to the refinements of life, seem to enjoy the journey as much as if it were a picnic. In truth it is better than that; for, while they are not exposed to the dangers of war, they participate in its excitements. The column has a singularly *outre* appearance. First, there will be a huge family coach containing ladies, with their personal baggage crowded about them; then an army wagon loaded with men, women and children, comfortably seated upon such articles of household truck as they are allowed to carry. Following this will be a country cart filled with negro women, for the negroes come along also, and hosts of little curly, bullet-headed youngsters, who gaze curiously upon the strange sights which meet their eyes.

General Hazen, whose name can never be mentioned but with inspiring recollections of the assault of Fort McAllister, tells me that the large number who accompany his Division are but little trouble to him, and that they have so quickly learned to forage for themselves that they are no expense to the Government. Two of the escaped officers, with a detachment of ten men, have charge of the train, which takes its assigned place in the column ; a few tents, which are in excess or have been captured, are pitched, when the column go into camp, and our little colony, with grateful hearts, go to their night's rest with the glad consciousness that they are step by step approaching a land of civilization and freedom.

In this life, so new and strange to the refugees, numbers of families become separated from each other. Portions of the army, who for days march upon separate roads, will at one time or another come together again, as at this place, for example, when three Corps, which have been marching upon different roads, unite at Cheraw for the purpose of crossing the river. The troops and trains, although really distinct to the initiated eye, may be mistaken for one another. I have seen the negroes, especially, wandering about as completely lost as if they were in an uninhabited forest.

THE DESOLATION OF WAR—FORAGERS AND FORAGING.

Our foragers spread in irregular and regular parties, skirmishing over the country. These enterprising characters were known by the names of "Bummers," "Smoke-house Rangers," and "Do-Boys." A bummer is an individual who by favor of a wagon-master becomes possessed of a broken-down mule, or else starts, if needs be, on foot, in either case, of course, armed with his musket. He makes his way into the enemy's country, finds horses in numbers by help of the negroes, hitches a team to a wagon, loads on it all the stores and supplies he can find in the nearest house, mounts his negroes on the rest of the horses, and returns with his spoils. He never objects to gold watches or silver plate "if he can find them in a swamp a mile from any house." These men were stragglers, not in the rear, but in front of the army, and they went before it like a cloud, being often twenty or thirty miles in advance of the head of the column. They would fight anything. Three "bummers" together would at any time attack a company of rebel cavalry, and, in favorable circumstances, would disperse them and capture their booty. With the exception of Columbia alone, every town in South Carolina through which the army passed was first entered by the bummers. At Chesterfield they were two days and a half ahead of the army, the whole Corps having congregated at this point.

At Robertsville we struck the Savannah & Augusta Railroad, and in obedience to the "file left" order, turned toward Augusta. Half a mile out I noticed the smoldering ruins of Colonel Lawton's fine plantation, the fence and negro shanties alone remaining undisturbed. The plantation hands were all at home, but before the column had disappeared but one or two of Lawton's blacks remained to tell the tale of devastation when the Rebel lord returned to his deserted grounds.

One thousand miles triumphantly traversed brought the captors of Atlanta, Milledgeville, Savannah, Charleston, Columbia, Fayettville and Goldsboro', into the very heart of North Carolina.

Some of the results of this campaign were fourteen cities captured, hundreds of miles of railroad destroyed, thousands of bales of cotton burned, 85 cannon, 4,000 prisoners and 25,000 animals.

After Sherman had destroyed the arsenal, machinery and other property that might be of service to the enemy, without resting his army at Fayetteville—as he would have been excused for doing, and as any other commander would have done—marched across the country to Goldsboro'! With his habitual but astonishing fearlessness, he moved for the north and rear of Goldsboro', for the purpose of flanking it. The move was a perfect success. Bragg and Johnston moved back on Raleigh. The flanking of Goldsboro' at once relieved the pressure which kept Schofield at Kinston.

Sherman's army moved forward, and without serious opposition captured Raleigh, the capital of the State.

The unfailing success of Sherman in driving the rebel army before him, from point to point, until he had reached a position so threatening to Richmond, compelled General R. E. Lee to send reinforcements to Johnston from Richmond. The enemy knew that unless Sherman could be checked both armies would be caged inside the fortifications of Richmond. But to reinforce Johnston was to present a strong temptation to General Grant to attack Richmond. The experiment was tried, "*ex necessitate*." Grant, with his eagle eye, saw the prey, darted down upon it and seized it.

MORE INFORMATION OF THE EARLIER HISTORY OF THE TWENTY-FIFTH MISSOURI.

Since the main portion of the book was in type, Lieutenant Colonel Van Horn has furnished the following facts concerning the earlier history of the formation of the Twenty-fifth Missouri.

The nucleus of this Regiment was composed of the commands of Colonel Peabody and Major Van Horn, engaged at the battle of Lexington in September 1861, taken prisoners, paroled, and afterward exchanged for the prisoners taken at Camp Jackson in May 1861.

Near the last of May, 1861, General Lyon, in command at St. Louis, authorized, by an order issued to the commanding officer at Fort Leavenworth, the organization of two Battalions of 300 men each, at St. Joseph and Kansas City, to be commanded respectively by Everett Peabody, and R. T. Van Horn, to be known as "United States Reserve Corps." The order farther directed that the two towns be garrisoned by regular troops till the volunteers were organized, mustered in, and armed. This was done, and Major Peabody at once began increasing his command to a Regiment to be called the Thirteenth Missouri. Attached to this command he also began organizing a cavalry detachment under Major Berry, but as this force had not been mustered in when the command was ordered to Lexington, it was left to help garrison Kansas City, and on the surrender to General Price of the balance of the command, Major Berry's was necessarily disbanded. This is the real history of the command of Major Berry, and why the Thirteenth Missouri under Peabody became extinct. The history of Van Horn's Battalion gives the history of both commands and their organization into the Twenty-fifth Infantry after Lexington.

This is the true story of the beginning of the Twenty-fifth Missouri, and is unknown to most of the old Regiment. Major Berry left Missouri before the war ended, and soon after the incidents narrated, and went to Oregon. He was seen by Colonel Van Horn in Washington while the Colonel was in Congress.

There were never any "Horse Guards" connected with the Twenty-fifth—they were volunteers from the beginning, and were called officially "United States Reserve Corps" till after their organization as a Regiment, after the State Government had been reorganized, and we had a Governor to commission offices. The fact that for nearly a year after secession we had no loyal Governor in Missouri is lost sight of by the writers in military affairs in the early part of 1861. Neither Peabody nor Van Horn had a commission issued under the authority of the State till in March 1862. If this fact was kept in mind, much of the confusion as to those early times would be avoided. It explains all the mystery as to the Thirteenth Regiment, Major Berry's command, and all other organizations, prior to the time when Governor Gamble took office under the Provisional Government of Missouri—when for the first time troops in this State were organized under State authority. Sterling Price was Major-General of the State Guard of Missouri, commissioned by Governor Jackson, when he took us at Lexington, and the cartel of exchange for the Camp Jackson prisoners was made with him as such, and not as a Confederate, for at that time he had not come under the Confederate authority.

A sentence of Lieutenant Newhard's, in relation to Lieutenant-Colonel Van Horn, is a mistake. He was well of his wound and was on active duty at the battle of Corinth—was in the council with Colonel Peabody and Major Powell, and party to all that was going on. Major Powell was Brigade officer of the day, and the order to take out those companies was given to him as such, to be taken out and stationed when he made his grand rounds. It was Lieutenant Newhard's impression that as he was not the officer in charge, it was from his wound—Colonel Van Horn's official report will show where Lieutenant Newhard's memory was at fault in this interval. Lieutenant Newhard's statement is a very clear one, and agrees in the main with Lieutenant-Colonel Van Horn's.

INDEX.

	Page.
Adams, Charles E.	15, 28, 30, 35, 49, 54, 72, 87, 99, 110
Adventure on the Front Line Before Corinth	51
Anderson, Jesse D.	10, 11, 15, 32
Anderson, John F.	59
Appendix	245
Argyle, Fort	163, 164
Armstrong, David	17, 40, 50, 63, 134
Ashton, La.	79, 80, 81, 83
Atlanta, Ga	142, 145, 146, 154, 257, 271
Averysboro, Battle of	173, 174, 292, 294
Bailey, T. W.	14, 49, 59, 66, 67, 68, 134, 146, 166
Ball's Ferry	159
Bannaker's Bridge	166, 287
Barfield, Miss Sallie and the Rifle	140
Barrow, W. H., Sergt.	37
Bates' Ferry	167
Battalions	72, 85, 105, 120, 146
Battle of Averysboro	173, 174, 292, 294
Bentonville	173, 174, 175, 295, 297
Corinth, Second	58
Cow Bells	17
Farmington	52, 57
Jonesboro	144, 257, 259
Lexington	26, 121, 127
New Madrid	28, 30
Shiloh	51, 122, 245, 257, 305
Baxter's Bayou	79, 80, 81
Bayne, Geo. G.	134, 146
Beadles, J. D., Care of	64, 65, 66
Beam's Cross Roads, N. C.	173, 174
Bear Creek, Ala.	101, 102
Beaufort, S. C.	165, 281, 283
Belgian Muskets, 69 Caliber	17, 22, 24
Belle Memphis Steamboat	61
Bentonville, N. C., Battle of	173, 174, 175, 295, 297
Berghoff, Dr. John T.	129, 130, 134
Berry, Major	120, 304
Besier, John C.	13, 33, 53, 59 63, 73, 85, 134
Bet of Col. Flad's	102
Bird's Point, Mo	32, 49
Bissell, J. W., Col.	9, 11, 13, 15, 20, 23, 26, 27, 29, 31, 33, 34, 35, 36, 39, 40, 47, 48, 50, 51, 54, 61, 64, 67, 68, 71, 75, 76, 77, 82, 83, 88, 90, 95, 97, 141
Bissell, J. H., Lieut.	72, 100
Bivins, Thomas E.	53
Black Bayou	82, 142
Bolivar, Tenn	63, 71
Book, John C., Dr.	100, 134, 146
Both Parties Mistaken	137
Box's Mill	136, 137
Bradley, S.	18
Bradshaw, R. C.	129, 134
Brackett, G. B.	13, 14, 54, 56, 59, 68, 71, 77, 105, 134
Bramble, John J.	130
Brant, —	13, 14
Bras, Frank	13, 14, 58, 67, 68, 134, 146, 166

INDEX.

Bristow, Geo. W., Sergt.	40, 44
Broad River	168, 169, 290
Brooks, J. P	58, 59, 66, 68, 79, 134
Brown, B. F.	12, 24
Brown, S. S.	134, 146, 161, 162
Brown, W. W.	134
Buzard, Benj. F	134, 147, 155, 157, 158, 159
Burial, Unusual	49
Camp Hasie	18
Genesee	17
Rochester	17
Mildred	20, 24
Julia	20
Campaign Through the Carolinas	105, 281, 303
Canonchee River	163
Canal New Madrid	35 to 39
Vicksburg	77, 81, 84, 106
Cape Girardeau, Mo.	15, 32
Cape Fear River	172, 291
Car (gun), Bullet-proof	97
Carlin, James	99
Carlisle, Henry	134
Carroll Station, Tenn	64, 76
Carver, ——	53
Centralia, Mo. Massacre, The	147 to 154
Charleston, S. C., Evacuation of	290
Chattahoochee River Bridge, Ga.	143 to 257
Chattanooga, Tenn	143
Cheraw, S. C.	170, 171, 290
City of Alton, Steamer	85
Citizens, Spies, etc.	57, 64, 88, 89, 90, 138, 141
Ordered from Atlanta	264
Claim, a Rebel	93
Claxton, William	134, 147
Clark, Aaron, Sergt	55
Clinton, Ga.	158
Coleman, Benj. F.	134, 146
Columbia, S. C.	167, 168, 169, 288
Comanche (Wm. Frazier)	25, 63
Commerce, Mo	30
Company A	21, 95
Companies, Formation of	10, 11, 12, 13, 14, 134, 135, 146, 147
Congaree River	167, 288
Connett, W. H	15, 24, 26, 59, 74, 98
Connor, Josiah	147
Corinth, Miss.	49, 52, 57, 100, 102, 104, 122, 131
Second Battle	66
Cow Bells, Use of	17
Coy, L. W	40, 58, 59, 79, 84, 88, 134, 149, 162, 165
Crescent City Steamboat	60, 77 to 86
Craig, Alfred	142
Cross, William	10
Cunningham, James	10
Cunningham, John S	67, 76, 134
Darby, Timothy	134
Daugherty, Frank	10, 51
Davis Mill, Miss.	72, 75
Dean, T. J	13, 14, 51
Detachments Companies A and I at New Madrid	50
Deer River	59
Dill, Hamilton, Major	124, 127, 128, 134
Disinfecting Steamboats	
Dodds, Jack, Co. F, Killed	50

INDEX. xi

Donnelly, Geo. K., Capt. 129
Duck River. 138
Dunn, James. 131, 147
Dunsford, Charles. 134
East Point, Ga. 145, 261
Edinger, M. D. 11, 25, 27, 57, 72, 74, 134
Edisto River. 166, 285
Eggleston, John Q., Dr. 134
Empress Steamboat. 29, 30
Engineers, Regular Change to. 66
Enlistment Circulars. 9, 12, 66
Enrollment. 9
Enler, Mathew, Sergt. 128
Eveans, Simon S., Capt. 124, 126, 128
Extra Duty Money. 10, 12, 29, 58, 82
Expedition to Macon Hills. 83
   Dyersville. 86
   Austin, Mo. 121
   Tracy Creek. 136
   Duck River. 138
   A Failure. 139
   Camden. 142
Farmington, Miss. 62, 57
Fayetteville, N. C. 172, 173, 291
Feuerbach, Henry. 10, 32
   Capture. 54
   Escape .... 73 to 108
Finch, John. 77
Fish at Grand Lake, La. 86
Flad, Henry, Col. 15, 23, 31, 59, 61, 67, 68, 72, 73, 75, 86, 88, 96, 97, 100, 102, 134, 142, 147
Flat Creek, Mo. 18, 20
   Tenn. 137
Floating Battery. 60, 63
Fog, In a. 277
Folsom, D. C. 11, 24
Folsom, Isaac Y 15, 66
Foraging. 70, 97, 146, 160, 273, 276, 302
Fort Argyle, Ga. 163, 164
Fort McAlister 164, 278
Fraude Max. 132, 134
Frazier, William (Comanche). 10, 25, 63
Gast, Paulus. 13, 83, 135
Gaines' Mill, Ga. 145
Gilchrist Bridge, N. C. 172
Giseke, Herman 134, 135, 147
Glenn, Addison N 135, 142
Goldsboro, N. C 175, 176, 298
Goodman, Thomas, Sergt .... 147 to 154
Goodrich, Soloman. 13, 68, 72, 85, 90, 96, 104, 134, 147
Grand Junction, Tenn. 71, 86, 88
Grand Lake, Ark 81, 86
Grand Movement by the Right Flank to Jonesboro. 257
Grant, U. S., Gen. 32, 63, 68, 76, 82, 95, 106, 122, 125, 177, 246, 303
Graves, Daniel B. 60
Griffith, —— Capt 11
Griffith, Platt. 54
Grow, Asa K. 11, 24
Grow, Devillo. 40
Gross, Dr. Mill, Tenn. 136
Gun, Car. 97
Guns, Siege. 32, 33, 34, 45, 53, 82, 83, 86
Gum Swamp. 171
Hahn, W. J. 135

Haines Bluff	107
Hamburg, Tenn	49
Hampton, James V	103
Hall, Adolphus	85
Harding, Chester, Col	122
Harrisonville, Mo	121
Haskins, L. G., Sergt	37, 40
Hasie, M. S., Maj	13, 15, 16, 31, 66
Hasie, Charles R	13, 51
Hawley, J. B	134
Henderson, J. D	134
Hendrick's Mill, Ga	155
Henion, T. W	12, 24, 29, 32
Hennings, Henry	34, 135
Hensler, J. E	132
Hequambourg, Alex. G., Capt	54, 57
Hight, W. E	135, 147
Hildebiddle, Chas. T	148
Hill, E. M	11, 25, 27, 29, 30, 49, 51, 60, 63, 68, 78, 102, 103, 107, 134, 146, 163, 164
Hill, William	14, 58, 66, 67, 68, 74, 75, 134, 146, 177, 178
Hillsboro, Ga	158
Historical Memoranda	108, 177, 179, 303
Hole in the Cash Box	21
Holman's Bridge, S. C	166
Holly Springs, Miss	71, 73, 74, 75
Honey and Persimmon Beer	93
Hooker, H. D	72, 134, 147
Hooker, James W	72, 100
Horseneck Swamp, N. C	173
Howard, O. O., Gen	147, 162, 259, 274
Hudson, H. E	15, 24, 58, 71, 73, 97, 134, 147
Hudsonville, Miss	73
Hunt, Rev. E. L., Chaplain	98, 102, 134
Injured	75, 78, 85, 98, 142
Iuka, Miss	100, 101, 102, 103
Iron Mountain, Mo	123
Irwinton, Ga	158, 159
Jackson, Tenn., Operations at and Around	57, 71, 75, 76, 87
Jacobson, A	15, 25, 50, 58
Jefferson City, Mo	17, 26, 27
Jencks Bridge	162
Johns, N	13
Johnsonville, Tenn	135, 136, 137, 138, 140, 142, 267, 272
Jones, E. L	10, 32
Jonesboro, Ga	144, 257, 259, 261
Kansas City Mo	120, 121, 304
Kilp, Anthony	134
King's Bridge, Ga	163, 164, 165
Klingler, Frederick	120, 131
Knapper, J. G	85
Knower, Charles, Dr	15, 22, 56, 61, 105, 134
Kotowsky, a Suttler	21
La Grange, Tenn	25, 75, 30
Lake Providence, La	78, 80, 81
Lamine Bridge, Mo	17, 25, 26
Lancaster, L. R	134, 147
Lape, H. T., Sergt	37, 40
Laurel Hill, N. C	171, 203
L, Company, First	132
Lewis, John	10, 54
Left Wing in the Carolina Campaign	282
Lexington, Mo	26, 121, 122, 123, 124, 303
Liberty Hill, S. C	169

INDEX.

Lochbiler, Christian........................... 135, 147
Logan, John A., Gen................................64, 70, 131, 168, 172, 296
Louisville, Ky.......................... 178
Lovejoy, Ga........................ 258, 265
Lucas, Stephen T.........................135, 147, 173, 174, 175
Lyle, W. K........................135, 147, 155, 159
Lynche's Creek, N. C........................169, 170, 290
Lyon, Nathaniel, Gen........................120, 122
Macon Bayou, La........................26, 79, 81, 83
McAllister, Fort........................164, 278
McClary, Ralph B. Dr........................ 135
McClure, James........................ 10, 53
McDonough, Ga........................ 155
McDowell, Steamer........................ 49
McLaren, John........................12, 24, 40, 58, 59, 67, 79, 135, 146
Marching Early and Late........................ 170
March to the Sea........................104, 155, 271
    Preparations for........................264, 270
    Sherman's Poem........................ 280
Marietta, Ga........................ 143
Mattis, S. W........................12, 59, 68, 76, 79, 135, 147
Memphis, Tenn........................75, 76, 77, 86, 99, 103
Merritt, A. J........................14, 55, 75, 85, 134
Midway, S. C........................166, 285
Millar, Wm., Capt........................120, 121, 128, 129, 135
Miller, John H........................ 129
Mills........................
Mobley, James........................ 148
Monticello, Ga........................ 157
Morgan, Morgan........................ 32
Morrison, Charles W., Sergt........................ 11
Mosquitoes........................49, 61
Moscow, Tenn........................71, 72, 75
Morton, John, P........................134, 159, 146
Morton, William, A........................134, 147
Morton, Marcus........................ 134
Muskets........................17, 22, 24
Mules........................ 25
Muster Out........................ 178
Murphy, John E., Capt........................10, 15, 59, 72, 134, 147
Murphy, John, Lt........................134, 147
Naming the Regiments........................9, 120, 133, 146
Nashville, Tenn........................103, 104, 105, 107, 135, 143, 267
Neal, W. A., Dr........................15, 134, 142, 146, 164
Negroes—See Slaves, Negro.
Neuse River........................175, 176, 295
Never Eat Hams........................ 87
Newberry, Oliver P........................ 129
Newhard, James M........................124, 127, 134, 146, 162, 305
New Madrid, Mo........................28, 30, 31, 49, 123, 131
New Market, S. C........................ 170
Nichols, Fred C., Maj........................122, 134
Nicholson, S. T., Capt........................12, 24
Nullings, Factory, Ga........................ 156
Numerical Strength........................15, 108, 135, 146
Obion River, Tenn........................59, 72, 76, 87
Observatory, near Farmington, Miss........................ 53
Ocmulgee River, Ga........................156, 274
Oconee River, Ga........................ 159
Odenbaugh, L., Capt........................15, 53, 59, 61, 66, 68, 73, 134
Ogeechee River, Ga........................161, 162, 163, 164, 165
Ohoopee River, Ga........................ 166
Orders, Official, etc........................106, 133, 146, 262, 269, 270, 287

INDEX.

Organization............................ 9, 15, 120, 121, 122, 133, 135, 146, 147
Orangeburg, S. C...166, 287
Otterville, Mo., Camp..19, 24
Parker, Daniel G........................59, 60, 72, 85, 88, 97, 103, 134, 147
Partisan, Rangers....................62, 63, 89, 90, 96, 97, 99, 138, 140, 142
Patten, W. G., Capt............................11, 24, 27, 29, 53, 54, 59, 95, 134, 147
Patterson, Mo...123, 131
Paysons, S. C...169
Peabody, Everett, Col........120, 121, 122, 123, 124, 125, 126, 127, 128, 130, 304
Pedee, River...171, 290
Penfield, S. M..130
Peters, Valentine..147
Percy, John H..40
Pilot, Knob, Mo...123, 131
Pillow, Fort...49
Pistol, How Large One May Look.......................................52
Pittsburg, Landing..122, 128, 130
Pocahontas, Tenn..86, 90, 97
Pocotaligo, S. C..165, 281, 283, 285
Poem, "Sherman's March to the Sea"..................................280
Point Pleasant, Mo..32, 49, 60, 63, 77
Points, John A..58, 135
Politics..25
Ponton Bridge, etc...155, 156, 270, 277
Poisoned at Sedalia...18
Pope, John, Gen.......................16, 19, 27, 33, 36, 38, 40, 42, 45, 51, 95
Powell, James E., Maj.....................122, 124, 125, 126, 127, 128, 305
Powder, Explosion of, at Cheraw.....................................300
Prescott, A. R......................14, 24, 40, 68, 70, 85, 86, 97, 134
Railroad Destroying..144, 145, 155
Raleigh, N. C..175, 176, 177
Randal's Mill, S. C...172
Randolph, M..................12, 24, 36, 39, 43, 53, 54, 56, 58, 66, 73
Reënlisting (Veteran)..105
Refugees and Loyalists...300
Reports, Official, etc.........................19, 47, 108, 128, 129, 248, 275
Return of Men Captured..72, 98
Richardson, Le Roy..21, 22
Ricketts, Joshua...................................10, 15, 59, 68, 73, 79, 85
Rivers Bridge, S. C..165, 284
River Patrol, Mississippi.......................................61, 63
River, Broad..168, 290
    Cape Fear...172, 173
    Canouchee..163
    Chattahoochee..143
    Coldwater...73, 88
    Congaree...167, 288
    Cumberland...101
    Duck...138
    Edisto...106, 286
    Mississippi...........................15, 29, 49, 61, 63, 77
    Oconee...159
    Ocmulgee...156
    Ogeechee.....................161, 162, 163, 164, 165, 274, 277
    Ohoopee..160
    Pedee..171, 290
    Saluda..167, 168, 288
    Tallahatchee..74
    Tassahaw..155
    Tennessee..49, 136
    Tuscumbia..55, 98
    Wateree...169, 290
Rock Fish Creek...172, 174

INDEX.

Rose, Cass... 148
Roster..180 to 244
Rowley, John D. 13, 59
Rowell, Charles T. 10, 15
Ryan, Richard A... 10, 53
Salkehatchie River, S. C.. 165, 284
Saluda River, S. C... 167, 168, 288
Salzman, Gustavus.. 134, 147
Sam Young, Steamer.. 77, 81
Sanders, Jack... 23, 77
Sandtown, Ga... 143, 258
Sand's Mill, Ga... 160
Sanford, N... 13
St. Joseph, Mo... 121, 123, 124, 131
St. Louis, Mo.. 10, 17, 28, 30, 123, 178
Sartain's Creek, Ga.. 160
Savannah, Ga... 165, 278, 282
Sedalia, Mo... 18, 20, 21
Senthouse, John... 78
Sherman, W. T., Gen................... 18, 63, 91, 101, 103, 125, 145, 177, 245, 257, 268, 281, 301, 303
Sherwood, Daniel B... 59, 71, 75, 102
Shelton, Charles S., Dr.. 15, 16, 44, 53, 74, 92, 100
Shiloh... 51, 122, 124, 128, 130, 245, 257, 305
Schilling's Bridge, S. C... 166, 287
Schmitz, Geo. F., Capt.. 123, 124, 127, 128
Shinn, Geo. W.. 135
Sickness... 17, 19, 24, 31, 41, 50, 60, 61, 68, 71, 76, 77, 103, 105, 136
Sikestown, Mo... 32, 33, 49
Simmons, Geo. F., Sergt.. 120
Simons, John, Steamboat... 61, 63
Singleton, John W... 129
Skull, Human, Found... 67
Slaves, Negro... 17, 25, 27, 68, 264, 272, 276, 301
Smithland, Ky... 103, 104
Small Pox... 136
Smith's Bridge, S. C.. 107
Smith's Saw Mill, Mo... 19, 20, 24
Smith, D. F... 77
Smith, James.. 18
Smith, R. G... 68, 81
Snider, John A.. 32, 71
Snyder's, Bluff, Miss... 107
Soper, Joseph.. 23, 77
Spears, Henry... 120, 121
Springfield, Mo., Why March Was Not Made... 20
Staples, C. A., Chaplain.. 15, 51
Starr, John S... 135
Station Fifty-three... 142
    Twenty-eight.. 142
    Fifty-seven.. 135, 136, 139
Steamboat Empress.. 29, 30
    Emily... 61
    Belle Memphis... 61
    City of Alton... 81
    Crescent City.. 60, 77 to 86
    McDowell... 49
    W. B. Terry... 36, 37, 38
    Sam Young.. 77, 81
Storey, Oscar F., Capt.. 135, 147
Sumner, H. M.. 20, 24, 68, 135, 146, 164
Sutler, S... 21, 83, 95
Tanner, Benj. R... 134, 147, 159, 164, 172, 173, 174
Tassahaw River... 155

INDEX.

Temperance in the Regiment	93, 96
Templeton, Thos. G.	12
Terry, W. B., Steamer	36, 37, 38
Thirteenth Missouri	120, 121, 122, 304
Proper	252, 255
Thomas, James	148
Thompson, Chas. R.	11, 51, 58, 84, 134
Thompson, Jacob E.	167
Thompson, Joseph	128
Tiller's Bridge, S. C.	169, 290
Trenton, Tenn.	72, 76, 87
Tressillion, Capt.	16, 65, 70
Turkeys, Hunting	22, 101
Tunica, Francis	103, 135, 147
Tuscumbia River	54, 55, 98
Tweeddale, W., Lt.-Col.	12, 35, 36, 39, 40, 43, 48, 50, 64, 67, 72, 75, 81, 85, 105, 107, 134, 147, 155, 158, 161, 164, 175
Twenty-Fifth, Mo.	103, 107, 108, 120, 122, 303, 305
Unionists	89 to 93, 97, 100, 276, 301
Van Horn, Robert T.	120, 121, 122, 123, 127, 128, 129, 130, 132, 134, 303, 304, 305
Vicksburg, Second Battalion at	85, 105, 106, 107
Campaign	77, 86
Vreeland, J. H.	10, 32
Wade, Chas. A., Capt.	129, 130
Waller, Jeff C., Sergt.	37, 40
Ward, J. D.	15, 24
Ward, Wm. H.	71, 135
Warrenton, Miss.	107
War Secretary Visits	20, 38, 44
Washington D. C.	177
Wateree River, S. C	169, 290
Watermelons and Whisky	
Watson, Thomas, Corp.	54
Waverly, Tenn.	135, 136, 142
Weather, Severe, etc.	24, 30, 50, 67, 68, 76, 77, 103, 104, 136, 158, 285
Webster, M. K.	71
Werth, G. L., Capt.	13, 37, 40, 59, 64, 66, 73, 76, 96, 101, 135
West, Stephen H	37
Whitcomb, A. D.	14, 59, 60, 66, 67, 76, 147, 164
White River Bridge	16
Wide Outs	23
Wilcox, N. W.	14, 36, 58, 64, 68, 77, 79, 88, 98, 99
Wilson, James	77
Winnegar, Eli	58, 71, 82, 102, 134, 147
Winnsboro, S. C.	169, 290
Women, Lewd	57
Wood, Chas. C.	79
Wright, Alpha, Chaplain	134
Wright's Bridge, Ga.	162
Yell, The Rebel	53, 145
Young, Lewis	10, 53
Young's Point	77, 81, 84, 106

www.ingramcontent.com/pod-product-compliance
Lightning Source LLC
Chambersburg PA
CBHW022020240426
43667CB00042B/1006